Post-War Identification

Post-War Identification

Everyday Muslim Counterdiscourse
in Bosnia Herzegovina

Torsten Kolind

Aarhus University Press |

Post-War Identification
Everyday Muslim Counterdiscourse
in Bosnia Herzegovina
© Aarhus University Press and Torsten Kolind 2008

Design and typesetting by Anne Marie Kaad
Printed by Narayana Press, Gylling
Printed in Denmark 2008

ISBN 978 87 7934 313 9

Published with the financial support of
Aarhus University Research Foundation
Danish Agency for Science Technology and Innovation

Aarhus University Press
Langelandsgade 177
DK-8200 Aarhus N
www.unipress.dk

International Distributors:
Gazelle Book Services Ltd.
White Cross Mills
Hightown, Lancaster, LA1 4XS
United Kingdom
www.gazellebookservices.co.uk

The David Brown Book Company
Box 511
Oakville, CT 06779
USA
www.oxbowbooks.com

Contents

Former Yugoslavian republics and autonomous provinces, 1945-1991

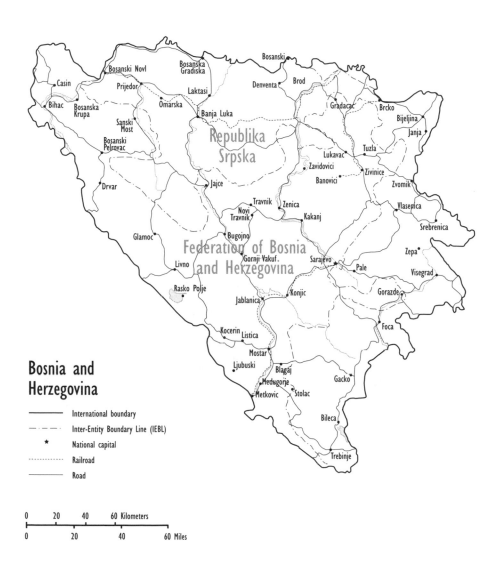

Bosnia Herzegovina after the Dayton agreement 1995, showing inter-entity boundary line between Federation of Bosnia Herzegovina and Republika Srpska (Serb Republic) and larger cities.

List of abbreviations

Armija BiH The Army of the Republic of Bosnia Herzegovina. (The largely Muslim army of Bosnia-Herzegovina).

CPY The Communist Party of Yugoslavia.

HDZ *Hrvatska Demokratska Zajednica.* The Croatian Democratic Union. (The Croat nationalist party. Though this is a Croat party, my informants always referred to HDZ and not to HDZ-BiH, when talking about Croat nationalist policy).

HDZ-BiH *Hrvatska Demokratska Zajednica – Bosna i Hercegovina.* The Croatian Democratic Union – Bosnia-Herzegovina. (The Bosnian Croat nationalist party).

HOS *Hrvatska Odbrambene Snage.* The Croatian Defence Force.

HV *Hrvatska Vojska.* The Croatian Army.

HVO *Hrvatsko Vijeće Odbrane.* The Croatian Defence Council. (The army of the Bosnian Croats).

IPTF The International Police Task Force.

JNA *Jugoslovenska Narodna Armija.* The Yugoslav People's Army.

LCY The League of Communists of Yugoslavia.

NDH *Nezavisna Država Hrvatska*; the Independent State of Croatia. The wartime fascist state run by a Nazi-installed regime led by Ante Pavelić.

OHR The Office of High Representative. (Created under the General Framework Agreement for Peace in BiH (the Dayton Peace Agreement of December 1995) to oversee implementation of the civilian aspects of the Peace Agreement).

OSCE The Organization for Security and Cooperation in Europe.

SDA *Stranka Demokratske Akcije.* The Party for Democratic Action. (The Muslim nationalist party).

SDS *Srpska Demokratska Stranka.* The Serb Democratic Party in Bosnia Herzegovina. (The Serb nationalist party).

SDP *Socijaldemokratska Stranka.* The Social Democratic Party. (Non-nationalist party, mainly supported by Muslims).

SFOR The Stabilisation Force. (A NATO-led multinational force overseeing the implementation of the Dayton agreement).

SBiH *Stranka za Bosnu i Hercegovinu.* The Party for Bosnia Herzegovina.

Acknowledgements

My book is based on research which was part of the research project 'Archaeological and Social Anthropological Perspectives on War and Society' at the Institute of Anthropology, Archaeology and Linguistics at the University of Aarhus, Denmark. This project formed part of the Danish Research Council for the Humanities' special initiative on the subject of 'Civilization and War'. I want to thank all the members of our research group for our inspiring discussions, seminars and workgroup sessions (see Otto *et al.* 2006 for an overview of the results of this research project).

I want to thank Ton Otto, professor at the Department of Anthropology and Ethnography, University of Aarhus, who supervised the PhD dissertation on which this book is based. His comments were always constructive, he was respectful of my way of thinking, and he supported me whole-heartedly.

I want to thank both Aarhus University Research Foundation and the Danish Agency for Science, Technology and Innovation for grants to fund the publishing of this book.

I also want to thank a handful of scholars whom I have come across during my research in Bosnia Herzegovina, and who have commented constructively on my work and inspired me intellectually. Dr Maja Povrzanović Frykman, who completed a thorough and critical reading of my manuscript for the PhD dissertation, and for inspiring conversations. Dr Xavier Bougarel for his useful comments on part of my work (Kolind 2007). Dr Mitja Velikonja, Dr Ivana Maček and Dr Stef Jansen for stimulating conversations at seminars in Aarhus and Lund, and fruitful email correspondence. Dr Hannes Grandits for our friendly and interesting exchange in Stolac and Mostar. And Dr Tone Bringa, whose works have inspired me a great deal, and for the invitation to the right seminar at the right time.

I want to express my greatest debt of gratitude to my informants in Stolac. For many years their lives have been a nightmare. They have experienced war, expulsion, fear, hunger and desperation; and after returning to their homes, many have felt uncertainty, bitterness and resignation. I was therefore amazed and impressed by how hospitable, sincere and trusting most of my informants were. Circumstances, unfortunately, do not allow me to mention any names. I do, however, wish to express a special thanks to my host family, who did all they could to help me in my research, as well as being thoroughly decent people. M for our inspiring talks and for your work in translating interviews. A for helping me with arranging interviews and for the kindness that you and your family showed me. H for your decency. M, your father, M and J for our good times together.

Last, I want to thank my lovely family, first of all my wife Jeanett Bjøn-ness and my two children Martine and Severin, my father Jørn Kolind, my two brothers Lars and Marcus, and my deceased mother Inger Kolind, to whom this book is dedicated.

Part I
Framing the question

Prologue: Chronology of the war

Stolac, the town of departure for this book and the site where I conducted field-work, is located in the south-western corner of Bosnia Herzegovina. Before the war, according to the population census from 1991, the municipality of Stolac had 18,681 inhabitants (Muslims: 43 %; Croats: 33 %; Serbs: 21 %; others: 3 %), and the town itself had 5,530 inhabitants (Muslims: 62 %; Serbs: 20 %; Croats: 12 %; others: 6 %). A large proportion of the Croats lived in the minor villages in Stolac municipality. When I did fieldwork among the Muslims of Stolac no census figures were available, but judging from the number of schoolchildren attending the school in Stolac, the town had a majority of Croats, the rest being Muslims. Only a few Serb families had returned. According to the daily newspaper *Dnevni Avaz* (8 December 2001), between 1998 and 2001 about 3,700 Muslim refugees had returned to the municipality of Stolac, and 1,700 to the town itself. Most of the Muslim returnees were confined to a few neighbourhoods in the eastern and southern part of the town, which were largely destroyed during the war.

Before the war Stolac was a beautiful and historical town, as can be seen from pre-war pictures. The town contained many buildings from the Ottoman period, including mosques, houses, housing complexes and bridges. Post World War Two architecture was finely adjusted to the cultural traditions of the town. Stolac also had a lot of light industry, with several of the factories employing between 200 and 1,000 people. In addition, there were banks, a shopping centre, a museum, a cinema, many cafés, a new hotel, a big market, a hospital and a high school. Today a large proportion of these buildings have been destroyed, the industry has fallen apart, and the Croat population runs nearly all the public institutions.

The war in Herzegovina

Bosnia Herzegovina experienced a fierce war from 1992 to 1995, a war which divided the country ethnically. The Dayton peace agreement of December 1995 retained Bosnia Herzegovina's international boundaries and created a joint multi-ethnic and democratic government. Also recognised was a second tier of government comprised of two entities roughly equal in size: the Bosniak/Croat Federation of Bosnia Herzegovina, and the Bosnian Serb-led *Republika Srpska*

(RS) (see map). The Federation and RS governments were charged with over-seeing internal functions.

The war in Bosnia Herzegovina was initially an act of aggression and ter-ritorial conquest instigated by Serbian political leaders. However, as the war progressed, it increasingly came to consist of several minor wars, one of them fought in Western Bosnia Herzegovina between Croatian and Muslim forces. This was the one that affected the inhabitants of Stolac the most. At the be-ginning of the war, Bosnian Croats and Muslims had joined forces, primarily because they faced the same enemy, the Serbs, who had already conquered large parts of Bosnia Herzegovina in the first month of the war. Croatia had already suffered from Serbian attacks, so in Croatia people felt sympathy for their neighbours. However, the alliance was a marriage of convenience, made up of rather different strategies.

The Bosnian Croats were divided between those living in central Bosnia, who considered themselves as much Bosnian as Croat, and the Croats living in areas dominated largely by Croats, mainly Western Herzegovina, who were eager to forge closer ties with Croatia proper, rather than with the other eth-nic groups of Bosnia Herzegovina. The Herzegovinian Croats only constituted around a third of the total Croat population of Bosnia Herzegovina, but when the war started they were the most influential. This influence was primarily due to the existence of what some have called 'the Herzegovinian lobby' (Do-nia and Fine 1994: 249; Grandits 2007: 107-9), a hard-core nationalist group of mainly émigré Croats. The Herzegovinian lobby had contributed greatly to the Croatian President Tuđman's presidential campaign in 1990 (Woodward 2000). Tuđman – himself strongly nationalistic, with his dream of annexing substantial parts of Bosnia Herzegovina[1] – rewarded his backers by supporting their desire to divide up Bosnia and make Herzegovina a part of Croatia. In July 1992, the Herzegovinian Croats, led by Mate Boban, leader of the HDZ-BiH (*Hrvatska Demokratska Zajednica – Bosna i Hercegovina*; the Croatian Demo-cratic Union – Bosnia Herzegovina, a strongly nationalist Croat political party) convened a self-proclaimed Presidency of the Croatian Community of *Herceg-Bosna* and declared a self-governing community (Donia and Fine 1994: 248-51; Glenny 1996: 192-9; Bennet 1995: 198-202).

1   By March 1991 Tuđman and Milošović had already met to discuss the partition of Bosnia Herzegovina between them, and on 6 May 1992 Tuđman sponsored talks between Mate Boban, the leader of the Bosnian Croats' strongly nationalistic and heavily influential political party HDZ, and Radovan Karadžić, leader of the Bosnian Serbs, at which time they considered a potential division of Bosnian territory (Bennet 1995: 200, Glenny 1996: 193-4).

The Herzegovinian Croats, despite the declaration of the self-governing community, lacked the strength to pursue the annexationist design and felt that in the long term an alliance with the Bosnian government was still the best way to realise their nationalist dreams. But it was clear from the start of the takeover of the HDZ-BiH by Mate Boban that the Muslim-Croat alliance was fragile: fighting broke out between Muslims and Croats at several places in Bosnia Herzegovina, and Croats started driving out Muslim inhabitants of villages under Croat control (Donia and Fine 1994: 250, Glenny 1996: 194, Cigar 1995: 125). For their part, the Muslims, who were desperately pursuing the goal of an autonomous unitary Bosnia Herzegovina, had no alternative but to form an alliance with the Bosnian Croats and uphold the best possible relation with Croatia. The Bosnian forces (of which the majority was Muslims) were ill-equipped and would have stood no chance if they were to face both the Serbs and the Croats. Furthermore, they depended on good relations with the HVO (*Hrvatsko Vijeće Odbrane*, the Croatian Defence Council, the army of the Bosnian Croats) in order to receive the illegal weapons supplies (illegal because of the international weapons embargo) coming through Croat-held territory, as well as food supplies to major Bosnian cities (Glenny 1996: 195, 228).

Croatia and Bosnia Herzegovina, then, were officially war allies during 1992 and the beginning of 1993, and in Herzegovina Muslims fought in the ranks of the HVO against the Serbs. But in spring 1993, the latent Muslim-Croat conflict escalated into full-scale war. A prime reason was probably the international community's Vance-Owen peace proposal, which, in addition to ratifying the carving up of Bosnia Herzegovina along ethnic lines, also allotted a proportionally large amount of territory to the Bosnian Croats. For the Bosnian Croats the Vance-Owen peace proposal was an incentive to consolidate their respective positions and assume full control of the area assigned to them under the plan, as well as to seize additional areas from the Bosnian government, including areas where Croatians were in a distinct minority (as in Stolac).

In many areas of Western Herzegovina the Bosnian Croats' policy resulted in open fighting between Muslims and Croats. The Croats wanted to cleanse the territories ethnically and unite them with Croatia, while the Muslims wanted to keep the areas under the control of a multi-ethnic Bosnian state. Some of the fiercest fighting of the entire war broke out between Muslims and Croats in Mostar. And in areas south and south-west of Mostar (among them Stolac) the entire Muslim population, including former Muslim co-combatants, was disarmed and arrested, then placed in horrendous prison camps (*logori*) or expelled to territory held by the Bosnian army. At the same time the Croats and Muslims were still fighting together against the Serbs, in Sarajevo for instance.

A year later the fighting between the Muslims and Croats was stopped by the signing of the Washington agreement by both parties on 18 March 1994. It was a federation agreement, and though not respected as such – the Croats did not dismantle their newly created republic of *Herceg-Bosna*, and joint command of the two armies remained a fiction – it was a step towards stopping the war in Bosnia Herzegovina. The Dayton agreement, which officially put an end to almost four years of total destruction and ethnic cleansing in Bosnia Herzegovina, was signed on 21 November 1995. The agreement was not a formal division of Bosnia Herzegovina (see however Mertus 2000), but in reality the country has been ethnically divided ever since. The Serb Republic is controlled and mainly inhabited by Serbs, and the Federation (between Muslims and Croats) is itself divided in Croat and Muslim areas and jurisdictions. As a case in point, today the country has in reality three different armies.

Today Bosnia Herzegovina faces huge problems. One of the hardest to solve has to do with the repatriation of displaced people. Between 100,000 and 200.000 people died during the war, and more than 2 million out of a total pre-war population of 4.3 million were internal or external refugees after the war.[2] So besides facing a completely ruined economy, a destroyed production apparatus, enormous unemployment, war traumas *en masse*, corruption and a general mood of despondency, the Bosnian people and Bosnian political system in cooperation with the Office of High Representatives (OHR) also have to solve the impossible puzzle of relocating people to their houses, houses which have in many cases been ruined or occupied. When the war was brought to an end, a pilot project facilitating inter-Federation returns in four towns was initiated. One of these was Stolac, where the Muslim and Serb populations were to be supported in returning. The return of the Muslim population to Stolac was met with resistance by the Croats, many of whom had fled to Stolac from central Bosnia during the war. These Croats feared for 'their' (the Muslims') property as well as their newly won political power in town. And on the ideological level, the Croats worried about the decreasing prospects for realising the independent state of *Herceg-Bosna*. Of the four pilot projects, the Stolac project has been the most difficult one to realise,[3] due to the immense obstruction from the Croats living in town. With this background in mind, I will now focus more closely on Stolac and offer some details.

2   The figure 200,000 is from UN sources, the figure 100,000 is from a recent research project at the Reserach and Documentation Center Sarajevo.

3   See OHR's HumanRights report 28, May 1998.

The war in Stolac

The war started officially in April 1992, when Serbian forces occupied Stolac. But many people sadly recall an incident six months earlier, when a war memorial from World War Two commemorating fallen Partisans was blown up.[4] The monument was located in front of the school. Today on the same spot the Croats have placed a bust of Ivan Musić, who was a leading Croat resister in the Herzegovinian revolt (1875-1878). The Serbian occupation of Stolac town did not meet any resistance. The Serbs set up their military camp outside town, but there was no fighting, and there was hardly any looting or killing as was the case in areas occupied by Serbs in eastern Bosnia during the same period. The occupation of Stolac had severe consequences though. Most of the Croatian population fled overnight, fearing the Serbian forces. The whole Serbian population of Stolac joined the Serbian army either compulsorily or voluntarily, and the Muslims secretly arranged a number of local defence units in order to protect their families if necessary. Some Stolac Croats have subsequently accused the Muslims of not having resisted the Serbian occupational force, but according to my informants resistance would have been suicidal, as the Muslims were too badly equipped to face what was the fourth largest army in Europe.[5]

Two months after the Serbian occupation, Croatian forces (the HVO and the HOS) conquered Stolac almost without a fight, and the Serbs withdrew to the mountains and hills east and southeast of Stolac.[6] Many of the Muslims regarded the Croatian takeover as a relief. They hoped and thought things would improve, and many believed the Croats' explicit statements about their desire for Muslim and Croatian coexistence, although on the other hand they also regarded the massive Croatian presence as a new occupation (*vlast*). Many Muslims from Stolac joined the forces of the Bosnian Croats (the HVO) because there were no units of the Army of the Republic of Bosnia Herzegovina (*Armija BiH*) in town: the closest was around Mostar, and service here would have meant separation from one's family. Soon after the Serbian withdrawal,

---

4   I do not know the reason for the sabotage, but see Bax (1997) for similar actions elsewhere in Herzegovina, where Partisan memorials were interpreted by local Croats as symbols of Serbian oppression.

5   Serbian forces in Bosnia Herzegovina consisted of Bosnian Serbs as well as part of the former JNA.

6   Several Muslims I spoke to saw the Croatian conquest of Stolac as part of a deal between the Serbian and Croatian forces about sharing the territory of Bosnia Herzegovina between them. As an example of such a deal people recall how in this period of Croatian/Muslim control of Stolac, Croatian refugees from Central Bosnia were driven to Croatian territory south of Stolac through Serb-controlled territory, that is, with the approval of the Serbs (see Glenny 1996: 196-8 for further elements of the political games influencing life in Stolac).

the Serbs started shelling Stolac, which caused several casualties, and fighting between HVO and the Serbs resumed.

The Muslims and Croats joined forces from June/July 1992 and for almost a year, though as mentioned above it was a marriage of convenience. There was sporadic fighting between Croat and Bosnian forces several places in Bosnia Herzegovina, though not in the Stolac area. Then in April 1993, the Croats started arresting leading Muslim intellectuals and local Muslim politicians in and around Stolac, as well as the few Muslims who held more responsible positions in the HVO. The arrests continued, and on the 1 July all adult Muslim men from Stolac were arrested, interrogated, beaten and driven to prison camps (*logori*). According to my sources the oldest person arrested was 90 years old, and the youngest 13. A few managed to escape through the mountains, and a few hid in the hills. According to my informants, the whole operation was carried out systematically by troops from the HVO and the HV (*Hrvatska Vojska*, the Croatian army).[7] To the Stolac Muslims the mass arrest came as a surprise. Although they had had a feeling that something was going to happen, my informants had generally been 'naïve' enough to hope that ethnic cleansing was not going to happen to them. Nevertheless, the Muslim men were forced into prison camps known as Dretelj and Gabela after the villages of the same name outside Čapljina, not far from Stolac. The camps were former JNA (*Jugoslovenska Narodna Armija*; the Yugoslav People's Army) hangars and ammunition warehouses, totally unfit for human habitation. The Muslims were crammed together in these extremely hot and totally dark buildings. They were beaten, threatened, starved and offered extremely low rations of water. And they were forced to listen to and also sing Croatian nationalist songs.

Women and children continued to stay in Stolac for about one month after the men had been expelled. It was a month of fear and uncertainty. Croats looted and burned down old Muslim houses, and terrorised the Muslim civilians. And the women and children had no information about their husbands, fathers and brothers. Then on 3 and 4 August, the women and children (and the men who had hidden themselves) were picked up in their homes, escorted to the school or a local factory where they were robbed, and then transported to the borders of Croat-held territory, from where they were forced to walk to the Bosnian-held territory of Blagaj. In Blagaj people searched for places to stay,

---

7   Though it is important to account for the many local strategies and motives in the war (see e.g. Bax 2000a, 2000b) when outlining episodes in the war in Southern Herzegovina, one also has to acknowledge that the expulsion of the Muslims from Stolac and other towns was orchestrated from above and formed part of a general Croatian attempt to annex and ethnically cleanse parts of Bosnia Herzegovina, see for instance Cigar (1995) and Glenny (1996).

in private homes, or abandoned houses: many families lived together in a few square metres.

Throughout the following year (1993-94) the women, children and elderly lived under miserable conditions. Both Croatian and Serbian forces shelled them, there was hardly any food to be obtained, and many contracted infectious diseases. Some managed to smuggle money or some basic food supplies past the Croatian search in Stolac, but these resources only lasted a short time.

Following the expulsion of the Muslims, Croatian forces started looting Muslim property in Stolac and destroying all signs of the town's Muslim heritage: the town's four mosques were blown up and the remnants were removed. Old houses, the town market, the town café, which had been built in traditional Ottoman style in 1986, and an office complex from 1990 were burned. Libraries, private as well as public, were burned, collections of carpets and rugs and other old irreplaceable antiques were destroyed.[8] The destruction of Stolac formed part of what can be seen as a general 'urbicide' (destruction of urbanity) in Bosnia Herzegovina (Coward 2002).

For the first three months after the internment, the prison camps were kept secret, but their existence was brought to public attention after the visit of the journalist Ed Vulliamy to the camps on 7 September 1993 (Vulliamy 1995: 277-86) and the visit of the Red Cross the day before. After the visit of the Red Cross, around 500 of the prisoners in the poorest condition were released, but only on condition that they were to be transported to territory outside Bosnia Herzegovina – that is, mainly European countries and the US. The rest remained in the camps. In the following month more were released, but many remained imprisoned until March 1994, when the Washington deal was signed. They could then rejoin their families in Blagaj and other areas; for a period of one year, they had not had any information about one another.

The return

As mentioned above, Stolac participated in a UN-sponsored pilot project to facilitate the inter-federation return of displaced persons. But such returns were difficult to realise, and many local politicians obstructed them. And the situation was particularly grave in Stolac. One must remember that the expulsion of the Muslims from villages in Herzegovina had formed part of a general Croatian war aim of creating ethnically clean territories, whereas return

---

8   See document *Crimes in Stolac Municipality* for a thorough statement of the destruction of historic monuments in Stolac. The document is also on the Internet: http://www.haverford. edu/relg/sells/stolac/CrimesSt.pdf

projects such as the one in Stolac attempted to remix these territories. In the eyes of many nationalist-minded Herzegovinian Croats, towns like Stolac had been conquered in war – so they and their contents were to be seen as booty.

In 1996, groups of Muslims began visiting Stolac for the first time since the war. They drove from Mostar by bus escorted by SFOR (Stabilisation Force; a NATO-led multinational force overseeing the implementation of the Dayton agreement). On their arrival in Stolac they were often met by angry Croats throwing stones, eggs and bread at the buses. According to my informants, the throwing of bread was an attempt to insult the Muslims, which alluded to the period during the war when the Muslims were starving to death. The Muslims could not walk the streets or visit their properties, and only some were able to visit relatives' graves. The visit was a shock for the Muslims. They had not seen the town after the destruction of all Muslim architecture; furthermore, the Croats had not cleaned up the town, and so rubble and garbage marred the face of the town. After the first visits many Muslims were disillusioned. Though they had initially looked forward to returning, many now had second thoughts. Nevertheless, workers protected by SFOR started rebuilding damaged and looted houses, preparing for the first Muslims to return. When the Croats realised that the Muslims were actually going to return, a wave of post-war violence started. Around 200 Muslim houses in the municipality were blown up or burned within a short time, and the work of the pilot project was sabotaged. Though the mayor of the town had instructions from the UN to support the return, and though the police force was officially neutral, not one of the Croats guilty of these crimes was ever caught. The Croats kept intimidating the Muslims hoping that they would not return and reclaim their property, and several episodes of physical violence were recorded.

Despite the difficulties and with a great deal of delay, the first sixteen Muslim families returned to live in Stolac in June 1997. The initial period was very difficult and horrifying. The Muslims did not dare walk the streets in the centre of town, as they were met with threats, comments and sometimes even direct assaults. The social network did not work; mostly people stayed indoors by themselves watching TV. There were no Muslim shops or cafés and nearly all the facilities (institutional as well as others) were controlled by and more or less reserved for Croats only. Many of the returning Muslims felt that Stolac was as a totally new town. The street names were new, the physical shape of the town was new, and there were new and unfamiliar neighbours. The situation was not unequivocally depressing. Croat shops soon started selling the products desired by the Muslims, and one of the Croat-run cafés welcomed the Muslims. People felt that some Croats (mainly old friends) were pleased with their return to Stolac. Slowly things started to improve: more Muslims returned, some

Muslims opened shops, and people began to feel safer – though the violent episodes and mining of property did continue and the police's detection rate was almost zero.

At the beginning of 2000, things improved further. Following the death of the Croatian president Franjo Tuđman in December 1999, the financial support from Croatia to the Herzegovinian Croats and their self-proclaimed independent state *Herceg-Bosna* dried up (Grandits 2007). This made them much more dependent on funding from the international community, funding that the OHR and UN could use as a political means of exerting pressure. And because Mostar was much more important for the leading Croat politicians in the HDZ than Stolac – which on the other hand held a high symbolic significance for the OHR – deals about such issues as the school and the return of Muslim property could be made. Furthermore, in April 1998, the Croat mayor of Stolac, Pero Raguz, became the first Bosnian politician to be sacked by the UN's High Representative Carlos Westendorp. And in November 1999 his successor Pero Pazin was also sacked, due to his own obstruction of the return of the Muslim refugees. Furthermore, the local police were placed under the close scrutiny of the international Police Task Force (IPTF). When I started fieldwork in September 2000, the situation for the Muslims in Stolac was thus markedly better than it had been only one or two years before. Despite the improvement of the situation and despite the feeling of the Muslims that the Croats had accepted their presence, at least on a pragmatic level, changes were slow. Stolac was still a more or less totally ethnically divided town, with the Muslims being discriminated against on all levels of society. Many of my informants compared the situation to a kind of apartheid.

The public sphere in Stolac

Institutionally

According to several employees in the OHR, IPTF (International Police Task Force) and OSCE (Organization for Security and Cooperation in Europe) I talked to, it was very difficult to make progress in Stolac municipality, as every attempt at establishing or facilitating inter-ethnic cooperation was obstructed by hardliners in the HDZ. Furthermore, according to the same sources, there was reason to believe that heavy and well-organised criminal activity emanated from institutions, companies and groups of persons around Stolac with connections to the HDZ. Upholding the nationalist policy of ethnic separation could therefore be a way for such corrupt Croats to profit financially. I will not evaluate these presumptions; but it does make sense that a rather influential and inflexible group of Croats was trying as hard as possible to uphold ethnic division in Stolac in as many areas as possible. When I did fieldwork, Stolac was ethnically divided on all institutional levels, and intense symbolic demonstrations constantly reinforced nationalist thinking and promoted ethnic stereotypes. In short, antagonistic Croats dominated the public sphere, where they clearly communicated the message: "Croats and Muslims cannot live together." I shall give some examples of how thorough the ethnic division and discrimination was on the institutional level at the time of my fieldwork.

All local public enterprises in Stolac had Croat directors, and they only employed Croat workers (only three Muslim men had been re-employed in their former jobs due to their much specialised skills). Croats ran the post office, the banks, the telephone company, the power supply, and the water company. As a result, Muslims used banks and post-offices in Mostar, and only a few Muslims had telephones in their homes. Furthermore, the post office only used Croatian stamps and Croatian currency (as well as DM: Deutschmarks). The municipal assembly elected in April 2000 was dominated by the HDZ and, despite the sharing of power principles laid down by the OSCE, Muslim town council members had been completely excluded from the local administration. Since the reunification of the cantonal police in the Herzegovina-Neretva canton in June 2000, the local police station had officially been multiethnic. Interethnic cooperation had in reality been very rare. Furthermore, according to the local representative of the IPTF Croats still dictated the majority of police activities and protected criminals from prosecution. He himself had to conceal his written documents on a floppy disc, as they would not be safe on his computer in his office at the police station. Since May 2000, Muslim school children had been permitted to make use of a small part of the local primary school, but classes for Muslims and Croat children were still held separately, and the secondary school as well as the school gym was for Croats only. Muslims were excluded from local public health care; the hospital built and financed with public funds before the war only treated Croats. The nearest TV antenna was turned so that it was only possible for the residents of Stolac to watch Croatian television unless they bought a satellite dish. A small town had been built on a field on the western side of Stolac, which was inhabited only by Croats. Croats occupied many Muslim houses, though the situation has improved since I left Stolac. In short, the self-proclaimed state of *Herceg-Bosna* was a *de facto* reality. In fact, in November 2000, the HDZ took the initiative to hold a referendum among Croats, in order to establish an independent state *Herceg-Bosna*. This referendum, which was invalid under the terms set by the OHR, was regarded by the Muslims in town as pure provocation.

Symbolically

The public sphere in Stolac was dominated by nationalist-minded Croats symbolically as well as institutionally. The public sphere was filled with nationalist symbols of all sorts. Again, let me offer some examples. Today the central mosque in town (*Čaršija* mosque) has been rebuilt; but when I did fieldwork, the whole area – where the mosque and all the old buildings connected to the marketplace area surrounding the mosque had been before – was laid out as a parking lot, and on one side there were three flags: the flag of *Herceg-Bosna*, and two flags with the Herzegovinian Croats' newly designed version of the coat of arms of Stolac. A big wooden cross had been erected outside the municipal office. Crosses were used by the Croats as territorial markers in various places in Herzegovina. On the outskirts of villages or areas ruled by Croats, one often saw two/three-meter-tall concrete crosses painted white. Inside the medical centre, there was a huge poster with a picture of the former Croatian president Franjo Tuđman, who supported the struggle of the Herzegovinian Croats. Inside all the public buildings I entered, I saw the *Šahovnica* (a framed checkerboard emblem composed of white and red squares, the Croatian coat of arms with strongly nationalist and at times fascist undertones) the size of a normal sheet, and several places also a poster of Franjo Tuđman. On the top of *Stari Grad* (Pasha Rizvanbegovic fortress, an old fortress and a cultural monument), there was a big Croatian flag that could be seen from almost any part of town. Nationalist Croat graffiti was abundant, though a lot of it originated from the time of the war. For instance, on entering Stolac one sees the sentence *Dobro došli U Stolac* (Welcome to Stolac) painted on a house, with the 'U' painted in a way that symbolises Ustashe.[9] However, the graffiti is rather faded. Streets and town sites have been given new names, which are all part of a Croatian nationalist discourse. Many Bosnian Croat cars had a BiH (Bosnia Herzegovina) sticker on the back of the car, but the letters were printed on a red and white checked background, the Croatian national symbol. Leading up to the general election in November 2000, many of the election posters of the Herzegovinian Croats featured fierce nationalist rhetoric. In short, Stolac was ruled by nationalist-minded Herzegovinian Croats. On the institutional level and on the public symbolic level, the Muslims have no influence. In all these arenas ethnic discrimination and nationalist symbolism prevails.

I have found it necessary to begin with this short prologue summarising the war in Herzegovina and Stolac in particular, outlining the return of the Muslims to

---

9   Ustashe is closely connected to violent Croat nationalist and fascist policy.

Stolac, and describing the incessant dominance of nationalist ideology in the public sphere. These matters are rather complicated, and I refer to episodes and periods throughout the book. The other main function of the prologue is to describe a town where nationalist thinking had come to be totally dominant because of both war aims and post-war policy. My informants' counterdiscourse, which is the focus of the book, has to be understood on the background of this dominance.

Introduction

The war in former Yugoslavia – mainly Croatia and Bosnia Herzegovina – and the fierceness with which it was carried out is probably still remembered by most Europeans. For many, this war inside Europe destroyed the feeling of living in a peaceful region, a feeling built upon a common European commitment to not letting the Second World War repeat itself: Never again! Some, though, succeeded in upholding the idea of everlasting European peace by ascribing the war and violence in former Yugoslavia to an endemic Balkan mentality: the Other within.

The war is now over, at least it officially ended with the Dayton agreement on 14 December 1995, and the people of the region are now trying to piece together a life – pieces consisting of war-related traumas, nationalist propaganda, ruined economies, disappointment, memories of pre-war life and so on. This book focuses on this puzzle of post-war life among the Muslim population of Stolac, a small town in Bosnia Herzegovina. More specifically, I will concentrate on how in everyday practices and narratives the Muslims of Stolac resist the ethnonationalist discourse that has invaded so many aspects of both public and private life throughout the last two decades. Their resistance is seldom outspoken, consciously articulated or organised; rather it consists of a steady insistence on not using ethnic or national categories and stereotypes when identifying themselves and others. And it exists in a hope for future inter-ethnic coexistence. I term this resistance counterdiscourse.

Many books and articles dealing with the war and pre-war period in former Yugoslavia have been published in the last fifteen years, and nearly all of these have analysed the role of nationalism. Some maintain that nationalist or ethnic tensions in former Yugoslavia ignited the war; others have demonstrated how such tensions were produced throughout the war and pre-war period to legitimise a fight for power. Hardly any, however, have focused on how ordinary people trying to hold on to everyday life have related to the discourses of nationalism outside the public sphere.[1] In this book I maintain this ethnographic focus; and, as my results illustrate, nationalist policy and ethnic identity and stereotypes in the light of the everyday life of the Muslims of Stolac

---

1 Bougarel et al. (2007), Jansen (2000a), Maček (2000a), Povrzanovic (1997) and Feldman et al. (1993) are important in this respect.

come to mean something else and also something less, as they have to live with the consequences of ethnic hatred in a much more direct way. My analysis thus partly contradicts structuralist theories of violence, claiming that violence results in the creation of unambiguous and clear-cut identities. By relating such an argument to *the way in which* actual victims of violence react to the creation of unambiguous identities, one sees that complexity, flexibility and inconsistent categories are what mark post-war/post-violence society.

Because the complex question of ethnicity and nationality in former Yugoslavian republics is so central for understanding both war and post-war life, I shall provide a short explanation:

1) In the former Yugoslavia, everyone had a Yugoslav *citizenship*.

2) In the former Yugoslavia, one could choose a *national identity* from the options given by the state, for example on census forms. However, the English term 'national identity' or 'nation' does not fully cover the term used in former Yugoslavia: *narod*. In Danish, my own language, there is a more or less equivalent term: *folk* (or in German *volk*). The national identities most relevant for this study are: Croat, Serb, Muslim and Yugoslav.

3) In former Yugoslavia, one had an *ethnic* or *ethnoreligious* identity (*nacija*). I use the terms interchangeably. This identity was more or less 'inherited' from one's parents. Though religious terms are used to designate ethnic identity, one cannot translate *nacija* as religious identity. In my study, I will be referring to the following ethnic or ethnoreligious identities: Catholic, Orthodox Christian and Muslim. And in general (but not always) Croats are Catholics, Serbs are Orthodox Christians, and Muslims are Muslims.

However, things are and were not as clear-cut as the above divisions indicate. In the book, I do not use the terms 'national identity' (*narod*) and 'ethnic identity' (*nacija*), and nationalism and ethnicisation in an entirely consistent and clear-cut manner. In the first place, my informants did not do this either, and in the second place the major aim of nationalist policy was to conjoin the two identities, so that the emotionally deep ethnoreligious identity could strengthen the more arbitrary national identity. This nationalist project did succeed up to a point: when my informants – who are Muslims – referred to a Muslim identity, it was not always obvious whether they were referring to ethnic (*nacija*) or national identity (*narod*); and often, it was my sense that they were not certain either. It is necessary to add a further remark on terminology. A 'Bosnian' (*bosanac*) is someone coming from Bosnia Herzegovina no matter what his ethnic affiliation. 'Bosniak' (*bošnjak*) means Bosnian Muslim. However, the terms however have a disputed history, see Chapter 10.

The structure of the book

Part I, *Framing the question,* consists of the Prologue, with factual information about war and post-war episodes in the Stolac area. Chapter 1 presents a thorough reading of contemporary anthropological perspectives on war and war-related violence, and my own research is placed in relation to this. In Chapter 2, I depict the way in which my informants' world has been unmade: primarily through ontological insecurity, the breakdown of mental categories, moral decay, and an all-pervading feeling of loss. Chapter 3 outlines the theoretical tools for analysing identification, discourse and counterdiscourse; the delicate balance is to establish the concept of counterdiscourse solidly enough for it to function as an analytical tool, and porously enough to avoid doing violence to the ambiguities of real life.

Part II, *Who are they, the ones who did this to us?* is about how the Muslims of Stolac identify possible Others when accounting for the war as well as for their present hopeless situation. My main argument is that their identifications of the Others resist the ethnicisation that came to dominate public life in former Yugoslavia and in the seceding nations. Chapter 4, therefore, outlines the emergence of this national thinking in former Yugoslavia, showing how it is rooted in the post-Second-World-War politics of Tito, but exploded throughout the 1980s as a way to gain power. Chapters 5, 6, 7 and 8 present the most important categories of identity which my informants employ when identifying the guilty party: immoral politics; decent and indecent people; un-cultured persons, and, lastly, a complex range of different ways of categorising Croats (my informants' main ethnic Other). All identifications avoid ethnifying the war and are part of the Muslims' counterdiscourse.

Part III, *Who are we, since this was done to us?* deals with my informants' identification of themselves as Muslims, an identity that has become increasingly important. Pre-war embedded practices of identification no longer suffice, so new and more conscious values have to be attached to their ethnoreligious identity. When identifying Muslimness, my informants avoid drawing upon the national and religious values promoted especially by Bosnian Muslim political elite throughout the war. Chapter 9, which should be read in continuation of Chapter 4, accounts for the emergence of this specific Bosnian Muslim national religious identity; and I argue that it came late, was contradictory, and can to some extent be seen as an elite project. In Chapter 10, I outline the features of pre-war processes of everyday Bosnian Muslim ethnoreligious identifi-

cation. I find it reasonable to conclude that this identification was very important, but also embedded in everyday life and characterised by respectful means
of inter-ethnic interaction. This insight is important later when I demonstrate
how my informants have objectified elements of such pre-war habitual patterns
of inter-ethnic interaction today, and when I estimate the changes that the war
has created in matters of identification. Chapter 11 illustrates how national and
religious identification is only of minor importance to the Muslims of Stolac.
Chapters 12, 13, 14 and 15 present the most important categories of identities
which my informants employ when identifying themselves: a strong local pa-
triotic attachment that includes all respectable citizens of Stolac; an ideal of
tolerance and inter-ethnic coexistence; shifting attachments to the discursive
construct of Europe-Balkan; and the 'role of the victim.' The first three resist
the nationalist thinking to various degrees. For my informants, their Muslim
identity is of utmost importance; however, the content of this identity relates
not to nationalist or religious elements, but to values stressing interethnic respect and coexistence. Only in the 'role of the victim' have I found elements of
an antagonist, essentialist ethnic identity.

The field

In a tragic but also important way, Bosnia Herzegovina serves as a contemporary example of how war and war-related violence is connected to processes
of identification. The war in Bosnia Herzegovina consisted of several conflicts.
One of them took place between the Croats and the Muslims in Herzegovina,
and it is this somewhat neglected war I look into. I choose Stolac as a field site
as the UN and OHR (Office of High Representatives) had a pilot project here
encouraging Muslims and Serbs to return. A local employee in the DRC (Danish Refugee Centre) helped set me up in Stolac with some of his friends; here
I rented a separate room on the lower floor of their house. In the beginning,
I ate alone and did not interfere very much in my landlords' lives. I did not
want to trouble them too much, and they left me alone so I could concentrate
on my research. Soon, however, our formal ways of interacting changed. I had
my meals in their house, we interacted a great deal, and I came to have a very
relaxed relationship with the family (children, brothers and parent), several of
their friends, and their home in general. I listened to their tragic stories and
their present problems, and they comforted me when I missed my wife and
children in Denmark. I conducted fieldwork from the middle of September
2000 to the middle of April 2001, taking a two-week break around Christmas to
recuperate (the sad and depressing life and fate of my informants having taxed
my energy) and for preliminary reflections on my data. My relatively short pe-

riod of fieldwork could not fully dissolve my role as an outsider, but in the end I did not think of myself as a total stranger. My fieldwork in Stolac was in a way rather traditional, but conducted in an untraditional situation. I participated in as many different situations as possible and interacted with as many people as I could. Some I only met or talked to once or twice, others I interacted with on a regular basis. As Stolac is in some respects a small town, I soon became acquainted with a lot of people, old and young, and heard stories about even more. Naturally, my data is marked by my role as an interested, educated, male, white Westerner. However, I never found that such roles excluded me from participating in any situations. And though much of my data is affected by, and some even came about as a result of, these roles, I also feel that I engaged in various situations where I could observe and listen or interact in a relatively relaxed manner without playing the lead: listening to people educate their children, watching television with informants, sitting in the café, drinking with some of my informants, walking around town talking with informants, participating in funerals, visiting people informally and so on.

I had five key informants with whom I interacted on daily basis:

– A schoolteacher in the mid-thirties. He lived with his wife, their small children and his parents. Like many of my informants, he was traumatised by his stay in a prison camp. He often told me how episodes from that stay troubled his sleep at night. Despite these tough memories, he spent a lot of energy trying to focus on positive aspects of the present, and he felt a heavy responsibility, due to his role as teacher and father, to refrain from instilling hate in the younger generation. This educational function, however, sometimes collided with the bitterness and anger which he also bore.

– A couple in their fifties. They lived with their grown-up sons. The husband was lucky to have work, which he conscientiously carried out. They had a nice house. All their furniture however had been stolen, and the house had been vandalised during the war. The couple was only slowly putting the house in order. As they sometimes said, they simply lacked the energy. The couple was bitter and often depressed, and they loved to talk about the past when they had experienced prosperity and happiness. They worried a lot about their children's future, as they feared there were only very few opportunities for them.

– A young man in his mid-twenties. He studied at the faculty in Mostar – a hard-working student. He lived with his parents and was an indispensable workforce in the home. He was very determined about asserting the future in a positive way. After four months of imprisonment in a Croatian-run prison camp he had been living abroad for four years, where he had been building up a life, and had a job and friends. Then voluntarily he had returned to Stolac. Living in Stolac, therefore, was for him a conscious choice and he wanted it to be successful. In contrast to his friends of the same age, he was interested in politics. And he believed, at least to a point, that a change on the political level away from nationalist politics was possible and could even improve ordinary people's situation and inter-ethnic relations in general.

– An old lady around seventy years old. She was living with her daughter. Although I regarded her as generally positive, she was also often very sad. She lamented her own situation: Stolac, the once so beautiful city where she had grown up, was now nothing but ruins. Most of all, though, she missed her son and her grandchildren. They were now living abroad and contact was rare. All her life she had been living with ethnic differences as a natural part of life, and she simply could not comprehend the present ethnic animosity in Bosnia Herzegovina, let alone Stolac.

An important part of my data stems from interviews. Some of the interviews only had one interviewee, but most of them were conducted in people's homes with much of the family and often also some friends present. The interviews were loosely structured. Normally, I introduced topics which I had found to be relevant when doing participant observation, and which helped steer the conversation toward subject matters I found important; but just as often the discussion took unanticipated detours, some of which became subjects for further conversations and interviews with other informants. In sum, I conducted twenty-eight taped interviews lasting on average one and a half to three hours. Often after I had turned off the tape recorder, people kept talking for an additional thirty minutes to two hours. I conducted the majority of the interviews with the same assistant, who vouched for me since I did not know all of the interviewees beforehand. In Denmark, I had taught myself Serbo-Croatian, or Bosnian, as Muslims in Bosnia Herzegovina call it today. And during at least the last three and a half months (the period when I also conducted the interviews), I felt I had an adequate command of the language. However, when I talked to people or overheard conversations, several shades of meaning got lost that were doubtless important. I therefore translated and transcribed all my interviews in Stolac into Danish with the help of an informant who spoke Danish almost fluently (he had spent four years in Denmark as a refugee). My interviews and participant observation therefore contributed to each other in various ways. Throughout the book I quote from both taped interviews and conversations written down post factum. I do not always point out whether I am dealing with the one or the other, only mentioning it when I feel it is significant. All the names of my informants are pseudonyms; however, the same pseudonyms are used consistently for the same persons, allowing the reader (at least to some degree) to get to know the different informants. On a few occasions, however, I have used two different pseudonyms for the same person, simply in order to prevent a potential identification. Only rarely do I offer individual characterisations of or personal information about my informants. I know it is detrimental to my presentation; however, the anonymity of my informants takes first priority.

My study has one great bias. Only on a few occasions did I talk to or otherwise interact with Croat citizens of Stolac. Some of my informants encouraged me to do so; however, I did not feel I could entertain credibility among either the Muslims or the Croats by pursuing such a strategy, and I did not have sufficient time to divide up my fieldwork. As a result, my analysis deals with the point of view of the Muslims of Stolac alone.

In addition to my fieldwork in Stolac, I also did research among Bosnians living in Denmark. I carried out ten unstructured interviews with Bosnians who had been granted residence permits. And for three months I visited Bosnians living in a camp for asylum applicants on a regular basis. I have not worked systematically with the data collected through my research in Denmark. But the research did function as important background knowledge for my later fieldwork in Stolac. It meant that I was already familiar with relevant cultural categories, personal stories about loss, strategies of resistance, repression and acceptance of ethnic thinking. And perhaps most importantly, the research in Denmark put my Stolac data into perspective, enabling me to see how fierce and unambiguous ethnic denunciation thrives best in exile, probably because people then do not have to live with the consequences of their own actions in quite the same way. In addition, socialising with Bosnian asylum applicants gave me a chance to practise my Serbo-Croatian.

Chapter 1

Anthropological perspectives on war and war-related violence

In this chapter, I identify important perspectives in contemporary studies of war and war-related violence, and place my own research in relation to these. The perspectives used, which I have labelled *instrumentality/structure, expression* and *experience/narrative,* have developed in relation to and at times as critiques of each other; they are not necessarily mutually exclusive, but reflect focuses on different phases of war and war-related violence. The first perspective attempts to explain the outbreak of war and violent acts; the second centres on the cultural meaning of violent events; and the last represents *experiences with* and *narratives of violence,* focusing on the effects of violence. The perspectives also reflect different analytical levels, falling from a macro to a micro level, which, some would claim, relates to the possibility of empirical comparison (Schröder and Schmidt 2001), an argument reminiscent of the 'verstehen' – 'erklären' contrast.

Instrumentality/structure

The anthropological literature on war and violence reflects broader developments in anthropological theory, in which the critique of evolutionistic and functionalistic theories has given way to theories focusing on the relation between structure and strategy. Functional explanations of war (Gluckman 1955; Turner 1956; Ferguson 1984; Vayda and Rappaport 1968) have been abandoned, and though evolutionary theories of violence are still present in contemporary anthropology (Keegan 1994; Carneiro 1996; Reyna 1994; Abbink 2001), many explanations favour at least some degree of agency/structure.

Instrumentality

In relation to the first part of the *instrumentality/structure* pair, the central argument is that violence does not occur randomly but is intended. Competition over scarce resources or competition for power does not automatically result in violence; rather violence is conceived as a deliberate outcome of conscious actors' strategic considerations. Violence is an instrument or a source of social power; it is action taken in order to reach certain goals (Hardin 1995; Turton 1997; Schmidt and Schröder 2001; Jabri 1996) – a thought echoing Carl von Clausewitz's famous dictum that war is politics by other means. When explaining the break up of Yugoslavia, for instance, such analyses have often highlighted the erosions of political power centres (both national and global) and explained violence as strategic action intended to cement or defend economic and political positions (Schierup 1991; Cohen 1993; Simić 1993; Malcom 1994; Nagengast 1994; Bennett 1995; Shoup 1995; Sofus 1996; Glenny 1996; Gallagher 1997; Gow 1997; Turton 1997; Brubaker 1998; Sunic 1998; Oberschall 2000).[1]

When discussing violence as a source of power, legitimacy becomes a central issue. Riches (1986) has argued that one reason why violence is a universal social and cultural resource is that "performance of violence is inherently liable to be contested on the question of legitimacy" (ibid. 11). Violent clashes in modern states – defined by their 'legitimate' monopolisation of violence (Giddens 1985) – could therefore be theorised as fights for or contestations of this legitimacy, as seen by the fact that often the very definition of the status of a conflict is strategically contested. For example, are we dealing with war, civil war, terror, defence or humanitarian intervention? The use of violence to contest legitimacy is usually accompanied by propaganda. In modern conflicts, the mass media have increasingly helped to create the demonic Other, on whom violence then turns (Allen 1999; Naughton 1994; Malešič 1993; Sofus 1999). Such propaganda often tends to produce a strictly polarised structure of 'us-them' that no-one can escape, that leaves no room for ambiguity, and where 'our' side is understood as morally superior (Löfving and Maček 2000; Schmidt and Schröder 2001). Discussing such propaganda, advocates of the instrumentalist perspective have often invoked it as an explicit critique of the so-called primordial perspective,[2] though the primordial perspective is seldom clear-cut (in relation to the Balkans, however, see Mojzes 1994; Kaplan 1993).

The instrumentalist approach to violence sometimes fails to notice that even though violence is a possible power strategy for local elites, strategic action is affected by broader global systemic processes. Mass communication and

---

1   Although, as argued by Sluka (2000), state violence should not (only) be seen as an instrument with which potential elites can seize power in periods of eroding state power. Rather, state violence tends to increase when the power of the state increases, as strong states do not have to take into consideration their ways of defending established inequalities, and violence is often the most economical means of protecting privileges. Therefore, according to Sluka, it is not disintegration of the Weberian state that explains contemporary excesses in state-related violence (as argued, for instance, by Desjarlais 1994; Brubaker 1998), but rather the opposite.

2   The argument is that violent conflicts are outbursts of latent ethnic, religious, cultural or other essential differences.

mass immigration have made local identification problematic; and along with growth in the global weapons industry and the rise in long-distance national-ism, this has increased the very potential for conflict (Anderson 1992; Turton 1997). Another dimension that fits into the instrumentalist perspective but which is also often neglected is that wars, even if they are the outcome of stra-tegic considerations, often create their own complex dynamic, inasmuch as war tends to develop into a kind of mental framework in which physical violence occurs. Bax (2000a; 2000b), for instance, describes how in Herzegovina already existing local conflicts escalate, change, and form their own dynamic in a war situation, because local leaders perceive the war as a framework for solving existing conflict by new means. War then comes to serve the different purposes of many actors, which may in turn account for the difficulties of putting an end to wars.

Structure

The instrumentalist approach, which focuses on the strategic use of violence, conflicts with *structural* theories; however, I have grouped them together be-cause they both attempt to explain the origin of war and violence. Structurally inspired anthropological analyses of war and war-related violence have prima-rily focused on the inherent potential of violence and war to create identities. In a condensed form, the line of reasoning goes like this: Identity is built on dif-ference, and when differences become too small, identity becomes threatened and violence then recreates or reinforces differences. This is Blok's (2000) argu-ment, for instance: following Freud, he calls violent practices aimed at destroy-ing similarities and thereby creating the Other, the: "narcissism of minor differ-ences." As he writes in respect to the eruption of war in former Yugoslavia:

> Once more we see the working of the narcissism of minor differences: the ero-sion and loss of distinctions and differences result in violence. (ibid. 41).

Violence as a technique to create the Other is also present in Malkki's (1998) study of Hutu narratives of Tutsi violence:

> Through violence, bodies of individual persons become metamorphosed into *specimens* of the ethnic category for which they are supposed to stand. (ibid. 88; original italics).

Violence, it is argued, creates the structural division on which identity is built: we are us because we fight against them, and vica versa. Consider also Har-rison's (1993) claim that violence in Melanesia has a structural function – that is, groups do not create war, war creates groups. As he sees it, both gift giving and violence create social relations, which are contrary to the view of Mauss, who saw violence as the failure of the gift (Corbey 2000, 2006). Sorabji (1995) has argued that the logic of the violence in many parts of Bosnia Herzegovina was to de-personalise social relations and annihilate existing cultural values of neighbourliness in order to install an ideology of nationalism. The violence was therefore often rather extreme and furthermore performed in local settings, so as to destroy the memory of ethnic coexistence. In a study of ethnic cleansing in Bosnia-Herzegovina, Hayden (1996) follows a different, but still structural approach. Inspired by Mary Douglas, he claims that in the nationalist ideologies of the new Yugoslav states reigned a vision of ethnic homogeneity that did not correspond to reality. The ethnic cleansing and the removal of populations that occurred during the war constituted an attempt to recreate the world to correspond to this vision. Finally, in his re-reading of Clastres, Bowman (2001) suggests that violence does not even have to be carried out physically to construct identity. Violence is a force that creates boundaries and may operate conceptually prior to manifesting itself in action. It is the imagining of violence that "...serves to create the integrities and identities which are in turn subjected to those forms of violence which seek victims" (ibid. 27), and it is the imagining of violence against the Other that is the medium through which (embedded) societies are represented to themselves.

So far we have two different explanations of war and war-related violence. In the first, violence is purely instrumental and contextual, which means that violence is never studied in its own right. Often such analyses inspired by political science explain war but do not account for what happens when violence breaks out. In doing so, they overlook the cultural framework in which violence is constructed and interpreted (see next paragraph); miss the possibility of operating with innate structural properties of violence; and often reproduce a Hobbesian view of human nature, which views violence as latent and erupting when the centralisation of power erodes. In the structural approach violence is perceived not as a source of social power, but as a source (either acted or imagined) of identity. Furthermore, the inherent logic of violence creates subject positions without the help of any concrete subjects. This perspective ignores the fact that the use of and reaction to violence can change the course of violent events. Claiming that violence creates unambiguous identities, therefore, only accounts for part of the process relevant for understanding the relationship between violence and identification. Violence plays a part in constructing a general polarised atmosphere of 'us and them', but this does not say anything about how people react or relate to such a dichotomised space of identity. Furthermore, even if we accept the idea that violence creates unambiguous identities, such consequences should not be confused with explanations of why violence occurs in the first place.

Expression

The next perspective to be found in contemporary anthropology of war and war-related violence focuses on the violent acts themselves, on the meaning they carry and the cultural landscape in which they are shaped and serve as communication. The perspective is based on the implicit assumption that the way in which one dies or is injured is significant and seldom coincidental. The studies grouped together in this second category therefore try to explicate (Geertz 1973) rather than explain violent events; one could say that they make a 'thick description' of the violent events.

Van de Port (1998) conducted fieldwork in a Serbian town in Vojvodina. His research was meant to be a study of gypsies, but then the war broke out and left him and seemingly everybody else in a condition of mental and existential chaos. But only seemingly. He discovered the existence of a cultural logic that he, following Taussig, calls implicit social knowledge, which was used to make sense of the madness of the war. This knowledge, which was neither conscious nor verbalised, was for instance manifested in the Serbs' ambivalent relationship to the gypsies. On the surface, the Serbs condemned the gypsies as uncivilised primitives, but below the surface the Serbs embraced the primitive, uncivilised, emotional craziness that they felt the gypsies represented. So in everyday life the 'civilised' Serbian citizens of Vojvodina showed distaste for the war-related barbaric and insane violence; but at night in the gypsy bars they embraced it because of the connection they felt with the implicit social knowledge which the gypsies embodied. Other studies have focused more on the violent acts themselves and shown how they can be loaded with cultural meaning (Feldman 1991; Krohn-Hansen 1997b). Malkki (1998), for instance, analyses the Tutsis' bestial, violent acts against the Hutus as attempts to dehumanise the Hutus, to associate them with nature and disassociate them from culture. And Olujic (1998) argues that war rapes in former Yugoslavia were not only physical assaults on the women, but also attacks on the male members of their family, whose honour was related to the female members' chastity. The individual body becomes in this way a metaphorical representative of the social body, and the killing or maiming of that body symbolically kills and maims the individual's family and ethnic group. The war rapes also reinforced the cultural notions of cleanliness and dirtiness associated with sexuality and ethnic affiliation. Through forced pregnancy resulting from rape, aggressors could 'purify the blood' of the attacked group by creating 'ethnically cleansed' babies belonging to the group of the invading fathers. On quite a different scale, Appadurai (1999) tries to understand contemporary ethnic atrocities worldwide in relation to a culture of modernity. Modernity and globalisation, he claims, have disembedded social relations and created uncertain and alienated identities. Violence thus uses the body to recreate certainty and intimacy in a grotesque way.[3]

Anthropological studies of violence that focus on expression and meaning try to understand the cultural anchoring of violent acts and how violence functions as communication. And sometimes such insight is used to explain the potential instrumentality of violence. A major challenge confronting anthropological studies of the expressive character of violence is to consider the ethical dimension thoroughly (see, for instance, Richard Jenkins' (1992) critique of Allen Feldman). In short, it is essential not to let the act of interpretation overshadow the experience of violence.

Experience/narrative

The third and most recent perspective in contemporary anthropology of war and war-related violence is mainly an ethnographic one. The centre of interest is not on macro-actors' strategic use of violence, the built-in potential of violence to produce identities, or the communicative aspect of violence. The focus is on actual victims' subjective *experiences* of war, violence and torture, and on the *narratives* people construct in their attempts to (re)create meaning, identities and social relations in a shattered world.[4] Concurrently with such analyses, the very possibility of the academic representation of such fundamental and groundbreaking experiences has been discussed. Analyses of actors' experiences of violence can, it is argued, be seen as a contradiction in terms, since the "experience of war implies a loss of the conceptual and epistemological framework that previously provided means to interpret the events of life and death of others" (Löfving and Maček 2000: 5, see also van de Port 1998: 27-8). At the same time, though, anthropologists have also insisted on the academic respon-

---

3   Analyses on such analytical levels are often rather speculative. One could argue otherwise and claim that violence itself has become a disembedded practice. As Bauman's (1994) study of the Holocaust shows, violence in modern bureaucratic systems has in fact been lifted out of concrete social relations and developed into a rational bureaucratic tool. Violence thus becomes devoid of meaning and purely instrumental –an instrument not of an actor, but of a bureaucratic system. In a similar vein, Pick (1993) argues that the acts of violence and slaughtering (both of animals and men) in Western Europe in the past 150 years have followed the overall pattern of systematic industrial rationality.

4   Studies of the experience of perpetrators of violence are very rare (Schmidt and Schröder 2001).

sibility to 'write against terror', and speak out against injustice (Scheper-Huges 1992; Taussig 1987).

Experience

Elaine Scarry's (1985) argument regarding the relation between torture and pain has served as an explicit or implicit theoretical inspiration in many of the ethnographic studies of people's experiences of war and violence and loss of epistemological framework (Feldman et al. 1993; Green 1995; Jackson 2002; Maček 2000a, 2000b; Nordstrom 1997; Povrzanović 1993, 1997; Scheper-Huges 1992; Van de Port 1998). Her basic contention is that the feeling of physical pain is an irreducible bodily experience that cannot be objectified by anything outside the body including language. This is why torture is such an effective instrument of power, because the inexpressible and non-communicative feeling of pain, the 'unmaking of the world', as she calls it, that takes control of the victim can only be alleviated through a new version of the world – another version of the Truth (see also Löfving and Maček 2000: 5; Frykman 2002). Based on ethnographic fieldwork in war-torn Mozambique, Nordstrom (1997) expands Scarry's idea of torture's 'unmaking of the world' to the general wartime situation experienced by civilians. Nordstrom sees the structure of this experience as bearing clear parallels to Bakhtin's idea of the grotesque:

> When the familiar and everyday are turned into implements of torture and murder, the familiar everyday world is rendered grotesque – not merely by the fact of the present terror and repression, but by the enduring nature of association. (p. 168).

She offers an example of a man who had his throat cut in the family's mortar by intruding soldiers, the whole village being forced to watch, and she asks if the onlookers will ever be able to use a mortar without having the drama run at the back of their minds. The strength of terror, she argues, exists in its ability to break down the everyday world and destroy the webs of significance into which people's self-identities are woven. In this way terror was used intentionally by all parties in the war in Mozambique to eliminate political will and military resistance among civilians. But besides unmaking the world, terror also incites different kinds of resistance: retelling the grotesque practices and linking them with the perpetrators, rebuilding broken social relations and institutions of the community, and imagining a world beyond that could function as a source of creativity in everyday life. When listening to the horrible atrocities to which people had been subjected, Nordstrom was furthermore impressed by the concurrent life-generating creativity of her informants. In sum this made her see how in Mozambique peace and solid social relations were built from the bottom up. In a related but less optimistic study of the siege of Sarajevo, Ivana Maček (2000a, 2000b) invents the concept 'the deserter's mode of perception' in an attempt to communicate people's war experiences. The deserter's mode is a process "… in which all individuals, faced with unexplainable violent disruptions of their lives, constantly engage in making sense of their situation" (Maček 2000a: 240). It is a sense-making process whereby people, in their attempt to categorise and understand the situation, easily fell victim to the nationalistic discourse that swept the country.

A problem with some of the ethnographies focusing on experiences of war and violence is that bare survival becomes labelled as resistance. This either romanticises people's coping strategies or expands and thereby weakens the concept of resistance. However, it does focus on a crucial discussion: whether the creative component is violence (as the structural perspective has it) or people's strategies and reactions toward violence. Does violence create identity, or is it people's reactions to violence that create or destroy positions of identity?[5] The focus on the disintegration of everyday life furthermore questions the concept of violence. Many scholars have asked: Is violence only physical? (See for instance Riches 1986; Nordstrom and Martin 1992; Nordstrom and Robben 1995; Simons 1999). I only want to add that violence does not need to physically attack the body to produce an 'unmaking of the world.' A constant threat of violence can disrupt the fabric of everyday life (see, for instance, Gilliland 1995; Ross 2001).

Narratives

It is difficult to uphold a division between, on the one hand, the experience of loss of meaning and, on the other, the narratives people use to explain and make sense of this loss, especially if both matters are only revealed to the ethnographer in communication. That is to say, what part of communication expresses the pure and unmediated experience of violence and what part is a narrative representation of it? In medical anthropology, the idea of pure existential experience has flourished (Kleinman and Kleinman 1995, Good 1994); the same can be considered true in experientially oriented war anthropology. The critical philosophical problem, however, is that experience must always pass through language to be visible/audible (Mead 1967). Some studies have nevertheless focused more on the *narratives* used to make sense of the violence experienced and the destroyed everyday world than on the 'pure experience'

5   A point raised by Ivana Maček (personal correspondence).

that the unmaking of the world can be said to represent – which may be due to the ethnographer's arrival after the violence has stopped (Zur 1998; Warren 1993; Malkki 1998; Mehta 2001; Jansen 2000a, 2000b; Das 1990, 2001; Perera 2001; Kolind 2006, 2007; Jackson 2002). In these studies, the concept of narrative[6] (or similar concepts) is often used to systematise informants' more or less ordered and identifiable versions of events and relate them to the overarching discourses in which they are cast. In a study of Hutu refugees' memory of violence, Malkki (1998), for instance, found what she calls a 'mythico-history', or cosmological ordering of the past, a 'world-making.' The Hutus construct themselves in their attempt to seize history, condemn the Tutsis' atrocities, and legitimise their own position in Rwandan society. Malkki (1998) does not try to sort out true facts from invented ones in these mythico-histories:

> Different regimes of truth exist for different historical actors, and particularly historical events support any number of different narrative elaborations. (p. 104).

What her analysis misses, though, is a consideration of other possible 'regimes of truth' or discourses that affect the Hutus' narratives. In a more phenomenologically inspired narrative approach, Jackson (2002) focuses on what he calls 'the politics of storytelling.' In the face of violent events and other disempowering circumstances, storytelling (narratives) – understood as "a result of ongoing dialogue and redaction within fields of intersubjectivity" (ibid. 22) – can be seen as a way to transform private meanings into public ones and to sustain a sense of agency, both vital aspects for human existence. In other words, the very act of putting experience into words (and thereby sharing it, making it part of the social) is theorised as a necessary human capacity to overcome the 'unmaking of the world' and recreate a meaningful life.

However, it is also possible to think about narratives and people's categorisations as less consistent and static than the prevalent use of narratives seems to indicate. When primarily focusing on the ability of narratives to order the world cosmologically and morally, one may overlook the more chaotic, fragmented and contradictory aspect of social life and its strategic uses, especially in post-war societies. The branch of anthropology inspired by Mary Douglas, which basically sees human activity as cosmological ordering of the world, may

---

6   By the term narrative I mean clusters of speech and action that are moral and cosmological and which have an internal structure that organises the past and gives directions for the future; these clusters draw on external sources (discourses) for their constructions (see Mattingly 2001).

overlook another feature of social interaction: the persistent situational and strategic mixing of categories. In a study of post-war Croatia, Jansen (2000b, 2006), for instance, shows how on the surface people reproduce the nationalistic rhetoric that has poisoned the whole area, but on closer inspection what looks like conformism is rather a manifestation of agents' situational and concrete strategies. For instance, a Croat family (from Bosnia) living in a Serbian house in Croatia evoked the authoritative nationalist discourse of 'language right' (even though the languages are nearly identical and even though before the war the family lived peacefully with their Bosnian Serb and Muslim neighbours), which allowed them "to resist subjection to another, possible threatening discourse, that of rights of property and return" (Jansen 2000b: 14). This example shows the intricate relationship between discourse and agency, or the way in which people's narratives of the war are both situational and strategic.

For some scholars the recent shift in the anthropology of war and violence focusing on experience and narratives is perceived as a blind alley. Schmidt and Schröder (2001) argue, for instance, that this "postmodernist shift in anthropological research on violence" (ibid. 7), as they call it, is a hindrance to comparative anthropology. Violence, they claim, can easily be compared to its causes, events and results, but not to its subjective experience of these things. I do not agree. I think that one can actually distinguish some core themes in this 'postmodernist' ethnography of war and violence: violence that 'works' via its erosion of the everyday, taken-for-granted world; ways of rebuilding meaning when people's worlds are shattered (a comparison that could be expanded to other areas of research; see, for instance, Cohen and Taylor 1972); and a theoretical discussion of resistance and the ways in which discourses interrelate with processes of recreating meaning through narratives.

Relevance to my study

I have outlined three different focuses of research in contemporary anthropology of war and war-related violence: instrumentality/structure, expression and experience/narratives. By focusing on processes of post-war identification (and its counterdiscursive aspect) among the Muslims of Stolac, I primarily adopt the last perspective. However, the other perspectives have also influenced my study.

In my historical account of the emergence of nationalism in Yugoslavia (Chapter 4) and more specifically in Bosnia Herzegovina (Chapter 9), I follow the *instrumental* perspective. While my aim is not to explain the war, I show how and why nationalist ideologies became so dominant. And one of the conclusions is that nationalist ideologies served to legitimise a rise to power. I use the *structural* argument only partly. In short, it is important to acknowledge that the war and war-related violence created a dichotomised space of identity. Ethnicity, which was only one identity among others before the war, came to the forefront throughout the war, increasingly determining everybody's lives, and the actual violence and threats of violence contributed massively towards this change. The ethnic identity of some of the Muslims of Stolac became a matter of life or death; for most it was the reason they were expelled, and for the returnees it was the cause of their discrimination in post-war Stolac. The total destruction of everything reminiscent of the Ottoman influence (see Prologue) in Stolac also contributed in a violent way to create the ethnic Other. However, this is 'only' the framework; in my analysis I focus on how my informants fill up this framework in their everyday life, that is, how they relate to the ethnic identities promoted by the war. The focus on *expression* is only of indirect importance to my study. I primarily use it as an ethical reminder. First, violence can have an exotic entertainment value, as seen, for instance, in entertainment films. I have therefore been careful to restrict my presentation of examples to those necessary to present my argument. Second, I try to refrain from only depicting my informants as 'victims of violence' and thereby 'othering' them. Instead I analytically approach my informants' use of the 'role of the victim' (Chapter 15). In Chapter 2, I follow the *experience*-oriented approach, demonstrating how the concept of 'unmaking of the world' is apt when generally describing my informants' experiences of the war and post-war violence. The focus on the unmaking of the world is important for two reasons. First, inspired by the epistemological discussion ascribed to this research approach, the validity of my own as well as my informants' representations can be questioned. If it is true that the unmaking of the world also implies destroying the categories normally used to communicate experience, then both my analysis and my informants' accounts are somewhat blurred. This does not make my analysis of my informants' post-war identifications irrelevant or invalid, but it has helped me to persistently focus on the very act of category building. My representation of Muslims' ways of identifying themselves and the Other therefore goes into detail with this process of reconstructing categories and looks into how they eventually build upon pre-war classifications. Second, my book is based on the analytical division of unmaking – remaking, with emphasis on the latter. By looking into the unmade world of my informants it becomes clear how profound the devastations of the war have been, and consequently how profoundly my informants have had to question, reconsider and remake their social relations, friendships, religious beliefs, moral values, conception of the nature of society, ethnic identities and so on. Cultural construction takes place everywhere, all the time; in Stolac, however, such cultural construction is so profound and extensive that it is apposite to term it remaking. And it is this process of remaking with emphasis on the question of identification that is my major focus. The theoretical background for my analysis of this process of remaking and identification, and especially for considering this as a counter-discursive practice, is presented in Chapter 3.

Chapter 2
The unmaking of the world

In order to fully understand the remaking of the world that my informants engage in – and especially the elements of resistance and counterdiscourse involved in this remaking – it is important to realise how profound and severe the unmaking of their world has been. As I will argue, the unmaking of my informants' world has forced them to re-question previously taken-for-granted social relations, values and moral categories: in other words, to re-identify themselves and the ethnic other. Both during and after the war, an ethnonationalist paradigm was the dominant explanatory device available for explaining people's misfortunes, as well as a central element in the remaking of people's shattered lives. An element of counterdiscursive resistance is therefore legible when people refuse to give ethnonationalist discourse the upper hand in the remaking of the unmade world.

In this chapter, I outline some of the central events and experiences in the unmaking of my informants' lives. First, however, some terminological clarification is necessary, for, as touched upon in the previous chapter, the distinction between the world's *unmaking* and its *remaking* is a necessary theoretical fiction. In the first place, attempts at holding on to mundane everyday practices – however much of a caricature this may seem – are characteristic of wartime life. Povrzanović tellingly calls this practice/strategy of attempting to stick to 'minimal normality' (Maček 2000a) 'imitations of life' (Povrzanović 1997: 157). The unmaking of the world and the remaking therefore take place simultaneously. However, the object of my study is a post-war society, not a war-time society. Though my informants' lives were still darkened by the shadow of the war, they no longer feared for their own lives. And despite their difficult social situation my informants still felt that in general things had improved since the end of the war. So, whereas in a situation of war it would be accurate to describe unmaking and remaking as simultaneous, in Stolac today people are more occupied with attempts at understanding, forgetting and forgiving. These forms of remaking are qualitatively different from the wartime 'imitation of life' which they superficially resemble. On the other hand, it is still important to acknowledge how destructive the tough post-war situation has been to people's hopes and dreams, as well as their meaning-creating narratives, which are still severely damaged. In one sense, then, a process of unmaking is still going on.

Analysing the unmaking of my informants' lives centres on two core aspects: the everyday world and epistemology. Firstly, by 'everyday world' I mean the non-conscious routine practices and categories one employs to make sense of events, including other people's actions. Moreover, such non-conscious acts and categories can often easily become the object of conscious reflection. It is this domain that much phenomenologically inspired anthropology has tried to analyse and conceptualise. For instance, the non-conscious constitutes a central component in Bourdieu's concept of *habitus* (1995) as well as Arthur Kleinman's 'local moral worlds' (1992). For an overview see Jackson (1996). The everyday routine world has also been a focus of ethnomethodology. For example, Garfinkel's studies (1963, 1967) have revealed the existence of an implicit everyday morality, a largely hidden taken-for-granted world with unwritten assumptions about the *do*s and *don't*s of social life, which is the basis for people's situational strategies. But Garfinkel's work also reveals how seemingly minor and in a way imperceptible changes in people's behaviour can radically disrupt the neat flow of social interaction, creating feelings of confusion. In a similar way, Goffman's extensive studies of face-to-face interaction have shown that the individual's use of social identities as well as the social expectations attached to such use (in sum *impression management*) is dependent on predictability in social interaction (*the interaction order*) (1971, 1974, 1983). In sum, the everyday world possesses a taken-for-granted-ness that is fundamental to processes of identification of oneself and the Other, and to avoid feeling bewilderment and confusion. And it is the damage to such everyday worlds with their predictable social routines and identities that constitutes a core element in many people's war experiences.

The second aspect of the unmaking of the everyday world relates to the loss or failure of epistemological frameworks. As mentioned, Scarry's work (1985) describes how the experience of torture is often non-communicative, because the categories and concepts its victims would normally use to communicate experience no longer suffice.[1] This is why the victims of terror and war-related violence often state that they cannot describe what happened, that they do not have the words, or that strangers will not understand (Maček 2001, Mertus 1997, Povrzanović 1993, Perera 2001). The ability to communicate experiences of violence is restricted because the mental categories normally used

---

1   Whereas in Scarry's theorising the experience of violence is a matter of the relationship between the individual and his/her body, in anthropological theorising the experience of violence is primarily a matter of the relationship between the individual and his/her society, for society constitutes the foundation of the life-worlds of individuals. Therefore, the unmaking of the world relates to more than the inability to express individual experiences. This term also encompasses the experience of what one might call 'social pain', the breakdown of social relations and categories (see for instance Ross 2001).

for making sense of the world are themselves shattered by the unprecedented events of war and violence (Zur 1998: 159-91; Nordstrom 1997: 153-75). In sum the world's unmaking forces its victims to redefine their social worlds from minor mundane practices to more overall values and ideals.

In the rest of the chapter, I will describe my informants' experiences during and after the war in terms of four aspects of the unmaking of the world. The destruction of the everyday world, stories and communication, and finally the all-pervasive feeling of loss.

The destruction of the everyday world

In pre-war Bosnian life, a normal day did not start with the question whether you and your family would survive or have anything to eat and drink. But during the war basic subsistence suddenly became problematic. A central theme in my informants' accounts from the war is how such fundamental aspects of everyday life became a question of life and death. Suddenly life was reduced to bare subsistence, and fear and desperation followed. I will present some of the recurrent themes in people's accounts of wartime life.

Leaving everything behind

The imprisonment of the Muslim men of Stolac happened more or less overnight. But before the women and children were arrested they had had six weeks to prepare themselves, knowing all this time that they were at great risk of being driven out like their men. Valuables were therefore hidden, for instance buried in the garden, and when the soldiers came to fetch the women many had packed clothes, photos and food in rucksacks, and they had hidden money and jewellery on their persons. Even after all this preparation, many women recall the experience of having to leave everything behind as really horrible. Material possessions gathered over a lifetime, along with the dreams, happiness and expectations connected symbolically to these objects, were left behind. Repeatedly I heard expressions such as "We were forced to leave carrying only a plastic bag". As one woman lamented "What can you put in a plastic bag?" To make matters worse Croat soldiers stole bags, jewellery and money from the women when they were searched before their actual expulsion from Stolac.

Violence

Both men and women experienced physical violence, including murder. They also experienced a constant threat of violence. These terrible experiences are central themes in their accounts of the war. For the men violence relates to the brutal interrogations before the internment as well as to the routine beatings of prisoners in the camps. Both the interrogations and the beatings killed several people. As a consequence of the visit of the Red Cross to some of the prison camps about three months after their creation, some of the most exhausted prisoners were allowed to leave – those who had lost the most weight. They were not allowed to return to Bosnia Herzegovina, but had to travel to third countries instead. Emir was one of these prisoners. When he was released, the Red Cross sent him to the small island of Korcula in Croatia. After about two months, Emir had recovered somewhat. As he concisely summed up: "There we were well, we were given food three times a day, we were not beaten, we had a bed to sleep in." Aspects of life that had been natural and unproblematic a couple of month previously had suddenly become issues of conscious concern. The women experienced the physical violence when they were searched and robbed by Croat soldiers. Violence also marks their ten-kilometre march from the place where the Croat soldiers set them off to Blagaj, a Muslim-controlled area. It was hot, people were scared, and they had to carry heavy burdens – baggage, as well as children or disabled parents in some cases – while the Croat soldiers fired into the air. About nine old women lost their lives on this march, probably from exhaustion. The experience of violence also relates to the time the women spent in Blagaj. One woman, Anvere, occupied a basement. The area was shelled all day, so she and her children had to stay indoors, and they only dared to tend the small vegetable patch they had for cultivating some lettuce or cabbage at night, and then very hastily.

Hunger

A third experiential theme relates to the hunger and thirst people felt, the diseases they contracted, and the lack of treatment available. In the prison camps the prisoners were given one loaf of bread every two weeks, as well as some soup, and almost nothing to drink. The camps were extremely hot, and the constant thirst was unbearable. Some people urinated in a tin can, filtered it through a sock, and drank it. Aziz told me:

> I was thirsty and nobody would give us water. They brought one milk-can of water to 500 people so everybody pushed and fought for the water. You opened your mouth, but there was no water. It was worse not to have water than not to have food. After the Red Cross had been in the prison-camp (*logor*) the Croats began to give us a little more water. But it was not clean water, it was dirty. The water was reddish. But we drank it, because we were thirsty. When you had to pee or go to the toilet, you did it where we slept, and we did it in buckets and some days you did not know if you should use those buckets to pee in or drink water from.

The women and children also starved after being driven to the Muslim-controlled areas. At first some could live on the food they had brought with them, but it did not last long. Some food could be bought, but it was extremely expensive. So the money some people had managed to bring with them was soon spent. Here are the words of Nusreta:

> It was a hard life, when we stayed there. So hard that we did not have anything to eat. Once we only had 350 grams of food for fifteen days. You were so hungry. And some of the old people, they starved to death. We ate grass. We soon learned to recognise every sort of grass, and that was one of the things that saved people, and then you ate fruit, grapes. Some got dysentery. A lot of people got that disease, because you drank too much water and hardly ate. The shells were falling all the time, and the shells killed people.

TK: Didn't you receive humanitarian aid?

Nusreta: We didn't receive much humanitarian aid, because the Croats would not permit it to pass through to us. They stopped the convoys […] and plundered them. It was very difficult […]. And the old people who could not search for food, they starved to death. There was this woman, one of the richest in Stolac, she lived alone in Stolac. When we were expelled she came to the same village as me and she also starved to death. Nobody could help her, or give her grass or grapes or other kind of fruit. It was terrible. I hope God will not give such a thing again (the saying *spomenulo se ne ponovilo se*: you can talk about it, but you do not hope it will happen again). Never again, it would be better to be dead than experience it again […]. I had a good friend, she took care of my daughter, she brought her some milk. Every night her son brought her some milk […]. One of her sons was at the front facing the Serbs, a Chetnik killed him. She and her family were very kind, and she saved my little daughter. We all had a hard time when her son was killed. It was like he was one of ours [one of the family]. I'll never forget how well they treated us.

Anxiety about one's family members

The last theme I will touch on here is the insecurity and anxiety people felt not knowing anything about the fate of family members. A related theme is the feeling of desperation caused by not being able to provide for one's children, because it was not possible to fed or protect them. It was not just in Stolac that men and boys were imprisoned. It also happened elsewhere in Herzegovina, and formed part of a Croatian strategy of ethnic cleansing. The women knew that similar things were going on in other places, but nobody knew exactly what was happening to their men, whether they were dead or alive, until the men were allowed to send letters through the Red Cross. In these letters, the men always wrote that they were well; they did not dare to write the truth as they feared the Croats would read the letters. Emir was one of the first to be released from prison camp. He was then 18. He was sent to Germany, where he sent a message using a radio telephone reporting that he was all right. But he did not see his family for the next five years. The men who were captives in the prison camps were also filled with worry and anxiety: they had no news about their families for anywhere from five to ten months, depending on how long they were detained.

Osman: I was in prison camp for six months and it was terrible for me because I was sick. During the whole time in prison camp I did not get two litres of water. And we did not have food enough, and everybody just wanted water and food. But I escaped it without any injuries, and I was not beaten. All the time I thought that they were going to kill me, all the time, even though I was not guilty of anything. The worst thing was not to know where my family was, if they were alive or not, and when I got out of the camp, I had to start looking for them.

It was terrible for parents not to be able to take proper care of their children. The children were hungry and frightened. They could not understand their situation and were exposed to great danger, and the parents could do very little to help. A woman called Fata recalls how providing for her children made everything else less important:

They shot at us from two different sides. During the war between Muslims and Croats I lived in Mostar and we did not have water in the houses and you had to go to Neretva [the river] to fetch water. And we passed the *Harem* [Muslim graveyard] on our way to Neretva, and we saw them burying the dead soldiers and civilians. You did not think at all that tomorrow or the day after tomorrow you might be buried the same way yourself. You did not fear. You knew you had to go to the river to get water, because the kids needed water, and you just *had* to make it to the river. It was like you did not care about being killed. We just walked without fear.

The themes in this section all focus on aspects of an everyday world that suddenly became problematic: food, shelter, security, and basic social relations. Together, they constitute a fundamental aspect of the unmaking of my informants' world.

The destruction of stories

Another aspect of the unmaking of the world relates to the destruction or questioning of the values and principles governing normal social life: what van de Port calls "the damage war can cause to stories" (1998: 109). The stories damaged by my informants' wartime experiences were not epic, but rather the simple tales that make everyday social interaction meaningful, understandable and predictable: You can trust your friends. Children are the most valuable thing in life. Criminals go to jail. In hospitals sick people are cured. War happens somewhere else. The family is a safe haven. Jackson (2002) has argued that the fundamental function of stories and narratives is to enable the individual to integrate his personal world and the wider world of others, in his words "transforming private into public meanings" (ibid. 15). He describes how narratives meet an existential human need for "sustaining a sense of agency in the face of disempowering circumstances" (ibid.). The unmaking or questioning of peoples' stories thus destroys the very foundation of self-identification and this sense of agency. However, unmaking relates not only to how such stories suddenly break down or slowly crumble away, but also to how one starts questioning the very foundation of (such) stories, that is, starts seeing them as only an illusion.

> It is interesting that questions of identity often arise [...] in the face of terror (warfare) and cruelty. It is perhaps here that people meet the most significant challenges to their sense of self and humanity. "Violence", as Allen Feldman has noted, "itself both reflects and accelerates the experience of society as an incomplete project, as something to be made" (Nordstrom 1997: 189).

The following examples from my informants' discourse will illustrate how their experiences affected the stories they lived by before the war. All of these people experienced the disintegration of stories which had formerly bestowed meaning on their lives. For the first time, they were led to reflect on values and narratives that they had always taken for granted.

Am I me?

Nusret is a sculptor, that is, he was a sculptor; he is not able to make art any more. Instead he makes tombstones – such is the irony of fate. Once he showed me some of the creations he had made at the academy before the war, and he was especially proud of a small, beautiful Virgin Mary sculpture. The first time I met him he was standing outside his house working. I started talking about my research, but he interrupted me before long. This is how I remembered part of the conversation afterwards:

Nusret: This country is not normal, nobody here is normal, but when nobody is normal you feel normal! People are crazy, insane. [...]

TK: Do you make sculptures now?

Nusret: No! How could I? I can't any more. Everything seems so unreal. It's abnormal, as I'm living in a fake world. I'm standing here watching the huge pile of garbage [a pile of rubble and garbage approximately two metres high and thirty metres long running along the road] and I don't care. It's as if it's not my concern, or as if it's completely normal, but it isn't. The destroyed, mined and burned-out houses, everything seems unreal or normal at the same time.

The first time I saw a dead man it was terrible, it made me feel sick, but later I could see ten dead people, it didn't affect me, I didn't care. When you have seen dead women and children and experienced all this madness, how can you make sculptures? I cannot. Nothing matters. How can I laugh? Well I can laugh, a lot, but it is not I who do it...it feels unreal. I'm destroyed inside. It's as though there's a distance between me and the world, it's as if it's not I who stand here talking or laughing.

What do children play?

Lamira told me that watching children's games during the war sometimes hurt her the most:

The boys gathered some old tyres, which should do duty as a bundle. The girls played women, they cried and kept asking: "Where are our men or brothers?" At one point in the game the boys would come out of hiding, dragging the tyres, they were pretending to be the men coming home from prison camps, and the women [girls] thrilled to see them. And then they would start all over again.

What is a school?

Normally it is a place where children are educated and socialise, but during the expulsion of the Muslim men and women, a school (as well as a hospital and a factory) was turned into a place for torture, robbery, humiliation and killing. Moreover, for many adults it was the very school they themselves had attended as children; the children had been students there only months before.

What is an enemy?

Normally friends and enemies are clearly distinguishable, but during war this changes. Mensur told me how in Blagaj the Serbs and the Muslims traded with each other. The Serbs sold coffee for DM 25 per kilo, which they may had bought for DM 6-8 per kilo, and the Muslim traders would then resell it for DM 50 to other Muslims, and after that the Muslims and the Serbs would shoot at each other again.

What is an ally?

Aziz told me that people were driven to eat grass during the war when there was nothing to eat. One day his mother was picking some grass in a garden when the owner (who was also a Muslim) came and kicked her out. He needed the grass for his cow. And another time when she went to a place where a little food could be bought, the owner told her that she did not have enough money to buy anything, but then he saw her ring and said she could have one kilo of food in exchange for it.

You don't kill children, do you?

Several people expressed feelings like Nijaz: "I cannot understand how one can kill children; one thing is if a soldier meets another soldier and it's a matter of life or death, but to kill a child, or like in Visegrad to throw them out from the bridge…old and children."

You teach your children to be good, don't you?

Senad's mother's experiences made her question the moral education of the Croats. On the day she and her family were driven from their home:

> …one of the Croat soldiers had a knife in the one hand and a hammer in the other, then another came and opened the door, it was a young guy the same age as my Senad [her son], and I thought about what I had taught my children and how they [the Croats] raise their children. And I thought, how could they hurt an elderly woman? I was forty-eight at that time. Then a couple of them came in and beat me and my maternal uncle's wife. My mother-in-law stayed in the house, and she begged for somebody to stay with her in the house, but they said that everybody had to go away from the house and then they burned the house with her in it. The worst is that we do not know where her bones are.

Normal people react to injustice, don't they?

Anvere: I lived with the children here in Stolac. Nihad was in prison camp. One day one of the kids found a little piece of paper, something from the UN. It told us things I did not even know. And when you watched TV there was nothing [no information about what was happening to the Muslims in Herzegovina].

They knew out in the world what was going on, but they didn't do anything and they didn't inform us either. We were an experiment, a political experiment.

You trust friends and neighbours, don't you?

The last example relates to the central value of inter-ethnic coexistence, condensed in the idea of neighbourliness (*komšiluk*). For many their betrayal by friends, neighbours and fellow citizens, with whom they had lived peacefully for many years (often their whole lives), was the most incomprehensible of many disillusionments. Here I will describe three examples, showing how such feelings of betrayal were expressed to me.

I

Nermin: I should never have thought that my friend, who lived together with me, would take the rifle and shoot at me. My best friend sang and drank together with the other Ustashes [term of abuse for violent Croat extremists], while I was locked up on the lower floor. He was my best friend from Stolac.

II

Ljubica: The people we had been drinking coffee and *loza* [grape brandy] with, it was they who picked up Nihad [her husband], and stole my jewellery. It was they who came and stole our things, they knew where they were.

III

Senad's father: The worst is that up until yesterday we were neighbours and we lived well together, but suddenly they looked upon us as wild animals who should be slaughtered. It is totally inexplicable that some people can behave like that.

Lamira's story

I will end this section with an excerpt from an interview with Lamira, a woman in her late 20s. The first time I met her was at her work. I introduced myself and told her about my study. We then went down to the canteen, where she started talking. We had coffee, but she did not touch hers for a whole hour, she just talked. She said that it had been a long time since she had last talked about the war, and that there was so much to tell. Sometimes, she said, she really wanted to talk and other times she did not even want to think about it. The excerpt consists of several small anecdotes about deceit and evil, which reveal how the world has been unmade. But there are also elements of pride and hope. Like Nusret at the beginning of this section, she said: "Often I feel like a bystander to it all. As if it is not I who have experienced it. It's like I'm standing outside looking in at myself."

I don't know where to begin. There is so much to tell. There are so many stories. In Stolac there is a hospital for skin diseases. We have such good air here. So before the war a lot of people came to Stolac to get treatment, and there were a lot of disabled staying there permanently. When the Croats expelled us they turned this hospital into a barrack and all patients were removed. The Croat patients were driven to Čapljina, the Serbians to the Serb Republic and the Muslims were put in cars, and several of them could not walk, they used wheelchairs. They drove them to a place at Buna, near Blagaj. They abandoned them there, so that they were outside Croat territory, some of them died. We had to transport them in sheets or pieces of cloth and put them up in houses in Blagaj, but there were no wheelchairs, and none of the treatment they had been getting, so a lot of them died.

One day we were told to leave our house and leave the key in the door. It was the third of August, and all the women and children were expelled (*proteran*). My father, my cousins, and all the other men in town had been driven to concentration camps a month earlier. We women and children were taken to *Željezara* [a factory in Stolac], There we were locked up in a room and robbed of everything, money and gold. [...]

I remember those women who came dragging big bags. Not real baggage, but for instance the kind of sacks you store potatoes in, they were dragging all these things, and they begged the soldiers to be allowed to bring them with them, they were weak women. And then there were the women who only carried a handbag with family photos. They were very aristocratic, and they didn't deign to look at the soldiers. They were proud, and 'If you want the bag, so take it.' They didn't want to beg for anything.

Afterwards we were put on trucks. Many of the trucks were stolen from Bosniaks, and many of them had previously been used for transporting animals. We were then driven to Buna, where we had to walk to Blagaj. It was terrible. It was a no-mans-land.

TK: Many people tell me that this walk of eight or nine kilometres was very terrible, why was it like that?

Lamira: There were dead bodies along the road, people died on that walk. I always thought that when you die, then you turn cold and stiff. But we were expelled in August, and it was very hot, and the dead bodies were totally swollen. And when we walked, the soldiers constantly told us to keep walking. And the people living in Blagaj said they didn't have room, so we had to keep on walking, walking…and we didn't have water or food. The disabled and sick we carried in blankets, and we kept thinking 'Is there room here for us?' At last we found an abandoned house, or what was left of it. Four families were staying in one room. There were thirty-five people in the house. There was one outdoor toilet, where you should see to everything. There was only very little water, water from the gutters saved in tanks. We had to live in the basement because they were shelling us. Next morning….We lived here for eighteen months. We had no food. We were starving and lost a lot of weight. It is hard to imagine, but try not eating for seven days, then you can imagine a little. And then there was the constant shelling.

In December 1993 – or was it January 1994? – We received aid from the air for the first time. It was American planes that were dropping relief supplies. I remember the night when they dumped those relief supplies; it was one of the worst nights in my life. We ran to the field. It was at night, but there were snipers. We ran to the packets that had landed in no-man's-land. You have to imagine the Croats one the one side and the Serbs on the other, and then we were in the middle in a hole [Blagaj is situated in a kind of valley], and they shot at us and shelled us. But the packets weighed about 500 kilos each, so we couldn't carry them back, we could just try to wrench something loose from the packets and then hurry back. People were scared, and some got wounded. I lost a friend that night. Snipers hit her. But the day after, it was absurd, because at night we hadn't been able to see what we had grabbed/taken back with us, and some had only got hold of chewing gum, so all the kids were walking around blowing big chewing gum bubbles, but there was no food.

When we arrived [at Blagaj] we had to describe our skills, and my mother and sister told the soldiers they could cook, so they were stationed in the kitchen. I said I could type, so I typed some documents on an old typewriter. Then I started to teach the kids. We didn't have any schools, but we tried to arrange some teaching, and I taught English. I had 130 pupils. We didn't receive any pay. It was voluntary. We only got some candles as payment, so we could sit at night and prepare the lessons, write down some exercises. My friend and I got a candle each, we shared it, so we had a spare one. Then there was a woman who had a baby, and she had some instant milk, but she breastfed her child, so we traded our candles for some instant milk.

There are many stories from that time, a lot of sad and a lot of beautiful stories. There was a woman who had one of her hands so badly injured that she couldn't use it, and she had to take care of her two children, she had to chop firewood and take care of everything with one hand. On one occasion my friend was wounded, and there was a man who had a wheelbarrow, we wanted to borrow it to drive her to a place where she could get some treatment, but he didn't want to lend it to us, he had to take care of *his* family. We lived like animals.

What else? In my class there was a very nice girl. She was so lovely and kind towards the other kids, she was so full of life. But one day she locked herself into a room and didn't want to speak to anybody, she withdrew into herself, into her own traumas. It was sad to see. There was an eleven-year-old boy without parents, he managed himself. Planted potatoes and harvested them.

Once we had a lot of glue, I don't know from where, probably Germany, then we made a lot of collages, on paper. We picked a lot of flowers and used them to make a tree, a hand or other beautiful things with this glue. We also made a two-metre-long letter to a school class in Bremen with drawings where we wrote who we were. There were a lot of beautiful things then.

When we buried our dead, we didn't have coffins, as there was no wood. The last one we buried in wood, was one we laid on a door, but after that it was decided that we should only use fabric, sheets and such, because we barely had enough firewood.

My father returned from prison camp in 1994, but he hasn't ever been the same since. He turned silent, introverted and sad. [...]

In 1994 I started on the faculty in Mostar. It was a long way to walk, eight kilometres each way. I was a teacher at that time, but I didn't have time and had to stop. I remember the day the radio reported: 'Today there are no dead.' It was unbelievable. They had been reporting who had died every day. That day it was as if the whole world opened itself to me. There was a German journalist who interviewed me and asked how I could be so happy when the whole town was destroyed and everything was in ruins, but I said he should try to imagine finally being able to walk the streets without being afraid of getting shot. He wanted to give me some money. He felt pity for me, but I said: 'Keep your money and write the truth about what has happened here instead.'

Sometimes I think it is all like an experiment. Like if you take two frogs and you put one of them into boiling water and put the other into cold water, which you then bring to a boil slowly. I felt like the last one.

Lamira's story, as well as the other examples I have presented, on a general level reveal that nothing is sacred: social relations and matters formerly taken for granted reveal their illusory character; meaning becomes problematic; agency vanishes; and institutions, practices and values change character. All in all this leads to a general need for reformulating moral behaviour, and re-identifying social belonging (e.g. ethnic identity).

The destruction of communication

Lamira's story is somewhat extraordinary, not in content, but in form. It has a chronological order and is coherent. Most Muslim women in Stolac would probably recognise the feelings and situations she depicts, but few would be able to express them so clearly. This brings me to the methodological problem of how to represent the violent memories and experiences of my informants, how to "write about the 'unmaking' and 'creating' of the world in a 'made' world of academic prose?" (Nordstrom 1995: 138). Theory and academic writing style have a structure and order which is removed from lived experience (Hastrup 1988), an order which is imposed on the world, "the academic will to order" as van de Port names it (1998: 25), an order which is especially intolerant of the chaotic experiences related to war, violence and the unmaking of the world. It is therefore unlikely that experience of war and violence can ever be documented in any real sense. Representations of human suffering will always have gaps in terms of experience, perception and the nature of pain itself (Perera 2001: 157-60).

Furthermore, the problem confronts not only anthropologists: it is also central for the victims of war and violence themselves. In essence, the problem is this: how can one communicate experiences when existing categories do not suffice, and when the categories themselves have been distorted by the unprecedented events of war and violence. In addition, victims of violence and terror are also often caught in a dilemma between wanting to forget and wanting to remember at one and the same time. For example, Warren (1993) has described how people in Guatemala did not want to talk about *la violencia* (a period of intense state violence) because they feared reprisals. At the same time, however, that period came up in all routine conversations, in part because it functioned as a temporal marker in people's conceptual world. My informants showed the same ambivalence: on the one hand they wanted to speak out, and to put their violent experiences into word to tell the world about them (thereby experiencing the imperfection of words); on the other hand, and at the same time, they wanted to forget, to be able to get on with life and achieve peace of mind.

Problems with forgetting

The evocative power of words was one reason why my informants wanted to forget. Telling someone about horrible events can make them come alive (see also Jackson 2002: 57; Perera 2001: 159). If people did choose to talk about experiences like internment in a prison camp, the horrible time in Blagaj, or the expulsion, they would often only say a little and then stop. They did not want to talk about it because it was like reliving the experience. We see this clearly in the following excerpt from my notebook about a man called Emir, who had been interned in a prison camp with three thousand prisoners and only thirty-three plates and spoons:

Emir: So nearly 100 of us had to share each spoon and plate. When the Red Cross arrived, we washed the spoons for the first time. We had very little time to eat, 15 seconds.

TK: Was it hot food?

Emir: Yes it was soup. We slept on the floor on the concrete. 500 in one hangar. There were no blankets, and if you had to pee, you just had to do it where you were.

He suddenly stops talking, I can feel that he is moving towards the limit of where he still can talk and keep things at a distance. I say that it is impossible to understand how people can do such things to others. He answers that if you could, you would be like them.

According to Anvere, people's and especially men's attempts at forgetting are rather general, as she straightforwardly ascertained about her husband.

Nihad he has not told me about the prison camp, he can't manage. No men tell about their experiences from there, well yes a little when they drink *loza* [grape brandy].

Like speech, television is a strongly evocative medium. Once the film *Welcome to Sarajevo*, which depicts the horrendous time during the siege of Sarajevo, was shown on television. Seeing the film with my hosts was a tough emotional experience. We all sat watching: nobody said a word except my landlady, who kept sighing. Her husband, who normally likes to eat the hot popcorn his wife makes, did not touch it. After the film nobody spoke, and we all went to bed. The day after several people asked if I had seen the film. Safet said that when he saw it everything came back to him. He told me how he had relived a lot of episodes from the war, and had not fallen asleep until 4 am. Nusret's father, on the other hand, said that he only saw the first ten minutes. He had seen it all in real life, he explained, and did not need to see it again.

My informants' intentions to forget were often sabotaged by the way the subject of the war would surface in many everyday conversations. Anything could function as a trigger of episodes from the war, as the following examples show. My father visited me for four days while I was doing fieldwork, and I remember how it struck me that on the first evening he was with me in my host family's company, we only talked for about half an hour about the things one normally converses with foreign guests about, such as climate, buildings, family relations, food and so on. At this point the conversation changed topic and we concentrated on the war and the present problems. It was impossible to carry on a 'normal' (non-war-related) conversation. Once Osman offered me a cigarette, a Bosnian cigarette labelled *Drina*. He asked if I knew the River Drina, and I said yes, it is located at Visegrad, which then led him to talk about the war, starting with the atrocities committed by Serbs in that town. And at a child's birthday party, my comments about the lovely food we were served led to a discussion about the lack of food during the war. Often people did not even need a cue. Experiences from the war often erupted spontaneously.

Problems with remembering: incomprehensibility

I will now turn to the other side of the dilemma in which my informants are caught: wanting to remember and put their terrible experiences into words. Remembering is blocked by the fact that people often cannot understand what has happened. It does not make sense to them. As I was told several times, "how should you be able to understand it, when we can't?" Many people explained that their memories were all like a dream: one is just waiting to open one's eyes and wake up. Some of the examples offered above already express this feeling of incomprehensibility. I shall here limit myself to two examples. During an interview, in which Fahrudin had been talking about problems related to rebuilding the ruined houses in Stolac, he suddenly said:

> There is one thing I don't understand. I was born here and I lived here until I was caught and put in prison camp, and then I returned and continued to live here, and I intend to die here. But I cannot understand what was going on in their heads. The people who expelled the Bosniaks from here. Those who committed this urbicide [I come back to this term], genocide. You should talk to them instead if you are interested in this social pathology.

When I asked Amela, a young schoolteacher, what she thought about the situation, she turned my question back on me:

> What do you as an anthropologist think about this situation? We live together in an area, Serbs, Croats and Muslims. We were raised in the same system and in the same social environment. Why do they have this will to kill? How can they have the will to kill a human being?

Problems with remembering: epistemology

A more fundamental problem confronting people's attempts to remember and communicate their experiences in a meaningful form relates to epistemology: how to communicate experiences when existing categories do not suffice. In addition, the difficulty of communicating traumatic events arises from the victim's experience of feeling disconnected from the life s/he lived before and his/her experience of being out of time. For this reason, "refugee stories are not like the stories we ordinarily tell. They do not carry us forward to any consoling denouement. They do not require others to listen to them or respond. There is no prospect of closure. There are victims, but few free agents. They may bear witness to an event, describe a journey, or recount a tragedy, but they suspend all consideration of salvation or justice" (Jackson (2002: 92). Furthermore, traumatic events are often remembered as bare facts disconnected from the world, as "an unbearable sequence of sheer happenings" (Arendt in Jackson 2002: 92). These events are therefore without meaning. This characterisation of refugee stories has parallels to some of the stories I was told. When people told me about, or rather tried to tell me about, such topics as prison camp, expulsion, separation from family and Blagaj, they lacked the right words and categories, and their stories sometimes sounded disconnected from time and were occasionally held in a prosaic, record-keeping style.[2] However, there are also differences. My informants were telling about events that had happened at least eight years earlier, and some of these stories had been given some kind of structure since then, they urged the listener to respond, and they included considerations of 'salvation or justice.' Even though (pace Jackson) people were unable to express the whole of their experience, and were frustrated because they lacked the right words, nevertheless they did develop ways of communicating (about) their experiences which gave them coherence, set them in a moral framework. A central strategy is what I will call 'amputation.' By 'amputation' I mean that when mental categories do not suffice and/or are invalidated, new categories are invented. While they cannot fully express war-related experiences, they function as a kind of symbolic shorthand.

Amputation: we ate grass

Often people said that they had to eat grass when living as refugees in Blagaj during the war. In 1993 and 1994 hardly any relief reached the area: the Muslim-

---

2   Factuality could be used as a way for the speaker to distance himself from the spoken. The only time I heard Emir's father talk about his stay in the prison camp, he mentioned that the first 41 days were the worst, then came the Red Cross, that he was in the camp for 168 days, that he lost 35 kilos, that they had one loaf of bread for 15 men and so on.

controlled area around Blagaj was like a tongue of land, with only one unsafe entrance. People were hungry or even starving. But how does one communicate the feeling and experience of starvation? It does not suffice to say 'we were starving' or 'starving to death', or 'we were extremely hungry', though I have heard all these expressions. Then people summed up the experience in the sentence 'we ate grass'. The expression 'eating grass' functioned as a symbol covering some of the feelings people had in relation to extreme starvation and fear. This symbolic expression could stand alone, without needing to be commented or elaborated on. Let me give two examples: One evening Nihad was jokingly talking about how they had made moonshine during the war, and we were all laughing at his story. Suddenly his wife said: "we had to eat grass." Then the laughter stopped, and we were all silent for a couple of minutes. Then we started talking about something else.

Amer told a story he had probably heard from his wife:

> The women went to the field to pick some grass, and they ate it. While they did this, the snipers were shooting at them. This was while we [the men] were in prison camp. Near the house where my mother lived, an old woman was out in the field, two times the snipers shot at her, they missed two times, but she did not hear, she was nearly dead. And then they shot her the third time. The women in the house were shouting at her to hide herself, but she did not hear, and then the third time they hit her. And all she did was to pick some grass from the field.

Amputation: losing weight

Another way of condensing and expressing the feeling of starvation and misery was to say how many kilos one had lost. "I lost thirty-five kilos in the first three months!" "Aziz lost thirty kilos in prison camp!" Again there is no reason to disbelieve this. The point, however, is the sentiment such a statement is able to carry. The accurate enumeration of the number of kilos lost is not a mere factual calculation, but rather a symbolic visualisation of hunger.

Amputation: film analogies

When they told me about the shelling, people sometimes made an analogy to film, saying for instance that when the Serbs starting shelling Stolac in 1992 it was like a movie, or it was like the things one had only seen in movies. Again, here, the analogy compensates for the inadequacy of the existing vocabulary. The merging of fiction and reality is a way to express such dramatic occurrences: the sound of a bomb hitting the ground, the sensation of immense tremors in the earth, the sight of people running.

Amputation: rather die than go through it again

People sometimes condensed their overwhelming, unwieldy and intangible feelings from the war by saying that they would rather die than go through it again. This might be considered as no more than a saying. However, the *way* people said it convinced me that at the moment of speaking they meant it seriously.

Amputation: this war was the worst

Another condensation: comparing this war to previous wars and then saying this war was the worst:

TK: You have survived two wars?

Džanana: Yes one in childhood and one in old age…But that war [World War II] was nothing compared to this war. *Božija milost*! [Meaning something like God's joy that God gives in abundance, which is the way Džanana compares World War II to the present war].

People would also make comparisons to Hitler, saying that he had not been as destructive as the Croats had been during this war. And not only old people who had actually experienced World War II made such comparisons. Even for younger people, evoking Hitler, the symbol of modern evil, and stating that this war was worse than what he did, was a powerful expression of the strength of their feelings.

Amputation: hero-tales

The last example relates to how remembering experiences can function as a way of recovering agency. I call the agency-generating stories told in Stolac hero-tales. The point is that when telling these rather tragic stories, the speaker introduces a little twist, so that he becomes an acting subject and not just an object acted upon by others. Hero-tales can be stories about escapes, hiding food in prison camp, dressing up like a woman and thereby tricking the Croat soldiers when they came to fetch the Muslim men, and so on.

A transcription of an interview can never convey the atmosphere in which it was conducted. This is a great disadvantage in this excerpt from an interview with Muhamed, as the atmosphere was full of humour and liveliness, and Muhamed's story was accompanied by vibrant gestures.

Muhamed: Did you arrive from Denmark by plane?

TK: Yes.

Muhamed: From Mostar to Sarajevo, Mostar to Sarajevo over the mountains on foot! Yes on foot…And we had noting to eat, no water, there was nothing.

Muhamed's wife: It was war.

Muhamed: Over the mountains. I had boots. My wife had only shoes. And there were a lot of stones, and they hurt your feet.

TK: How many days?

Muhamed: Four days and four nights. Halfway through Bosnia on foot, and we returned to Konjic on foot. And we returned to the house in the evening, washed a little … [and then he uses body language to show how they then made love]. We were not tired [laughing}, but after making love, we were tired [laughing]. […]

TK: When was that?

Muhamed: In 1994.

Wife: Tell him about when we were married.

Muhamed: The wedding was at ten o'clock in the morning … No wedding outfit … [only] uniform…we washed ourselves…My wife had smartened herself up you know, and all the time shelling, snipers; take cover. I said to my wife…it is normal at a wedding that you shoot in the air. I said 'Here is a gun so we can shoot, for real.' [Laughs]. But the shells were falling so we could not shoot [What he means was that they did not need to shoot, because all the shells were a salute in themselves]. Then we were in the basement, only the four of us. Me, my wife and the best men (*kum i kuma*). Nobody else. 10 o'clock in the morning. We signed the papers and then we were ready to go to another house and…you know [laughs.] And we had no wedding ring. My wife made *pita* [traditional dish] out of tinned food, then we had half a litre of *sliva* [plum brandy], and at 4 o'clock in the afternoon I had to go…to the front…yes…that's how it was…love.

The unmaking of the world is not 'only' about how the everyday world is destroyed and values and social relations damaged. It is also about how communication of the violent experiences is itself problematic. People want to forget but cannot do so because the memories keep surfacing. And people want to remember and talk about it all, but cannot do so because they are not able to understand what happened, and when they try words and categories do not suffice, so new but still insufficient ones have to be invented: the amputated telling from the world's unmaking.

The all-pervasive feeling of loss

The final element in my informants' experiences of the world's unmaking relates to a seemingly trivial, but nevertheless central point: the unmaking of my informants' world is not restricted to either a discrete period in time (the war) or to a bounded set of core experiences. Rather, it must be seen against the background of a total and all-pervasive feeling of loss:

- Loss of future or belief in a future (dreams, plans, wishes).
- Loss of nation state (Yugoslavia, and the identity: Yugoslav).
- Loss of a functional society (school, doctors, pension, law and order, industry, education).
- Loss of a safe society (ethnic violence, Croat intimidation and discrimination of Muslims).
- Loss of material goods and material status (house, clothes, not being able to buy birthday presents for one's children, money).
- Loss of status and dignity (an old ethnology professor from Mostar now walks about the streets in ragged clothes trying to earn some money by guiding the few tourists).
- Loss of family members (refugees in other countries, killed).
- Loss of the sense of psychological security (war-related traumas).
- Loss of a native soil (for everybody Stolac is a new town, virtually nothing is as it was, personal contacts are gone, and the town has become ugly).
- Loss of the past.

Even though this list covers many aspects of people's sense of loss, it still cannot capture the pervasiveness of people's feelings of bereavement. Stolac is a sad and depressing town, with a gloomy atmosphere. And though people are friendly, hospitable and refreshingly humorous (albeit blackly), the place drains their energy. I felt this myself. Sometimes I felt that Stolac was nothing but a sump of sadness and despair, despite the optimism, creativity and courage that sometimes also existed almost schizophrenically.

One example of the persistent attack on the everyday world is the way people seldom distinguished clearly between peace and war. People for instance said 'after Dayton' instead of peace, or they said 'the present situation.' They seldom remember the date of the Dayton agreement, but they remember the exact date they were released from prison camp and the day they returned to their home in Stolac. Sometimes people say they wish for peace to come (implying that the present situation is not peace), or they simply say outright that the war is not over. This is from an interview with Suljeman:

Suljeman: It is impossible to live here. When was it the peace came, 1995?

TK: Yes, in 1995.

Suljeman: Then six years have passed and there is no progress. Things have not become better, no industry, nothing.

One day while I was talking to Nusret's father outside a small shop, a man about my age stopped by. He lived in a village one kilometre away, where the power supply had not yet been fixed. I asked him if they were going to get electricity soon, as a US-funded project was fixing the electricity lines around town. He said:

Yes, but they say that about everything: 'Just wait a little, just wait.' For my part the war has now been going on for eight years, and they are just wasted years. I've not accomplished anything, it has only been waiting time, and I'm still waiting, but for what? They say things will be better, but a lot of my years have been wasted. To you this is maybe interesting, but to us it is tragic. I have no job, nothing to do, and we've been living without electricity since we returned.

It is difficult to describe the sad atmosphere I often found in Stolac, An atmosphere that contributed to people's general feeling of loss. Nevertheless, I will here quote a few excerpts from my notebook to give an impression of how the town appeared to me.

I

I am just returning from Nota [a small café]. I don't know what it is, but something has happened to the way I see things today. From being exciting and interesting – and myself having positive energy – things have changed. People are strange. The town is strange, a dump. Down at Nota, for instance, five to six people sit. There is a only little light. Two individuals are talking. Some drink coffee and half-sentimental Bosnian music fills the room. The room is no more than twenty-five square metres. The cables in the bar are hanging down. An old 16-inch TV stands on the bar, it is dirty. One of the 'waiters' sits in a corner kissing his girlfriend. Jamezdin is sitting in the dark, alone, like he has totally given up.

TK: What did you do today?

Jamezdin: Nothing!

He has no coffee, *nista* [nothing]. Osman sits on one of the four plastic chairs, which, placed around a plastic table, make up the regular table for those who play cards in the evening. The room is like a bunker someone has tried to fix up a little. On the way out we talk a little about football, and about good and bad Danish football clubs. They know them better than I do. The worn football programme in the bar, showing dates for matches and the odds, is the only thing livening the place up. One of the young men turns on the TV, but there is nothing, only static.

II

Stolac is a hole. There is nothing in the town. The tired unshaven man sitting in the post-office, staring and saying *sutra* [tomorrow] when I ask if I have mail. Cafés with room for one hundred but with only ten guests. I met the guy without teeth on my way back, we talked a little…about nothing.

III

It is as though everything, in one way or another, has been ravaged by the war. Houses are shattered and collapsed and just standing as empty gaping ruins: bushes and grass grow in many of them. Goats are grazing there. Other houses, inhabited, are filled with holes after shell splinters, they lack windows, and plastic or planks cover the window openings. Houses about to be built – but the money has run out – are left half-finished, but inhabited anyway. Laundry is hanging outside, and a satellite dish hangs on the rough wall. Outside in the garden there is an old lady, dressed in black. Her child or grandchild gets into the old ramshackle and rusted Opel Cadet in the driveway, starts it and drives away, the noise from the leaky exhaust pipe filling the air. I pass a small bridge, the metal railing is torn by shell splinters, and it is rather rusty. Below is an old factory, all the windows are broken, the drainpipes are gone, so the walls on the north side are mossy as the rainwater just runs down the building's sides. The roads are filled with potholes, but people still drive extremely fast. I meet a young girl, about twenty-five, in a pink pullover, I say hello and smile, she smiles back showing all her missing teeth. The Muslim graveyard [*Harem*] is overgrown by twining plants, the Croats haven't touched it, but time has. Nobody has tended it for the last five to seven years. All this decay is in glaring contrast to the few new and very stunning three-storey houses and a totally new Alfa-Romeo or Mercedes driving by.

IV

At the café I noticed many have bitten-down nails. Coffee, cigarettes and bitten-down nails.

And finally, two quotations that communicate the feeling that the unmaking is still on-going. One day Anvere said to me:

Nicolas [my second name], you can't understand what the war has done to us. At first sight everything may look normal, but it's not. Nothing is normal. The war has changed everything.

Another day she talked about the time in Blagaj. This is how I recalled the conversation afterwards.

Anvere: In Blagaj I lost thirty kilos in the first three months. Imagine! Fear and there was no food. All the time I had to think about how to get food. Alen [son] did not come out of the basement where we lived for half a year, he would not, he was scared. I had to go out to get food. But there was nothing to buy. There were no shops. Sometimes you could buy a little from those who had something, some of their homemade stuff, a little meat or some honey. But it was expensive. If not, I had to pick grass, we had nothing else. We cooked it and ate it. And we were scared all the time…And the things Nihad experienced in the prison camp, he has not told me. He can't bring himself to tell me, and I can't stand to hear it.

Nihad: It was terrible; you can't understand how it was. One day or one week you could maybe endure, but when it continued week after week, month after month…I saw people dying in front of me, we were scared, it was…

He stops. Nihad is not a man who talks a lot, but at this moment I simply do not think he can manage to say more, and I do not ask. His face is ash-grey, and his whole body is somewhat fallen apart. When he stops talking he lowers his glance, and it stays there. His wife then said:

Anvere: And the fear we had hasn't left us. When I gave birth to Amer in 1997, I think I passed on that fear to him; he was like…wild and restless [she cries].

TK: Yes, but he is a good boy now, he has a good life now.

Anvere: Yes, but I passed on that fear to him, and now what does he have to grow up for? There is no future, no work, nothing.

This last section has showed how – owing to the unhealed traumas of my informants and the present depressing situation – the unmaking of the world is still going on. I have termed it the existence of an omnipresent feeling of loss. Let me stress again that my depiction of Stolac and people's mood is just one side of the coin. The other side is hope, successfully forgetting the past, optimism, laughter, humour, determination and energy. But when the coin is flipped, this side often lands face down.

The aim of this chapter has been to give an account of central themes in my informants' experiences related to the unmaking of their world. The very foundations of existence (property, security, food and family relations) have been affected. The stories and values governing normal social life were also damaged, which led people to question not only ontology, but also moral principles and social relations, especially ethnic relations. Furthermore, the unmaking of the world means a loss of epistemological frameworks, making both the remembering and communication – as well as forgetting and repression – of traumatic events equally problematic. Lastly, I have tried to capture my informants' general and all-pervasive feeling of loss.

The chapter is a necessary introduction to the rest of the book, in which I concentrate on my informants' *remaking* of their world. I intend to analyse the contours of the mental landscape (what I see as their counterdiscourse) they have created in order to explain and give meaning to the devastating experiences of recent years. It has been necessary to show how profoundly people's world has been unmade in order to make it possible to contextualise how fundamental the question of identity is in this process of remaking for the Muslims of present-day Stolac. It is my argument that the unmaking of people's world forces them to first question and then recreate a number of the central categories of human experience: social relations, moral values, the everyday world, and group identity (especially ethnic). I will be treating many of my informants' questions and uncertainties concerning these fundamental issues under two primary headings, touched upon in each part of the rest of the book. Firstly: Who are they, the ones who did this to us? And secondly: Who are we, since this was done to us? The question of the identity of the Other will be the theme of Part II, and the question of my informants' own post-war identity will be the theme of Part III. However, before looking at some of the answers people have come up with in detail, I will outline the central aspects of the analytical framework for my discussion of the remaking of the world.

Chapter 3
Remaking, identification, and counterdiscourse

Remaking

As an introductory remark one could argue that the concept of *remaking* is not theoretically solid enough to demand specific focus. After all, what we are dealing with is an aspect of cultural construction. Remove the *re-* and one has a commonplace anthropological focus upon how people *make* their world. I more or less agree. In her study of war and the consequences of war, Nordstrom (1997) argues differently. Her informants' world was totally destroyed, and as she analyses it they had to rebuild it from scratch: "[normally] people do not create worlds anew but fine-tune the ones they are born into. Very few empirical data exist to show how people's worlds are newly crafted" (ibid. 13). Though it is analytically tempting to envisage war-torn societies as areas of cultural *tabula rasa*, cultural construction can never be studied from scratch (Connerton 1989); and as my study demonstrates, people draw upon already existing cultural categories and habitual practices when remaking a world. Nevertheless, I still find the concept of *remaking* illuminating, as we can use it to direct attention to the intensified need that people who are victims of war and violence have to adjust experience to larger narratives (and vice versa). As I showed in the previous chapter, many aspects of my informants' everyday world were unmade during the war and post-war period, and the unmaking is still taking place. Therefore, the material and mental remaking of this shattered world is necessary in order for the Muslims to live on. The difference in relation to 'ordinary' studies of cultural construction is then quantitative and not qualitative.

I will introduce four themes central to the study of practices of remaking in post-war societies. These themes are: a) *officially sanctioned public spheres* for narrating experience; b) creation of a predictable *everyday life*; c) *agency*; and d) *identification* of oneself and the Other. My study mainly focuses on one of these themes – identification – though the strength of the analysis consists in letting the different themes interact.

Officially sanctioned public spheres

The first thread relates to the general human need for connecting individual stories to larger collective or supra-individual ones in order to express and order experience (Jackson 2002: 11-37). More specifically, the focus relates to experiences with officially sanctioned public spheres, which give explicit recognition to one's suffering. That is, which enable one to express grief, recount experiences, facilitate a sort of intellectual grasp on events and obtain some kind of satisfaction for the injustices experienced. In post-traumatic societies, such a requirement is of special importance, as many of the existing narratives are often destroyed or no longer valid, and because people's experiences often exceed the explanatory potential of remaining narratives. In some countries hit by war or conflict, official attempts at creating such organised arenas for communicating loss and injustice have been made. Consider for instance the work done by the South African Truth and Reconciliation Commission (Buhr 2000; Fiona 2001). Or take the example of Nigeria, where the deliberate and widely accepted displacement of the process of reconciliation from the national to the community level has occurred (Last 2000). When we look at Stolac and Bosnia Herzegovina, though, such officially sanctioned space is already colonized from the perspective of my informants.

As already shown, the official public space in Stolac is totally dominated by nationalist-minded Croats, and the message communicated is clear: We won the war! Stolac is Croatian and has never been otherwise! Ethnicity is a hindrance to interaction! The Muslims' perspective is unimportant![1] Since I left Stolac, the central mosque in town has been rebuilt. I imagine this is a great blow for the nationalist-minded Croats. On the other hand, I do not think it is seen as a great victory by many of the ordinary Muslims. As I demonstrate throughout the study, the counterdiscourse that the Muslims produce, though it is about identifying the culprits and gaining recognition for their own suffering, is not a fight over national symbols. Rather it is about resisting the nationalist discourse altogether, which in Stolac is almost impossible. Furthermore, this counterdiscourse does not exist in the publicy sphere. It exists rather as an implicit, loose and often non-conscious practice.

One might expect that the International Criminal Tribunal for the Former Yugoslavia in the Hague would function as an official criminal justice system, redressing the Muslim's grievances. However, it is not regarded as such. In gen-

---

1   The term space should also be taken literally. I had an informant with whom I often walked about Stolac discussing various matters, and it was always very obvious when we passed Croat cafés or houses, or walked in areas mainly inhabited by Croats. He lowered his voice, or stopped talking, sometimes in the middle of a sentence, and I could sense his uneasiness.

eral people feel that the work of the tribunal is all too late and too slow. Furthermore, they feel that the tribunal fails to indict the right people. Several of the war criminals from the war and post-war period are still walking the streets, and some are even employed in the public sector.

One could also imagine that the West or the international community in some way could work to officially recognise the grievances of the Muslims. Many Muslims, however, have an ambivalent relationship towards the West, for instance reflected in their attitudes towards the Dayton agreement, which ended the war. Naturally they are relieved that the war ended, but on the other hand they are also resentful over the neutrality of the agreement. All groups are treated equally, which means that no groups are treated as having suffered more than others, which is directly contrary to the experience of the Muslims of Stolac. In general, people accept or appreciate the international presence in Bosnia Herzegovina, but they do not find that this presence guarantees or constitutes a public sphere communicating their experiences.

Everyday life

Attempts at creating or relating experience to officially sanctioned collective memories often run counter to another characteristic of post-war remaking: the need for rebuilding an everyday life. This is the case because forgetting is often a central element in this process. In order to live on, restore a belief in a future and create an everyday life not permeated by hate and implacability, a strategy of active forgetting is often pursued in post-war/terror communities (Das and Kleinman 2001; Jackson 2002). The tension between creating spheres for articulating experience (remembering) and on the other hand consciously setting the past aside in order to live on (forgetting) was very clear in Stolac. Sometimes it was a generational matter. For instance when the older people persistently talked about the war, and the younger people deliberately tried to avoid any focus on it. But the dilemma was felt by all and manifested itself through often outright contradictory statements. In a study of post-war life in Bombay, Mehta and Chatterji (2001) observed the same relationship between forgetting and the resumption of an everyday life:

> The altered everyday is marked by a new knowledge and memory of loss, but also a practical wisdom of negotiating this loss. It tells one that reparation cannot take the form of justice, coexistence is possible only if the past is deliberately set aside. (ibid. 238).

It seems that condemnation, hate and a feeling that justice is all or nothing is characteristic for people living 'outside', either abroad or outside the relevant community. The reason is, I believe, that they do not have to live with the consequences of their own condemnations. In post-war communities the different parties have to develop some kind of 'working consensus' or unspoken agreement about social interaction. In this light we can understand the technique of a Muslim woman who told me that she never discussed politics with her Croat colleagues. The only things they deliberately talked about were cooking and children. The rationale behind such a strategy seems to be related to the integrity of the situation – upholding the 'order of the interaction' – that is, a mutual protection and confirmation of the identities presented (Goffman 1983; see also Kolind 2002a). But naturally the creation of a working consensus is not easy: for example, if one has lost everything, including family members, and then has to co-exist with the guilty party or members of the 'guilty' ethnic group. Often, though, people have no alternatives. On several occasions I heard people in Stolac say that they could not yet live together with the Croats, but they could live alongside them. The implicit assumption was that as time passes the ethnic groups would learn to live together again. Last (2000), in his work on reconciliation, the restoration of sociality, and the establishment of the trust necessary for cooperation in post-war society, has isolated four main areas necessary for the recreation of an everyday life:

1. The establishment of a framework of security.
2. Reopening the pathways of exchange, social as well as economic.
3. Symbolic cleansing of the land.
4. Offering of credible grounds for hope.

Looking at Stolac I would say that people are beginning to feel safe, as incidents of ethnically related violence diminish, and as inter-ethnic economic exchange in the town grows. However, social interaction is still rare and difficult, and as three and four have only been partially realised.

The rebuilding of an everyday world, one can see, is not about ideology. It is about establishing predictability, creating a 'working consensus', and burying memories. It is about being able to send the children off to school, to get personal finances to hang together, feel safe, (re)build friendships, buy a car, have a cosy café where one can socialise, cultivate the garden, keep the sadness at bay, fall in love, take care of the parents, dream. As Das and Kleinman (2001: 15-16) have put it when writing about similar matters:

> We are looking not necessarily for a grand narrative of forgiveness and redemption but for the small local stories in which such communities are experimenting with ways of inhabiting the world together.

Agency

A third element relevant for analysing post-war practices of remaking relates to agency. Above I mentioned the importance for victims of warfare to be able to connect their experiences to larger collective narratives in order to gain recognition for injustice and in order to grasp the violent interruption of their lives. The implication is that experience only exists when narrated. However, the representation of experience does not account for the whole picture. According to existentialist-inspired writers, people also generate strategies aimed at sustaining a sense of agency, especially in the face of disempowering circumstances. Jackson (2002) analyses storytelling not solely as an attempt to understand the world conceptually. Rather: "Storytelling reworks and remodels subject-object relations in ways that subtly alter the balance between actor and acted upon, thus allowing us to feel that we actively participate in a world that for a moment seemed to discount, demean, and disempower us" (ibid. 16). Jackson relates this to a general existential imperative, understood as the need "to be more than a bit player in the stories of our own lives" (ibid. 15). It should go without saying that this existential imperative is intensified for victims of violence and war.

Returning to Nordstrom's (1997) study of civilians' reactions to the terror and warfare in Mozambique, she found that the creation or sustaining of agency constituted a central element in her informants' counter-practices. She furthermore noticed how this agency-creating activity was closely linked to a strong code of human ethics. The result of this combination was, she argues, to disprove the Hobbesian dictum that life is reduced to a free-for-all; a mentality of unstructured survival in situations of destruction of institutional structures and governmental support. Instead, people's 'worldbuildings' (ibid. 13) were characterised by the making of durable social relations and by mitigating the onslaught on the self and one's status as a political subject, which the terror had aimed at (see also Howel 1989).

In the previous chapter, I introduced a number of 'hero-tales.' These can be seen as examples of agency-creating activity. Though the existential imperative will not be my central focus, it can be used to put the data I present into perspective. The counterdiscourse I analyse is probably not only about resisting nationalist discourse and creating meaning in a shattered world. It is also about restoring a sense of control over relevant elements in one's life. The focus upon counterdiscursive elements will tend to make people's practices a little too conscious and ideological and treat them as a little more coherent than they are in reality, whereas a focus upon existence and agency will make them look individual and idiosyncratic. Furthermore, such idiosyncrasies – when taken together and related to a code of human ethics or a will for coexistence, which I found in Stolac – can be seen as part of a human ability to create sociality. We must not automatically depict the sociality in post-war societies as a Hobbesian nightmare. Fulfilling the existential imperative (by not giving up, but resisting the destructive force of violence) coupled with a will for coexistence can – as in Stolac – very well be the force or potential in local everyday interaction that can help rebuild society from below.

Identification

The last, and for this book most central theme relevant for studying processes of remaking relates to everyday identification. *Everyday* identifications are distinguished from the officially sanctioned public sphere by being more undefined, non-conscious and implicit. Officially sanctioned public spheres can function as a means of connecting individual stories with supra-individual collective stories, but as I pointed out above such official spheres are not present for the Muslims of Stolac. The question is what happens when relevant officially sanctioned public spheres for representing experience do not exist.

Various anthropological studies of ordinary people's reactions to violence and war have focused on precisely this relation between individual and collective memory. They have analysed various strategies for transforming private into public meanings. That is, creating integration and balance between one's personal world and the wider world of others, which seems to be especially problematic when justice in a legal sense has not (yet) been achieved; as is also the situation for the Muslims of Stolac. Such alternative or dissident collective memories and cultural representations (alternative or dissident in relation to the officially sanctioned public sphere) do not need to be coherent, ideological, fixed or totally conscious in order to work. In fact, they do not even need to be new. Often already existing cultural categories and narratives are used or remoulded in order to grasp experience and explain people's changed reality. Alternative collective memory can take the form of culturally sanctioned ghost stories, which are used as instruments for remembering the past terror in an otherwise politically dangerous milieu (Perera 2001). It can also consist of traditional narratives or tales commenting on a local social situation of distrust, which mitigate the consequences of the internalisation of violence in local society (Warren 1993). Alternative narratives can also function as a critique of an officially sanctioned nationalism by indirectly operating with a different period of time (Jansen 2000b). Or they can be explicit and conscious political expressions such as painting murals and graffiti (Sluka 1992b).

In Stolac, I found people to be primarily occupied with two kinds of identification. First, they persistently tried to answer the question: *who are they, the ones who did this to us?* This was about being able to hold someone responsible for it all, and though ethnic identity was officially presented as the most important identity overall by all sides throughout the war, ethnic identity did not suffice for my informants in answering the question. The second question was: *who are we, since this was done to us?* Again, one might presume that ethnic affiliation would be central in answering the question, and in a way it was. But when ethnicity was used as identification, it was often not the public nationalist discourse's version of ethnicity, which focuses on territory, blood, language, history etc. Rather, it was one characterised by a local ethic stressing inter-ethnic respect; and what is more, non-ethnic identification existed as well, in narratives that stressed coexistence and local solidarity. Identification among the Muslims of Stolac should be seen as part of a counterdiscourse that partly rejects the nationalist discourses and partly offers alternative interpretations of relevant aspects of those discourses. Identification and counterdiscourse will be the theoretical focus of the remainder of this chapter. The discussion will be conducted in light of the two central aspects: discourse and resistance.

Discourse

Discourse has become a more or less catch-all concept in the social and cultural theorising of recent years. However, I find the concept illuminating, and the definition offered by Hajer (1995: 44) is helpful. Discourse is:

> … a specific ensemble of ideas, concepts, and categories that are produced, re-produced, and transformed in a particular set of practices and through which meaning is given to physical and social realities.

This definition is probably a little too broad and in the following I will try to narrow it down somewhat.

Constraining qualities of discourse

Foucault has contributed extensively to the popularity of the concept of discourse. When writing explicitly about discourse, he emphasised both enabling and constraining qualities, but his historical analysis has mainly highlighted the constraining power of discourse at the expense of the reflective powers of individuals (Hajer 1995: 42-52; Dreyfus and Rabinow 1982). According to Foucault, his overall intention was to produce "… a history of the different modes by which, in our culture, human beings are made subjects" (Foucault 1982), subject positions which are the results of objectifying practices. His analysis of the construction of *the delinquent* (Foucault 1991) – which simultaneously was a study of the working of the disciplining power of modernity – is an example of this. That is, a symbol of how identities are manufactured and internalised. In

Panopticon people are not related directly to each other, but produced as subjects in front of the gaze. Furthermore, not only are subject positions the results of the working of the formative power of modern discourses. Our very notion of the individual, the subject itself, is also regarded by Foucault as a modern construction produced through various practices (Foucault 1994). As Nikolas Rose has termed it, we have 'invented ourselves' (1996). The constraining effects of discourse are summed up by Hajer (1995: 49):

> Discourses imply prohibitions since they make it impossible to raise *certain questions* or argue certain cases; they imply exclusionary systems because they only authorize *certain people* to participate in a discourse; they come with discourse forms of *internal discipline* through which a discourse order is maintained; and finally there are also *certain rules* regarding the conditions under which a discourse can be drawn upon. (My italics).

When looking at the nationalist discourses in former Yugoslavia such constraining features are relevant, as will be shown in Chapters 4 and 9. Questions about the possibility of interethnic coexistence have become increasingly impossible to raise. Politicians, religious persons, military personnel, nationalist-minded journalists, and others, were the voices making up the discourse; whereas ordinary people's more ambiguous everyday voices, as well as criticism of the nationalist programmes, were silenced. New elements were increasingly incorporated into the discourse, and were all related to the same agenda: national identity. As regards the last element of the quotation above, one could say that during the war there were hardly any conditions under which the nationalist discourse could not be made relevant.

There are, however, also problems involved in viewing discourses as only being constraining and producing subjectpositions. Even though the nationalist discourse of former Yugoslavia became almost hegemonic, it is also essential, especially when doing ethnographic research among the receivers of such massive ideological impact, to focus upon the ways ordinary people receive, resist, reject and also reproduce, in sum reflect on 'constraining' discourses.

Reflection

Inspired by Foucault, Hacking has studied how modern science has been engaged in 'making up people', that is, producing knowledge in relation to groups of people. Unlike Foucault, though, Hacking sees such subject positions or 'human kinds' (Hacking 1995: 354) as real. Real in the sense that people who are classified can react to these classifications, and real in the sense that intentional action is action under description. When people respond to the classifications that have entrapped them, the classifications have to be readjusted: "…our clas-sifications and our classes conspire to emerge hand-in-hand, each egging the other on" (Hacking 1986: 228). Hacking calls this process of feedback 'dynamic nominalism' (ibid.; see also Pedersen 1989). Contrary to Foucault's analysis, power is dynamically linked to its outcome; power does not operate as an ex-ternal principle saturating everything but not itself explained (Foucault 1994: 97-109; Dreyfus and Rabinow 1986: 207). Although modernity has probably ac-celerated the production of identities (subject positions), and though Hacking only considers modern scientific discourses, I think we can expand his insight into a general characterisation of human identification. The very relation be-tween objectified identities and reflection can be seen as part of a general hu-man social adjustment.

Mead (1967, 1982) theorised human reflection or self-consciousness as an ability man has developed throughout evolution in order to sustain interac-tion, a capability realised through verbal socialisation. The metaphysical im-material subject existing in Descartes' *cogito* – the impossibility of which Lacan (1956:80) has described as: "I see myself seeing myself" – is replaced by Mead by a social self, for whom:

> Thinking [or reflection] is the same as talking to other people, except that it is done inwardly, with one self rather than with others. (Mead quoted in Baldwin 1986: 31).

Consciousness and reflection originate from the human ability to use symbols or language and let them stand in for interaction-experience. Humans are – contrary to animals – capable of reacting to symbols. We are able to envisage the result of a given action before it has been realised. Thinking is internalised experiences with interactions put into language/symbols. Reflection is thereby built into sociality, as we can only see the consequences of our actions through the eyes of 'the other.' As Mead stated:

> The individual experiences himself as such, not directly, but only indirectly, from the particular standpoints of other individual members of the same so-cial group as a whole to which he belongs. For he enters his own experience as a self or individual, not directly or immediately, not by becoming a subject to himself, but only in so far as he becomes an object to himself just as other individuals are objects to him or in his experience; and he becomes an object to himself only by taking the attitudes of other individuals towards himself within a social environment or context of experience and behaviour in which both he and they are involved. (1967: 138).

Mead operated with two sides of this social self. The 'Me', which is the organisation of other's attitudes in the self, and the 'I', the subjective attitude of reflection itself gazing on the objective image of the self and its own responses
(Mead 1967; see also Burkitt 1991: 28-55). These two phases of "self-reproducing
activity" (Shotter 1989: 139) are in constant dialogue, and the one cannot exist
without the other. Furthermore, the 'Me' is not only internalised experiences
with concrete others, but also relative structured accumulations of experiences
with what Mead called generalised others. That is, general attitudes, values and
morals, or one could say discourses. Contrary to Foucault, though, Mead does
not perceive such discourses or generalised others as being purely restrictive;
rather they are seen as conditions for actions. Only through action (the 'I'),
do these structures come alive – get reproduced or transformed. And the 'I'
on the other hand can only act on the background of experiences with such
generalised others. Discourses then are without a doubt constraining; they produce subject positions and they offer and even prescribe a vision of reality. On
the other hand – though some macro-actors are more capable than others of
constructing the discourses others have to relate to – discourses or generalised
others enter the individual's social self as interaction-experience and are used
in social interaction. I do not argue that ordinary individuals are capable of
transforming discourses at will, but rather that they can relate themselves and
their actions to them, thereby resisting, rejecting, reproducing or surrendering
to them.

Mead's theory is important when investigating my informants' relations
to the massive nationalist discourse penetrating so many aspects of their life.
No doubt this discourse produced subject positions, that is, it produced 'nationalists' out of neighbours, colleagues, and friends. But this did not occur
automatically. People reflected upon the new identities, a reflection based upon
former experience with social interaction, and, as I will show throughout my
study, this reflection altered, modified and even resisted the subject positions
created by the nationalist discourse.

The impossibility of discursive closure

Mead's theory operates with two forms of consciousness: 'consciousness *qua*
experience' and 'consciousness *qua* awareness' (see Natsoulas 1985). The former
refers to unreflective everyday acts. That is, dispositions, knowledge and experience not immediately accessible to us in language. This is similar to what
Giddens has termed 'practical consciousness' (1987: 52-73). Only when such
habits and routines are consciously put into language do they enter a self-re-
flective process, the 'conscious *qua* awareness', which only happens when daily
interaction becomes problematic. When social adjustment is unproblematic,

one is not forced into the subjective attitude that demands objective reflection upon oneself and one's actions. However, when the everyday is questioned, the taken-for-granted part of social life becomes conscious and at the same time changeable. As Giddens (1987:63) writes: "These latter forms of cognition cannot be translated into discourse without the influence of some kind of distorting mechanism."

In ex-Yugoslavia this translation into discourse of non-reflected elements was astoundingly massive and fast. In only a couple of years, nearly all aspects of not only political life but also people's everyday life had become articulated in the context of a nationalist discourse. Music, food, history, territory, traditions, family relations, literature, language, greetings and so on all became incorporated into the discourse and interpreted through its nationalist lenses. In only a couple of years nationalist thinking became almost hegemonic. Vukovic (1993) recounts how he was rejected by close friends at the beginning of the war in Sarajevo, not because of his ethnic background, but because he refused to enter the nationalistic discourse and define national loyalty.

One question remains: are discourses – no matter how massive they appear – capable of becoming completely hegemonic?[2] Following Laclau and Mouffe, discursive closure is logically impossible, as this would imply a world of fixed meanings and an unchangeable status quo (Jansen 2000a: 11-14). Guha (1997) displays the same kind of logical reasoning. Though his analysis is developed in relation to the colonial situation in India, I think we can generalise some of his insights. According to Guha, power is a logical relation of entailment between dominance and subordination, as it is not possible to think of the one without the other.[3] Each of these positions is in turn constituted by a pair of interacting elements: domination by coercion and persuasion, and subordination by collaboration and resistance. Domination and subordination imply each other *logically*, as do coercion and persuasion on the one hand and collaboration and resistance on the other; whereas the relation between the two pairs is *organic*, that is, a contingent empirical relation. Therefore, the power relation domination: subordination differs from one society to the other according to the organic composition of that power relation. As Guha writes (1997: 22): "There can be no ideal structure of power that is not subject to and modified by the contingencies of history: no Nazi fantasy of total force that is not disturbed by nightmares of dissent, no populist utopia of total consent that is not traversed by a constable's beat, if not trodden by army jackboots." He takes hegemony as

2   This line of reasoning is inspired by Jansen (2000a).

3   Or as Foucault (1990: 101-2) has it: "Where we have power there is resistance." Power relations simply need a multiplicity of points of resistance to be articulated against.

an example. Hegemony is a condition of dominance in which persuasion out-weighs coercion, but is still organically related and open to resistance (through the logical relation of domination and subordination). It also follows that there can be no hegemonic system under which persuasion totally supersedes coer-cion. Were that to happen, there would be no domination, hence no hegemony (Guha 1997: 20-23).

Discourses then often strive to become hegemonic, to define everything in their own image, but they will never succeed. There will always be an el-ement of instability, contingency, and potential dissident alternatives. This is similar to the point made by Scott (1990: 4-5) that the dominant part never controls the stage absolutely, but their wishes normally prevail. What may look like hegemony or dominant discourses is more a result of both parties – both the dominant and the subordinate – on the public scene tacitly conspiring in misrepresentation (ibid. 2); but behind the public scene resistance or hidden scripts always exist. Possible alternatives will always exist. In Stolac I found people submitting to the nationalistic discourse, but they also resisted it. Resist-ance, the second central element of the identifications I found in Stolac, is the theme I will focus on next.

Resistance

Rigorous scientific discourse claims that our categories and analytical concepts should have precise and definable edges, and be strict, recognisable and invari-able from one situation to another. This is not the way Keesing sees it. In his discussion of resistance as an analytical metaphor, he concludes that while it is useful in characterising a range of phenomena it will never be able to fit all situations equally aptly, as well as not being precisely definable (1992: 217-25). According to Keesing, the *force* that resistance resists can be a concrete physical force, as well as an abstract, general and unclear one. Resistance itself can be the attempt to push back, but also the passive slowing down of the impinging force, or even partial compliance with it. Individuals as well as a collective can be the ones who resist (slow down, partially comply), and finally resistance can be overt and conscious as well as indirect and involuntary. He concludes:

> Images and metaphors may be more or less apt, more or less useful; they can scarcely be incorrect. If we expect our technical terms to be precise, resist-ance will not serve us well in theoretical analyses. If we see our theoretical discourse as inevitably cast in everyday language, then we will abandon false hopes for precision and prescriptive definitions. (ibid. 224).

Bearing this dilemma in mind, I shall now clarify the way the term resistance is used in this study. Let me start by noting that I tend to use the concept counter-discourse instead of resistance. That is, I see the counterdiscourse of the Muslims of Stolac as a resistance to the dominating nationalistic discourse.

Counter

I shall start by discussing the first part of the concept counterdiscourse: 'counter'. The counterdiscourse I analyse only exists in relation to the nationalist discourse. Even though the counterdiscourse reflects and is based upon deep-seated cultural and moral values (see below), it is only when such 'traditions' are viewed in relation to more macro-political changes, such as the rise of nationalism in Yugoslav public life, that they take the for of resistance (Nordstrom and Martin 1992). As such, counterdiscourse can be compared to Scott's (1990) use of the concept *hidden transcript* to analyse resistance. The hidden transcript is, as he sees it, derivative, in the sense that it consists of those practices which mainly contradict what dominates the public scene (ibid. 4-5). Labelling the Muslims' resistance as being *counter* is a way of giving it form analytically. It follows, therefore, that my informants, simply by *not* using ethnic or nationalist categories to explain the war, violence, and people's misfortunes, are resisting the nationalist discourse. Such 'non-ethnic condemnations' (Kolind 2002a) resist the nationalist rhetoric, not by speaking against it, but by avoiding it. I did find in Stolac articulate and conscious resistance to nationalist thinking, and such 'anti-nationalism' (Jansen 2002a) is part of the picture. But the major part of the counterdiscourse I analyse is more intricate, implicit and subtle, and exists precisely in avoiding the worldview offered by the nationalist discourse, and by suggesting alternative interpretations and alternative contexts for understanding social life. Instead of blaming the ethnic Other, people use and construct other categories of blame: *politicians, not-decent people, the uncultivated, the rural population.* And instead of identifying Muslim identity by reference to nation, blood, territory, history and so on, as the nationalist discourse has it, my informants evoke *localism, ideals of tolerance and coexistence,* and *Balkan mentality.* The counterdiscourse I encountered in Stolac is not a winning or well-defined analytical discourse. Sometimes it became articulate and ideological, but mostly it was not open and direct. It is not even possible to locate persons who can act as pure representatives. The force of the counterdiscourse exists rather in being able to *recontextualise* the narratives of destruction, loss and violence (see also Das and Kleinman 2001: 6) - thus offering alternative non-nationalist contexts for explaining and identifying.

Culture

However, the counterdiscourse of the Muslims of Stolac is not just defined by being 'counter-.' The non-nationalist identifications – the recontextualisations – that the Muslims make rest upon already existing cultural categories and social identities, as well as drawing upon experiences from pre-war habitual inter-ethnic interaction. In other words, the recontextualisations characterising a large part of the Muslims' counterdiscourse are not arbitrary. The counterdiscourse, though defined by being *counter-*, also has its own internal dynamic, coherence and constraints. There is no incompatibility between defining the Muslims' counterdiscourse in its 'counter-ness' to the nationalist discourse, and concurrently analysing how counterdiscursive practices are anchored in cultural values and patterns of habitual pre-war inter-ethnic interaction. In fact, the interesting point is to see how embedded cultural practices and values become metamorphosed into more or less conscious resistance to a nationalist paradigm. Though I agree with Martin (1992: 186-7) that when, as is often the case, resistance is "encoded in cultural forms rather than expressed in consciously organized social movements [...] the anthropologist is left to discern the element of resistance in a culture of domination."

Working out where to position oneself in this field of tension is a challenge. One finds oneself caught between analysing resistance only as sets of ideas called into being by the situation of domination itself, and on the other hand only looking at cultural traditions and practices and neglecting the meaning and actions that the domination is able to call forth. Ortner (1995) may well be right in stating that 'resistance studies' of recent years are characterised by a certain degree of 'cultural thinning'. Consider for instance Fox's (1985) study of Sikh identity formation during colonialism. Here political strategies of resistance are only analysed in relation to the actual logic of the situation in which they are unfolded.

In short then, the nationalist discourse which has been striving for hegemony in pre- and post-Yugoslavia has called forth novel practices of resistance and defiance. On the other hand, pre-war cultural categories and social practices have been elevated from a non-conscious level to a much more conscious and focused field of battle, in which they have changed character as well as becoming practices of resistance against the nationalist discourse. For example, I show how the Muslims of Stolac explain violent and warlike behaviour as stemming from people being *uncultivated*, a categorisation not just originating in the present situation, but deeply rooted in a Yugoslav cultural dichotomy between the urban and the rural.

Authenticity

Operating with culture in relation to categories and practices of resistance makes it possible to clarify a related discussion: the question of authenticity of resistance. According to Scott (1990), the hidden transcript in which practices of resistance are located is not just a space (physically as well as mentally) where dissident thoughts and actions can be conducted. It is also an authentic space where "a natural impulse to rage, insult, anger, and the violence that such feelings prompt" can be articulated (ibid. 37). In the public transcript the subordinate has to act and also suppress true feelings, whereas in the hidden transcript he can display his real self and genuine emotions (ibid. 28-44). Scott's concepts have clear associations to Goffman's (1971) distinctions between frontstage and backstage behaviour, where frontstage is the place one consciously plays different roles and is observant about other people's reactions. Backstage, however, one can tear off the mask and act naturally: "Here the performer can relax" and "reliably expect that no member of the audience will intrude" (ibid. 115, 116). Though appealing, Scott and Goffman's differentiations between real and pretended actions, real and pretended selves, are analytically problematic. First, anthropological studies have shown how the (Western) notion of authentic selves is a cultural construct (Geertz 1983; Shweder and Bourne 1984; Selby 1974), and furthermore how emotions are not universal, but constituted through discourse (Rosaldo 1984; Lutz and Abu-Lughod 1990). Operating, then, with true selves showing true and natural emotions, seems to reflect rather than analyse power relations, that is, the primarily Western construction of the individual (Rose 1996; Taylor 1992; Hacking 1994; Foucault 1994). It is probably wise to operate with two different spheres of action, as Scott and Goffman do; but rather than differentiating between degrees of authenticity, one should realise that both spheres are socially constructed. In both public and private spheres social expectations about proper behaviour exist. Such a thing as a 'natural response' does not exist analytically.

In Stolac I found that people communicated dissimilar and occasionally opposing views depending on the situation. Sometimes people could even utter rather contradictory views in one and the same sentence. For instance, a person could say that he felt that the three ethnic groups of Stolac belonged together, that they had always existed together and that were they still able to do so. In the next sentence he could then say that one should never forget what happened during the war, and that during the war the Croats showed their true nature. Now, which is true? I think both statements are. Neither of them is a more transparent reflection of true emotions and feelings than the other. Instead of operating with different spheres, reflecting different degrees of authenticity, I work with different discourses: the nationalist discourse and its counterdiscourse. In fact a chief characteristic of post-war life in Stolac is ambiguity, existing due to this persistent struggle between two opposing discourses, taking place in people as well as in different situations. People, therefore, are not schizophrenic: but social situations are.

Operating with discourses instead of poses and real actions is inspired by such work as: Gal's (1995) thorough review of Scott's study, and her own study of bilingual communities in Hungary (1993); Jansen's (2000b) analysis from Zagreb and Belgrade of nationalism opposed to anti-nationalism, both seen as discursive practices; Mehta and Chatterji's (2001) research on the time after communal riots in Bombay; and Abu-Lughod's (1986) study of two contrasting discourses among Bedouins of Egypt. Common to all of these scholars is that they analyse seemingly contrasting and ambivalent practices and their relations to power, but without resorting to essentialist explanatory models such as 'human nature' or 'authentic impulses.' Instead, practices showing conflicting values and contrasting stances, such as my example above, are "... evidence of the coexistence of deeply felt yet contested discourses" (Gal 1995: 413) – one being no more real than the other. As Abu-Lughod (1986: 238) wrote about one of the discourses she analysed, a discourse of honour: "...the cultural ideals set by that code for the individual are not empty acts of impression management but the stuff of morality." There is no real individual lurking behind the scenes, as is the case in Goffman's work, and no natural impulse coming out in the hidden transcript as Scott sees it.

Consciousness

Lastly, I shall discuss consciousness in relation to resistance. The question is, in what way and to what extent were my informants aware that their actions and thoughts constituted a collective, more or less coherent alternative opposing the nationalist discourse of the war and post-war period? To what extent does the counterdiscourse gets its substance, coherence and form through my analysis?

In Stolac I found that people occasionally criticised the nationalist thinking very consciously, and they intentionally tried to communicate alternative ways of interpreting the conflict, as well as trying to envisage an alternative future that included inter-ethnic coexistence. A counterdiscursive consciousness existed. Sometimes, though, such consciousness turned into a servant of the very nationalism it tried to resist, as when ideals of coexistence, tolerance and forgiveness were seen as constituting the core elements of Muslim mentality. Ideals which the other ethnic groups, due to their ethnicity, did not adhere to.

However, conscious resistance to the nationalist discourse in Stolac is only part of the picture, and I would say a minor part. Another way, then, of addressing the questions posed above is to ask whether people resist without knowing it. According to Keesing (1992), it is important that one does not restrict the study of resistance to only focusing upon conscious political acts. Such a view is contrary to for instance Lagos (1993), who criticises a tendency in anthropological studies of hegemony to define almost every form of cultural alterity as resistance. The point which Lagos tends to miss, however, is not to confuse form and function, since it is not what people do, but how actions are interpreted by others that matters (see e.g. Abu-Lughod 1990). Furthermore, as Keesing (1992: 216) writes:

> On the one hand, if we define resistance so flexibly and broadly that subalterns are resisting when they are not aware of it, or when outwardly they are passively accepting the terms of their domination, we have taken a term that – in its common use at least – implies conscious agency and intentionality and so bleached it that these qualities disappear. On the other hand, if we insist on a more strict definition, and observe a subordinated population through time, we find overt resistance bursting forth at historical moments when circumstances allow [...]. Resistance seemingly then emerges out of apparent quiescent acceptance, consciousness burst out of unconsciousness.

Whether the counterdiscourse I analyse has the potential to become a more political ideological resistance, only time can tell. Nevertheless, I think it is important to focus upon the many minor actions, thoughts and practices people perform without clearly knowing why, though still having a feeling of expressing alternatives, indignation, bitterness, and even despair. Though I do not accept Scott's (1990) idea of 'human nature', his establishment of a field of everyday resistance open for anthropological research inspires me. People in everyday life are not ideologues, and especially not in war and post-war situations, where they are more involved in strategies of survival and remaking. However, such necessary strategies can constitute patterns and visions that transgress their local anchoring. This is a vital element in hidden transcripts as well as the counterdiscourse I analyse. Even apparent conformity to dominant nationalist ideologies can entail elements of or potential for resisting the self-same ideologies, as shown by Jansen (2006) in his study of a small Croatian village.

I would like to state that one should be careful not to romanticise resistance. The image of people collectively uniting for one just cause against oppression is probably only an image, seldom a reality. Interwoven in the counterdiscourse of Stolac are a lot of personal strategies and ambitions, personal hurts and fantasies. According to Ortner (1995) it is important to integrate such personal projects and strategies into the analysis of resistance. I have chosen not to do so. I do not think six months of fieldwork enables me to see through people's acts and say what they are really up to. Naturally, I did encounter examples of inconsistencies between what people said and what they did, between what they said they did and what they did, and between what they said they would do and what I thought they would do. However, I do not feel I have the knowledge necessary to distinguish practice from ideology (or one could say the real from the posed) in order to reconstruct individual(s') (real) strategies and motives. In fact I do not think anybody has, and perhaps not even the individual himself. I therefore find it more apposite to operate with discourses and inconsistencies between them (recall the discussion above about human nature).

I shall give an example that illustrates the problem. Mustafa was a man who often talked about interethnic tolerance. He was very conscious about raising his children in a non-antagonistic way, and he stressed the importance of financial interaction between the different ethnic groups as being an important step towards reintegration. Now, Mustafa also has a small family business also serving Croat customers. Should I then analyse his statements about inter-ethnic coexistence as (only) being a result of his financial enterprise? In a way this would make sense, but then how many of his utterances and practices are formed by his financial interests? Does he at all believe in inter-ethnic coexistence? Instead of engaging in such guesswork, I analyse and outline the counterdiscourse. I do not try to discern how people use it. Furthermore, it is my belief that this counterdiscourse is 'the stuff of morality' as stated above, not empty impression management. The counterdiscourse is about values and social recognition. One cannot step outside the moral values of the counterdiscourse. One can step over into – and alternate between – the nationalist discourse, but there is no 'real' position from which the Muslims (or I) can judge their behaviour.

My attempt to outline the contours of the counterdiscourse of the Muslims of Stolac, or one might say my focus upon the counterdiscursive elements of the mental landscape of my informants, is furthermore a personal choice. The vast majority of the literature produced on the break-up of former Yugoslavia deals with nationalism in the political sphere. Many learned studies explain, analyse, describe and criticise the emergence and articulation of nationalism in Yugoslavia; but hardly any have examined everyday resistance to nationalism in any detail. Outlining and representing the contours of my informants' counterdiscourse, therefore, is also an attempt to counterbalance this dominant focus. This, though, is not the same as accepting all the statements of my informants at face value. In order for the counterdiscourse to be taken seriously, I persistently point out any ideals and values that seemingly communicate tolerance and coexistence but in fact only underline the nationalist discourse they are supposed to resist.

My general analytical tool in this book is *remaking*, and *identification* is the element of remaking that I focus on in particular. I have theorised identification as being part of a *counterdiscourse*, and the counterdiscourse I have isolated by discussing *discourse* and *resistance*. I have discussed four themes relevant for understanding the element of resistance in the counterdiscourse. Firstly, more than an explicit articulation of opposition to nationalism, a substantial part of the resistance exists in persistent recontextualisations of the narratives of destruction, that is, by introducing alternative agendas for explaining and understanding. Secondly, the recontextualisations – though obtaining analytical status as resistance only by being counter – are often routed in existing cultural categories and social identities and draw upon experience from pre-war habitual inter-ethnic interaction. Taken together it is interesting to see how 'neutral'/non-conscious cultural categories and practices change character, not so much because their content changes, as because the context changes. Thirdly, instead of analysing resistance as being more authentic and real than subjection, I operate with various discourses. Conflicting statements and practices are therefore not evaluated in relation to their authenticity, but analysed as indications of the coexistence of deeply felt yet contested discourses. Fourthly, acts and statements need not consciously resist the nationalist discourse in order to be analysed as part of the counterdiscourse.

Part II
Who are they, the ones who did this to us?

Introduction to Part II

I have now given an account of my informants' experience of how the world has been unmade, and I have outlined the theoretical assumptions necessary for analysing my informants' remaking of their world, most crucially the concepts of discourse and counterdiscourse. These subjects will be in focus in the remainder of the book, with a principal focus on the counterdiscursive practises of my informants. In Part II I shall start by outlining the rise of the dominant discourse: the nationalist ideologies that swept through most of former Yugoslavia prior to the war. I shall also describe the major characteristics of these ideologies, which have attempted to – and to a certain degree succeeded in – making ethnic identity the most salient issue in all aspects of social and cultural life. On the basis of these ideologies, the nationalist politicians of the region have pursued a policy of ethnic separation. Despite 'successes', the Muslims of Stolac exhibit resistance to the nationalist ideologies and the separatist policies based on them. Though resistance is sometimes expressed explicitly, mostly it is implicit and unspoken, existing as a counterdiscourse. The hallmark of this counterdiscourse is an insistence on not using ethnic categories when explaining and holding Others responsible for the tragic events of the war. Instead of relying on the dominant antagonist national ideology, people try to facilitate interethnic coexistence by for instance remoulding and reusing already existing cultural categories that indirectly communicate interethnic tolerance. So although ethnic thinking has pervaded everything, at the same time a myriad of small practices and ways of thinking and explaining try to reject the ethnic categories, or at least make them less important. One of the most central issues in this struggle is to answer the questions: Who are they; the ones did this to us? What kind of people could commit such terrible acts? In Chapters 5 through 8, I introduce four different categorisations, which are all part of my informants' attempts at answering these questions. The categories refer to: unmoral political action, non-decent people, uncultured people, and finally a complexity attached to ethnic labelling. People's attempts at resisting ethnic thinking, however, are not always successful. There exists a persistent struggle between the nationalist discourses and counterdiscursive practices, a struggle played out in the everyday life of the Muslims of Stolac. This ambivalence is at the heart of post-war life in Stolac.

Chapter 4
Yugoslav nationalism

In this chapter, I identify and discuss the most important discursive framework in which my informants have been caught: the discourse of nationalism in the former Yugoslavia. The chapter focuses upon the historical emergence as well as the contours of the nationalist discourse that swept through the former Yugoslavia prior to the war, conquering the political, cultural and public scene.[1] Nationalist movements and ideologies existed even before the creation of the First Yugoslavia in 1918, but starting in the period immediately preceding the latest war and lasting throughout and after the war, nationalism has been the language through which nearly all disagreements and discontents have been expressed, especially so in the political arena. Outlining the discourse of nationalism is necessary to fully appreciate the element of resistance in my informants' counterdiscourse. The nationalist discourse has been so amazingly all-encompassing, and has penetrated nearly all aspects of people's lives with its focus on such ideologically charged themes as blood, territory, language, and origin. My informants resist the discourse of nationalism not by consciously and openly rejecting it, but by continuously avoiding it as a context of reference for explaining their present situation as well as the terrible events they have endured.

A rather confusing and tangled picture emerges when we look at the history of Yugoslavia. Borders have shifted and been easily penetrable. Populations, political and religious ideas, merchants, commodities and armies have been in constant movement and provoked the redefinition of borders and have challenged the different states. Conquests, wars, displacements, spontaneous drifts and urbanisation are some of the grounds for the huge movements of populations throughout the history of the Balkans (Malcom 1994; Sofus 1996; Allcock 2000: 145-70). The linear, uncontested and progressive evolution and realisation of national identities belonging to a people and a territory which the politicians and intellectuals of the former Yugoslavian states refer to does not have a solid foundation in historical fact as revealed by historical research. The different historical myths on which current national constructions rest are pre-

---

1   In the first chapter of part III, I will examine the emergence of nationalist discourse among the Muslims of Bosnia Herzegovina in more detail.

cisely that – mythical and not historical. Indeed, it is often difficult to establish the objective historical link between a given people and a given territory, as the history of the Balkans as a whole indicates that their forefathers probably lived somewhere else.

The First Yugoslavia

The emergence of national consciousness in the Balkans was inspired by the general nineteenth-century European search for the authenticity of 'The People', an authenticity which was variously defined in terms of such abstractions as language, territory, blood, mentality and history (Knudsen 1989). The cultural and ethnic movements in the Balkans sought to carve discrete national cultures and languages out of the linguistic and cultural continuum characteristic of the region's peoples (Sofus 1996: 253). The establishment of national centres of education, increased schooling, the establishment of print media in most of the major cities, the standardisation of national literary languages and the codification of national folklores were all important components of the development of national consciousnesses (Cohen 1993: 1-45).

The Serbian national movement was probably the most successful of these early Balkan national movements. The creation of an independent Serbian Principality in the 1830s, together with the intellectual national Romantic Movement, really boosted Serbian nationalism. Though still formally subjects of Turkey, the Serbs could see that full independence was only a matter of time, a goal they reached in 1878. For this reason, the unification of all Serbian people in a strong, independent state was the chief goal of the Serbian elite of the middle decades of the 19th century (Cohen 1993: 6). Support for a Yugoslav state first arose in the twentieth century, but the idea that the people of the region shared a common ethnic background emerged during the nineteenth century, at the same time as the Serbian nationalist movement flourished. It was primarily Croatian intellectuals who promoted the view that Serbs and Croats had more things in common than dividing them – for instance their language – and that the distinct Serbian, Croatian and Slovenian identities were merely the results of tribal divisions. The 'Yugoslavism' that the Croats advocated was moreover presented as an alternative to dependence on the Austro-Hungarian and Turkish empires (Cohen 1993: 1-45; Lampe 2000: 39-194). The Serbs however, were for their part ambivalent about the issue of a common South-Slavic state called Yugo-slavia (*Yugo* means south). On the one hand, the proposed unification of the south-Slavic peoples had an aura of romanticism. The union was also seen by some as a shortcut for reaching the goal of Serbian independence from Turkey. On the other hand, many of the more nationalist-minded Serbs believed that such a union would weaken the sovereignty and strength of the Serbian people.

Then with the First World War came the disintegration of the old empires. The result was, if not a literal vacuum of power, then at least a real possibility for the emergence of a sovereign Yugoslav state. The Croats were still the primary advocates of the idea, now because their territorial possessions and sovereignty were threatened by a possible Italian invasion. For their part, the Serbs were more reluctant, but the formation of the 'Kingdom of the Serbs, Croats and Slovenes' in December 1918 was realised to a certain extent on the premises of the Serbs. In addition, This Kingdom was an elite project with very little popular support, and it consisted of some rather disjointed territories, populated by rather different peoples, with different religions, histories and political aspirations (Lampe 2000: 39-194).

The union of the South-Slavic peoples was a rather unstable undertaking. The greatest disagreements existed between the Slovenes and the Croats on the one side and the Serbs on the other. The Slovenes and the Croats considered the Serbian influence in the coalition to be too dominant: they wanted a federal state with greater independence given to the different republics. The Serbs, on the other hand, wanted a centralised Serbian-dominated state and did not want to divide the Serbian population, which would have been the result if greater independence were given to the different republics because 30 percent of the Serbs lived outside Serbia. The Serbs succeeded in imposing a unitary state model in 1921, but the Croats and Slovenes did not accept it and declared it invalid.

The greatest resistance to the Serbian-dominated centralisation project was lead by Stjepan Radic and his Croatian Peasant Party, who sought Croatian autonomy through mainly peaceful means. But the Serbian political domination also produced more violent forms of organised resistance, such as the terrorist Croatian independence movement Ustashe (meaning uprising). In 1928 Radic was murdered, an incident that created turmoil and violence. In 1929, in general frustration with the conflicting parties' inability to find any agreement and as an attempt to keep the country together, King Alexander dissolved the parliament and instituted a strongly authoritarian regime, while focusing on promoting pan-Yugoslav ideas and sentiments. But his nation-building project failed, and in 1934 he was killed. The conflicts between the different parties were still deep, but after decades of struggles and ineffective rulers, in 1939 the Croats and the Serbs finally signed a treaty which recognised Croatia as a partially independent nation inside Yugoslavia with extensive rights. And for the first time sporadic feelings of 'Yugoslavism' began to evolve (Cohen 1993: 1-45; Malcom 1994: 136-56; Bennett 1995: 16-42; Sofus 1996). Then came the Second World War, and political extremism revived.

The Second World War

The history of the Second World War in Yugoslavia is so complicated that I will not even try to do justice to it. I will only offer a very general picture, in order to illuminate the post-war politics of Tito, as well as the historical basis for some of the current explanations for recurrent Balkan violence.

In 1941, the South Slav Kingdom surrendered to the Axis forces, and on 10 April of that year the Germans proclaimed a new independent Croatian State (NDH: *Nezavisna Država Hrvatska*; the Independent State of Croatia. The wartime fascist state run by a Nazi-installed regime led by Ante Pavelić), including the whole of Bosnia Herzegovina. In reality this 'independent' state was nothing more than a German puppet state. The extremist terrorist movement Ustashe was given control of the state, and this organisation's pre-war nationalist dream of a strong and independent Croatia was partly fulfilled. The issue of the Jews was of only secondary concern to the new rulers,[2] who rather saw the 'Serbian minority' in Croatia (the territory of NDH) as their main problem. This 'minority' actually constituted almost a third of the population: 1.9 million out a total population of 6.3 million (Malcom 1994: 176). Ustashe started a regime of terror, attempting to eradicate the ethnic Serbs through such measures as forced conversion to the majority religion, Catholicism,[3] expulsion to Serbia, and literal slaughter (Denich 1994: 374).

The Serbian inhabitants of Croatia and Bosnia Herzegovina (the territory of NDH) were taken by surprise when Ustashe members started their deportations and massacres of civilians. The Serbs, though, soon organised themselves in two resistance movements, which however were at war with each other as well as the Croats. The so-called Chetniks formed a unit based on the remnants of the pre-war Yugoslav army. The Chetniks were led by Draža Mihajlović, who supported the restoration of the monarchy. The other resistance movement was the communist Partisans led by Tito.[4]

The Chetniks engaged in massacres and deportations of both Croat and Muslim civilians, and massacres were also carried out by non-Chetnik Serbs in Bosnian villages. However, none of these massacres were a part of the implementation of an official policy of genocide like the Ustashe's attempted 'cleans-

---

2   Though secondary, the anti-semitism of the NDH state was catastrophic for the Jewish population of Croatia and Bosnia Herzegovina. Only 4,000 of the original 36,000 Jews survived the regime's persecution and extermination (Lampe 2000: 212).

3   For the Vatican's rather controversial role in supporting the Nazi puppet state NDH, see Dedijer (1992).

4   Tito's real name was Josip Broz. He was born in 1892 in northern Croatia, which was at that time part of the Austro-Hungarian Empire. His father was a Croatian peasant, and his mother a Slovene (Bringa 2004).

ing' of the territory of NDH (Malcom 1994: 175-78; Lampe 2000: 201-33; Denich 1994: 375).

Generally speaking, the Bosnian Muslims' position during the war was very complex. Before the war they supported the Croatian political programme of decentralisation, which would have granted the Bosnian Muslims some kind of independent state. The Muslims were against the national aspirations of the Serbs, which also entailed anti-Muslim rhetoric before the war. But the behaviour throughout the war of Croats and Serbs alike did much to encourage Muslim distrust and hatred. During the war the Ustashes killed Muslims, Chetniks made raids on Muslim villages, and even the communist Partisans had dead Muslims on their conscience. At the beginning of the war some of the Muslims supported the Croatian state and the Germans, and a volunteer Muslim SS division[5] was created with an eventual full strength of 21,000 men. Many Muslims thought that supporting the Germans could protect their villages from attack. When this strategy failed, many of them switched sides and joined the Partisans. Tito, the leader of the Partisans, stopped the attacks on the Muslims seeing the advantages of enlistment Muslim in the Partisan ranks.

For a long time Tito was prepared to cooperate with the Germans, as he knew that the liberation of Yugoslavia by the Allies would entail the restoration of the monarchy. But the situation changed after a number of heroic battles in the summer of 1943 in Montenegro, after which some of the British officers who had witnessed the strength and fighting spirit of the Partisans sent admiring reports home. This led the Allies to shift their support from Mihailović and his Chetniks to Tito's Partisans, and on 6 April 1945, the Partisans liberated Sarajevo. Many Muslims were relieved, for they had neither been absorbed into a greater Croatia (the Ustashes' plan) nor a greater Serbia (the Chetniks' plan), and they were now promised a solution in which Bosnia could continue to exist (Malcom 1994: 173-94).

The Second World War was nothing less than a human disaster in Yugoslavia. A huge number of people died, of all nationalities and ethnic groups – over a million by the end of the war. Whole villages were wiped out. Ethnic cleansing, either by deportation or extermination, had been carried out – 8.1 % of the Bosnian Muslims were killed during the war. Military or paramilitary associations crossed ethnic lines to set Serbs against Serbs, Muslims up against Muslims. An estimated 250,000 people (anti-Partisan forces and associated civilians) were killed by the Partisans, either in mass executions or in the Partisan-run concentration camps in 1945-46, Slovene 'home guards', Ustashe

---

5   The principle of recruiting volunteer SS divisions was well established in other occupied countries like France, Belgium, Holland and Denmark.

soldiers, Serb and Muslim Chetniks, Bosnian Croats, Serbs and Muslims were among the victims (Malcom 1994: 173-94). More than half of the over one million people who died during the war had been killed by their fellow Yugoslavs. Nobody came through the war untouched. Fear and distrust were rampant, and ethnic and religious dividing lines were sharpened. On the foundations of hate, loss, confusion and political and ethnic divisions, Tito hoped to rebuild and modernise a unified Yugoslavia. The task was not easy, to say the least.

The Tito era

After winning the war three main problems faced Tito and his Partisans (organised in the CPY, Communist Party of Yugoslavia). One was to deal with the 'ethnic question': the politicisation of ethnicity that had emerged in the period between the wars, and which had intensified during the Second World War. A second task, obviously related, was to invent some kind of overarching national identity, a new version of Yugoslavism, which could suppress the traumatic memories from the war. The third challenge was to modernise the country and rebuild it economically, as post-war Yugoslavia was totally devastated and underdeveloped. I think it is fair to say that Tito and the CPY never managed to either separate or solve these problems (Sofus 1996: 256).

Tito and the CPY's solution to the first problem was the creation of a federation with six republics and two autonomous units. The leading principle of the federation was to be so-called Yugoslavism, which was a fusion of socialism, a belief in Yugoslavia as a common project, and respect for the cultures of the different ethnic groups. This solution imposed by the communist regime to deal with national tensions was not the outcome of any deep respect for the complexity of the country's ethnic composition. It was rather a pragmatic strategy for keeping the country together and avoiding conflicts. In short, nationality was a tactical question for Tito. As he saw it, the Second World War had not been about nationality. It was not Croats against Serbs or Muslims, but communists against anti-communists. In this view, the Second World War had been an anti-fascist struggle and a proletarian revolution. And in fact the communists succeeded in drawing followers from all Yugoslavia's Slav people. The Communist party was for everyone, irrespective of national origins (Bennett 1995: 51-3).

As Milovan Djilas, one of Tito's closest allies in the wartime communist struggle later said about the communists' pragmatic relationship to the issue of nationality:

We looked on the national question as a very important question, but a tactical question, a question of stirring up a revolution, a question of mobilizing the national masses. We proceeded from the view that national minorities and national ambitions would weaken with the development of socialism, and that they are chiefly a product of capitalist development [...] consequently the borders inside our country didn't play a big role. [...] We felt that Yugoslavia would be unified, solid, that one needed to respect languages, cultural differences, and all specificities which exist, but that they are not essential, and that they cannot undermine the whole and the vitality of the country, inasmuch as we understood that the communists themselves would be unified. (Quoted in: Cohen 1993: 24).

As a consequence of this ideology, the territorial borders inside Yugoslavia were drawn rather randomly – which, as we have seen, would later make them highly disputed. One of the reasons for splitting up Yugoslavia into republics and autonomous provinces was to divide the power among the different ethnic groups and thereby limit dominance by any one ethnic group, especially Serbian, and thus avoid internal rivalry. The geographical and political divisions made by Tito were meant to both reflect and defuse the reality of Yugoslavian ethnic diversity.

The regime institutionalised two categories of populations in Yugoslavia: national groups (*narod*) and nationalities (*narodnost*). The first group consisted of those recognised as having their homeland inside Yugoslavia, whereas the other group was made up of those assumed to have homelands outside Yugoslavia. But as always, categories were one thing, reality was another. The ethnic map of Yugoslavia did not lend itself to a neat division of republican borders. Serbs also lived in the republic of Croatia, three ethnic groups lived in Bosnia Herzegovina, Serbia's Sandžak region had a Slav-Muslim majority, and so on. Nevertheless the six republics were constituted: Serbia, Croatia, Slovenia, Macedonia and Montenegro, and finally Bosnia Herzegovina with its heterogeneous population of Croats, Serbs and Muslims, where no *narod* was in the absolute majority. The second grouping, the nationalities (*narodnost)*, consisted of Albanians, Bulgarians, gypsies, Romanians and others. It was never entirely clear exactly why some groups were recognised as nations and others as nationalities. The Muslims, for instance, were only recognised a national group in 1974 (see Chapter 9); and Kosovo, with its Albanian majority, was only granted status as an autonomous province, as was also the case for Vojvodina with its large Hungarian population.

It is hard to say whether Tito's ambitious project of creating a Yugoslav communist state uniting all citizens in an atmosphere of 'brotherhood and unity' (the official post-war Yugoslavian motto) was a success: it depends on who you ask. The ones who achieved the most benefits from Tito's organisation of Yugoslavia were the country's smaller peoples, for example the Muslim Slavs, who were shielded from the potential aggression of Croatian and, in particular, Serbian nationalism. Tito's system allowed these people to thrive culturally and evolve confident national identities. As a result, sympathy with Titoism survived longest in these areas (for instance Bosnia Herzegovina). On the other hand, the Serbs and the Croats – at least from the 1970s onwards – saw Tito's policies as a hindrance to their national ambitions (Bennet 1995). Furthermore, the degree of identification with Yugoslavism was much lower in the countryside than in the cities. In fact, several authors have gone so far as to argue that local identification, communitarism and personal alliances were far more important than federal or even republican and/or national identifications; especially in the countryside. Yugoslavism was a rather peripheral phenomenon (Allcock 2000; Bougarel 1996; Sunic 1998).

From 1945 to 1980

The time from 1945 to Tito's death in 1980 can, according to the political scientist Lenard Cohen (1993), be divided into five periods (see also Shoup 1992).

The first period lasts from 1945 to 1952. During this time, Tito was inspired by Soviet communism and its strong centralisation of power. Despite Yugoslavia's federal structure, the country soon became highly centralised – Tito's power was immense (Bennet 1995: 54). Tito also thought that high levels of industrial growth and a fair economic distribution among the republics would create a common feeling of Yugoslavism. He initiated a Soviet-inspired five-year plan, which promoted the development of heavy industry at the expense of agriculture and other primary-sector economic activities (Sofus 1996: 258). Expressions of religiously based ethnic affirmation were harshly suppressed in this period as part of an attempt to prevent any ethnic and/or religious tensions. The Catholic Church was treated with special harshness, as some of its clergy had cooperated with the Ustashes. But Islam was also heavily repressed, primarily because it was seen as backwards and 'Asiatic': Islamic courts were suppressed, elementary schools teaching the Koran were shut down, and teaching children in mosques was made a criminal offence (Malcom 1994: 195).

In 1948 Stalin expelled Yugoslavia from Cominform, and the period that followed, from 1953 to 1962, was characterised by more humane socialism and greater liberalisation of the political system. After the break with the USSR and the power it represented, Tito could no longer afford to ignore the deeply established group sensibilities in Yugoslavia, and the period witnessed a growth in local authority. The regime also began to realise that the creation of a common feeling of 'Socialist Yugoslavism' would be a long-term enterprise that was dependent on education and political socialisation as well as rapid economic growth. However, inter-ethnic conflicts were still most often suppressed and swept under the carpet.

Then from 1963 to 1971 came a period of what can be called 'pluralist socialism.' Yugoslavia was experiencing rapid economic growth, a continuous increase in living standards, and a growing international recognition due to its non-alignment policy. However, the progress was partly financed by loans from the West, and Yugoslavia's constantly fragile economy was partly shored up by these loans. One must remember that by virtue of being a socialist country not dependent on the USSR, Yugoslavia was an important ally for the West in the Cold War period. Nonetheless, in the 1960s the economic imbalance began to have visible effects: an inflexible economy due to the one-sided investment in heavy industry, high inflation, and increasing economic inequality between the republics. The rich republics like Slovenia and Croatia were in the north, and the underdeveloped areas like Bosnia Herzegovina and Kosovo were in the south (Cohen 1993; Ramet 1992b: 136-76). At the same time, Tito's state-sponsored Yugoslavism, the idea of a transcendent ideological consciousness, began to be regarded as reactionary by leading communists. Inter-group conflicts were no longer taboo, in fact different and conflicting interests were seen as a normal phenomenon during a socialist revolution, and decentralisation and regionalisation were seen as more viable political solutions to such conflicts than centralisation and uniformity. In effect, by the end of the 1960s, the republics and provinces of Yugoslavia had begun to emerge as important centres of political authority and power. The mix of increased economic problems, dissatisfaction with marked regional imbalances, and greater scope for expressing national aspiration enabled a shift from a focus on economic problems into a focus on national identities. Yugoslavian politicians increasingly used the 'national question' in order to gain support for economic programmes (Ramet 1992b).

Then from 1972 to 1973, Yugoslavia experienced a short period of governmental re-centralisation, an attempt to handle the growing inter-ethnic disputes. But this direct attack on nationalist movements – jailing of leading figures, banning of nationalist propaganda, purging of official ranks and so on – was followed by the 1974 constitution, which in some ways moved in the opposite direction. It invested the Yugoslav republics and provinces with autonomous statehood. In this way Tito attempted to neutralise the nationalists' appeal by delegating even more authority from the federal to the republican level. Unfortunately the consequence of this reform, which also allowed inter-ethnic conflicts to be articulated publicly as long as they were not politically subversive, was a politically ineffective society. Furthermore, the federal government was on a rotation basis between the different republics, resulting in an inconsistent federal policy, as regional politicians used their short periods of power to cultivate regional and personal interests. The period witnessed growing corruption, regional chauvinism, and conflicts among the different republics. Tito's policy of regionalisation was intended to legitimise the power of the federal government, but the consequence was the opposite. The new constitution combined with a growing economic crisis produced a society fragmented along regional and ethnic lines.[6]

In the last years up until Tito's death the republics, rather than the federation, had became the real loci of power. And national identities served as a means of expressing regional economic conflicts, which could not be expressed in the rhetoric of a unified communist federation (Bowman 1994: 152). To some extent Tito managed to suppress ethnic conflict and deal with the so-called 'national question', which primarily concerned the conflict between Serbian and Croatian nationalist and territorial aspirations. After all, his regime managed to keep the peace in the country for forty-five years. The ideological project of Yugoslavism did succeed to some extent, though this is hard to evaluate.[7] However, his policy of decentralising power along republican lines (later to become national lines) would have devastating consequences in the years after his death. Though domestic political relations in the 1970s were generally calm – at least compared to what was to come – due to high rates of economic growth, it was apparent to many that national tensions would re-appear at some point, either following the death of Tito or provoked by an assertive leadership in Serbia (Shoup 1992).

After Tito: nationalism explodes

On the 4 May 1980, Tito died in a hospital bed in Ljubljana (Slovenia), leaving the majority of the country in grief (Bringa 2004). The huge economic and political problems and the nationalist power struggles that would haunt the country for the next eleven years had been developing for a while. Paradoxically, it

---

6   Some observers see this continued decentralisation and regionalisation of power as a poor substitute for the kind of genuine democratisation which might have facilitated the evolution of non-nationalistic opposition politics, thereby preventing the war (Denitch 1994; Dimitrijević 1995).

7   Although 'Yugoslavs' only accounted for 5.4 % in the 1981 census – Yugoslavs mainly lived in the cities, where local/religious/ethnic identifications mattered less, and in Bosnia Herzegovina (7.9 %) with its very mixed population – the Yugoslav identity was never meant to replace national identities or compete with them. Rather it was part of Tito's general attempt to create an all-embracing Yugoslavism under which national identities could exist.

was Tito himself who laid the foundations for nationalist strife by regionalising power along republican lines: while intended to solve the 'national question', this solution meant that divisions and tensions would come out into the open after Tito's death.

Throughout the 1980s, Yugoslavia experienced high unemployment, a huge foreign debt ($20 billion in 1987), high inflation and serious food short-ages. Salaries dropped, and the standard of living plunged.[8] This growing eco-nomic crisis destabilised the country so much as to threaten its very existence. Inefficiencies in economic production and failure to adjust to a changing world economy led to slow economic growth rates, undermining the country's abil-ity to respond properly to the crisis. The average annual GDP growth rate fell from 6.1 % in the period 1973-1979 to 0.4 % in 1980-1984, and the real personal income growth rate fell from 6.1 % in the period 1965-1972 to 2.7 % in 1973-79, and -2.0 % in 1980-1984 (Cohen 1992: 31). Looking at the economies of the in-dividual republics comparatively, deep inequalities also became apparent, with Croatia and Slovenia having the lowest unemployment rate, the largest GDP, and generally speaking the healthiest economies. Despite this relative prosper-ity, these republics also expressed great dissatisfaction with Yugoslavia's policy of income redistribution, which benefited the poorest republics and autono-mous provinces such as Bosnia Herzegovina and Kosovo (Ramet 1992b: 136-76; Allcock 2000: 89-100). The burden of subsidies to the 'underdeveloped south' made it easy to blame the backward parts of Yugoslavia for the economic dif-ficulties that these more prosperous republics faced. Slovenia and Croatia were not alone in blaming other republics for their own republics' economic difficul-ties. The political elites of all the republics and autonomous provinces began blaming other republics for their difficulties, together creating a 'culture of par-anoia.' The enemies 'without' of the Cold War period were replaced by enemies 'within' of other Yugoslavian nations and nationalities (Allcock 2000: 96).

Under Tito's rule strikes had only occurred on rare occasions, but after his death they became more common. In 1989 for example, 1,900 strikes involving 470,000 workers were reported (Donia 1995: 199). Though these strikes were not all economically motivated – several were staged by the nationalist regime in Serbia – they did reveal a growing popular dissatisfaction with the economic developments in Yugoslavia. In addition, a series of financial scandals involving party members and major Yugoslavian companies revealed an economically

---

8   The economic crisis and decline in salaries and living standard greatly revitalised the country-city network, as owning a piece of land could alleviate the worst consequences of the crisis (see for instance Simic 1973: 108-26; Allcock 2002: 140-4).

and politically corrupt Yugoslavia controlled by economic strongmen who could do whatever they pleased without any interference by the state.[9]

The increasing economic crisis was thus paralleled by a political crisis. Party members and citizens in general lost confidence in the capacity of the ruling communist party to solve the country's difficulties and maintain Yugoslavia's territorial cohesion. This loss of legitimacy is illustrated by the communist party's declining membership, especially among younger people. This crisis of confidence grew in intensity as each of the eight republics and provinces became more autonomous and unwilling to implement the decisions made at the federal level. And though the mid-1980s saw a relatively high degree of turnover in the party elite, with younger ambitious leaders replacing the older Tito-era communists, this new generation – even though it was preoccupied with solving the country's economic problems and renewing the socialist regime's legitimacy – nevertheless still sought to acquire political support by appealing to the regional concerns of local communities (Cohen 1992: 45-51; Janić 1995). The League of Communists of Yugoslavia (LCY) increasingly lost legitimacy and cohesion. Republican interests had gradually undermined the federal institutions of the ruling Communist Party, to the extent that the LCY was little more than a loose association of republic-based organizations by the end of the 1980s.

Milošović

The Serbian leader Slobodan Milošović arose out of this economic and political crisis. I shall briefly sketch his rise to power and the nationalism he promulgated. Milošović did not single-handedly invent Serbian nationalism as such. Rather he both exploited and catalysed the smouldering nationalism which the economic and political crisis had intensified. Milošović was born in Serbia in 1941. He became a member of the Communist Party at the age of twenty-eight, but only entered politics in 1984 at the request of his friend Ivan Stambolić, chairman of the Central Committee of the Serbian Communist Party. Though Milošović soon gained a reputation as a strong advocate of Serbian interests, it was not until Milošović's famous speech in April 1987 in Kosovo Poljo, where he told the Serbian minority that "Nobody, either now or in the future, has the

---

9   Bosnia Herzegovina, for instance, witnessed an immense and rather symptomatic economic scandal in 1987. By accident it was revealed that Agrokomerc, one of the largest enterprises in Bosnia Herzegovina, was built on unsecured promissory notes valued at $875 million, and from one day to the next 50,000 workers' paychecks were invalid. The unsecured debt of Agrokomerc was part of a greater fraud involving 200 party members in Bosnia Herzegovina and Croatia, and it was argued that the practice of Agrokomerc was widespread throughout Yugoslavia's industry (Donia 1995: 195-8).

right to beat you," that he really discovered the political power of nationalistic rhetoric (Ramet 1992b: 227). After this Milošović managed to oust Stambolić from the Serbian presidency and began his own climb to power.

His first step was to establish full control in Serbia. As a way to achieve this goal he sought to gain control of the media. Among other things, he fired journalists and editors at the renowned publishing house Politika and replaced them with supporters of his own political views. Before long other leading publishing houses were following the nationalist editorial line set by Politika. By so doing the media soon began to play a central role, both articulating and also creating nationalist tensions and antagonisms. Increasingly the media played on a fear of the ethnic Other, as well as attacking the Yugoslav ideology of 'brotherhood and unity' (Malešič 1993; Sommelius 1993; Naughton 1994). At the end of the 1980s a moral panic was created by the Serbian media, a panic mainly based on fear of the Kosovo Albanians and their presumed attempted genocide on the Serbian minority population in Kosovo. The official Serbian press printed stories of Kosovo Albanians raping Serbian women and destroying Orthodox Christian monasteries. Milošović also created a close alliance with the Serbian Orthodox Christian Church, thus adding further weight to the authenticity of Serbian nationalism. Furthermore, the media encouraged devotion to a mythical version of Serbian history, heroising the Serbs' fight against the Turks 600 years before in particular (especially highlighted was the defeat of Prince Lazar in 1389). In short, an image of the suffering and glory of the Serbian nation was constructed (Bowman 1994; Sofus 1999; see also Čolović 2002a). A cult arose around Milošović, making him the first really strong man after Tito, and it became increasingly difficult to criticise Milošović and retain a job of importance (Ramet 1992b: 228).

Milošović's next step, after having established full control in Serbia, was to gain control of the two autonomous provinces Kosovo and Vojvodina. Right from the beginning of his rise to power, Milošović had maintained that Serbia was discriminated against in Yugoslavia. An example of this injustice was the two autonomous provinces, which Milošović claimed ought to have been Serbian by rights. These arguments were added to the old Serbian nationalist claim that Montenegro was in reality the coastal part of Serbia. Through the extensive use of orchestrated mass demonstrations as well as by putting immense pressure on local leaders, Milošović managed to gain control of Kosovo and Vojvodina in addition to Serbia itself by mid-1989. He had also installed his men in Montenegro, and made Macedonia his ally. Furthermore, he sent agents to Bosnia Herzegovina to attempt to subvert the republic from within (Ramet 1992b: 231-233).

As a result of these manoeuvres, at the end of the 1980s Serbia found itself with four out of eight votes in the collective presidency which had replaced Tito after his death, which gave a right of veto over all federal decisions. The collective presidency, which was meant to mediate differences between the republics, was thus increasingly reduced to an instrument of Serbian nationalist leadership and became increasingly delegitimised in the eyes of the republics who had not supported the Serbian line (Denitch 1994: 61).

Milošović's takeover of the Serbian Communist Party and the collective presidency was closely linked to another central step in his rise to power: the rebuilding of a strong Yugoslavia through a strong Serbia. Milošović himself called this project an anti-bureaucratic revolution, a campaign intended to cleanse the state apparatus of inefficient bureaucrats. More to the point, his project was directed against the decentralisation of power along republican lines laid out in the 1974 constitution. Many Serbs flocked to Milošović, the strong man who, rebuilding a powerful and proud Serbia, would also restore the decentralised, disintegrating and corrupt Yugoslavia. His fervent nationalistic rhetoric gained him immense support for the claim that the disintegration of Yugoslavia was an attack on legitimate Serbian interests: as the largest ethnic group in Yugoslavia, Serbia should not be reduced to just one republic among others.

Milošović's rise to power in Serbia and Yugoslavia in general represented a break with previous post-war politics in Yugoslavia. His use of mass rallies and the threats of the crowd was a new weapon that radicalised the political climate.[10] In combination with his anti-bureaucratic revolution, Milošović's intimidating Serbian nationalism and the project of the 'Serbianisation' of Yugoslavia were increasingly regarded as a threat by the other republics.

Slovenia

I shall now examine Slovenia, Croatia and Bosnia Herzegovina's response to Milošović's nationalist policy individually.

While Milošović worked for the centralisation of Yugoslavia, Slovenia went in the opposite direction. Their goal was to achieve independence from Yugoslavia gradually. However, nationalistic rhetoric was also part of their strategy. The Slovenian goals of decentralisation and eventual independence

---

10   In a Belgrade rally in 1988 in support of Milošović an estimated 800,000 to 1.3 million Serbs were present (Cohen 1992: 52), and also in 1988 100,000 Milošović supporters marched to Novi Sad (the capital of the autonomous province of Vojvodina) to 'convince' the communist officials to resign in favour of Milošović supporters. The same strategy also paved the way for the resignation of the anti-Milošović government in Montenegro (Sofus 1995: 264).

were partially motivated by Yugoslavia's economic subsidies to the poorest republics and autonomous provinces. The Slovenes wanted to keep 'their' economic surplus for themselves.

Slovenia had been advocating pluralism since the mid-1980s. Slovenian society, in particular, had witnessed a growing liberalisation as exemplified by the emergence of non-governmental alternative movements, especially youth movements. Many Slovenes, therefore, saw Milošović's centralisation of Yugoslavia as a threat to Slovenia's sovereignty. 'One republic, one vote' was the slogan for the federal power structure they advocated, instead of the majority vote in terms of population Milošović campaigned for – which favoured the Serbs, as they were the largest group in Yugoslavia. The disagreement between Slovenia and Serbia about the degree of centralisation of Yugoslavia intensified in the late 1980s: the political debate was laden with nationalistic and republican rhetoric.

The situation reached a crisis when, in November 1989, the Slovenes denied Serbian demonstrators entry into the republic of Slovenia. The Serbian communist leadership responded by threatening to terminate governmental and business relations with Slovenia. Slovenian discourse was becoming increasingly not only anti-Serbian, but also anti-southern. Though they theoretically supported the Kosovo Albanians' right to autonomy, the Slovenes also feared an influx of poor migrants from the south, and the Slovenes therefore tried to set themselves apart culturally by connecting to Europe and dissociating themselves from the Balkans.

After the Slovenes walked out of the Yugoslav Communist League's Extraordinary Congress in January 1990 together with their Croatian colleagues, Yugoslavia in reality ceased to exist. The first genuinely free governmental election in Yugoslavia since 1938 was held in Slovenia soon afterwards, in April 1990. The communists lost, while the winners were former communists who had become nationalists more or less overnight. Soon elections followed in the other republics. Some commentators have described the atmosphere of elections as virtually millenarian: "People felt that if they took the magical draught of democracy proffered them by the West, they would instantly move into a new, and far better, world" (Bowman 1994: 145). The elections were all based on the assumption that legitimacy came from 'the people' rather than the self-ordained communist leadership, but the central question arose: who are the people? The answer given by the winners of the elections was that 'the people' were the dominant ethnic groupings of the respective republics (Bowman 1994: 145-6).

Slovenia prepared for sovereignty, and in July 1991 the republic proclaimed its independence. The Yugoslav army, which had supported Milošović's centralising line and was by this stage Serb-dominated, was sent in to regain control. But after a mere ten-day long relatively bloodless confrontation, the army was withdrawn. The first period of independence was not easy, and the country was hit hard by the Slovenian economy's isolation from its traditional markets in Yugoslavia. Xenophobia and nationalism grew, and as a consequence, so did the nationalist right-wing party (Cohen 1992: 59-94; Sofus 1996: 265-7).

Croatia

Whereas the route to independence was relatively easy for Slovenia, Croatia's road was harder and nationalistic rhetoric and political goals had much more influence. While Slovenian protest had been directed against the communists and the policy of centralisation, the rhetoric of the Croatian opposition was markedly anti-Serbian and outright nationalist. Croatia's first multiple election took place just a week after the election in Slovenia. One of the best-financed political alternatives to the communist ruling party was the Croatian Democratic Union (HDZ), led by the historian and former communist Franjo Tuđman, who had also fought with Tito's Partisans.[11] The HDZ had already existed illegally for a year, with branches all over Croatia and Bosnia Herzegovina. Tuđman and the HDZ won the election. Despite only getting a little over 40 % of the votes, the HDZ received nearly 70 % of the seats in the Croatian legislature (Cohen 1992: 95, 100).

Tuđman had spent several years in jail in the 1960s and 1970s because of his nationalist activities. His version of Croatian nationalism was based to a large extent on an attempt to rehabilitate aspects of the Ustashe-led Independent State of Croatia (NDH) from the Second World War. For instance, he understated the scope of the genocide of the Ustashe regime, and he encouraged the public use of many of the symbols of the controversial NDH State, in particularly the checkerboard emblem composed of white and red squares, the *Šahovnica*. This symbol, which replaced the communist red star after independence, had also figured on the flag of the fascist Ustashe state, and even though it dated back to the Middle Ages it was hated by many Serbs as a reminder of the Ustashe regime's atrocities and oppression. Tuđman also initiated a revival of the wartime linguistic innovations of the NDH, stressing the dissimilarities between the Serbian and Croatian dialects.

Tuđman advocated an independent Croatia, claiming that the Croatian people had the right to self-determination and sovereignty. However, he specified that the Croatian state ought to reclaim Croatia's 'historical borders' – that

---

11   $8 million was raised in support of Tuđman's victorious campaign for presidency; a good proportion of these funds came from returning émigrés (Woodward 2000).

is, the borders drawn by the NDH state. These borders annexed the territory of Bosnia Herzegovina. Tuđman had revitalised the old claim that the Muslims of Yugoslavia had originally been Croats, and that Bosnia Herzegovina and Croatia therefore formed an indivisible geographical and economic entity (Malcom 1996: 218; Denich 1994: 377-80; Bowman 1994: 155-7; Sofus 1996: 267-9).

In several ways Tuđman can be seen as the Croatian Milošović. Like Milošović, Tuđman and his regime used the media to deliberately create or exaggerate ethnic hatred (Bennett 1995: 148; Malešič 1993). Like Milošović, who had succeeded in stirring up the Serbian masses with a nationalistic programme advocating a strong Yugoslavia under Serbian dominance, Tuđman employed a fierce and antagonistic ethnic rhetoric to offer his people a vision of the restoration of the Croatian-led fascist state of World War II. And finally, Tuđman served as a unifying symbol for the many Croats who had come to fear the growing Serbian nationalism.

One of the dangerous aspects of Tuđman's nationalism was that it both rhetorically and legally reduced the huge Serbian minority of the republic to second-class citizens.[12] Tito had cautiously defined the republic of Croatia as 'the nation-state of the Croatian people and the Serbs in Croatia', giving the two peoples the same rights. By contrast the new constitution (from 1990) reduced the status of the Serbs to that of a minority. On several occasions Tuđman stated that the Serbs of Croatia had the right to live there, but also had to accept that they were a minority. In Yugoslavia there had existed a distinction between 'state' and 'nation' ('nation' being ethnically defined), which secured the equal right of all the citizens of the state, no matter what their nation. But in the nationalist constitutions of Slovenia and Croatia this distinction was erased, and the state was legitimised on the basis of the sovereignty of the ethnically defined nation. Other national groups could be citizens, but could not expect the same right to participate in the control of the state (Hayden 1996).

The conflict between the new Croatian regime and the country's Serbian minority, who understandably feared the anti-Serbian policy of the state, was essential in leading Croatia and Serbia into war (Grandits and Leutloff 1999). When Croatia voted for independence, the Croatian Serbs of the historically important Krajina area claimed independence, maintaining that they had the right to belong to Serbia proper. Milošović and his propaganda machine supported the uprising of the Krajina Serbs, telling people in Serbia that their brothers in Krajina were in danger of losing their lives to the Croats (Bow-

---

12   One tangible sign of this was the purging of Serbs in Croatia from administrative positions.

man 1994: 156). Whether Milošović's consideration for the Krajina Serbs was genuine, or whether he had ambitions of creating a 'Greater Serbia' now that Yugoslavia was disintegrating, we can only guess. However, it is beyond doubt that conflict regarding the Serbian minority population in Croatia was also a fight for power and influence.

Milošović and Tuđman were officially enemies, but they both pursued the same strategy: nationalism as a way to power. One of the few non-nationalist politicians of this period was the federal president of Yugoslavia, Ante Marković, who persistently emphasised the need for economic reforms. Both Milošović and Tuđman had an interest in de-legitimising his influence. Together they managed to transform the moral discourse of Tito's Yugoslavia, epitomised by 'brotherhood and unity', into a violent discourse of ethnic, religious and nationalist antagonism. Visions of a 'Greater Serbia' or 'Greater Croatia' built upon ethnic homogeneity and to be realised through the annihilation of the ethnic Other became ruling ideologies (Bowman 1994).

Bosnia Herzegovina

In 1991 Bosnia Herzegovina had 4,3 million inhabitants, of whom 43.7 % were Muslims, 31.4 % Serbs, 17.3 % Croats and 5.5 % Yugoslavs.[13] With its complex mix of different ethnoreligious groups, the republic had for a long time had the potential for interethnic tensions. But at the same time, it was almost absurd to imagine civil war in this particular republic, as the ethnic groups were mixed together throughout the country. Bosnia Herzegovina has no 'natural' ethnic borders. Splitting up Bosnia Herzegovina into ethnically homogeneous regions would require huge forced resettlements and/or ethnic cleansings. Though this was exactly what was to come, in the early nineties hardly anyone could imagine it, even in their worst nightmares.

When Yugoslavia recognised Bosnia Herzegovina as a republic after the Second World War and gave equal rights to all its ethnic groups – Serbs, Croats and Muslims[14] – it was believed that the political tensions caused by Serbia and Croatia's competing claims to the territory would be defused. Unfortunately, this was not to be the case under Milošović and Tuđman. Even though Milošović's appeal to Serbian nationalism had originally focused on the rights of the Serbian minority of Kosovo, he gradually began to focus on the 'difficult situation' of the Serbian enclaves in Croatia and Bosnia Herzegovina. When Tuđman then started talking about reconsidering the territorial borders of Bos-

13   'Yugoslav' was a category invented by the communist regime. People could choose to define themselves primarily as Yugoslavs and thereby support the regime's nation-building project.

14   Though the Muslims were only recognised as a constitutional group in 1971, see Chapter 9.

nia Herzegovina, politics in Bosnia Herzegovina became more pronouncedly ethnic. In the summer of 1990 the actions and demands of the Serbs in the Krajina region spread into Bosnia Herzegovina, as the Serbs started expressing their desire to establish a Serbian republic in the Krajina area, which would annex territory from both Croatia and Bosnia Herzegovina (Glenny 1996).

The Muslims were caught in the middle by the claims made by both Croatia and Serbia to the territory of Bosnia Herzegovina. Fear of the two large neighbours' territorial claims, coupled with Serbia's nationalist scare campaign against the 'Islamic fundamentalists', led the Muslims to organise themselves in the Muslim Party of Democratic Action (SDA), led by Alija Izetbegovic. Right from the start, the SDA's ideology was somewhat contradictory. On the one hand, they argued for the preservation of Bosnia's unique ethnic and religious heterogeneity. On the other hand, the party promoted a strong partisan Muslim ethnic and religious identity: in this respect, they took part in the nationalist fantasies spreading all over the former Yugoslavia. This tension has subsequently been central in the political life of Muslims in Bosnia Herzegovina (Bougarel 1997).

In the free election of 1990, all the major parties in Bosnia Herzegovina were organised along ethnic lines, and the election itself was a thinly disguised ethnic census: people voted not for competent political leaders, but for ethnic representation. Misha Glenny (1996: 147) reports how easy it was to identify the different ethnic districts by the symbols hanging from all the buildings when he drove through Bosnia Herzegovina just prior to the election: the green crescent (SDA), the *Šahovnica*[15] (HDZ-BiH), and the four Cs (SDS[16]). All the parties argued for the preservation of Bosnia Herzegovina. Their disagreements related to how and to what extent the republic should be connected to Yugoslavia. The Serbs wanted a close connection to Yugoslavia, whereas the Muslims and the Croats argued for a loose connection.

After the election the SDA's leader, Alija Izetbegovic, formed a 'government of national unity' composed of a formal coalition between all three major parties, and government posts were shared between them. Though dedicated to the Muslim case, Izetbegovic was also dedicated to the preservation of Bosnia Herzegovina, and he tried very hard to make the three ethnic groups cooperate. For a while it seemed as though he would succeed, but there was no room for pan-ethnic identifications. Tensions grew, the nationalist aspirations of all

---

15 A checkerboard emblem composed of white and red squares. The Croatian coat of arms with strongly nationalist, in some respects even fascist undertones.

16 *Srpska Demokratska Stranka*. The Serb Democratic Party in Bosnia Herzegovina (the Serb nationalist party).

three ethnic groups increased, and with the declaration of independence in the spring of 1992, the country would be cast into war (Cohen 1992: 139-63).

The Serbs played a major role in Bosnia Herzegovina's tragic fate. In June 1991, when Izetbegovic was still trying to keep the country together, the ethnic-Serbian party SDS declared three areas of Bosnia Herzegovina to be autonomous Serbian regions, and Milošović helped to arm these breakaway areas. And when independence was declared in 1992, it was Serbian forces and snipers who started the siege and shelling of Sarajevo, and it was Serbian irregular troops who oppressed and killed the mainly Muslim population of eastern Bosnia. All these actions were part of a clear strategy to integrate Bosnia Herzegovina into a Greater Serbia, and they enabled the Serbs to gain control of 60 % of Bosnia Herzegovina only six weeks after the outbreak of the war there.

The politics of the nationalist Croats also played a part in the destruction of the republic of Bosnia Herzegovina. When the citizens of Bosnia Herzegovina voted for independence in the spring of 1992, the Muslims and the Croats were in favour, whereas the Serbs boycotted the election. But the ruling political party of Croatia, the HDZ, strongly supported the platform of a faction of Herzegovinian Croats led by Mate Boban, who wanted a part of Bosnia Herzegovina to be annexed by Croatia. And on 3 July 1992, the Herzegovinian Croats did in fact establish a self-governing community of Herceg-Bosna in Herzegovina (see the Prologue).

Alija Izetbegovic's political programme was more compromise seeking, less antagonistic and less aggressive than those of the Croats and the Serbs. Nevertheless, he and the nationalist-minded Muslims also played a part in the dissolution of Bosnia Herzegovina. Whereas both the Croats and the Serbs had a 'mother country' to turn to, or rather political powers that to a great extent decided on the politics of 'their' respective ethnic groups in Bosnia Herzegovina, the Muslims had no allies.[17] The Muslims had to navigate between the political ambitions of both the Serbs (Serbia) and the Croats (Croatia). For many Muslims the destruction of Bosnia Herzegovina was therefore tantamount to the eradication of the Bosnian Muslims. In this situation Izetbegovic had to choose between Tuđman and Milošović. That is, he could seek independence for Bosnia Herzegovina, knowing that Croatia would probably make claims upon Herzegovina. Alternatively, he could let Bosnia Herzegovina enter into a federation with rump Yugoslavia, knowing that the Muslims would be reduced to a minority in a Serbian-ruled state. When the Bosnian Muslims and Bosnian Croats declared independence for Bosnia Herzegovina it was not the

---

17   Though parts of the SDA openly cooperated with Muslim countries and thereby sought legitimacy for a more radical Muslim identity (Sofus 1995: 272).

cause of the war, but at the very least Izetbegovic should have taken the threat represented by the Serbian population of Bosnia Herzegovina more seriously. He underestimated their fear of living in an independent Bosnia Herzegovina led by what they considered to be Muslim nationalists (Shoup 1995; Sofus 1996; Cohen 1998; Simić 1993; Mojzes 1998a).[18]

Nationalism for all

The wars that spread throughout Yugoslavia in the early 1990s like wildfire were to a great extent ignited by political leaders, all former communists, who were using nationalism as a way to (re)gain power. Tuđman and Milošević were enemies, but their ideologies and their methods were the same.[19] In fact, one could maintain that their ideology and method involved exactly the same thing: ethnic cleansing. That is, territorial invasion and 'cleansing' were legitimate as a necessary attempt to create homogeneous and ethnically clean areas.

The nationalism that started in the political sphere soon spread throughout all aspects of society. There was a revival of interest in and politicisation of national literatures and national history. For example, the literary work of the Nobel Prize winner Ivo Andric was greatly politicised. The Serbs saw him as a great Serbian writer, while some Muslims depicted his work as following "the Balkan Greater-Serbian agenda which aims to obliterate Muslim Europeans" (Karic 1999: 53-63). The nationalist cultural revival was also reflected in the production and growth of underground cultural groups. Cultural production in general increasingly referred to and was consumed by the inhabitants of the individual republics. As such it both reflected and contributed to the disintegration of a common cultural frame of reference (Ramet 1992a: 29-30). Over the course of the war this tendency escalated. Laušević (2000), for example, analyses how radio and television music broadcasts became a strong symbol of national belonging. Tchaikowsky's Symphony in B-minor became Serbian if performed by the Belgrade Philharmonic Orchestra, and could therefore not be aired on Muslim-controlled Sarajevo Television. Bands and genres were furthermore strongly associated with the different ethnic groups. Musical instruments were invested with national identity. Modes of singing, sound and tempo, indeed every possible element in the musical performance was reinterpreted and given ethnic identity (Laušević 2000; Čolović 2002b).

The disintegration of a shared cultural world was also reflected in the tendency of the different nationalities in Yugoslavia to read their own newspa-

---

18 See Chapter 9 for details of the policy of the Muslims of Bosnia Herzegovina.

19 Milošović and Tuđman met as long ago as 1991 to discuss the division of Bosnia Herzegovina (Glenny 1996: 194; Doina 1994: 248-56).

pers, a tendency that also spread to Bosnia Herzegovina. Croats read Croatian newspapers, Serbs read Serbian newspapers, and so forth (Ramet 1992a: 57-81). Furthermore, the press increasingly communicated a provincial republican perspective at the expense of a Yugoslav viewpoint, as well as contributing to the massive demonisation of the ethnic Other (Denich 1993; Bringa 2002).

The period also witnessed a politicisation of gender relations. One example relates to mixed marriages. During the communist period such marriages were praised as triumphant results of the ideology of 'brotherhood and unity', while with the coming of the nationalist ideologies they were increasingly condemned as unclean and as defiling the purity of the nation. The period also saw a growth in aggressive masculine images and an increased oppression of the rights of women (Ramet 1992a; Morokvasic 1998). This escalated throughout the war, as women and their bodies became symbols of male-directed battles over ethnic identity. The rape of women was often used or presented as the symbolic rape of territory and ethnic identity (Meznaric 1994; Olujic 1998).

Resistance?

It is difficult to evaluate how deeply the nationalist discourses of this period in the former Yugoslavia invaded the minds of people. Such themes as nationality, ethnic Otherness, self-determination, territory, ancestral blood and so on were factors everybody had to relate to: one could not opt out. One could not go about as if nothing were happening. But was the nationalist mindset internalised by individuals? Not much has been written about opposition to nationalism prior to and during the war. The few studies that do exist, however, indicate that some resistance existed.

Cohen's (1992) analysis of the free elections in the former Yugoslavian republics, for instance, shows that the electoral system in both Slovenia and Croatia substantially enhanced the winning nationalist parties' relative positions in the distribution of legislative seats, and it appears that quite a large number of voters opposed the nationalist parties. Additionally, Denitch (1994) maintains that the development of a unifying Yugoslav-wide political force was never allowed to develop, as no Yugoslav-wide federal elections were ever permitted. Only elections on the republican level came about, and their very existence in itself indicated opposition to the Yugoslav federation.

Another indication of resistance to the nationalist ideologies relates to a survey conducted in the winter of 1989-90, which showed higher levels of inter-ethnic tolerance in the ethnically mixed and conflict-ridden republics of Croatia and Bosnia Herzegovina than in the ethnically homogeneous Slovenia, indicating that the strategies and rhetorics of ethnic cleansing were to a large extent part of a political project (Hodson et al. 1994). This is also argued by

Hayden (1996): "Extreme nationalism in former Yugoslavia has not been only a matter of imagining allegedly 'primordial' communities, but rather of making existing heterogeneous ones unimaginable" (ibid. 783). Therefore, he maintains, the war was fiercest in Bosnia Herzegovina, as this republic had the most heterogeneous population.

In a study of some of the anti-war initiatives which took place throughout the war, Devic (1997) concludes that resistance to ethno-nationalism emerged in a certain cultural milieu, but that the majority of individuals in former Yugoslavia shared this resistance. Evidence for this widespread resistance includes the rather substantial anti-Milošović protest demonstration in Belgrade in 1991, as well as the anti-war demonstrations in Sarajevo just before the outbreak of the war (Cohen 1992; Malcom 1996). On the basis of such popular resistance, Devic predicts that the new nationalist regimes of former Yugoslavia will not be able to generate enduring hegemonic cultures, simply because they do not have enough public support.

Finally, even during the war in Bosnia Herzegovina, when nationalist propaganda was most passionate and when people were actually experiencing the disastrous and deadly consequences of the war, deliberate resistance to ethnic thinking existed alongside pronounced nationalism (Maček 2000a; see also Povrzanović 1997).

I have given an account of some of the historical threads leading to a situation in which nationalism conquered the public discourse in Yugoslavia in the 1980s and early 1990s. Though resistance to the nationalist discourse existed, nationalist and ethnic thinking came to dominate public discourse completely. Ideologies as well as everyday practices of inter-ethnic coexistence and tolerance were damaged. Heterogeneous communities were made 'unimaginable', multi-ethnicity was unmade. Territory and ethnic nationality were seamlessly linked. Disbelief in inter-ethnic coexistence meant that territories were cleansed not only of the individual ethnic Other, but also of physical symbols of the ethnic other and of ethnic heterogeneity.[20] Central to the ideology of nationalism was the demonisation of the ethnic Other. Fear of the ethnic Other was promoted and increasingly came to dominate the everyday world, a process in which the media played a very central role. In short, it seems that no spheres of life escaped the nationalist discourse. Marriage, cultural production and consumption, the press, history, language, literature, religion – everything had become coloured by the idea that ethnic origin was the most important aspect of life. I

---

20   The term 'urbicide' has been employed to denounce the deliberate destruction of the city as a symbol of ethnic heterogeneity (Coward 2002).

will now turn to the central question of the degree to which this omnipresent nationalistic discourse affects the way in which the Muslims of Stolac understand their world. In particular, I will focus on the extent to which my informants have been able to resist the ideology of ethnicity and to produce alternative identifications and narratives.

Chapter 5
Politika

In this and the following three chapters, I introduce four categories through which my informants' resistance against the discourses of nationalism is expressed. The first one is *politika*. *Politika*, or 'politics', is a central component in the lives of the Muslims of Stolac: during the last decade, the politics of the region and towards the region have had catastrophic consequences, among them the politicisation of everyday life. Moving beyond the common understanding of politics as 'realpolitik', I will analyse *politika* as a category of moral action created and used by the Muslims of Stolac in order to resist the invasion of everyday life by ethnic thinking, and to account for the ungraspable aspects of the life produced by the war (see also Kolind 2007).

Politika as a moral category

Politicians and the field of politics in Stolac are associated with a certain moral (or rather immoral) universe, a universe sharply contrasted to the life and ethics of ordinary people. This view of politics is probably related to the lack of political modernisation in Yugoslavia, where civil society as a mediating level between everyday life and state politics never seems to have developed (Allcock 2000: 245-308, 351-76; Sunic 1998). It also relates to the prohibition of collective criticism in the former Yugoslavia. Though some freedom of expression was permitted – the young could indulge in familiar Western-style 'sex, drugs and rock-'n-roll' experiences – attempts at organised collective opposition were suppressed. Some intellectuals on the urban scene had what Drakulić calls a 'contract with the government', whereby they refrained from criticising the government in exchange for certain cultural and material liberties, and because they felt 'at home' in Yugoslavia (Jansen 2000a: 109; Drakulić 1995). As a result of the absence of civil society and critical public opinion, large parts of the Yugoslav population did not participate in political decision-making; contact with the political system took place in the form of fixed patron-client relations (Allcock 2000: 245-308, 351-76; Devic 1997: 144-5; Sunic 1998). Apparently, this distance between politics and everyday life has grown throughout the war and post-war period (see UNDP 2000; Maček 2000a: 161).

The Muslims of Stolac are very direct when talking about the moral universe of *politika*: politics are the pursuit of power for the sake of power: politicians are people who think only of themselves, they are cynical, scheming and untrustworthy (see also Helms 2007).

I

Mehmed: I do not like politicians and neither do I like politics (*politika*). I'm a tolerant man, who respects differences. I respect you, that is very important and it is human, even though there are differences between you and me; simply a tolerance, the tolerance of life, it is very important. But politicians as politicians, they always lie.

II

Munir: We have to look forward in these times. But we do not have the power to change the situation here. The politicians we had during the war and who are here now, they are very rich, they made money during the war as well as today, and therefore it is very hard for them to loosen their grip on power. And they all say they work for the people, but they are only working for themselves

When I asked Emir about the meaning of the word *politika*, he smiled a little, showing that there was much more to the word:

> Politics is something that is above you: something ordinary people do not understand or have any influence on. *Politika* is something the people far away are doing, the ones who do not have to live with the consequences of their actions; it is cynical and egoistic acts. For instance our people [Muslim politicians] in Sarajevo are requesting people to return to Stolac, so when the year has passed they can say: 'Look, now a thousand Muslims are living in Stolac, now the Croats can no longer say that this is Croatian territory.' But none of them ever come down here to see how we live, or just to talk to us, they do not care about ordinary people, what we think or feel. We have a saying 'politics is a whore' (*politika je kurva*), they are only doing it for themselves, like a whore is only doing it for money.

Politika is also linked to corruption and criminality. Politicians are often seen as not only cunning, but directly involved in criminal activities such as fraud and bribery, smuggling, drug trafficking, and incitement to actual physical violence. As a young man in his 30s said:

We have a saying: 'Those Tito jailed, they were not there without reason.' Now they are all in power, all the ones Tito or the communist rule jailed. The criminals have risen to power. They are now presidents, governors and ministers.[1]

In general, *politika* represents an ethically devalued universe consisting of immoral actions and immoral persons sharply contrasted to another category of persons I will come back to in the next chapter: *pošteni ljudi* (decent people).

Politika as resistance

Using *politika* as an explanatory device constitutes a withdrawal from using ethnic stereotypes, and as such resists the dominance of ethnic identities created by the war's violence and the post-war political situation. In using the cultural category of *politika*, the Muslims of Stolac insist on blaming not the Croat or the Serbian Other, but the politicians: the war was not caused by a Serbian aggressive mentality but was due to Slobodan Milošević, and it is not because of the Croats that they have suffered and still suffer, but because of Franjo Tuđman and the HDZ. To put it simply, there is an element of resistance in merely avoiding ethnic categories as explanatory devices.

It is also possible, however, to find components of a more conscious critique of the nationalist ideologies and practices which clearly and unambiguously maintain that Muslims, Croats and Serbs cannot live together because of differences in mentality. Contrary to the discourse of nationalism, the Muslims of Stolac assert that if it was not for politicians and the force of *politika*, ethnic identity would never have become a determinant factor and the war would never have occurred. They stress that politicians stir up ethnic divides and fears in order to maintain power, that they manipulate people, and that without the present politics the citizens of Stolac could easily live together again. They also say that their society does not function because of the lack of political will, and that if politicians would sit down together and work for the future of Bosnia Herzegovina, many of the current economic, social and legal problems would be solved. I shall offer some examples.

Mehmed, who holds an important post in Stolac, told me how all the present problems come from the political sphere, and that ordinary people do not have problems interacting. He then told me about his backgammon board, beautifully engraved with a picture of Stolac a hundred years ago. A Croat had borrowed the board a couple of days before our conversation, a man who, as

---

1 Let me just add that Izetbegović, Tuđman and the Bosnian Serbian leader Šešelj among others served time in prison in pre-war Yugoslavia, sentenced for spreading nationalist propaganda.

Mehmed said, "sits here playing and drinking coffee." It is not without reason, I thought, that he mentioned the engraving. Stolac a hundred years ago was the Ottoman Stolac, the Stolac that Croats destroyed during this war – so the engraving could easily be read as a Muslim nationalist symbol. The fact that the Croat borrowed it, on the other hand, indicates that he did not perceive it as a nationalist symbol, but rather a symbol of *the Stolac spirit* of coexistence and ethnic tolerance (see Chapter 12).

The next example is an excerpt from an interview with a family in which we were talking about the religious dimension of the war. Here it is the young man in the house (who is studying in Mostar) who speaks:

> Religion was a cause, but it is the politicians who provided the words. We feel the differences, but it is only when the politicians put words to them that they become a matter of conflict. Because it is the politicians who control the army, they are the ones who decide.

Another example comes from an interview with an old woman:

> Džanana: Before [the war], we had good relations with Orthodox and Catho-lics. It is interesting that after this war, which was so terrible, we have come back to this town where Croats have occupied everything. And despite all that happened, we still have contacts with our neighbours and we live and work together, we are a people who have lived together for a thousand years. Many of the politicians are guilty for what happened; they keep repeating that we cannot live together. They say that people cannot live together, but in spite of that we do.

This image of interethnic relations is perhaps a little romanticised. The woman had contact to some old Croat friends, but she also had a very complicated relationship with her neighbours, who were Croats from central Bosnia occu-pying her son's house. And I often heard her criticising these neighbours. The woman's critical remarks, however, never used ethnicity as a framework, but rather the category of *not-decent people*, which I return to in the next chapter. Such ambivalence (both criticising and wanting to tolerate the ethnic Others) is not atypical. Rather it is a hallmark of post-war life in Stolac.

The Muslims of Stolac also talk about how the Croats or Serbs were forced by the politicians to participate in the war and in actual acts of violence. Simi-larly, they often state that violence and discrimination did not occur because people in general had gone mad or because ordinary Croats or Serbs are evil. People committed immoral acts because they were placed by politicians in situations beyond their control, in situations without choices. Again ethnic difference is presented as a positive factor in daily life that had been twisted and manipulated by the politicians. Ahmet told me about an incident from the Serbian occupation of the Stolac area in 1992. Every Serb capable of carrying arms was forced into uniform, and anyone failing to turn up at the barracks was picked up. He continued:

> When the Serbs withdrew from Stolac they were on the hill just behind our house, at that time we were communicating with the Croats. We knew that the Serbs would withdraw in a couple of days, but just in case we armed ourselves so that they would not come down and hurt women and children. Then my father came and whispered to me and Omer that if we see Goran [a Serb friend forced in uniform], we should not shoot at him. But it was war and we were afraid of going out of the house, but even so he said that we should not shoot at him. Everything happened at night where you cannot see when a man is coming with a gun, nonetheless my father said that we should be careful not to shoot Goran. This is how my father is, and this is the way he taught us to be.

Goran has returned to Stolac. He tills the soil with Ahmet's father and they are still good friends. This is a story of friendship, but it also reveals how people distinguish between a man's real character and what he is forced to do by the politicians.

People's use of *politika* and other non-ethnic categories was occasionally a source of frustration for me. Sometimes when people were describing a situation where, for me at least, the guilty party was very apparent, I was the one to use ethnic identity as a way of blaming, not my informants. There was the time when my landlady said that no Orthodox churches were destroyed during the war, but that everything Muslim was. I responded by saying that there are many idiots in the world. But I was surprised by her answer, just as I was many times before and after. Instead of agreeing she said: "Yes, but it is not everybody. Like under the rule of Hitler, not everybody was a Nazi, but the war forces one to do things, politicians and the political situation force one."

The use of *politika* as counterdiscourse, however, should not be confused with actual practice of interaction. There are small islands of inter-ethnic interaction, but the Croats, Muslims and Serbs mostly keep to themselves, and I am not sure whether this would change overnight if the political climate were changed. This does not mean that people's construction and use of *politika* is pretence. Instead it should be seen as a part of the (new) world that people creatively try to (re)construct around themselves, a world making sense of a senseless past and present, and offering guidelines for future behaviour. It is thus possible to say that the use of *politika* is also political. It is a social vision, an attempt to create a picture of a future Stolac rid of the immoral force of *politika*, a place where the Muslims would have the same opportunities and rights as the Croats, and where the different ethnic groups could co-exist as they did before the war.

The use of the cultural category *politika* represents a critique of the ethnicisation of the world. But a tension exists when the Muslims state that all politicians are scheming and power-seeking, but 'their' politicians are even worse than 'ours', and when political parties are seen as in fact representing the mentality of the ethnic groups they claim to represent. Then the Muslims of Stolac suddenly identify with 'their' own political parties. In other cases, they say that people have been brainwashed and manipulated by nationalist politicians, but that Croats are much easier to manipulate and that 'they' are manipulated in many more spheres of life than Muslims are:

Nedžad: In the Bosnian areas SDA loses every time, so that the SDP, SBiH and the other [non-nationalist parties] get more and more votes, and SDA fewer and fewer. But in the Serb Republic the SDS gets the most votes, and in the Croat areas HDZ gets most of the votes [...] I am also in favour of those changes [against nationalist parties], but they [Croats and Serbs] are not. They think that national parties will help them, but if they could understand, they would see that the politic of nationalism is losing.

What we have here is a critique of the politicians, and especially the nationalist ones who, as I was often told, do not really help ordinary people. However, it is also an indirect critique of the ethnic Other. It is an example of how ethnicity is not only resisted by blaming the politicians and referring to the immoral state of *politika*, but also used as a framework for explaining the present lack of interaction (because the Croats are not in favour of changes). It is exactly this ambivalence that is so characteristic of post-war identification in Stolac.

The results of the general election in November 2000 in Bosnia Herzegovina provide an example of this ambivalence. Considering the anti-nationalistic attitude of my informants, it would be reasonable to assume that the majority of the Muslims would vote for the SDP, the only real non-nationalist political party in Bosnia Herzegovina.[2] But this was not the case. The question then is, how are we to understand the contradiction between attitudes and actions, between what is said and how people actually behave? Are the Muslims of Stolac cunning because they say they want to cooperate, coexist, and get rid

---

2   One could say that the *SBiH* is also a non-nationalist party, but in Stolac it joined a coalition with the SDA.

of the nationalists, while at the same time many of them vote for nationalist parties?

First, though some Muslims vote for the SDA (the Bosnian Muslim nationalist party) because they are nationalists, the SDA is itself split: there is a division between religious nationalists and secular pragmatists, dating far back in Bosnian Muslim politics. It is fair to say that the SDA itself embodies the tension between ideals of ethnic coexistence and ethnic separation, which is also reflected in many of my informants' statements,[3] (I return to this issue in Chapter 9).

Second, client-patron relationships are still prominent in local politics in many parts of Bosnia (see above, see also Grandits 2007). In the elections of 2000 in Stolac, the two candidates who got by far the greatest number of Muslim votes were Kemal Isaković and Suad Sefo, both nominated by the SDA. They were also two important figures in town. Suad Sefo was the manager of a big factory with 700 employees before the war and now works at the local government offices (*opština*). He has a good reputation and is a respected man. Kemal Isaković is also a person who people approach to ask for favours. He told me himself how the system of patronage makes it very hard to be in politics because people come to him all day long and expect that he can sort out their problems (get a phone line, get more funds for reconstruction, arrange jobs etc.). People vote for ideals, but they also vote pragmatically, for a particular person whom they respect and can ask for favours. In any case, neither Kemal Isaković nor Suad Sefo are nationalists – they are more like local patriots.

Third, it is my impression that many of the young Muslims in Stolac did not vote: they did not care about politics or often did not have any knowledge about it. For them politicians were all the same. Still others do not dare vote for the non-nationalist SDP because they fear what would happen if they voted for a non-nationalist political party and the other ethnic groups did not. This is an extract from an interview with a young man. I had asked him about what he thinks of politicians:

> They are all the same, all corrupt. There was a test where all the politicians' toilets were inspected, and all the samples showed trace of cocaine or heroin. Imagine! It is not normal; it is crazy, all the politicians are using drugs. They are all corrupt, when donations come from abroad; they end in the politicians' pockets.

3   Thanks to Xavier Bougarel, who made me aware of this point.

TK: What about the SDP?

Young man: No it is not my party, maybe SDA. To be honest I do not care to vote, but I have to vote to counterbalance the Croatian parties.

TK: How many political parties exist?

Young man: There are HDZ, SDA ...

He stops. I do not think he is aware of more parties, except the SDP. He simply does not care. Indifference towards politics is not restricted to the young. Meeting Džanana on her way back from the polling station at the general election, I asked her whom she had voted for:

> I don't know, there were so many parties [on the registration list], but one has to vote, for things to get better, they say ... If only we have peace so things can be better.

I am not inferring that all the politically conscious people vote for the SDP and the rest for the SDA. Rather my conclusion is that many Muslims have a complex relationship to the nationalist programmes. Although, in the ballot-box people can only place one mark, in their daily life they can place many – and these may well be contradictory. This tension between nationalism and everyday identification I shall analyse in the chapters to come.

Politika as externalisation of the ungraspable

Sometimes the use of *politika* as an explanatory device extends beyond the simple rational use I have described so far, and is established as an almost independent force or agency operating in the world. It is used to explain, or more correctly to put aside events and feelings that are too radically other to be comprehended. In such cases, *politika* is not necessarily somebody doing something. It is rather a free-floating autonomous power by reference to which the unmaking of the world is given a conceptual place. This force is used to explain the unexplainable or grasp the ungraspable. People have experiences – and here I am referring to both war traumas and present social and personal problems – that cannot find relief or expression through ordinary language. There are no public symbols or representations that could absorb or give meaning to them. Thus people resort to existing cultural and moral categorisations, which they mould to function as some kind of representation of the disintegrated and unmade world. *Politika* is such a moral category used to exorcise the madness from everyday life.

Once when I was driving through the southern part of town with Nihad, we were looking at some of the ruined houses. He told me how the Croats had blown up Muslim houses following the expulsion of the Muslims. He then said:

> There were good houses here before. Now they are destroyed. Look! They all need new roofs. Before – at least in the area where I live – Croats, Serbs and Muslims were living together. We all lived together. I had good friends who were Muslims, Serbs and Croats. Everybody was having a nice life … it is *politika*!

For my informants it was incomprehensible that Croats, Serbs and Muslims could be friends at one moment and at the next moment become enemies fighting each another.

Here is an excerpt from an interview with an elderly man, which illustrates how *politika* is used to absorb the madness of the war:

TK: Did you imagine that war would come?

Osman: No, we could not imagine that. I do not have a lot of schooling, I only have my primary school, but I consider myself to be a clever man. But I never could imagine that such dreadful things should happen. I never thought that war would come. Before the war we never fought or quarrelled. And then suddenly we were expelled (*proteran*). Nobody really knows what happened, we [Muslims] experienced it our way; maybe the Muslims in Bosnia [central Bosnia Herzegovina] said that they [Croats] also had to go to their people [that is, that they were expelled themselves]. *Politika*!

An old woman I visited a lot during my fieldwork often told me about the war, or rather tried to tell me about the war, but it was as if she never succeeded in creating a story that could explain or give meaning to all the losses she had experienced. This is a short extract from my notebook:

> She is talking about life during the war, and it is obvious that it is sad, tears are running down her cheeks, and her speech is halting. The story doesn't have a clear line or structure; if there is one it is: we were expelled, we came to Jablanica to the refugee camp, we stayed there, we did not know what had happened to our men, fathers or sons, there were continuous bombardments, we had only a little food, it was hard, and then we returned. The war is described very personally, in total contrast to a political science analysis. *Politika* is continually evoked to account for this unexplainable element.

In this excerpt I was trying to discover the narrative structure in the woman's utterances. Many other war stories exhibit a similar discontinuity of events, memories and feelings. *Politika* is a way to link all these fragments, to give them some kind of framework and meaning. Abrupt flashes of memory are linked together and integrated, not by an overarching and coherent narrative, but by an abstract force creating havoc and escaping the understanding of ordinary people.

Along these lines it is possible to synthesise a structure representative of many of the stories I heard in Stolac, a structure with *politika* at its core: "We were living happily together, then came this insane war, it could be so nice here, but – *politika!*"

Politika as a way of analysing

I have some hesitations about analysing my informants' use of the category *politika*. To put it simply, I take political science analyses of the war as valid academic work, but when ordinary inhabitants of Stolac use political reasoning as a frame of reference, I see it as either part of a counterdiscourse or as a narrative strategy. Similarly, the Croatian ethnologist Maja Povrzanović (2000) has pointed to how Croatian ethnologists from Zagreb have been treated as informants rather than colleagues by visiting scholars from the West, despite the fact that this group of Croatian scientists had produced substantial anthropological research in relation to the experience of war and exile. In this last section, I shall offer examples of how *politika* was used not primarily as counterdiscourse or a way to externalise the ungraspable, but as a valid political commentary and way of analysing events.

With regard to the outbreak of the war, people believe that responsibility lies with the politics pursued in former Yugoslavia as well as the various nationalist leaders, and they criticise the international community's policies of non-interference. They see Europe and the United States as liberators and as guarantors of the present peace in Bosnia Herzegovina. At the same time, they believe that the shifting political strategies of Europe and the West in general played a part in igniting the war. Europe and the West are sometimes depicted as having acted like cynical passive spectators for far too long: if only they had intervened earlier thousands of lives could have been saved. People sometimes have a feeling of having been a part of an experiment, as they call it, just small and unimportant pieces of a great jigsaw puzzle. The war was called down upon them, they feel, by forces far outside their reach, and some of these forces are international politics and alliances, in which Germany supports Croatia, France and Russia support Serbia, and no-one really supports the Bosnian Muslims. One elderly woman put this view very clearly:

> We have these three nations in Bosnia and then somebody from outside [outside former Yugoslavia] comes and bites us and stirs up strife.

Another example of Bosnian political analysis comes from an interview with Fahrudin, in which he gave a complex account of the political forces involved in the recent conflict:

> The history of this war should not be sought here in Bosnia Herzegovina. The war was brought from the West. Let me try to explain it to you. When I was hospitalised in Sarajevo and when I worked as a police officer [during the war], I ate beans two years older than my father. They were produced in 1934 in the United States. And we paid the United States for these beans, and we paid for the uniforms we had. And the biscuits we ate during the war were leftovers from the Vietnam War. This project *opremi i obuči* [literally: teach how to use] is a project where all the weapons, Kalasnikov and so on, we used during the war, are to be destroyed. And instead we get their weapons, M16's. And these M16's are very bad weapons. [...]
>
> They take something from you in order to give you something else and they get paid for it. The Americans have emptied their warehouses, sold arms to the Bosnian people, and now their military industry can get started again. That's why I say that the war was brought upon us. And here there were people ready to take up arms and start a war. The vision of a greater Serbia and greater Croatia existed of course beforehand in the heads of some Serbs and Croats. But I cannot understand why, if we could live peacefully for fifty years, we couldn't continue. If the EU had been against the war in Bosnia Herzegovina and Kosovo they could have stopped it earlier. They could have solved the problems if they wanted to... And the Americans, they also wanted to get closer to Russia. Before [the war] United States had offered 24 billion dollars to Tito, the size of all the national debt of Yugoslavia. In return they wanted an island in the Adriatic Sea, *Vis,* which they wanted to be their military base. But Tito didn't want that island to be a military base, and with this war the Americans obtained that island and in that way got the money from their humanitarian aid back.

Also the Romanov dynasty [the Russians] wanted access to one of the three warm oceans: the Black Sea, the Indian Ocean or the Adriatic Ocean. They have problems with the Turks, they have no real chance of getting to the Indian Ocean, so they tried to get through Serbia to the Adriatic Ocean. But the Americans were here to hinder it. They arrived first and made a base here in Yugoslavia. The greatest wish of America is to get to the Balkans and they did.

When it comes to political explanations focusing on the internal Yugoslav political scene, it is primarily the former Serbian leader Slobodan Milošović and the former Croatian president Franjo Tuđman people blame for the war (although sometimes the former Bosnian president Alija Izetbegovic is also made responsible). People claim that these 'enemies' were actually co-operating in an identical game for power using the tool of nationalism. This is an example from a conversation I had with Nihad:

Nihad: In 1991, we could hear Dubrovnik being bombed and towards the end of 1991, Serbian military trucks drove through Stolac. And in September 1991 the Serbs arrived and made a military camp here in Stolac. But we did not think there would be war [he laughs a little]. In April 1992 the Serbs occupied Stolac, and they were not met with any resistance. They just came and said, now Stolac is occupied. The night before their arrival all the Croats had fled, only Muslims were left. The Croats then came back on June 16th and HVO [the army of the Bosnian Croats] shot a little and then the Serbs withdrew without fight. I think there was a deal between Tuđman and Milošović. Because there were no fights. Nothing. The HVO just came and almost the same day the Serbs were out of town.

TK: But wasn't it often the Serbs' tactic to position themselves on the hillcrests and then bomb a city?

Nihad: Yes, but the frontlines between the Serbs and the Croats during the war ran exactly like the borders of the old NDH state [The fascist Croat puppet state during the Second World War].

I have shown how *politika*, besides being related to 'real-politik', is also a cultural category of immoral actions and persons sharply in contrast to the values of ordinary people's everyday life. It is used as a means of explaining and criticising without resorting to ethnic identity. *Politika* is furthermore constructed as an autonomous force accounting for ungraspable aspects of the unmade world.

Chapter 6
Pošteni ljudi – decency rather than ethnicity

On the moral scale adhered to by the Muslims of Stolac, *politika* is opposed to the category *pošteni ljudi*. Whereas *politika* alludes to actions and persons existing in a separate and rather abstract sphere, the kinds of actions and persons referred to by *pošteni ljudi* are embedded in local and face-to-face relations. *Pošteni ljudi* means something like decent, honest and straightforward people. To behave decently is to be able to provide for oneself and one's family, to be honest and hard-working, to be self-sacrificing, to be considerate toward other people and to pay visits to them, and also to remain the same no matter what pressures or temptations one is exposed to. It refers to an inner substance or character, and sometimes also to religious devotion; implying that if one is a true believer one is also a decent human being. As one woman put it, "I only believe in God and decent people; money – one day you have some, the next day you have nothing." This utterance came as she talked about how her daughter and son-in-law were to come to visit her from Germany but she did not even have a bed or mattress on which they could sleep. She and her husband themselves slept on a bed without a mattress. Before the war, her house had been fully equipped. What the woman meant, in other words, was that war can strip people of their material possessions, but not of their decency. Honesty and hard labour are other central values attached to decency. Mensur, one of my key informants, once told me this little story:

> During and just after the war there were several abandoned Croat houses, which were being robbed by Muslims. I said to my father: 'Shouldn't I go and take something, there are TV's and everything, there's furniture, and they have robbed us of everything,' but my father said no. I then said: 'Everybody else is doing it, why can't I, think of what they have done to us.' But my father said 'No!' And today I am glad he said that, now we have a clear conscience. We can hold our heads up high.

With *pošteni ljudi*, as with *politika*, the Muslims of Stolac have an important tool that can be used to evaluate behaviour without resorting to ethnic categories. Insisting, therefore, on evaluating behaviour by reference to decency and not ethnicity forms an important part of the Muslims' everyday counterdiscourse. Just as with *politika*, though, it is not always clear to what extent people succeed in resisting the ethnicisation of their world. The use of the category *pošteni ljudi* sometimes becomes characteristic not of a person, but of an ethnic category, as expressed in statements like: We (Muslims) are decent people, they (Croats/Serbs) are not (See also Kolind 2007).

Decency and moral disapproval

The category of decency and the values attached to it can be used as a way of criticising certain people and certain types of actions in a way that resists 'ethnicifying' social relations. One day Nihad, Anvere and I were talking about Villa Ragusa, a house in a beautiful setting by the river, which before the war had been the local *dom culture* (House of Culture) where young people enjoyed themselves on Saturday nights and where musical performances were held. During the war, a Croat family called Raguz rented the house very cheaply under some rather unclear circumstances and turned it in to a fashionable restaurant serving rich Croats and international personnel visiting Stolac. What was more, the Raguz family is extremely influential, and they are said to have played a role in the destruction and looting of Stolac, as well as the deportation of its Muslim population. So the restaurant is perceived as a symbol of the destruction of the town, the humiliation of the Muslims, and the enrichment of local Croat politicians. As Nihad explained:

> I knew Martin Raguz[1] when he didn't even have enough money to buy cigarettes, and a friend of mine has been in his flat in Sarajevo. It was stuffed with genuine paintings, and his daughter plays tennis. But in fact he comes from a village, they were not poor, but certainly not rich. The only reason why they have become rich is criminality and corruption, because the wealth they have … cannot have been obtained by decent work, because you do not become rich by that. You cannot become rich by working with your hands. You can live well, sure. We have lived well. We have always had food on the table, in the summer [before the war] we could go to the seaside, I was able to build my own house, but we have not been rich. Even if I had worked twenty-four hours a day we would not have been rich. You do not get rich by decent and

---

1 Martin Raguz, one of the leaders of the HDZ and one of the most prominent Croat politicians in Bosnia Herzegovina. He was briefly appointed Prime Minister of Bosnia Herzegovina between October 2000 and February 2001, and then, on 3 March 2001 the 'coordinator' of the self-proclaimed 'Croat self-government' (see Grandits 2007).

honest labour. If I had been rich, I would have had someone to build my house for me. It took me seven years to build my house.

By referring to decency and, implicitly, to the category of *pošteni ljudi*, Nihad was condemning the owners of Villa Ragusa. But everything they represented and all the actions they have been involved in were not explained with reference to an intrinsic Croat mentality but to their personal indecency, in sharp contrast to Nihad's own work ethic.

Another example comes from an interview with a Muslim couple whose flat was occupied by Croats. They lived in very straitened circumstances in a small and rather miserable rented house. They had a piece of land outside the town which they cultivated by hand. Before the war they had a tractor and a rotary cultivator, today they are gone.

Husband: The other day I saw my tractor in my neighbour's field. I didn't say anything. Puuuh! But it is not normal, it is not normal to go into another man's home and just take his things… You can't be normal.

Even though the man who had stolen the tractor was a Croat, the theft is not condemned with reference to ethnicity. His action is instead considered anomalous.

Džanana

Džanana was an old woman with a beautiful wrinkled face. She lived with her daughter who was hard of hearing. They returned to Stolac in July 2000. Their house had been partly rebuilt by the Danish Refugee Council after having been burned down by Croats in 1996. It consisted of two sparsely furnished small rooms, a toilet and a kitchen. They lived on their pensions, which were always delayed by several months and amounted to KM300 per month (*Konvertibilna Marka*, Bosnian convertible mark, €1 is approximately KM1.95), which also had to cover expenses like transportation and medicine for the daughter's cancer. They grew some vegetables in what used to be the flowerbeds in the walled garden around the house. Džanana was friendly, but also very sad. She often told me about her wartime experiences: the violent expulsion when she was only allowed to bring one plastic bag of clothes, her exhausting flight through the mountains to rejoin her daughter, her seven years in a refugee camp, her tremendous yearning for her son and grandchildren who lived in Denmark and who had nothing to return to, how everybody lived peacefully and was well off before the war, and the miserable situation in Stolac, where she had had to start all over. It was clearly hard for her to comprehend the events of the last eight years. She often heaved a deep sigh and wiped away her tears with her dishtowel, especially when she was talking about her grandchildren; she repeatedly showed me the two pictures she had of them while kissing their images. For her, decency was a very central value, and both the war and post-war Stolac were characterised by the total absence of decency. In her accounts of her experiences, she often clung to and repeated her few experiences of decency: the recurrent story about Camilla, a worker in the refugee camp who was 'so nice', the 'Danish people' who were helping her son, and the visits of neighbours when she returned to Stolac. She never condemned the Croats as a group, not even when she was talking about the people who lived next door in her son's house. The blame was always on individuals who behaved badly: people with hearts of stone, as she expressed it. The following excerpts from the interviews I did with her show some of her moral standards.

TK: What was the relationship between the Croats and the Muslims like?

Džanana: It was beautiful. Everybody lived together having a good relationship to each other. We helped each other. I had a neighbour whose name is Marko [a Serb], and his wife was called Gordana, further down the road I had a neighbour called Boris [a Croat]. When they expelled us, I gave the keys to my house to this Boris, saying: 'Just try to save my son's house,' he then replied that he didn't dare, 'I do not dare.' That's how it is. When I returned to Stolac for the first time after the war, everything was burned to the ground. What a sight. You can see it in this picture, before there was a huge door at the entrance.

When they came and told us to leave I just took a bag, and what can you put in a bag. I thought that this war would be like the wars before; you leave for a little while and then return to your house. But we were gone for seven or eight years, it was not easy. And we lived in two square metres, Mala [her daughter] and I. Nearly eight years. We lay on the floor like sardines in a tin box, no matter who was next to us. We suffered a lot. I didn't at all expect to survive, because it was a very tough life. But we lived.

[During the war] I didn't know anything about my children. Mala and my son's wife were in Čapljina along with the grandchildren. Mirsad [her son] was in prison camp.

TK: How many months?

Džanana: Six or seven months. I don't know precisely. It was very difficult. You think a lot, and sometimes I feel that it is only by luck that I didn't lose my reason.

TK: Where did Mirsad go after the prison camp?

Džanana: He didn't weigh much, and those who lost a lot of weight in the prison camps, they were sent abroad. And he chose Denmark. And he is satisfied. He says they are really decent people. They are decent people, they welcomed us. They sent me a letter of guarantee [some kind of residence permit], so we could go to Denmark as well, but I didn't want to go. I said to Mala that she could leave. I just thought that I would return to my house as quickly as possible. I think that was nice of those people, who received the Bosnians well, and they gave them an opportunity to live in a proper manner. But I never wanted to go to Denmark. And when I didn't, my daughter wouldn't either. That's how it is.

TK: And then slowly the Muslims began to return.

Džanana: They [the Croats] don't understand that you should not take another person's property. This [house] is mine; I have paid for it with my blood. Isn't that so? My husband worked for forty-one years, forty-one years! And now once again we have been reduced to beggars. One came with a chair [she refers to the help she and her daughter received when they returned to their empty house], the other with a table, the third brought some curtains, and sometimes I just wanted to cry. I just remember myself and my life and everything I had, but anyway. You forget everything when you survive.

Last night I said to someone that things are not going the way they are supposed to. You have to understand that we returned to an empty house and no one came and asked if we had what we needed [she is thinking of politicians and other potential patrons]. They only come and knock at your door when you have to pay for electricity, water and other things. And that is not humane. I didn't leave because I wanted to, but they [the politicians] do not understand. I do not like that. It is very important to offer one's help, such things I will keep in my heart as long as I live. I will not forget that. You have to do good things where you can, that's how it is, my son.

TK: What was the standard of living like before?

Džanana: The standard of living was good, everyone who wanted to work, they worked. Everyone had the opportunity to live well. My husband was a secretary in the town government, and he was also a judge. But when he returned from work he also worked in our little garden, and he did it so we could have our own produce, so that we didn't have to buy it at the marketplace. And then my son started to work and his wife worked also. My daughter Mala also had a job. And I repeat, everyone who wanted to work, they lived well. It was only the lazy who didn't want to work.

TK: And you had enough money?

Džanana: Yes, we invested a lot in the house. And now I judge myself; why should we have so much. Upstairs we had two rooms and the same downstairs. Now I'm having a hard time, it ought to be the best time and the children should be with me, so that I wouldn't miss them. Now things are difficult, they should be here helping me […].

There are people who have hearts of stone, who do not have feelings. I tell you it like it is. And I will tell my children not to forget the good things people have done towards them. And those who did the evil things, they have done them towards themselves. The evil things will one day strike back at them […].

When we returned to Stolac for the first time to visit our house, the people who were living in the house [Croat refugees from central Bosnia occupying her house] said that we could not enter the courtyard. Then I said: 'It is mine not yours, my destiny is the same as yours, but your destiny is not the same as mine, because I was a refugee, but I did not live in another person's house.' I demanded of this Franjo that he should give me a room, but he did not want to hear of such a thing. There are five rooms, but we could not have a single one … that's how it is … I think that the children learn from the parents and behave the way the parents do. When my daughter-in-law entered our house, she said: 'Look, there is our lamp,' then Maja [the Croat], who was then living in the house, said: "No it is our lamp", then my daughter-in-law said: 'Yes, it is yours now, but it was ours.'

Džanana sometimes complained about the children of the family living in her son's house. Džanana's house and her son's house are both located close to one another inside a walled courtyard with only one gated entrance. Today Džanana has got her house back, but her son's house is still occupied by the same Croats. Džanana says that these children always slam the door to the courtyard and that they never greet her, but then again, she said, neither do the parents. Furthermore, they will not agree to lock the gate at night, even though, according to Džanana, they know, that she and her daughter are two elderly women living alone. Finally, Džanana relates that they have not once offered to help her. Nevertheless, Džanana, as the excerpts from the interviews show, does not relate this behaviour to her neighbours' ethnicity, only to a lack of morality and decency.

When we were in the refugee camp we received a lot of help from Denmark. We didn't get new clothes, but it helped anyway. You just washed them [the used clothes] and wore them. Sometimes I would say that maybe someone died in those clothes, and now we are wearing them. But we accepted the help, because we did not have anything.

When we returned [to Stolac] we were living in darkness, so I went to the power station [the power station is in Croat hands, and the withholding of a power supply is used as a way of harassing the Muslim population, as it is with telephony] and asked if we could get electricity, and they said that it could take close to two years.

TK: For electricity?

Džanana: Yes. So I said it is not necessary to wait that long, you can see there is light in the street lamps. Then came Mirsad [her son], and he probably knew some of them, so they came and we got electricity. And because of that I feel that I lost some of my humanity. Whereas I would have helped them straight-away. I could not behave in that way. I couldn't. But that's the way it is, what can you do? [She feels degraded having to ask for such a standard thing as electricity].

And then he [the electrician] laughed at me and Mala because we moved into a house that was so damp. He said that one should not move into a house the first year. But I wanted it very eagerly, to move into my own house, no matter how it was. We paid with our lives, it is not easy to move into such a morass. The water installation is very bad [in general she felt that the house was very unhealthy to live in]. He said that you should give the house to your enemy so he can live there the first year. Then I said: 'If I don't want to move into such a house, neither should my enemy. I don't want to burden anyone' [...].

I then asked if they [the Danish Refugee Council] could also rebuild a room upstairs. But they wouldn't because we only live two persons in the house. But they said, in order to get more rooms, we should just pretend that more people lived in the house. But I don't want to do anything dishonest. I just want what I am entitled to, I don't want anyone to come afterwards and hit me in the head. That's how it is, my son. My father used to say: 'You should be tired of hard work, but not of hunger' [umorio se od rada a ne od gladi]. You have to work in order not to fear the future [...].

TK: What was your father's occupation?

Džanana: He repaired pots. Before you did not have plates and ordinary pots [of metal], you used something very different [stonewarepottery], and when it broke, he repaired it. When you make *bosnaski lonac* [traditional Bosnian dish] you make it in a big pot and then cover it with paper, so the aroma won't get out, and you simmer it over a low flame, it is marvellous. But later things changed. The times are changing. If only you could know how beautiful Stolac was. Now only the remnants are left ... The children have to take good care of each other, no matter who they are. It has to be as it was before. Madness came into people and told them that they cannot live together, how can it be true? We can. If we were able to live together before, why can't we live together again? It was *politika* that did it all. They were only clinging to their office, and that is ugly. Ugly [...].

TK: I have seen a lot of *Šahovnica* [the Croatian chessboard coat of arms, an important nationalist symbol], did you have these before in Stolac?

Džanana: Before the war there were none, but it doesn't matter that they are hanging there. Maybe some of their [the Croats'] dreams come true with that flag. What do I know? The most important is that we have peace. It doesn't matter they are hanging there, but it is not nice.

TK: What do you think about the future? Will Serbs, Croats and Muslims be able to live together?

Džanana: It has to be that way. In my opinion it has to be as it was before, for us to live well together and forget all the troubles one has lived through. But I do not know if everybody thinks that way. But I wish it could be that way, that it could be as before.

I was often surprised that Džanana, who had suffered (and still suffered) so much, hardly ever condemned people or their actions by reference to ethnicity. For Džanana the most important things in life were to behave decently, to work hard, respect other people, and live with her family. When we discussed the neighbours who had behaved badly (see above), I had to ask her about their ethnic identity, and when she answered, she said only: "They come from somewhere in central Bosnia". On other occasions she would refer to their town of origin. I could then infer that they were Croats. Naturally, she herself knew they were Croats, but this knowledge was of no use to her in explaining their acts, instead she made allusions to proper behaviour and decency. Similarly, when she talked about the lack of concern shown by the people at the power station in Stolac – all of whom are Croats – her reproaches were directed at the inhumanity of these people, not their ethnicity. Finally, whenever Džanana explicitly commented on the potential for future coexistence she expressed wishes for a future together with Serbs and Croats and she talked about the need to forget the past.

People reveal their true nature during hard times

During the war, many people had been disappointed. I heard many stories of how friends and neighbours, especially those of other ethnic backgrounds, had suddenly let people down, did not help when needed – neither during nor after the war. They failed to share surplus goods, and they did not even come to visit. Though such stories were common, former friends or neighbours were seldom criticised explicitly. Instead, the situation was outlined, leaving moral judgement to the listener. This aspect of moral judgement very often referred to values associated with the category *pošteni ljudi* and the saying that people reveal their true nature during hard times[2]. Armin's mother originates from a *mahala* (neighbourhood) where many Croats had settled well before the war and where her *prvi komšija* (first neighbour) had been a Croat:

Armin: We had a good relationship with their children. My wife went to secondary school with their daughter, and we were *kumovi* [witnesses] at their wedding. We spent a lot of time together. They came here and we visited them. We were together at least every second or third week, but today we do not see each other. We haven't heard from them since the war. I know they are rich, they have an apartment in Jablanica, and they drive a BMW. But we haven't heard from them. I am not going to contact them and, you know – it would be a little like apologising – to ask if we are going to see each other again. But if they come to our place, they will be welcome; they will get everything they need. But they never called us or tried to help us even though they are rich.

It was not only Croats who were judged with reference to the moral category *pošteni ljudi*. Nihad only spoke about the time he was interned in the prison camp very rarely. One time, though, he told about his fellow Muslim prisoners:

And the same is true about life in the camp. Here people also revealed their true essence. We were in that big hangar, and we did not get any food, and almost no water. And there were some who did not share what they had, if they had more than others, and some made a kind of territory of their own in the

---

2 *Čovjek upozna svoje prijatelje u nevolji*: You get to know your friends in misfortune.

hangar. Once I gave a little piece of bread to an old man who was sick. I don't think he has forgotten that. Then I ate nothing. But there were several who behaved egoistically. It is in such situations that people's true essence shows.

Decency and war-related behaviour

The moral universe surrounding the category *pošteni ljudi* has direct bearing on the judgement of war-related actions. Stolac Muslims accept that people were forced into uniform, that soldiers shot at each other, in short, that there was an immense pressure on everybody. *Pošteni ljudi* is used to categorise the people who behaved decently in such a situation. The day the male Muslim population was expelled from Stolac, some of the men escaped and others hid in the hills. For those who hid it was terrible to watch helplessly as fathers and husbands were taken away, their children and grandchildren calling out desperately. It was equally unpleasant in the weeks afterwards to live in a state of uncertainty, knowing that the Croats could come back at any time. Amer was one of those who hid himself. One day when Croat soldiers returned to his house, he knew he had to give himself up, as much as anything for the sake of his family:

> In front of the house was a Croat whom I did not know, he was from some-where in [central] Bosnia. He made a lot of noise and wanted to shoot us. But there was another one with him, one of my former colleagues, whom I had helped to build his house. And when I recognised him, I knew he was not going to hurt me. So I walked out of the house and talked to him. Then we smoked a cigarette together, and he said to me: 'Amer, nothing is going to happen to you or to your family, you just have to think carefully' [not to do anything rash]. Nobody touched me.

Amer stressed the fact that his former colleague 'did not touch him', and that they were smoking a cigarette together: implying that this man had no choice, and did not enjoy the situation either. In an interview with a couple in their sixties, the husband had a related story to tell.

> Osman: When I was in prison camp, if one of the Croats had a chance to hand me a piece of bread, he would do it, but I also knew that someone was watching him, and that if he helped me it would get him in trouble. That is how the dev-ilish politic was. You can't say that all the Croats are the same, not at all. There were some decent Croats, whom I knew from before the war, and when I went to work [outside the hangar] they would help me. And even if they could not give me anything to eat, then just a kind word would be enough, after such a word I would be in a better mood when I came back to the hangar. If every-

body had been the same [if all the Croats had been evil] nobody would have survived the camp. If you kill innocent people what will your God say? There is always somebody who thinks in that way, even if he has the chance to beat or hit someone he will not do it.

This insight into the political situation and the acceptance of the fact that some of the Croats could not have behaved otherwise, is the reason that the Muslims do not necessarily have problems interacting with Serbs or Croats whom they know fought in the war. But there is a very sharp dividing line: people can in no way accept or be together with those they know committed war crimes. Generally the Muslims feel that all war criminals should be convicted, no matter who they are. As a mother said while her son was listening: "Anybody who has committed war crimes should go to The Hague, even if it were my own son."

Explicit use of decency

Using the category *pošteni ljudi* to go beyond ethnic thinking is often done implicitly. Sometimes, however, it is also done explicitly. An elderly couple – the husband is Serb, the wife is Croat – stated this critique of ethnic thinking very unambiguously (showing that the counterdiscourse in not reserved for the Muslims only).

Marko: My oldest son married a Croat girl and the youngest a Muslim girl.

Olga: Even though they are not Serbs those two daughters-in-law are the best in the world. First of all you have to be a decent person, next comes if you are Croat, Muslim or Serb. If you have to pray to your God, you can do it in the house, you don't have to go to church. The most important is that people are decent. All the people I knew before I talk to now, if they are decent people (*pošteni ljudi*). I never had anything to do with the evil people. So if there was someone who said that I couldn't talk to the good people no matter if they are Serbs, Croats or Muslims, I would feel like I was dead.

In the interview from above, where Osman discussed the decent behaviour of some of the Croatian warders in the prison camp, the subject of decency came up again:

Mila: Ordinary people [*narod ko narod*] are not guilty for what happened, but they are the sufferers. The war was not good for anybody.

Osman: The decent people, they were not ready for what happened. I never thought I would leave my home [*ognjište*: the home fires]. Before the war we lived well together with both Serbs and Croats. We were like sisters and brothers. And suddenly, as they say, the devil came between us, and people started to quarrel. We left Stolac without a fight. I don't know how it happened other places, but here in Stolac we were just expelled [*proteran*]. We lived well before the war, but I am not embarrassed by what I did [that is, living peaceably with the Serbs and Croats].

Decency and the legitimisation of interethnic interaction

The categorisation of actions and persons with reference to decency and non-decency instead of ethnicity can also function as an important tool in facilitating interaction with people of different ethnic backgrounds. The category *pošteni ljudi* can go beyond ethnicity, not suppressing it but rendering it less important. An obvious case is the relationship with former friends and neighbours of different ethnic backgrounds. As in many other places, rumours and gossip are very important sources of information in Stolac. People generally know where their neighbours were during the war, whether they have relatives abroad and where, what their children do for a living, who their children's spouses are, and all kinds of other information conducive to good relations. Even so, people do not know everything, especially when it comes to Serbs who spent the war in the Serb Republic or in Serbia, or Croats who remained in Stolac during the cleansing and looting of the city. Categorising those people as decent removes the uncertainties that always hangs over what they did during the war, where their sympathy lay then and now – in short whether one can trust them again as one did before (see also Jansen 2007). Often when Stolac Muslims are talking about renewed interaction with friends and neighbours of different ethnic background, they unequivocally stress that these people are *pošteni ljudi*. One can say that the category of decency fills in the hole of insecurity that has been left behind by the lack of social knowledge. In some cases, in a kind of reverse logic, the Muslims of Stolac state that the very fact that people returned shows that they did nothing wrong during the war.

Munta: There is this woman, her name is Anita [a Croat]. She used to deliver milk to us before the war. She came and asked how we were doing, she said she had heard that we had returned and she just wanted to ask how we were. All the decent people they came – when we moved back – and asked how we were... We never before noticed who these people are; whether they are Serbs, Croats or Muslims, the most important is to be a decent person. To have character. Nothing else. But somebody did not like it [that the different ethnic groups lived together]. Even today people are shouting that we must be divided, that we can't live together. But I can live together with everybody. As long as the situation is just. Because we are used to it [living together]. For instance some Serbian neighbours returned; and they at once ran to us and asked how we were doing. The kids were always together, I don't know...

Emir, one of my key informants, used the values attached to the category *pošteni ljudi* in this way to legitimise renewed interaction with former friends:

The Croats have a lot of saints, nearly one for every day. Every family has approximately three patron saints, which they celebrate, for instance St. Nicolas, St. Johanna. And when they celebrated them, we used to bake cakes and bring them along for visit. The Serbs did this as well. We have some good friends in Berković [in the Serb Republic]. They celebrated their patron saint recently, then my mother baked cakes and my brother and I went there and visited them, it was the first time we had seen them since the war broke out. When they saw us they started crying. And they then came a week later and visited us, and celebrated that we had moved back in our own house, and they brought presents. They are some very decent people. We own some land together. They took care of it while we were expelled from Stolac. And during the war in 1992, when you couldn't buy anything, nothing, not even potatoes, this man came with a sack of potatoes, he came in full uniform. They are decent people. Our friendship goes way back. My grandfather had a good friendship with their grandfather … The reason why we are able to have such a good relationship is that I know they did not do anything during the war.

As the quotation show, it was important for Emir to legitimise his family's friendship to the Serbs by labelling them decent. After the war, ethnicity continued to pervade everything, including friendships and love relationships. Cross-ethnic relations are no longer unproblematic, and must be clarified each time in a way that is not necessary when Muslims interact among themselves. Against this background, the category *pošteni ljudi* helps resume and legitimise these *a priori* tense relationships.

Decency and Muslim identity

I have shown how values attached to the categories *pošteni ljudi* and *poliitka* are used as a way of resisting the ethnicisation of the social landscape. In using these categories, people try to dissociate ethnic identity from moral character. However, this dissociation can never be absolute. Ethnic categories also help the Muslims of Stolac to make sense of the unmade world by reshaping some kind of coherent identity as Muslims. This is a tension people struggle with in their everyday life. And sometimes *pošteni ljudi* is, contrary to the examples given so far, used not as part of the counterdiscourse, but to underscore the relevance of ethnic identity, as the following examples show.

Before women and children were expelled from Stolac, they were gathered in central places in the town: the school, the former hospital for skin diseases and a factory. There they were robbed and mistreated. Anvere had her jewellery stolen by a man from the town. Anvere's husband Nihad now works with this man.

Nihad: Therefore they [Croats] are insecure, because they know what they have done, and they know that we know it. If he had strength of character he would give Anvere her jewellery back, but they do not have character [he raises his voice and I can feel he is angry].

Munta – who stated in the quotation above that she could live with anybody as long as the situation was just, and that all the decent people came and asked after her when she came home – was sometimes clearly reproachful towards the Croats as Croats, thereby highlighting ethnic differences:

Munta: Stolac was not a big town, but it was always beautiful. The streets were clean. Now I see all that dirt and all the litter in the streets.

Daughter: There were four mosques, now there is nothing left, there is only one left in *Uzinovići* [a part of town] that was repaired when we came back.

Munta: And they [the Croats] call themselves believers, and they tell everybody that they believe in God. There is only one God, and if I respect my own, it means that I also respect yours. What have God's holy houses done – are they guilty?

The point is not that Munta or Nihad are being inconsistent in making such contradictory statements about their views on ethnicity and decency. Rather, such tensions are omnipresent: they form an overarching framework that determines the greater part of my informants' narrative practice.

Chapter 7
Nekultura – culture rather than ethnicity

Both *politika* and *pošteni ljudi* can be seen as fundamental to a moral scheme
of evaluation which enables my informants to disapprove of actions and people without resorting to the dominant ideology of ethnicity as an explanatory
framework. Categorising friends of another ethnic affiliation as decent also
enables them to legitimise and facilitate interethnic interaction. The third and
final non-ethnic category of moral judgement used by my informants refers to
'levels of culture.' Together the three categories: *politika*, *pošteni ljudi* and *nekultura* make up some of the building blocks of Muslim counterdiscourse.

The uncultured Other

The Muslims of Stolac often see themselves as cosmopolitans and emphasise
that a lot of prominent and well educated people have come from their town:
the former Bosnian Minister of Culture, Dr. Fahrudin Rizvanbegović, along
with well-known writers like Mak Dizdar, architects, doctors and athletes. They
proudly talk about the festivals held outside Stolac at the old *Stećci* [1] before the
war, to which poets came from all over the world. I was told that once even J. P.
Sartre participated. And people also stress the sophisticated beauty of their pre-
war town. As a foreigner coming from Western Europe to Stolac for the first
time, you would probably not associate this small provincial town, where everybody knows everybody else with urbanity, fashion and modernity. But this
is how the people of Stolac themselves regard their town, as an urban centre of
culture; and they clearly distinguish themselves as citydwellers from farmers
and country people.

One day Ljubica asked me if I had been to the newly reconstructed café
in town, and how I liked it. I answered that it was OK, I liked the big piece of
rock integrated into the café, but besides that it was not that cosy (*udoban*). She
told me that the rock had also been there before the war, however she had also
heard that the café was not that cosy even then – but after all it was owned by
someone from some village, with the implication that the lack of taste shown

---

1   A medieval cemetery, with some of the finest so-called Bogomil tombstones in Bosnia, though
one should rather call them Bosnian tombstones (see Donia and Fine 1994: 23-5).

by such country bumpkins was not surprising. When Emir and I talked about the café, he told me that the people who hung out in the café were people who liked to hear modern folk music (*novokomponirana narodna muzika*) – that is, farmers without style. On another occasion Emir told me that at the weekend people from the countryside came to town to drink and make trouble.

> We can sit in their cafés and they in ours[2], but not in the weekend, then you cannot be there, then all the people from the villages come, all the wild ones. But it was also like that before [the war]. People from the country came maybe twice a month and drank a lot and behaved like total idiots.

The categories that structure these two anecdotes relate to the conceptual division between *kultura* (culture) and *nekultura* (non-culture/uncultured). This moral dichotomy, which had already been common in Bosnia Herzegovina before the war, was used to evaluate all kinds of acts, situations and people, from individual behaviour to national cultures, from the tiniest village to the pulsating metropolis. It is possible to make a whole scheme of binary oppositions building on this opposition: primitive:civilised; peasant:middle-class; wild:civilised/domesticated; uncontrolled:controlled; countryside:city; Balkan: European; oriental:Western; backward:modern; dirty:clean and so on (see also van de Port 1998: 61; Jansen 2000a: 132). A central feature of this conceptual division is its relation to context. The dichotomy *kultura:nekultura* constitutes and enables a scheme of moral evaluations articulated in a geographical terminology, but in practice not reflecting fixed geographical patterns. The Stolac Muslims, for example, clearly judged people coming from the small villages around Stolac as farmers and as lacking culture (*nekultura*): they start fights in the cafés in Stolac on Friday and Saturday nights, they only have seven years of schooling, and they envy those living in the town. However, when my informants compared Stolac to Sarajevo or Mostar, they themselves represented the less cultured party. I had some informants I sometimes went out with on Friday or Saturday night. Mostly we would stay in Stolac, but sometimes we drove to the larger city of Mostar, and it was noticeable how our behaviour changed. We were much more focused on not behaving primitively or foolishly in Mostar than in Stolac. One of these informants proudly told me one night in *Galerija* (the Muslim café in Stolac) that: "In here you can do what you want, nobody cares or resents you." This was not the case in Mostar. Bringa (1995) has made similar observations about the situational aspect of the moral division *kultura*:

---

2   It is not a widespread practice as far as I have observed, and mostly it involves Muslims frequenting two to three specific Croat cafés.

nekultura. Her informants in the village where she conducted fieldwork distinguished clearly between those from the upper part of the town, who were poorer, less educated and more traditionalist, and those from the lower part who were more 'modern'. However, this did not mean that people coming from the upper part of Bringa's village were automatically labelled as uncultured. Depending on the person, the social situation, the actual behaviour in question, the strategies of identification (association or distancing), the location or the matters discussed, the labels were used differently.

In relation to my study, the division *kultura:nekultura* is an important non-ethnic set of categories, which the Muslims of Stolac used in order to explain the war and make sense of their ruined lives. It is a dichotomy which my informants used to condemn blameworthy behaviour and locate responsibility without resorting to ethnicity. As an informant explained while talking about causes of the war: "The wild people came and exterminated the cultivated ones." In other words, the war can be seen as a conflict between uncultivated country people and cultivated city dwellers. This is from an interview with Mustafa and his wife:

Mustafa: None of the intellectuals with a good education started this war. I have an interesting explanation for this war. It was a man who told it to me. He said that this war was a war where the asphalt [symbol of civilisation] fought against the *opanak* [traditional peasant shoes]. Those from the villages try to come down [from the mountains] to the towns by every possible means. And the only way they could come down to the towns was by creating a crisis and then a war.

Wife: A lot of people from the villages around Mostar moved to Mostar during the war, and now it is impossible to make them return to the villages. They occupied someone's flat and now they live there.

Mustafa: It is the same in Stolac, where those coming from the villages occupied someone's house or flat, and now they don't want to go back to the villages. And before the war they tended the sheep.

Fahrudin is a man who cares about Stolac and knows a lot about its architecture. He also took part in the reconstruction of some of the Muslim houses when people started returning in 1997, and he witnessed the reconstruction project being obstructed by violent Croats.

There are still some unfinished problems with houses and flats. And this war, like other wars before, was a fight between those from the town and those from the villages. A fight between the urban and the rural. Many of the Croats living in Stolac, they have their own houses in the villages around Stolac, but they do not want to go back. It is crazy. They do not like their own, but rather something which is not theirs. He does not want to go back to his house in Dubrave, but wants to stay here in Stolac in my house or yours.

Once when Nijaz and I were walking through the centre of Stolac, where the old Sultan Selim's mosque (1519) had been located, he told me as he had done several times before that:

> ...this was the place where the mosque was, and here was also a Muslim cemetery [*Harem*].

TK: It must have been huge?

Nijaz: Yes, it was very huge, and there were bazaars all around.

TK: What did they [the Croats who demolished the mosque] do to all the stones [which the mosque was built of]?

Meda: They blew it all, loaded them on trucks and drove them away, into the mountains. It is uncultured [*nekultura*]. For certain.

Another time, after coffee at Café *Galerija*, Nijaz and I passed a place where there was a lot of broken glass and broken bottles. Nijaz commented: "Balkan; it is the Croats from the small villages in central Bosnia. *Nekultura*, they have no culture."

The black market

A couple of kilometres outside Stolac was a black market where stolen and contraband goods were sold. The market opened during the war. Everybody knew about its existence, including the authorities. Some years ago it was partially closed down by the international community before that it had been a huge market where people came from all over to buy and sell.[3] Before the market was partially closed down it was also a place where stolen goods from the looted Muslim houses were sold: windows, furniture, electrical articles, doors etc. − or so I was told. The young Croat from Stolac who ran the market is now wanted by Interpol. The market was nothing more than a big parking lot, recently constructed by filling large parts of the River Bregava with stone, sand and gravel. This really annoyed many of the Muslims in Stolac, for the market ruined a place popular for swimming, destroyed the gardens of the Muslims who live nearby, and sand was continuously washed out into the river, which made it muddy and drove away the fish. Though reduced in scale, the market is still operating. The market was a rather unpleasant place − noisy and dirty. There were some primitive and unappetising fast food stands selling *ćevapčići* [grilled meat] and chicken, and one could buy lukewarm cola or beer all over the market. When people tried out the cars, they drove around the parking lot making the tires spin and jamming on the brakes so that dust filled the air. This, naturally, is my subjective experience, but I think it corresponds with the experiences of many of the Muslims in Stolac. For them the black car market is a provocation and a disgrace for the town, especially considering that before the war Stolac had an active, charming and very popular market (*Tepa*) in the centre of town, where all kinds of agricultural products were sold.

When my informants talked about the black market or when I asked about it, they always described it or categorised it as *nekultura*. This word sums up their feelings about a number of the market's negative characteristics. It was started by Croats, what is more Croats from Stolac: here household effects stolen from Muslim homes by Croats were sold. Here the Croats have violated the unwritten rules about how to treat the river, which in turn symbolises the corruption and decay of Bosnian society. In short, the market could very well be taken as a symbol of Croat aggression, of Croat lack of culture. However, people never once associated the black market with Croats or Croat mentality or Croat discrimination. Instead the market was described as uncivilised,

---

3   Here follow some passages from an article in the New York Times in 1999: "The used car market in Stolac, which convenes every Sunday in the Croat-controlled part of Bosnia, has one of the largest collections of stolen vehicles in Europe, according to the international police [...].
    On one recent Sunday, some 400 cars, most with forged registration papers and German, Swiss and Italian license plates, were being sold for large wads of German marks. The gangs that bring the cars into Bosnia oversee the sales [...].
    The Office of the High Representative has outlawed the market. It pressed in January to have the market's organizer, Jozo Peric, arrested. But the local Croatian court released him a few days later and dismissed the charges. Now Peric is in hiding. When federal tax officials showed up last year to try to carry out an audit, they were beaten so badly they were hospitalised." (Hedges 1999).

ugly, typically Balkan, criminal, mafia-like, and so on: in sum, *nekultura*. The Muslims' attitude towards the black market thus showed very clearly how the cultural category *nekultura* was used to condemn and explain immoral actions in an ethnically neutral way – actions which might easily have been associated with Croat political discrimination, post-war violence and Croat mentality: ethnic identity.

As with *politika* and *nepošteni ljudi*, my informants' use of the category *nekultura* dissociates ethnicity from blameworthy behaviour. Their use of these categories runs counter to the rhetoric of nationalism and is part of the Stolac Muslims' counterdiscourse. The resistance to nationalism consists of the attempt to facilitate coexistence and interaction with the ethnic Other by persistently judging behaviour by reference to non-ethnic cultural categories.

'The revenge of the countryside'

The cultural construction *kultura:nekultura* and the marked division between the rural and the urban on which my informants drew when evaluating and criticising behaviour as well as character are deeply rooted in the Yugoslav cultural and sociological processes of industrialisation and modernisation.[4] Yugoslavia was a very agrarian and underdeveloped country for most of its history. When industrialisation and the processes of economic modernisation did finally occur, development came rapidly. One can get an idea of the late development of Yugoslavia by looking at the infrastructure of the area in the 19th century. Mobility in Bosnia, as in most of the Ottoman territories, was then very poor: there were hardly any railroads, and the road network was primitive. Though the Ottomans had begun a programme of constructing improved trunk roads through the Balkans, they had not reached Bosnia by as late as 1877 (McCarthy 1993). According to the 1895 census, 88 % of the Bosnian population was engaged in agricultural production (Donia and Fine 1994: 76-7). This had not changed much by the middle of the 20th century: in 1948, 73 % of the Yugoslav population still lived on farms (Bougarel 1999: 165). As the country had not yet experienced land reform, semi-feudal relations were still characteristic in agricultural production (Donia and Fine 1994: 166). Then after the Second

---

4   One does need to beware the Eurocentric aspect of the concept of modernisation, as well as to consider how processes of modernisation and industrialisation are directly related to the absence of the same processes in other places. What Andre Gunder Frank calls the 'development of underdevelopment' is central for understanding the underdevelopment and late industrialisation in Yugoslavia. The backwardness of the Balkans, therefore, relates to their historical structural position vis-à-vis Europe and not to some reactionary force in the Ottoman Empire or the religion of Islam (Allcock 2000: 27-67).

World War things began to change rapidly. Yugoslavia went through an intense phase of urbanisation and industrial and cultural development. By 1981, only 27 % of the population was still living on farms (Bougarel 1999: 165). This massive urbanisation and industrialisation, along with the quest for education and culture that started with the Tito era, created the basis for the *kultura:nekultura* tension. The cities witnessed a massive influx of immigrants from the countryside, and though Yugoslavia was officially a classless society, the process of instant urbanisation produced a clash of cultures (see e.g. Simić 1973). Suddenly it became important for city-dwellers to distance themselves from the rural background of their parents, or the latest newcomers, or perhaps even their own background and origins. Many of the 'original' citydwellers saw their lifestyle polluted by the ignorant farmers, and a cleavage of identification evolved in which education became the paramount distinguishing factor (Drakulic 1995; van de Port 1998; Jansen 2000a; Ramet 1996). The modernisation/urbanisation process thus moved the traditional antagonisms between town and the countryside into the towns themselves, and made them much more conscious and significant.[5]

From the 1960s onwards, Yugoslavia experienced a period of 're-traditionalisation.' Allcock (2000: 351-81) has shown how the process of modernisation is not the same as the passing of traditional society: customs rooted in peasant society – in relation to family life, land ownership and patron-client relations – continue to provide important resources for living in the present. Re-traditionalisation, though, is something else: here traditions become a matter of the politics of identity. This politicisation of tradition or peasant identity is central to the resurgence of the nationalist ideologies that began in the 1960s and which ultimately culminated in the Yugoslav war. The nationalist ideologies of both Milošević and Tuđman linked national identity to the soil and nature, as well as to notions of an unspoiled, unsophisticated ruralness and to the 'authentic' cultural practices originating in the countryside. At the same time, genuine national identity was contrasted to the decadence, bureaucracy and heterogeneity of the cities (Bringa 1995: 149-53; Donia and Fine 1994: 186; Jansen 2000a: 113-16). The success of the nationalist politicians was consequently largely due to support from the countryside, and the relatively sparse opposition against the nationalist crusade was located in the cities (Jansen 2000a: 113).

---

5   Besides the socio-economic background Bougarel (1999) has shown how the discursive opposition between 'civilised' towns and 'barbarous' countryside/mountains has its roots in 19th century Yugoslav literature. The opposition was then articulated as lying between the mountains and the towns.

In sum, Yugoslavia before the Second World War was very rural and underdeveloped with marked but rather unproblematic cultural dividing lines between the cities and the countryside. With the rapid urbanisation following industrialisation and the focus upon education and *kultura* of the Tito era, these cleavages moved into the cities and became much more articulate. Then came a resurgence of nationalism starting in the 1960s, which initially drew support from those who were marginalised by the economic modernisation and who therefore experienced an identity crisis: that is, the rural population and the disintegrated urban population.[6] On this loosely sketched background, one can begin to understand the antagonistic relation between the urban and the rural, the cultured and the uncultured, the decadent and the authentic. These tensions have led many city-dwellers of all ethnic affiliations to perceive the recent conflict as one in which primitive peasants have sought to destroy urban civilisation in Bosnia and Croatia (see also Frykman 2001), an interpretation Bougarel (1999) has termed 'the revenge of the countryside.' Towns like Mostar and Sarajevo, relatively untouched by the fighting of World War II, were deliberately destroyed in the recent war. Serbian forces on the hillcrests around Sarajevo deliberately bombed the town's cultural monuments. And the Old Bridge in Mostar from 1556, the symbol of tolerance and ethnic coexistence, was continually shelled and finally hit by Croatian forces. One might see these major cities as living proof against the nationalist dream of ethnic homogeneity. The cities were ethnically mixed and a cosmopolitan attitude prevailed. The term *urbicide* has been employed to describe the conscious destruction of cities like Sarajevo, Mostar and also Stolac. As Jansen defines the term urbicide, it does "not only refer to the physical destruction of cities, but also, and maybe more importantly, to the killing of *urbanity*" (Jansen 2000b: 117). In other words, the target of urbicide is *kultura* (see also Bogdanović 1993; Coward 2002).

When the Muslims of Stolac continue to mourn the onslaught on their town and other cities of the former Yugoslavia, and when they blame the uncultured people from the countryside for the war and the present discrimination in Stolac, they are also expressing feelings of loss related to everything *kultura*

---

6   In fact, one can see the antagonism between town and the village/mountain as a result of an unsuccessful and incomplete modernisation of Yugoslavia. First, the "...various militias [in the recent war] attracted first of all the neo-urban strata of the population, disintegrated in the urban economy and culture, whereas the urban elites formed the principal support of the pacifist movement" (Bougarel 1999: 165). Second, the recurrent emergence, throughout Balkan history, of different militias living on the fringes of the shifting empires, alternating between armed rebellion against the state and armed service to the state, shows how the state has not been able to monopolise violence. In the recent war, as throughout the Balkan history, various more or less independent militias undertook military operations which the established military units were not willing or able to perform.

stands for: the ideals of education, cultivation, beauty and coexistence. Alija was a man who loved Stolac and who worked hard (see below) to make it a pleasant place to live once again. This is from an interview with Alija:

Alija: Lenin always said that one has to beware of socialism coming from the countryside. In the villages around Stolac, people live in their own world, they never wanted to send their children to secondary school or university. They have had their own world, which was different from ours, and there is a hatred between these two worlds. We Stolac people [*Stočani*] take care of the town. Before the war, if somebody came from Europe or another place, he came here to see the *Begovina*[7] [and all the old houses and antiquities, and people enjoyed seeing this. But these people who lived outside [of the town] Stolac, they didn't like it, and this is why they did all these things].

Emir: For instance they burned down the mosques and razed Begovina because they think in a different manner.

TK: Those from the villages?

Alija: Yes.

Nekultura as ethnic condemnation

As was also the case for the categories *politika* and *nepošteni ljudi* there is also ambivalence attached to my informants' use of *nekultura*. One could argue that using the category *nekultura* in remaking the world is just an implicit way of blaming the Croats, as the Croats constitute the majority of those coming from the countryside. It is impossible to fully distinguish those situations where categories like *nekultura*, *politika*, or *nepošteni ljudi* are used as the basis for implicit ethnic condemnation from those situations where they form part of the counterdiscourse by implicitly criticising the ethnicisation of the social landscape. But as argued previously, this uncertainty is not due to the lack of analytical tools. Rather, the nationalist discourse and my informants' counterdiscourse are interwoven and often hard to separate for people themselves. Blaming the ethnic Other and the wish for ethnic coexistence exist simultaneously. Here is an example of the category of *nekultura* used as an implicit way of blaming the ethnic Other. The speaker tries to establish an objective link between being Croat and a lack of education/*nekultura*. This viewpoint is presented as a neutral statement of facts, while I hear it more as a moral evaluation.

---

7 The *Begovina* ('house of the bey') was a residential ensemble of substantial architectural and historical value dating back to the 19th century. It was set on fire in 1993.

Muhamed: Stolac has always been special. A lot of intelligent people lived here, with many different ideas. Before the war there were, according to the census, 603 Croats in Stolac. And not many of them had important positions, or a university degree. And the situation changed totally after the war. Now they [Croats] produce diplomas as they produce ordinary papers. Now in Stolac there are eight or ten constructional engineers, but before the war no Croats had such an education. They needed people with education and then they just handed out diplomas; if one wanted a diploma, one got one.

As Muhamed sees it, Croats are generally less educated (than Muslims), hereby linking ethnicity and culture.

I have so far presented three categories which the Muslims of Stolac employ when trying to remake their shattered world and placing the blame for the devastating events of recent years: *politika*, *ne-pošteni ljudi*, and *nekultura*. *Nekultura* – as an element of the Muslims' counterdiscourse – works by putting ethnicity aside as a relevant factor in understanding the war and instead introducing culture, civilisation and urbanity as the most salient factors, all connected to the post-Second World War process of modernisation.

Chapter 8
Complexity in ethnic categorisation as part of the counterdiscourse

The Muslims of Stolac operate with several categories of Croats, and different moral value is attached to each category. Heterogeneity and not uniformity is the hallmark of what it means to be a Croat in the eyes of the Muslims. One of the aims of nationalist policy and violence was to reduce categorical complexity and create clear-cut ethnic identities. The complexity attributed to Croat ethnic identity, therefore, is part of the Muslim counterdiscourse. In some situations, Muslims state that the Croats are all fascists and have always been and that history is only repeating itself. On other occasions they stress that you cannot lump all the Croats together because only the ones from outside Stolac create trouble. It is not that some of the statements are false and others true. The identifications are context-dependent: they mirror the persistent tension in the Muslim community between tolerance and hate, condemnation and explanation, remembering and forgetting.

Croats from central Bosnia

One of the categories of Croats in Muslim discourse consists of 'Croats from Central Bosnia'. Before the war the Croat population in Stolac town made up 12 % of the total town population (in the whole municipality they made up 33 %; many of the Croats lived in the countryside). No figures were available during my fieldwork, but my estimate is that Croats were in the majority, even after many Muslims had returned. Many Croats, mostly from central Bosnia, have moved to Stolac during and after the war, a displacement that on a general level has been part of a broader political strategy of making a slice of Herzegovina (*Herceg-Bosna*) part of a greater Croatia (see Prologue). One could encounter a sad example of these policies when driving from Mostar to Stolac. Here one could pass through a small, newly built village looking like a ghost town. Between thirty and forty new houses had been built in a barren and grey landscape that made growing vegetables very difficult. Here several Croat families from central Bosnia lived, struggling to make a living. There were no shops of any kind – only these almost identical houses, all cement grey. The houses were only partly finished and will probably never be finished now, since the Herze-govinian Croats no longer receive funding from Croatia.[1] And this village is not unique. The Muslims of Stolac were well aware of the broader ethnic game the central Bosnian Croats were a part of:

Dino: Before only few Croats lived in town. These new Croats, they do not know Stolac, but were sent here by Tuđman, who paid for them, they came from central Bosnia. Before they were Bosnians, suddenly they became Croats.

However, some of my informants also feel that it was a little too easy for leading Croat politicians to convince the Croats to come and live in Stolac.

Suljeman: I have heard several times from those Croats from Bosnia now living in Stolac that they had been told that they could stay in our houses, that they were theirs. And this is how they think, they come to one's house and then it is their house. It is as if they were blind; they did not ask any questions. It is very easy to manipulate them. Often they think that they are the only ones who exist, that there is no Europe, no America, no universe, only them. It has been nearly impossible for them to understand that the Muslims were to return to Stolac, because they were told that we would never come back.

Even though my informants knew that the presence of the many central Bos-nian Croats in Stolac formed part of a political game, they were not always certain about the real circumstances behind the Croat population movements. Some Stolac Muslims were aware of incidents of Muslim violence and intimi-dation against Croats in central Bosnian villages; experiences which may have made them want to leave. In general, though, the Muslims of Stolac believe that the Croats moved by their own free will, or, more precisely, by the will of the nationalist politicians in Croatia and in Herzegovina. A prominent member of the SDA in Stolac had this interpretation.

---

1   Herzegovinian Croats do not have the same sympathy from the citizens in Croatia that they did before. After being perceived as spearheading the struggle for a Greater Croatia, they are back to their pre-war status as backward, uncivilised farmers from underdeveloped Herzegovi-na. Furthermore, many people in Croatia have been provoked by these boorish people driving in big Mercedes and engaging in luxury consumption financed by the Croatian government, while ordinary Croats have been getting poorer and poorer (Jansen 2000a: 120-3, 144; Grandits 2007).

Salko: Some of the central Bosnian Croats return home, some go abroad, and some are building houses down there [central Bosnia], and I hope they will leave [Stolac]. The only thing a Croat has here is the house HDZ[2] gave him. In Bosnia where he lived before, he has his house, his fields, his animals, his apples, his plums; he has a life waiting for him. And it is a fact that no Croats from central Bosnia were expelled. Tuđman wanted them to come here, because then it would be easier to divide Bosnia. I think Tuđman made a huge mistake. He could not move all the Croats from central Bosnia. Some of them wanted to stay there, even though it was a very fierce war. Did you hear what happened in the village Arkućer? There was a massacre in a village close to Vitez, and everybody was killed, even small babies, and it was Croatian soldiers who did this, and why did they do it? Only because they hoped it would provoke a big hatred in the Muslims, the Bosniaks, and that the Muslims then would drive the Croats out of there. And then they [Croat politicians] could say that: 'we cannot live together', that: 'we [the Croats] are expelled from here'. The Muslims were to drive out the Croats and then Bosnia was to have been divided. But things do not always go as planned.

The main issue associated with the presence of Croat displaced persons from central Bosnia in post-war Stolac is housing. I have met several Muslims in Stolac who lived in a rented house or with relatives because their own home was occupied by refugees. These Muslims obviously want the occupiers to leave, saying that they have no right to settle in their houses or flats. The Muslims of Stolac often say that it is precisely this group of Croats that is making trouble, burning down houses, beating up Muslims, vandalising the Muslim café, and generally intimidating the Muslims in the hope that they will give up the idea of returning to reclaim their property.

The line of reasoning is clear. Croats from central Bosnia were told that Muslims would never return. Suddenly, however, Muslims started to return and, even though the first step was to rebuild destroyed Muslim houses, it was clear that the repossession of occupied houses would be next thing to happen. Croats from central Bosnia occupying Muslim houses are therefore the ones who have the most to lose by the return process. Even so, many Muslims have a contradictory attitude towards them, feeling some pity for them as well. The Muslims can see the dilemma the displaced Croats are caught in, and say that the Croats have been betrayed. As Armin put it when talking about a friend whose house were occupied by central Bosnian Croats:

---

2   HDZ, though the name of a political party, is also a general term people use for influential local Croat rulers, see also below in the section about HDZ.

> They [the friend] pay KM150 [€75] in rent; they have built their own house, but now a family from Konjic lives there. The problem is that if they [the Croats] have to leave they will have nothing.

Or Munir:

> The central Bosnian Croats have been double-crossed. They were told that if they stayed [in central Bosnia], the Muslims would come and kill them, but if they came here to Stolac, nobody would touch them. In a way, I feel pity for them.

He laughed, not maliciously, but at his own words. On the one hand Munir thought that the Croats, coming as occupants, are only getting what they deserve; on the other hand, he could not help sympathising with them. I did not talk with many Croats in the course of my fieldwork, but Davor was one of them. He ran a small kiosk in Stolac. He came from a small village in central Bosnia, but fled to Croatia in 1995 and came to Stolac in 1997. He told me that he believed that Croats, Serbs and Muslims could probably live side-by-side again, but not together; history has shown that the fall of the Ottomans resulted in war, the fall of the Austro-Hungarians, the Kingdom of Yugoslavia, the fall of Tito – all resulted in war. He did not want his children to experience the same things; therefore, the ethnic groups had to live separately:

> We have different identities; we are different peoples with different language and culture. It is the same with Denmark, they are members of the EU, but they are still a people and it is important for them to be, they are not German or French.

He felt it was wrong that Croats took Muslim property, and he found that Stolac had become an ugly town. He said that even though he is Croat, he is a Bosnian Croat, and that he wanted to go back to his own town, but there was no work there. In Stolac he was able to support his wife and child. He was not proud of living in a Muslim house, but had nowhere else to go. When I talked to him, he had been told by the authorities (representatives of the OHR in Mostar) that he had to leave the occupied house in one month; but the house promised him by the HDZ was not yet finished, and there was no more money to build with.

Another arena of conflict is more cultural and relates to social knowledge. There is a feeling shared by all Muslims of Stolac that Croats from central Bosnian do not know the local culture and codes of behaviour; they simply do not fit in. One day I met Muhamed at one of the small bridges [ćuprija] in Stolac.

We admired the River Bregava for a while, then he started talking about the central Bosnian Croats:

> Today a lot of people from *Kakanj* [in central Bosnia] and other places live here, but they do not feel at home. When you meet them, you do not know who they are, they do not know you. In summertime when we sit down by *Bregava* – there is only one *Bregava* in the world – in summertime, we sit by the river and grill and bathe and have a good time, it is wonderful. But the Croats from central Bosnia, they do not know it [the river]. They are insecure towards it. They do not value it. There is a field down there where we play football, and afterwards we go and drink from the river; without the river there would be no town. But they do not appreciate it in the same way. I would never throw anything in the river, never. [Today there is a lot of garbage in the river, the riverside is becomming overgrown, and the wreck of a car mars the eastern part of the river].

Many Muslims think that a lot of the problems and tensions in the city would be solved if these strangers would only go back to their own villages, just as it would also be better for themselves to return to their place of origin. Emir explains why:

> The places where they come from, there everything is very primitive. Have you been north of Sarajevo? There are only mines. People work in the mines all day, they do not have running water in the houses, and the weather[3] is awful. Then they come down here and experience how wonderful it is here. Therefore they do not want to go back again. But they are different; they come from a different culture. Many [of us] would like to ask them to return, but that is also difficult.

Muslims attach various stereotypical characteristics to the Croats from central Bosnia: they say they are backwards but sly at the same time, having left miserable central Bosnia for pleasant Stolac. The point is, however, that such stereotypes are related to specific situations and experiences and, furthermore, that the problem with these people in the Muslims' eyes is not that they are Croats, but that they are strangers occupying someone else's houses.[4]

---

3   The Muslims of Stolac are generally very proud of their 'Mediterranean climate' as they like to call it.

4   Related problems exist elsewhere in Bosnia. In Sarajevo, for instance, there are tensions between Muslims from Sarajevo and Muslim refugees from eastern Bosnia (Steffanson 2007).

Croats from the countryside

Sometimes Croats from central Bosnia are merged into a larger category of the 'Croats from the countryside'. This in turn is linked to the central distinction between *kultura* (culture) and *nekultura* (non-culture), analysed in the previous chapter. Muslims of Stolac often use this distinction to explain the war and make sense of their ruined lives, to condemn bad deeds and locate responsibility. The wartime violence, 'urbicide', and the present lawlessness are thus basically seen as a struggle between people from the countryside and people from the town. Croats from the countryside living in Stolac are therefore considered illegitimate occupiers of both Muslim private houses and the urban public space.

Fahrudin: Those people living in the villages always wanted to move to town. Formerly this took place more normally. You bought a piece of land in the town and built a house. And you paid for it and it was yours. But those living here now, they want what they have taken over and do not want to give it back to the owners. So your house becomes my house.

Salko: It is a hard process to tell the Croats from the villages around Stolac to return to their properties. They have realised that it is much easier to live here than in their own villages. It is very hard for the young ladies to go back to their villages. The only thing waiting for them is cows and fields.

Like the central Bosnian Croats, the Croats from the countryside around Stolac are presented as uneducated strangers hungry for the options a town like Stolac can give them. Some Muslims think that the original Croats of Stolac accept the presence of both Croats from the countryside and from central Bosnia since, otherwise, they would become a minority again, and would then have to face the consequences of their own misdeeds. The point to bear in mind is that while this category of people constitutes a more or less well-defined class of Croats, their main characteristics relate not to their Croat ethnic identity but to a narrow-mindedness stemming from their lack of education and 'non-culture'. Its potential for resistance rests in its ability to disconnect ethnicity and bad deeds, and to make possible interaction with the ethnic Other by blaming only some particular Croats for the war. In this way it constitutes an element in the Muslims' counterdiscourse.

Croats from Stolac

'*Naši Hrvati*' ('our Croats') and '*naši domaći Hrvati*' ('our local/homegrown Croats') are expressions used about yet another category of Croats: '*Croats from Stolac*'. Local patriotism constitutes an important source of identification for the Muslims of Stolac (see chapter 11), and the 'homegrown' is more or less the icon of this identity: it is by definition superior. Even though it is not always consciously intended, therefore, the utterance '*naši domaći Hrvati*' has positive connotations. The class of Croats from Stolac is also in definitive opposition to that made up of Croats from both central Bosnia and the countryside, who clearly are not 'homegrown'.

When Muslims have social relations with Croats it is mainly within this group of people who they knew before the war. It is, however, not easy to resume relations in an ethnically segregated town like Stolac. Some Muslims told me that the HDZ forbids the Croats to mingle with the Muslims, sanctioning against fraternisation by means of access to jobs, houses and scholarships. Nihad, for instance, told me that when he came back to visit Stolac for the first time after the war he met several old Croat friends and acquaintances, but everybody turned their faces away, except for one man (a former colleague) who greeted Nihad. Naturally, this pleased Nihad, but the Croat was fired from his job a couple of days later. People also recount how when they returned to Stolac, former Croat friends would not dare to pay them a visit in daylight; only at night did they go to their Muslim friends' houses and welcome them back. According to Nihad, however, relations between Croats and Muslims have improved.

Nihad: Those who hid and turned their faces away now greet you.

Anvere (his wife): But it is only the *domaci* who do it, not the ones from the villages or central Bosnia.

Some consider that Muslims and Croats from Stolac have much more in common than Croats from Stolac do with Croats from central Bosnia: people originating from Stolac want to talk to each other, they are glad to see each other again, and they want to hear what happened during the war. Some Muslims also emphasise a level of understanding and respect between themselves and Croats from Stolac which outsiders do not understand. I asked Alija if the hostility against the Muslim café in the centre of town, which has been vandalised twice, was shared by all Croats.

The Croats living in Stolac before the war, they don't have much against it [the café], because they understand that we will be staying here in the future, and therefore there has to be something for us also. But the others living around Stolac [from the countryside] and those coming from central Bosnia, they are against [the café].

A common attachment to the town, which unites all 'true' citizens of Stolac, is also stressed when talking about Stolac Croats. The total destruction of the city is hard to grasp, and many Muslims express the idea that the wrongdoers must have come from outside. Some of them even consider that, if it were not for all the Croats from the countryside or from central Bosnia, the Croats who are originally from Stolac would return to their pre-war attitude and everything would be as it had been before. As Mensur expressed it, "If we only had real Stolac people [*pravi Stočani*], people born here in Stolac, then we would not have any problem. These people come from outside." Salko, a leading member of the SDA in Stolac, told me about his experiences during an interview:

It is a huge problem that the Croats in the leadership of HDZ here in Stolac come from the villages around Stolac, that they are not real Stolac natives. They do not feel as if Stolac is their own, you have probably noticed. Walking around Stolac, one can see it [garbage and car wrecks in the streets, ruined houses, graffiti etc.] I was asked, when the last mayor was sacked [a Croat], I was asked which mayor do you Bosniaks want. I said I very much wanted a Croat from Stolac [*gradski, urbani Hrvat*; a native, urban Croat]. One living here, who will notice that there is a lot of garbage that needs to be removed, one who feels for the town. Our last mayor Pero Raguz, he lived in Čapljina [some 40 km away], when he finished at work he closed the door and went home. And the other mayor [the one before Raguz] he was also from Čapljina. Now we have Kuzman, he is a little different. He wants to talk, he wants to drink coffee, sit together. He is married to a lady who comes from Stolac itself, and his wife has a big influence on him, and therefore he behaves differently than the other Croats. I knew him before I was married, and met him a couple of times when I was in prison camp. He was a hardliner in HDZ, but his wife and father-in-law have influenced him a lot. His wife was born in Stolac, and has lived her entire life here, and she definitely loves the town.

There is a dilemma embedded in such semi-romantic feelings, since Muslims also know that some of the Croats from Stolac participated in the expulsion of Muslims, and even in some of the atrocities, but they do not always know who did what and, more to the point, they do not know how the Croats feel about the expulsion of the Muslims. Did they support it or were they too afraid to stand up and oppose it? Croats from Stolac are therefore simultaneously seen as *pravi Stočani* who identify with the town and respect the Muslims, as well as the very people who let their former friends down. I asked Emir if it had been people from Stolac who picked them up them when they were expelled:

Emir: The majority of the Croats from Stolac participated in catching us, but those giving the orders, they were not from here. Those who gave the orders came from somewhere else.

TK: Were they forced to capture you?

Emir: I think that the greater part didn't want to, but there were also those who did it very gladly. The Croats who lived here always had to prove that they were real Croats. The Croats living in 100 % Croat-dominated towns think in another way than Croats living in mixed towns.

The ambiguous feeling towards the Stolac Croats also results in different strategies of interaction.

Osman: In the beginning [when he returned] it was a kind of tough with the Croats. But I walked proudly in the streets, and I was also pleased if some Croats greeted me. I just went for a little walk to see if there was somebody who would say something to me. In the beginning only a few would say something, even though I smiled to them and hoped they would say something to me, but now it is different. Now I go to town and meet the people I worked with before and we shake hands and greet each other, as if nothing had happened.

When I referred to this strategy of 'smiling to the Croats' in the course of a conversation with another informant, he commented that he would never humiliate himself by doing that:

They owe us an apology. They are the ones who did something wrong, not me. If I met someone in the street, whom I knew did something wrong – and here everybody knows what everybody has done – then I would pretend that I did not see him.

In Stolac lived a native Croat whom people labeled as a little crazy. In a way, he symbolised the dilemma that the category 'Croats from Stolac' entails. Ivan was a small, thick-set man who rode around Stolac on a woman's bike, and he was related to some of the powerful Croats in town. He stayed in Stolac during the whole war. I sometimes met him on the (Muslim) bus going to Mostar talking to everybody including himself, and he seldom payed the fare. People felt a little embarrassed in his presence; at the same time, they had sympathy for him. He was not crazy before the war. At that time he worked at the hospital. Some people said that the war was what drove him crazy. Emir told me that Ivan cycled around Stolac shouting at the Croats who 'did something' during the war: "I know what you have done, I know who blew up the mosques, you are criminals." Once he came to Mostar in the Muslim part of town wearing a cap with a *Šahovnica*,[5] but nobody said anything. Some 'big Croats' (*veliki Hrvati*, powerful and strongly nationalist Croats) lived opposite Ivan, I was told that they took part in the destruction of the mosques. In the window facing towards these Croats, Ivan had a big poster of Franjo Tuđman,[6] he said that he would not remove it until these big Croats were caught and sent to The Hague. He wanted to show that he was a bigger Croat than they were. Once Ivan gave a list of all the Croat war criminals to one of my informants while all the 'big Croats' sitting in the café nearby were watching. He also sometimes went to the police station shouting out who did what. Occasionally he kicked the supposed wrongdoers in the shins or placed small notes in their cars. As people said, he was a good Croat and he was crazy, but not totally crazy.

Muslim attitudes towards Croats from Stolac depend on the situation, therefore. In my view, the category of 'good Croats from Stolac' is especially invoked in statements about the legitimate presence and property claims of the Muslims in post-war Stolac, and about the possible expulsion of all its non-native citizens. Speaking more generally, the category of the Croats from Stolac is also an attempt to reconcile the tensions between forgiveness and hate, oblivion and remembering – between resistance to the world's ethnicisation and the use of ethnic categories to make sense of the world. By creating the category of the 'Croats from Stolac', the Muslims have constructed a group of people they can interact with without persistently having to question the very foundation of the interaction. That is probably why it is important for the Muslims to insist that the Croats from Stolac are 'glad to have them back', or for example that some

---

5   The Croat coat of arms and strong nationalist symbol.

6   Posters of Franjo Tuđman are placed several places in Stolac in public buildings. For many Croats he is a hero, supporting the Herzegovinian Croats' fight for an independent state, *Herceg-Bosna*. For the Muslims such posters signal ethnic violence and implacability. Ivan's deliberate use of Croatian nationalist symbols is also a reinterpretion and challenge to the meanings attached to Croat identity. He showed that he was proud of being a Croat, but at the same time he distanced himself from the ethnic violence and the implacability; he did interact with the Muslims.

Stolac Croats attended a Muslim's funeral because 'they can't forget the good times we had together either.'

Croats from Croatia

One might expect that the misdeeds of Croatian soldiers during the war and the physical and political violence that have taken place even after the Dayton agreement would have affected the Muslims' general image of the Croatian Croats; after all, a lot of the more organised violence and a lot of the propaganda were orchestrated from Croatia. Croatian army groups operated in Herzegovina, and the military objective of Croatia and the Herzegovinian Croats was to make Herzegovina part of a greater Croatia. It therefore surprised me that I never heard anything really negative about Croatia or about 'Croats from Croatia'. It appeared to me that for many Muslims of Stolac, Croatia was still a part of their sense of self. In this connection, it is important to remember that such attractions as the beautiful coast of Croatia and the old town of Dubrovnik are less than an hour's drive away from Stolac. Before the war, the coast was not thought of as Croatian but rather Yugoslavian, and people in Stolac were proud of its beauty. In a way, people still reckon Croatia – especially the coast – as theirs. On a number of occasions people asked if I had been to the coast, and said that: 'You should go, it is so beautiful down there'. Also they would tell me about their splendid summer holidays and weekends there.

One example of my informants' positive attitude towards Croatia relates to Croatian television. As part of the discrimination against the Muslims in Stolac, they were not able to watch Bosnian TV programmes unless they had a satellite dish. The annoyance people felt, though, was due more to the intention to discriminate than to a preference for Bosnian TV programmes. Even when the OSCE sponsored an all-Bosnian Muslim TEST channel that was broadcast two hours a day, people still supplemented it with Croatian news programmes. Even those with a satellite dish often preferred Croatian programmes because they felt the quality of the programmes was better – better movies and better documentary programmes. Young people preferred Croatian channels because they showed the most exciting sports events, and the Croatian basketball league was clearly better than the Bosnian one. In short, though people did miss watching television programmes from Sarajevo and the local channel from Mostar, they were still seen as only a supplement to Croatian programmes. Many mornings while my hosts and I were eating breakfast, the TV would be on in the background, and my landlady loved the programmes with food recipes and folk culture, many of which could easily be disliked on ideological grounds, as these programmes were obviously intended to be part of a Croatian nation-building process centred on shared cultural values. When the weather forecast was sent, lovely pictures from the Croatian coast covered the screen; we all agreed that the coast was picturesque and unique.

People also generally respected Stipe Mesić, Croatian president since the elections in 2000. They appreciated him as a responsible politician, especially because, as the Muslims put it: he believes that the Croats in Herzegovina have to realise they live in Bosnia Herzegovina and not in Croatia. My informants' positive attitude towards Croatia is also apparent from the experiences of those who had recently been at the Croatian coast, who said that it was easier and more relaxed to interact with the Croats there than in Stolac. "They know what they are, and do not have to prove it all the time, in opposition to Stolac, where the Croats persistently have to prove they are real Croats," as Alija said. This corroborates experiences people have had when visiting pure Croat cities in Herzegovina. Once Emir told me how he and his brother had made a business trip to Ljubuški, a pure Croat town next to the Croatian border, a forty-minute drive from Stolac:

> We had been in Ljubuški one day to sell firewood. When we came to the town, we were quite nervous, because virtually only Croats live there, about 95 %. But when we arrived at the market where you sell firewood on Mondays, then we said that we came from Stolac and our names were Emir and Senad, then they knew we were Muslims [most Muslim first names reveal one's ethnicity], but they were friendly. They helped us get the firewood sold and we drank coffee together. It was fantastic sitting and drinking coffee with Croats like that. It was incredible talking so pleasantly with them; they were kind to us. And later we met them at *Hrgud* [the mountain east of Stolac where they go to fell trees for wood] and we helped each other. Before going to Ljubuški my mother had said that we should try to sell the firewood here [in Stolac], and if we didn't sell it, it couldn't be helped. She didn't think we should leave, but we did.

The category 'Croats from Croatia' adds yet another piece of complexity to the general ethnic stereotype of Croats, and is as such part of the Muslims' counter-discourse.

Ethnic denunciations

I have argued that Stolac Muslims use non-ethnic moral judgements, that is moral classifications and condemnations through reference to non-ethnic cultural categories such as *politika*, *pošteni ljudi*, and *nekultura*. This is not to say that ethnic denunciation does not exist. Sometimes Muslims harshly criticise

Croats in general. Such stereotypes are obviously not counterdiscursive in that they show that ethnic thinking has in some way become automatic. Nevertheless, such statements should be seen as but a part of the overall complex categorisation of Croats, as they are clearly related to specific situations and experiences. For example, when people say that 'all Croats are fascists', this does not mean that they are incapable of different and diverging utterances in other situations, as we have seen in the nuanced judgments above. The Muslims' ethnic denunciations, therefore, constitute but one category of Croats among others.

It is, however, not clear for me to what extent I am able to fully objectify the Muslims' ethnic denunciations. While conducting fieldwork in Stolac, I became aware of how I myself interpreted the local world by using ethnic stereotypes, as some incidents from my fieldwork show. Once I drove by car with my family from Denmark to Stolac. Passing through the Serb Republic I was afraid of harassment and of being robbed by people in the area. And I remember the relief I felt on entering the Federation. My wife was surprised by my nervousness. When trying to explain the causes of my fear, I realised that a lot of the fear must have come from the stories I had heard from my informants about the evil deeds of the Serbian people. Reflecting on this fear and the stereotypes I had internalised, I recalled the insecurity I had felt when watching football matches at the stadium in Stolac, which is only used by Croats. I had thought that all these Croat spectators looked the same, with their military haircuts and arrogant grins. I also remembered the nervousness I had felt when sitting in Croat cafés or walking in Croat-dominated parts of Stolac in the evening, in contrast to the feeling of security I felt in Muslim areas. I often felt that Croatian shop clerks were unfriendly, and I felt hate and anger watching Croats drive by in their big, expensive Mercedes. Some of these feelings were probably generated by the misery I saw among the Muslims for which the Croats had been responsible, and the horrible stories I heard in Stolac about the Croat misdeeds. However, I also think that simply being among Muslims in Stolac had caused some of these stereotypical reactions to become a part of me.

For these reasons, I find it reasonable to assume that ethnic stereotyping does exist among the Muslims of Stolac at a level too deep for me to objectify. I will therefore turn to the generalisations I *can* objectify and see how such ethnic stereotypes relate to specific situations. I begin with a list of related negative categories used to describe and generalise about the Croats one wants to criticise: HDZ, nationalist, war-criminal, violent, fascist, rich, corrupt, criminal, *veliki Hrvati* ('big Croats'), arrogant, undemocratic, Ustashe, exile-Croat, nonconciliatory/provocative. In what follows, I will elaborate on the most important of these categories.

HDZ

The HDZ (*Hrvatska Demokratska Zajednica*; the Croatian Democratic Union) is a prominent player both in local politics and also in the Muslims' categorisations. To the Muslims, the HDZ is much more than a political party. It is the quintessence of Croatian discrimination, corruption, violence, fascism, uncompromising attitude and nationalism. Therefore, saying that 'the Croats are all members of the HDZ' is a strongly negative and ethnically charged utterance. But at the same time, it also expresses a resignation on Muslims' behalf. In their daily life, they long for progress in relation to coexistence with the Croats, work opportunities, the economy, political stability, etc. But more often than not, they experience retrogression, sudden outbursts of violence, nationalist manifestations, scandals of corruption, and economic recession. So saying that all Croats are members of the HDZ is not primarily a declaration that all Croats are fascist; rather it is a way to say that they do not try to change the present bad situation in an active way. For instance after the general election in November 2000, when 90 % of the Croatian vote had fallen to the HDZ, some Muslims felt betrayed by the Croats. The election confirmed their belief that the Croats either did not want to resist, or did not have the courage to resist the nationalist politics that had ruined the country. In short, identifying Croats with the HDZ is directed both at the Croats' passivity and their active misdeeds. Furthermore, it is a way for the Muslims to criticise Croats for being easy to manipulate. Suljeman's reply when I asked him if the war had changed people's mentality confirms this interpretation:

> No! That's my opinion. It is not easy to change one's mentality, maybe the young and the children. Maybe it happened for the small children, because they grew up in such times. It is easy to convince a Croat child who goes in a Croat school that they have to learn to speak Croatian and learn the Croatian history. Most of them are confused.

In January 2000, there were demonstrations in Split (Croatia) against the trial of the Croatian officer Mirko Norac, who was accused of having killed civilian Serbs in 1991 in the village of Gospic in Croatia. I watched the demonstrations on TV while one of my informants laughingly commented: "Look, there are lots of Herzegovinians, [he knew them by their banners], the HDZ arranges the demonstrations and gives ignorant farmers a free journey and KM50 (€25) if they participate."

The church

The Catholic Church is also depicted by Muslims as a major manipulator of the Croats, in close cooperation with the HDZ. They say that on Sundays the priests tell the Croats how to vote, what to say, and what to think. Related to this is the view that Croats are not really true believers, they only pretend to be. As some Muslims say 'God is only one.' This saying means that it does not matter *what* God you believe in, the important thing is *that* you believe, as true believers will always behave righteously towards their fellow men. The crimes of the Croats against the Muslims are therefore proof of the weakness of their faith. Muhamed made the following associations:

> After the Second World War, the Chetniks left something in the Serbs, and Ustashe left something in the Croats. And even though this war is over, many people have been killed, and everything could happen again. Like when you are weeding, if you don't remove the roots it can grow again, the right thing is to remove the roots, but this hasn't been done after this war. Right now, if all the UN forces were to withdraw, the problems would come again. That's how it is. We are sick and tired of this. But I don't think it is the same with them [the Croats], that's the kind of people they are, that's the truth. They love neither Muslims nor Serbs, nor Englishmen, nor Americans, nor Chinese, nor Danes, nor Finns, they only love themselves…They want to show the whole world that they are the greatest Catholics in the world. A real Catholic is what you are in your soul, you cannot show that. You just have to go to church and pray to your God and be a decent human being, and in that way, you show yourself. For instance if I take a gun and shoot a couple of people and go to the mosque and say *Allahu Akbar* [Allah is great] and then I am forgiven…but it doesn't work that way.

'Pure fascism'

The Croats are perceived as being generally better off than the Muslims, taking all the jobs and controlling the local political scene. Despite this, Muslims say that Croats are always complaining of discrimination by the 'international community'. This is felt to be a provocation by the Muslims of Stolac, since they consider themselves the ones who suffered and who still face severe discrimination. At the time of the election in November 2000, the HDZ made a very controversial election poster with the slogan: *Opredeljenje ili istrebljenje* (Determination or extermination). The OHR banned the poster a week before the election for being too provocative and aggressive. Some of the posters in Mostar were removed, or white semi-transparent pieces of paper were placed over the second part of the slogan. Nevertheless, in many other places, the posters were not removed and fliers printed with the same slogan were abundant. The symbolism of the poster focused on the threat against Croat national identity, represented by what was seen as forced coexistence with the other ethnic groups, and the inability to express and maintain Croat national characteristics. From this nationalist viewpoint, it was the Croats who were the victims. The slogan was also an attempt by HDZ leaders to restore ethnic loyalty in a period when HDZ domination was decreasing (Grandits 2007). One evening I talked to Nihad about this poster, and this is how I recalled the conversation afterwards:

Nihad: It is a provocation. Have you seen the poster with the slogan *Opredeljenje ili istrebljenje*? What is that? It plays on people's fear: extermination [*istrebljenje*]. We are the ones who were exterminated. They are fascists. But the slogan has been forbidden. Nicolas [my second name], have you seen the crosses put up in different places [the three-metre-tall white or grey concrete crosses placed in the countryside in Herzegovina].

TK: Yes I have seen them, those white ones along the road?

Nihad: Yes, and in front of the municipal office [*opština*], why do they have to do it? If they want them in their garden or on their houses it is up to them, but not these public places, why do they have to do it? It is simple provocation. When I was in prison camp, we were forced to kiss the Croatian flag, and it was painted on our foreheads. The old man Rizvanbegovic, they painted a cross on his forehead. Who do they think they are? And the street names, they are changed, before the road was called *Begovinska* now its name is *Banovinska*. It is pure fascism [*čisti fašizam*].

He then went on talking about the day when he was picked up by Croatian soldiers and placed in prison camp.

Croat nature

Specific experiences can lead Muslims to invoke negative Croat character traits, such as deceitfulness or moral cowardice. One central experience is, naturally, the feeling of betrayal. Once trusted friends and acquaintances suddenly let people down, either by participating in the violent expulsion of the Muslims or simply by failing to act, even to warn those they knew. Such deceit is difficult to come to terms with. Sometimes Muslims explain this shift in attitude by ascribing it to the Croat mentality, along the lines of, 'They let us down because they are that kind of people and we were stupid to trust them.' Once Safet told me about an episode from the local post office where he had been to get his driver's licence. The clerk working there was an old Croat acquaintance. Safet was therefore astonished when he was formally asked to give his name. "But you know me", Safet responded: "and then he asked me about my name once again." Safet's friends were also amazed; they know that before the war Safet and this man had coffee together several times.

Safet: When I was caught, and was sitting on the truck, I saw him driving the car behind us.

Sernad: We have had coffee with thousands [meaning we had many Serbian and Croatian friends].

Safet: When the war started, he [this Croat] said that Muslims are good and Serbs evil, *šta ćeš?* [what can you do?]

Omer: Do you remember when I told you that Croats are not good?

The last sentence is Omer's way of indicating that he knew that the Croats were bad all along, and that they always will be. Today, distrust is very pronounced between Stolac Muslims and Croats. When I asked Muslims whether it was possible for the two groups to live together again, many responded that it was too soon. The feeling of not being able to trust Croats is one of the major obstacles to (re)building relations with them. In addition to being deceitful, Croats are also sometimes depicted as born nationalists or as having a tradition for committing genocide, as expressed in the following excerpt from an interview with a father and his son. Here history is used as a frame of reference linking up Croat atrocities in the Second World War and in the recent war.

Aziz: During the Second World War exactly the same happened to the Serbs here in Stolac as has happened to us now from the Croatian side. The Croats caught the Serbs and threw them in big mass graves in the ground. For instance they tied together thirty people and threw them in these holes, and that's why they escaped from the Croats during this war.

Senad: It happened in '41 and '42.

Aziz: During Second World War the Croats killed a lot of Serbs from the Stolac area, and during this war they did nearly the same to us.

The Muslims are confident about their own righteousness, and some believe that the Croats must also understand they have behaved inexcusably, but are just too ashamed to admit it. Feeling this way is part of the Muslims' attempt to piece together their world. Right and wrong still exist, even in the minds of the Croats, even though the war has made one doubt.

Muhammed: I don't want you to think that we are lying to you. If you sit down with a Croat family, they may tell you something totally different, therefore it would be the best to take a Croat family living in Stolac and a Muslim one also living here, then both families can tell each other what they have to tell. I believe every Muslim family would agree to such a conversation, but no Croatian families would.

Mensur: Sure.

Muhammed: They wouldn't go along with it because they are ashamed.

Context-dependent condemnations

Fierce statements resting on ethnic stereotypes are often expressed during talks about nationalism, war-related violence, and post-war political discrimination. The fact that a Muslim says, for instance, that 'all Croats are fascists', or that 'they will never change', therefore does not demonstrate anything. It is important to take such utterances in their context and to know what the same person says about Croats under different circumstances. Sometimes Stolac Muslims state that all Croats are and have always been fascists, and at other times they insist that you cannot group them all together because only Croats coming from outside Stolac cause trouble. This suggests that even though the war and war-related violence have clearly carved out different ethnic identities, these identities remain complex, fragmented, inconsistent, and very much related to the situation in which they are employed and in which they function as ordering devices. I shall give some examples where the relevance of such contexts as nationalism, war-related violence and post-war political discriminations are particularly visible.

One day, I was having coffee with Nusret and his father in their house. Nusret's father was talking about classical Bosnian architecture. Then on a sudden impulse he fetched a book from his bookshelf which documented the massacres of Muslims committed by the Germans and the Chetniks during the Second World War. The book was published in 1991. It was a horrifying read. The inhabitants of entire villages were killed: the old, the young, everybody. Small children were thrown in the air and run through with bayonets. Nusret's father showed me the names and age of the victims; everything was systematically registered in the book. Nusret carefully attended his father's words. His father showed his grandfather's name, as well as the names of other members of his family who were massacred in a village not far away. He showed me pictures of soldiers 'practising' throat slicing on civilians. Nusret was laughing, but a sad laughter indicating madness. By showing me this, Nusret's father meant something like: 'Look how crazy these Chetniks were, and still are, they are barbarians.' The pictures he displayed illustrated Chetniks with the typical long hair and long beard. "They looked the same during this war," Nusret commented. His father also told us about some episodes from the Second World War where Croatian soldiers dressed as Muslims (at that time the different ethnic groups dressed differently) decimated Serbian villages. They were disguised so that the Serbs would afterwards take revenge on the Muslims: but the trick was revealed because some of the survivors had noticed how the Croats addressed each other by their real, non-Muslim names. We then got up and Nusret asked if he and I should step outside in the nice weather. He then started the car and drove towards the Serb Republic; the unmarked border was located only a couple of kilometres down the road. He asked if I had been there before, I said "no." "OK, let's go" he said, "but we will stay in the car, I will not get out." "Why not?" "No, it is not entirely safe." We passed the black market in the no-man's-land between the Serb Republic and the Federation: "Here the criminals sell all kinds of things." We continued driving and after a couple of minutes: "Now we are in the Serb Republic, in Chetnik-land, just look," he was pointing at a huge pile of garbage by the roadside (not actually any larger than the one in his own street). "You can see they are different." We drove the tour in order for me to see these 'others' that his father had been depicting just five minutes earlier with the book. Nusret said that he was not feeling well, that we had seen enough and that we should return. But the sightseeing was not over. Coming back to Stolac we continued through the town and stopped at a hillcrest overlooking a new part of the town where forty or fifty new Croat houses were under construction.[7] Nusret: "I will show you something very symbolic, these are Croat houses funded by HDZ and the former power in Croatia, that is a way of doing ethnic cleansing." On our way back we passed the site in the centre of town where the old mosque from 1519 used to be located. Nusret: "Now it is a car park, and over there [he pointed] where the HDZ is now holding a meeting [regarding the referendum of November 11, 2000, where Croats were to vote for the independence of a Croatian miniature state *Herceg-Bosna*], that was a Bosnian house before; before all these houses were Bosnian. By the way, the president of the

7   These new houses were built to accommodate some of the Croats who came from central Bosnia. They are situated systematically on a big piece of flat land. I was told that one never erected houses here before the war, because it was some of the best farming land in Stolac. The building project was not finished when I left Stolac; like many other of its kind it stopped when Tuđman died and the new government took over in Croatia.

Bosnian Croats stated this morning that from this day forward he will have nothing to do with either the West or Bosnia Herzegovina." Nusret clearly signalled with a shake of his head what he thought about that. I know that he saw the referendum as nothing more than a provocation. Passing the only Muslim hairdresser in town, he read aloud the graffiti spray-painted on the shop's white wall: 'This is not Croatian state but nonetheless Croatian property' [*Ovo nije hrvatska država, ali jest hrvatski prostor*].[8] The guided tour was over and it had shown me the enemy in no uncertain terms, as well as the innocent victims. We had seen the Chetniks and we had seen the Croat fascists and their symbols.

Knowledge is always contextual, and I am aware that this 'sightseeing' tour was an explicit statement caused by my presence as a 'war tourist.' But this does not make it untrue. The point is rather that it was not the whole truth, but rather part of a wide-ranging and contradictory way of categorising the ethnic Other. The context of the sightseeing was the stories Nusret father's had told, and in addition the tour was influenced by the impressions we received driving through Stolac – seeing the spot where the mosque had been, the meeting attended by the HDZ elite, and the nationalist graffiti. Nusret was clearly sincere in his feelings and statements denunciating the Croats and Serbs. But on other occasions he could also be rather neutral when talking about Croats, for example when he stressed that interacting with the Croats at the coast was unproblematic. I also know for a fact that he still had a couple of Croatian friends in Stolac. So the stereotypical image he presented to me during the sightseeing tour was just one statement about the Croats among others, even though it was a central one.

Another example of how fierce condemnation of Croats is tied to the (speech) situation comes from an interview with Muhamed, a friend of his, and his mother. The ethnic condemnations first appeared when the talk turned to the subject of violence.

Muhamed: First they captured the men who were ready to take up arms, and then only women and small children were left. A lot of people didn't want to leave, they just wanted to stay in their houses. With force they dragged them to the lorries, the elderly and the children, and drove them to Blagaj or Jablanica. It was a terrible sight. A lot of children, the elderly who didn't have anything to

---

8   The message of this graffiti has to be understood in relation to the Croatian politics of ethnic segregation. The Croats wanted Stolac to be only for Croats. Then the Muslims started to return, their presence protected by the SFOR, and today there can be no doubt that they will stay. But the local HDZ do not to accept this fact; they therefore continue the segregation where it is possible. The graffiti can be seen as communicating something like: 'OK, you have come back, you have opened a café, some shops and now this hairdresser, but Stolac is still ours!'

eat or drink. When they were arrested the soldiers checked them to see if they had money or gold. They had to undress completely, they [the soldiers] took their golden rings and bracelets, and afterwards they had to walk ten km from the lorries [to Blagaj]. Most people knew that something was going to happen [before they were expelled]. Some were relieved, because it is hard to face the thought of somebody knocking at your door, beating you up and plundering you, every day. Maybe they might rape the women or the girls.

Mother: All the women were searched at the school.

Friend: It happened one or two hours before they were expelled.

Mother: We had to go into a classroom where three or four Croats were sitting, and then they checked us. And then a girl came in, maybe fifteen, sixteen, seventeen years old, and she said 'no!' and then they said she had to take off all her clothes so they could check if she had money hidden in her underwear. I have seen such situations myself.

Friend: They are sexual maniacs.

Mother. There was a girl just before me and she had to take off all her clothes even though she was only 15 years old. When she came out she was crying and she told the others what they [the soldiers] had done to her. The little girl was daughter of [X].

TK: Was it planned or was it impulsive?

Muhamed: Everything was planned, everything. Today some of the men who did these things have expensive cars and they own some of the cafes in Stolac. Do you know how such a man will end up? Like an animal [*živina*, vermin]. Such people don't die, they rot to death. [*krepati*; there is no equivalent English word, but humans *umiru*, animals *krepaju*].

Like Nusret, Muhamed was usually a tolerant person who tried to avoid fierce accusations. He just wanted to get on with his life, provide for his family and stay out of trouble. But the context of the speech provoked his fierce burst of anger directed at the Croats.

The last example: one night the TV news had a story about some Croats who had mined a Partisan graveyard in Zagreb, and an HDZ politician made some nationalist comments justifying the mining. This incident really angered my hosts for several reasons. The war in Stolac had in some way started with the mining of the Partisan monument at the centre of Stolac, and furthermore for the Muslims, Tito's Partisans were in general seen as liberators and figured as an important part of their national imagining (of Yugoslavia). Finally, the destruction of the memorial was also a way of rejecting the past and the time of ethnic coexistence.[9] My hosts started making generalisations like 'fascist', 'bastards', and so on – at that moment Croats were truly the enemy.

'Good Croats'

The last category I will introduce is more consciously linked to resistance. It relates to the identification of '*good Croats*'. It struck me how many people had one or two stories about some 'good Croats' they knew. It was as if people collected such stories. I deliberately use the term 'stories' because they were commonly told in a clearly dramatic form. Here are some examples.

I

One day when visiting Ljubica and Armin I was served some lovely white wine, which I commented on.

Ljubica: Yes, it is homemade, my aunt brought it, she got it from her neighbours, they are Croats! Yes! My aunt told me how when she was riding with *Bregavatrans* [the Muslim bus company], two Croatian women boarded the bus.

TK: Was it the first time she saw Croatian women in the bus?

Ljubica: Yes. And it was two women my aunt knew. One of them was one of her good friends, but it was my aunt who had to make contact [*prva zvala*: called first], they did not do it. They hadn't talked for ten years, and my aunt said: 'come and sit!' and then they talked. Now it is difficult to make the first step, but one side has to do it. This woman and my aunt gave birth at the same time, they were at the hospital together, and then my mother did not have enough milk in her breasts to give to her daughter, and then she was given milk by this Croat woman. Yes that's how it was then, and you don't forget such things.

II

Miho told me that he has a piece of land outside Stolac where he grows grapes. Luckily it was not destroyed during the war because the Croat who owns the neighbouring field took care of his field. A vineyard has to be continually maintained; otherwise it becomes useless. Miho was therefore very grateful towards this Croat, who also lent him some machinery when he returned, because Mi-

---

9   The Croats who blew up the memorial, however, probably also had other motives (see e.g. Bax 1997).

ho's own had been stolen. What he did not mention was that this Croat harvested grapes from Miho's field for many years and had probably come to think of it as his own – though I do not want to belittle the significance of the unproblematic transfer of the land.

III

Mensur once told me about a Croatian friend who went to his house and removed the furniture after Mensur and his family had been expelled in 1993. When Mensur returned almost five years later, the Croat gave the furniture back. As Mensur explained: "He knew what was going to happen [the looting of the Muslim houses], and that we would need the things when we returned, because when we would return there wouldn't be anything, he is a good friend today." On another occasion, Mensur told me about how he had in fact phoned this friend to ask him to remove and take care of his possessions. Nevertheless, Mensur reckons it was a remarkable act.

IV

This is an excerpt from my field notes:

> Meliha told me yesterday that a Croat took care of her clothes and some tablecloths and that she got them back after the war. It was one of these stories about the 'good Croats.' I said that it sure was a nice thing to do, and after a while Meliha said: "Yes, but she also took some tables and wardrobes from the house, and she hasn't returned these things." This was a new twist, not so black and white: obviously, this Croat had spotted an opportunity to enrich herself, and Meliha knows this – why then did Meliha start by telling the story of how the Croat had helped her?

I do not dispute the correctness of the story. It seems that people sometimes deliberately omit negative aspects, but this is not the point. People could still choose not to speak about 'good Croats', or they could read events differently. So when informants presented me with such anecdotal accounts I saw it as a more or less deliberate choice which served at least two functions. First, these stories work against the erosion of the moral world that the war and war-related violence have caused. They express the idea that good and righteous action still persists even in a world which seems to be completely morally flawed; it is still possible to believe in the goodness of a fellow person, even one of different ethnic background. Second, these stories resist the ethnic generalisations and stereotypes which I outlined in the previous section. The use of Croats' individual names has faded away after the war at the expense of the general expression 'they', a development some Muslims explicitly acknowledge. The narratives about 'good Croats' can be seen as working in the opposite direction, as attempts to reinstall the personal pronouns and personalise the relationship towards those Croats one still feels or wants to feel connected to. It is a strategy that attempts to personalise relations which the war-related violence has depersonalised.

This chapter has focused on the production by Stolac Muslims of various categories of Croats. What this intra-ethnic categorisation shows is an internal complexity full of contrasts and differences: there are 'evil fascists' on one side and 'good Croats' on the other, Croats belonging to the city and Croats perceived as foreigners, Croats from the beautiful Croatia and the greedy and uncultured ones from the countryside. Even when Stolac Muslims make fierce and generalising condemnations, these are rather specific and linked with discussions of violence or discrimination. It is therefore possible to view this complexity as part of a Muslim counterdiscourse resisting ethnic categories: stated simply, the complex and fragmented way the Muslims of Stolac use the ethnic label 'Croat' is also an implicit denial of its very relevance.

Summary of Part II

The chapters making up Part II have been the first of two steps showing how the Muslims of Stolac remake their unmade world (the next step is taken in Part III). For most people the war came as a shock. The three ethnic groups had lived unproblematically side-by-side, and on a daily basis ethnic affiliation was simply not relevant. Most people had had a job or were following a course of study and generally speaking had few worries. Then suddenly the war came like a bolt from the blue and totally destroyed people's lives. In order to make some sense of it all, now that the war has ended, a central question has been: who are they, the ones who did this to us? I have outlined four answers to this question, which also constitute four categories of people. The first is *politika*, through which an abstract and morally loaded class of people is constructed to account for the war. *Pošteni ljudi* is another cultural classification, operating at the local and everyday level, used for evaluating concrete actions and persons. Thirdly, 'people from the countryside' and more generally 'people without culture' (*nekultura*) make up yet another non-ethnic grouping used to account for the war. Finally, the Muslims of Stolac distinguish between various kinds of Croats, identified with reference to dissimilar values and mentalities. This very complexity is a challenge to any monolithic representation of the Croat ethnic identity.

These categorisations are part of the Muslims' counterdiscourse, which argues for the possibility of future existence among the different ethnic groups. The element of resistance in this counterdiscourse is the shift away from ethnic categories towards non-ethnic cultural and moral categories in order to condemn actions, claim properties, explain misfortunes and changes, and make the world predictable and possible to live in once again. This 'shift' I have also called recontextualisations of the narratives of destruction. The resistance, or the recontextualisations, therefore, need to be seen in relation to the overwhelming nationalist discourses outlined at the beginning of Part II. Here I showed how the nationalist politics and the war profoundly changed the landscape of identification at all levels of social life, and how ethnoreligious identity had been foregrounded in both the public and private spheres to become the most important identity, determining or influencing nearly all others. There were thus two contrasting discourses present in the lives of my informants: a nationalist antagonistic discourse seeking to make ethnic affiliation as well as ethnic segregation the most important aspects of life, and on the other hand the counterdiscourse which worked to downplay ethnicity and facilitate interethnic coexistence. The counterdiscourse is not an ideological, deliberate or even fully conscious endeavour, it is rather a steady reintroduction and reshaping of already existing cultural categories. Furthermore, it is impossible to fully separate those situations in which categories like *politika*, *nepošteni ljudi* or 'Croats from the countryside' are used as the basis for implicit ethnic condemnation, from those situations in which they are used as implicit critique of the ethnicisation of the social landscape. This is not due to a lack of analytical tools, but because these two implicit and sometimes explicit tactics are interwoven and hard to separate, even for people themselves. Blame and exclusion of the ethnic factor exist simultaneously with a desire for ethnic coexistence and dissociation from the exclusiveness of nationalist politics and rhetoric. This tension constitutes one of the central features of the everyday life among the Muslims of Stolac in their attempts to make sense of the world, which the war and war-related violence have unmade, and it results in a feeling of personal and societal confusion. As already stated, people may act and appear in self-contradictory ways, not because they are schizophrenic, but because the social situation is.

Part III
Who are we, since this was done to us?

Introduction to Part III

I never thought of myself as a Muslim. I don't know how to pray, I never went to mosque, I'm European, like you. I do not want the Arab world to help us, I want Europe to help us. But now, I do have to think of myself as a Muslim, not in a religious way, but as a member of a people. Now we are faced with obliteration, I have to understand what it is about me and my people they wish to obliterate. (A young Bosnian Muslim soldier; quoted in Vulliamy 1994: 65).

In Part III I examine the ways my informants identify themselves as a group. Before the war, Muslim ethnic identity was primarily related to practices embedded in the routines of everyday life, partly non-conscious, and only one aspect of identity among others. With the war this changed. Ethnic identity became a matter of life or death, Muslim ethnic identity became *the* most important identity, and Muslims became much more aware of themselves as constituting an isolated and defined group. On the basis of these changes one might expect that a religiously based nationalist identity highlighting difference and arguing for ethnic segregation would prevail among the Muslims of Stolac, but this is not the case. I will analyse four different types of identification among the Muslims of Stolac, making up the second half of the Muslims' counterdiscourse. Taken as a whole, the identifications reflect a world characterised by complexity and contradictions rather than clarity and simplicity; a world that rests upon pre-war everyday inter-ethnic experiences and cultural categories rather than the more recent ideological discourses of nationalist exclusion. Inertia seems to be a leitmotiv.

In Chapter 4, I outlined the emergence of Yugoslav nationalism. In Chapter 9, I will concentrate on the emergence of a specifically religious nationalism among the Bosnian Muslims before the recent war, a nationalism which intensified during the course of the war itself. Familiarity with these developments will clarify how present group identifications among my informants form part of a counterdiscourse, in the sense that they do *not* draw on this public religious nationalism. In Chapter 10, I analyse pre-war ethnic identity in Bosnia Herzegovina showing how ethnicity was a part of everyday life instead of separate and politicised; present Muslim identifications rest upon this pre-war habitual understanding of ethnicity. Chapter 11 shows how neither national nor religious identifications have colonised the minds of the Stolac Muslims, and Chapters 12 to 14 analyse the ways the Muslims identify themselves today. In Chapter 15, I introduce a theme that complicates the analysis presented in previous chapters: this chapter shows how the Muslims' use of 'the role of the victim' clearly sets the different ethnic groups apart, thus running counter to the counterdiscursive ideals of ethnic tolerance and coexistence.

Chapter 9
The rise of Muslim national identity in Bosnia Herzegovina

This chapter outlines some of the important moments in the history of Bosnia Herzegovina central to the rise of Bosnian Muslim national identity. The Ottoman conquest of 1463 resulted in the imposition of *Islam* in Eastern Europe. The occupation by the Austro-Hungarian Empire of Bosnia Herzegovina in 1878-1918 motivated a *politicised ethnoreligious Muslim identity*. The politics of Tito supported a *secularisation of Muslim identity*. Finally, the period from the death of Tito in 1980 up to and including the recent war saw *the conjunction of religion and nationality for the first time* in Muslim religious-political life. The outline of the rise of Muslim nationalism in political life will not stand alone. Using anthropological pre-war data, I will outline the central elements in everyday Muslim identification. This analysis shows that although the maintenance of ethnoreligious differences was central to Muslim everyday identification, such differences were not considered primary. They were perceived not as a hindrance to interaction but rather as the very foundation for coexistence. Furthermore, ethnoreligious identity was established by practices related more to embedded localistic value systems than to objectified nationalist religious symbols. This traditional pre-war way of creating, preserving and respecting ethnic differences is a cultural resource that the Muslims of Stolac draw upon today in their attempt to make sense of the war and post-war situation and identify the ethnic Other and themselves.

The introduction of Islam

In 1463 Bosnia was conquered by the Turks, and Islam and Turkish traditions, values and customs were introduced to the area, and by the end of the 16th century a majority of the Bosnian population had become Muslim. The writing of the history of the Bosnian Muslims has focused on how and why this conversion and transformation of their society took place, and historians have attempted to answer the question of what the Muslims were before they became Muslims. Especially the last question has been rather politicised, as it has led to a discussion of the authenticity and origin of the existing Muslims of Bosnia

Herzegovina. Nationalist-minded Serbs and Croats have made claims on the Muslims and the territory of Bosnia Herzegovina. Some Croats maintain that Muslims in reality are 'islamicised' Croats, while some Serbs hold that Bosnian rulers were at one time vassals of the Serbian kings. And according to Muslim nationalists and others promoting the idea of an independent Bosnia Herzegovina, the Muslims were originally Bogomils.[1] Maintaining that Bosnian Muslims are descendants of the Bogomils legitimises contemporary claims about the territorial and cultural uniqueness of the Bosnian Muslims. The process of Muslim nation-building that these claims have contributed to is seen as following a course similar to that of Serbs and Croats, although with a delay. I will not discuss the authenticity of the Bosnian Muslims.[2] Instead, I start my account

1   In the early Middle Ages – primarily due to political controversies with Hungary, which was trying to gain control of parts of Bosnia with the support of the Pope – the Bosnians broke with international Catholicism and established their own church. The status and theology of this relatively independent Bosnian church have been highly debated in modern times, and historical interpretations have often been highly political. In 1869-70, the Croat historian Franjo Rački attempted to prove that this Church was derived from a Bulgarian heretical sect called the Bogomils, which preached a Manichaean dualist theology in which man only could free himself from the temptations of Satan by following a highly ascetic way of life. The theory was popular. First, it could explain the mass conversion of Bosnians to Islam at the time of the Ottoman invasion. It was argued that after having held out for centuries against the Catholic and Orthodox Christian churches, which made claims on the Bosnian church, these Bogomils finally decided to convert to Islam. Second, it could account for the many medieval gravestones (stecći) found in many parts of Bosnia Herzegovina. These unique stones with special engravings were then interpreted as a distinct Bogomil art form. The theory, however, has been highly criticised since. Today it is understood that many factors were involved in the spread of Islam, and one of these was in fact the absence of strong religious organisations. Furthermore, members of all three religious communities who could afford it erected the engraved stones. Instead of speaking of Bogomils, one should therefore rather talk about the Bosnian Church, which probably never had a huge membership. It was more of a monastic organisation than a Church with a strong hierarchy. However, sources from that period and area are extremely sparse (Bringa 1994; Friedman 1996; Donia and Fine 1994; Malcom 1994). The Bogomil theory is nevertheless still popular, especially among Muslim nationalists (Höpken 1994; see for example Karić 1999: 88-99, for a contemporary philosophical-political identification with the Bogomils).

2   Recent scholarly studies of the history of Bosnia Herzegovina have had as their hidden (and sometimes more open) agenda an attempt to legitimise the existence of the Muslims and/or Bosnians of Bosnia Herzegovina and their legitimate demand for an independent state by referring to both the long existence and the special cultural traditions of the area, especially the tradition of coexistence (Pinson 1993a; Donia and Fine 1994; Malcom 1994; Friedman 1996). These studies were published in a period during the war when the Muslims in reality were in danger of annihilation, and when the international community was reluctant to respond to the Muslim cry for help. As the editor of one such book writes in the introduction: "One of the goals of this conference [upon which the book is based] was to present sufficient historical material to show that this group [the Muslims of Bosnia Herzegovina] has existed long enough to warrant serious consideration by the world". This chapter makes use of these studies, but I am aware that they are also a part of the present politicised construction of the past. See Allcock (2000: 323) for a similar remark.

of the rise of Muslim national identity in Bosnia Herzegovina at the time of the decline of the Ottoman Empire, focusing on the Muslim elites and their self-understanding at that time, and then move on to the Austro-Hungarian occupation.

The mass conversion to Islam during the Ottoman rule should rather be called an *acceptance* (Donia and Fine 1994: 44) because it was rather superficial: people did not change their customs profoundly, instead merging Islamic symbols and practices with already existing Christian practices, a syncretism which was accepted by the Turks (Velikonja 2003). In any case, the Christian church was not strong in Bosnia Herzegovina, so one cannot really talk about the changes in the Bosnian practices as conversion *per se*. Three factors were central for the widespread acceptance of Islam by the population of Bosnia Herzegovina. Economic opportunism was one factor. One central institution was the system of boy-tribute, where young boys were either kidnapped or given up voluntarily to be raised as true Muslim believers inside the Ottoman system. In return they were given an education, which meant that they could later return to their villages as high-ranking soldiers or as officials. Secondly, slaves taken from other parts of the Balkans were often given their freedom if they converted to Islam. And finally, the impressive Muslim cities of the Ottoman Empire – among them Sarajevo – with their beauty, sophisticated lifestyle and wealth, probably tempted some to convert to Islam in order to become part of this way of life (Malcom 1994: 43-69; Babuna 1999: 198). In 1870, in the Bosnian Province 870,128 out of a total population of 1,746,399 were Muslims (McCarthy 1993: 58).

But what characterised Bosnian Muslim identity under the Ottomans? According to Friedman (1996), Bosnian Muslims were caught between two different set-ups. On the one hand, they felt some kind of solidarity with the Turkish conquerors. They shared the same religion, and more importantly, the Ottomans were the guarantors of Muslim feudal holdings, in return for which the Muslim landowners supported the suppression of anti-Turkish rebellion. On the other hand, Bosnian Muslims exhibited a local patriotism that set them apart from the Turks, making the Bosnian Muslims mistrusted and not fully accepted. This is reflected in the use of names. The Bosnian Muslims were called (by the Turks) and called themselves *Bošnjak*, a name that emphasises their regional origins and interests. Bosnian Christians called them *Turci* to distinguish them from Bosnian Christians, while the Bosnian Muslims called the Ottoman Turks the negative name *Turkuš*. But if the Bosnian Muslims identified themselves and were identified by the Turks as different from the Turks, thereby stressing their local origins, they were also set apart from their Christian neighbours. Being feudal landowners who often exploited their serfs (*kmets*), who were largely Christian, they risked serf resistance. In other words they were caught between two exclusive identities: *Bošnjak* or part of the ruling Muslim elite (by being feudal landowners). In addition, the Bosnian Muslims were not even a homogeneous group internally, as tensions existed between Muslim landlords and Muslim serfs. The Ottoman period, therefore, was not characterised by a strong and coherent Muslim identity; instead the category 'Muslim' was internally fragmented, split along both religious and economic axes. The Bosnian Muslims did develop some common cultural traits during Ottoman rule which distinguished them from non-Muslims in Bosnia. In addition, it is evident that there was a kind of common Bosnian Muslim class interest, as the landholding group was predominantly Muslim. However, these common traits and interests did not add up to a real ethnic self-awareness, and as a consequence, there were no national aspirations as such (Friedman 1996: 29-57).

The Ottoman period did not witness any major violent conflicts in Bosnia until the turn of the twentieth century. The Ottoman Empire was declining, and in response to pressure from the European powers, the Ottomans tried to modernise Bosnia by reducing some of the privileges of the Muslim aristocracy. But the Muslims resisted and tried to hold on to their position, and in fact increased the pressure on the serfs. This provoked armed rebellions from angry peasants, mainly Serbs, but also some Muslims, the largest of which (1875-78) brought about the intervention of the Great Powers of Europe and the end of Ottoman rule. Though these peasant uprisings were economic in origin, the nature of the rebellion changed when Serbs began making religiously motivated attacks on Muslim villages, inspired by the escalating nationalism in Serbia. The Muslims retaliated with counterattacks on the Serbs. It was thus not until the end of Ottoman rule that Ottoman Bosnia witnessed its first explicitly religious armed conflicts, conflicts which were rooted in the worsening economic conditions of Bosnian serfs, most of whom were Serbs. In 1878, the Austro-Hungarian Empire conquered Bosnia Herzegovina, and though economic/religious conflicts between serf/Serbs and landowners/Muslims had been going on for some years by this time, it was only under Austro-Hungarian rule that a politicised Muslim identity really began to emerge. The different religious communities classified as *millets* had existed during Ottoman rule, but religion, or Muslim identity, had never been used as a basis for making political claims uniting all Muslims (Donia and Fine 1994: 35-71; Friedman 1996: 29-57; Malcom 1994: 43-136; McCarthy 1993; Velikonja[3] 2003).

---

3   Velikonja, though, argues that in important ways, politicised ethnoreligious identities started to emerge as early as the end of the Ottoman rule.

Austro-Hungarian rule and the emergence of a politicised ethnoreligious Muslim identity

The Great Powers of Europe supported the occupation of Bosnia Herzegovina by the Habsburg Monarchy in 1878. However the Austro-Hungarians were not really interested in the area. Although rich in natural resources, the region was under-developed and unstable. But because of expanding Serbian and Croat nationalism and a fear that the Serbs, together with their Russian allies, would come to control the greater part of the Balkans, Austro-Hungary accepted the mandate to occupy Bosnia Herzegovina granted in *The Treaty between Great Britain, Germany, Austria, France, Italy, Russia and Turkey, for the settlement of affairs in the East*. The occupation did not proceed as easily as anticipated. Initially only the Catholics (Croats) welcomed their Austro-Hungarian co-religionists, and in fact the Catholic Church became more active than ever before under the Austro-Hungarian regime. The Serbs for their part feared that the occupation of Bosnia Herzegovina would be a step towards the occupation of Serbia, and the Muslims were rather insecure about what their new status would be, after belonging to the ruling class for centuries. At the end of the military operation Austro-Hungarian had engaged 268,000 soldiers and suffered the loss of 6,000. The losses of the population of Bosnia Herzegovina are not known (Karčić 1999: 75-80).

The Austro-Hungarians did modernise Bosnia Herzegovina. Infrastructure was developed, industries set up and education supported. Nevertheless, in 1910 after 30 years of occupation, 87 % of the population was still employed in agriculture. Only relatively minor land reforms were introduced, disappointing Bosnia's Christian peasants and resulting in sporadic violent peasant uprisings. The preservation of the status quo meant that Muslims continued to represent the majority of landowners and free peasants, whereas Orthodox Christians and Catholics were mostly tenants and sharecroppers. According to the 1910 Bosnian census, there were 10,463 landowners, 136,854 free peasants, 79,677 customary tenants and 31,416 tenants who also owned their land. Muslims constituted 91 % of the landowners, 55 % of the free peasants and 4 % of tenants who also owned their land (Karčić 1999: 88-89; Malcom 1994: 140). So when the Muslims discovered that their new rulers would not change their privileged position in any major way, they came to support the Austro-Hungarians to some extent. However, the structure of the agrarian relations increasingly became a great source of conflict and politico-religious mobilisation of the Muslims.

Initially the Austro-Hungarians tried to promote a common Bosnian identity (*bošnjaštvo*) to counter the growing Serbian and Croatian nationalism, but this ideological project was never successful. Instead the Muslims slowly began to develop a feeling of distinctive identity as a response to the experience of living under a non-Muslim regime, while trying to maintain as many privileges as possible against Austro-Hungarian attempts to reduce the influence of the different Muslim institutions. Muslims from Mostar were the first to organise continued political action. The incentives leading these Muslims to seek greater political influence were religious issues, for instance some controversial conversions of Muslims to Catholicism. The Muslim elite transformed the discomfort attached to these conversions into anti-Croat and anti-Austro-Hungarian protests directed against what they presented as a general repression of Muslim cultural and religious rights. And the protests against Austro-Hungary gradually increased. However, the Muslim community was still far from homogeneous and unified. Three main groups existed in this period: the intellectuals, the landowners and the clerics. The complex rivalries and conflicts within the Muslim elite, as well as between the Muslim elite and elites of other ethnic groups and the Austro-Hungarian administration, contributed to the formation of Muslim political consciousness: the persistent discussion of what constituted Muslim rights and interests in relation to a non-Muslim regime and how these were best promoted gradually produced a politicisation of Muslim identity which had not existed before (Babuna 1999).

One of the most important developments in this period was the creation of a Muslim political party in 1906 (*Muslimanska narodna organizacija*: MNO). The party was formed in order to promote the interests of the Muslim community (mainly the landlords), but it was also encouraged by the Austro-Hungarians, who believed that the creation of moderate political parties could hinder the increasing Serbian nationalism in the area, and decrease the confrontational line of the Serbs and the Muslims towards the regime. The result was the creation of a myriad of ethnically based parties in Bosnia Herzegovina. For the first time *Muslim interests* were organised, objectified and generalised in a formal institution (a party), instead of *the interests of private Muslims* being pursued through the exploitation of personal networks (Pinson 1993b).

Although the MNO campaigned for cultural, educational and religious autonomy for all Muslims in Bosnia Herzegovina, it represented the views of the landowning class to a great extent. For instance, the MNO cooperated with wealthier Serb peasants to prevent land reforms that had been promised to the peasants, including the Muslims. These kinds of alliances greatly undermined cohesion among Bosnian Muslims. As Friedman (1995: 72) concludes, "The earliest Muslim political party was thus controlled by those who deemed class interests, rather than solely communal [ethnic] interests, to be paramount."

When the ethnically based parties were created in 1907, nationalist movements in independent Serbia and Croatia respectively influenced both Serbian and Croatian political parties in Bosnia. Both groups asserted the same

– though mutually exclusive – claim on the Muslim population, maintaining they were Islamic Serbs or Croats, and that the territory of Bosnia Herzegovina should therefore be joined with Serbia or Croatia. Neither the Serbs nor the Croats constituted a majority in Bosnia Herzegovina, so without the Muslims they would have difficulties making territorial claims. The Muslims alternated between calling themselves part of the Serbian or the Croatian nation, but the ultimate failure of the Serbs and the Croats to represent Muslim identity speaks of the existence of a relatively solid Muslim identity and of specific Muslim interests. The Muslim political discourse was centred on religion and Muslim cultural rights, and the MNO managed to obtain relative religious autonomy for the Muslim community in 1909. However, despite the existence of an emerging Muslim self-consciousness, the Bosnian Muslims did not tie Muslims' cultural and religious rights to national consciousness, as they lacked the nationalist outlook which would have been encouraged by an autonomous or semiautonomous neighbouring political entity. Instead they continued to promote multi-nationalism, as they believed this was in their best interests. From the outset the actual politics of the Bosnian Muslims were thus very pragmatic, a feature which in fact endured up until the late 1980s (Pinson 1993b; Donia and Fine 1994: 93-120; Malcom 1994: 136-56; Friedman 1996: 57-89; Babuna 1999).

Several commentators see this political pragmatism as a hallmark of Bosnian Muslim mentality. They identify a Bosnian Muslim cultural core or tradition which is characterised by tolerance, a tolerance which was "betrayed" during the recent war (Donia and Fine 1994). This account is a simplification. Interethnic tolerance existed on the everyday level, and political pragmatism was an important element in the strategy of Muslim politicians, especially when trying to manoeuvre between Croat and Serbian national claims. But as we shall see, radical and dogmatic (at times pan-Islamic) religious thoughts also began to play a central part in the political life of the Bosnian Muslims.

The communist regime and the secularisation of Muslim identity

In the 1920s and 1930s Muslim religious identity, which had experienced relative freedom during the Austro-Hungarian period (ending in 1918), was increasingly threatened by the territorial and institutional claims made by both the Serbs and Croats in *The Kingdom of the Serbs, Croats and Slovenes*. The Bosnian Muslims increasingly lacked a strong identity and a clear perspective. In this climate of repression, a relatively radical pan-Islamic group, the *Young Muslims* (*Mladi Musliman*), emerged for the first time. They advocated the creation of a greater Islamic state and the reawakening of Islam in Bosnia Herzegovina.

The Second World War put a halt to the group's activities, but after the war – during which Muslim political allegiances had been rather changeable – the Young Muslims re-emerged in more than thirty cities in Bosnia Herzegovina. Their success, however, was short-lived and their existence was threatened by the communist regime's repression of all religious communities after the war. Muslim religious and educational institutions were closed down and privileges linked to the 1909 Statute of Autonomy were attacked. In the agrarian reform of 1946, the Muslims' privileges linked to the semi-feudal agricultural system were abolished. Together with the state's confiscation of clerical property, this deprived the Muslims' confessional community of its material basis. Instead of pursuing an abstract pan-Islamic state, therefore, the Young Muslims concentrated on fighting the new repressive state and trying to create a Muslim national consciousness (Bougarel 1997: 533-5; Banac 1993: 129-41). The Young Muslims were soon attacked. The first arrest came in 1947, and with the trial of the principal leaders of the group[4] in Sarajevo in 1949, which led to the death sentence for four others, the organisation broke up (Bougarel 1997; Friedman 1996: 146-77; Höpken 1994).

At this time the communists were very wary of any national uprising which might undermine the fragile post-war situation. Muslims, therefore, were not recognised as one of the constituent groups of Yugoslavia on an equal footing with the Serbs and the Croats. They were only accepted as a minority population with special cultural and religious characteristics. This policy is reflected in the censuses from the post-war period. Though it was possible for Muslim respondents to identify their religion as Orthodox Christian, Catholic or Muslim, their nationality[5] was to be designated as Serb, Croat or 'undetermined'.[6] That is, Muslims were Muslims by faith whereas their nationality was either Serb or Croat, the category 'undetermined' implying that they had not yet settled their relationship. Looking at the census figures it is not clear to what degree and in what way (or if) the Muslims in general perceived themselves as constituting a coherent national group, but it is clear that they did perceive themselves as religiously distinct and that they did not recognise themselves as Serbs or Croats. In the 1948 census 890,094 of Bosnia Herzegovina's people classified themselves

---

4   Among them Alija Izetbegovic.

5   As stated in the Prologue, the English word 'nation' does not fully cover the status of the different groups in Yugoslavia. The Bosnian term *narod* – more or less the same as the German *volk* – rather means a people, political group, or Nation.

6   Those who were members of the Communist Party were forced to align themselves with one of the other of the two nationalities (Höpken 1994: 229).

as Muslim by faith; of these 788,384 chose the option of registering themselves as 'Muslim undetermined' (Donia and Fine 1995: 176).

The communist regime's constitution of Bosnia Herzegovina also reflected the uncertain status of the Bosnian Muslims. After some intense disputes, it was agreed that Bosnia Herzegovina should be given the status of a federal republic instead of merely an autonomous province like Vojvodina and Kosovo. But where the other five republics were defined as republics consisting of one nation, Bosnia Herzegovina was a republic made up of 'parts of the Serbian and Croatian nation as well as the Bosnian Muslims' (Höpken 1994: 228).

Then in the beginning of the 1950s, the policies of the Communist Party concerning the Muslim community changed somewhat. These 'undetermined' people were now to make up the core of the party's new strategy of promoting Yugoslavism, a general national identity for all the people of Yugoslavia. The option 'Muslim, undetermined' was changed in the census form to 'Yugoslav, undetermined', and results of the census from 1953 show that the majority of the Muslims chose this category. The attempt by the League of Communists of Yugoslavia (LCY) to create an overall nationality was soon abandoned, however, and in the 1960s their approach to nationalism took a new direction. Concurrently with the suppression of the more radical forms of Bosnian Muslim political organisation (such as the Young Muslims) and the general ban on explicit public religious expression, the communist regime embarked on a strategy of supporting another branch of Muslim political life. The communists' legalisation and support of *Islamska Vjerska Zajednica* at one and the same time 'created' a Muslim community that was both secular and supportive of the communist regime. *Islamska Vjerska Zajednica*, renamed *Islamiska Zajednica* (Islamic Community) in 1969, became the official religious representative of the Muslims of Bosnia Herzegovina, or as Bougarel writes: "It became for the Muslims of Bosnia Herzegovina a veritable substitute national institution" (1997: 540). The secularisation of Muslim political life represented by this development posed a problem for the more devout Muslims, particularly the former members of the Young Muslims, who had by now completed their prison sentences. The slow but sure integration of this branch of more radical and religiously devout Muslims into the Islamic Community created two distinct wings in Muslim politics: a secular Muslim nationalism on the one side, and a revival of Islamic religious belief on the other (Bougarel 1997: 540-3; Malcom 1994: 200).

Although the communists supported the secularisation of the Muslims, Muslims still did not constitute a nationality in constitutional terms. Finally, in the 1960s, things started to change.[7] A first sign of the new recognition came in 1961, when Muslims in the census could declare themselves 'Muslim in the ethnic sense', though they were not yet fully 'national' like the Serbs and the Croats. A lot of discussion then followed in the LCY concerning the future status of the Muslims of Yugoslavia, and in 1968 the central committee of the League of Communists of Bosnia Herzegovina stated that: "Experience has shown the damage of various forms of pressure and insistence, in the earlier period, that Muslims declare themselves ethnically to be Serbs or Croats because, as was demonstrated still earlier and as contemporary socialist experience continues to show, the Muslims are a separate nation" (in Ramet 1992b: 179).

Then finally in 1971, the nationality 'Muslim' was formally recognised in the census form. In a way this was the ultimate fusion of religion and nationality for the Muslims of Bosnia Herzegovina – a fusion made by Orthodox Christian (Serb) and Catholic (Croat) Bosnians' nationalist movements of the late 19th century – and it was a rather unique constellation among the world's contemporary national identities. As Banac (1993: 146) has noted, the peculiar composition of Bosnian Muslim socialist nationhood allowed one to be a Muslim by nationality and a Jehovah's Witness by religion (as is commonplace in the town of Zavidovići). The designation of Muslim nationhood was fully accepted by the Muslim population, as can be seen in the census of 1971, 1981 and 1991 (Donia 1995: 178; Ramet 1992b: 180).

The recognition of Muslim national identity was part of the communist regime's strategy of secularising the Muslims. In addition, it was related to the regime's new views on national identity in this period of increasing regionalisation of power (see Chapter 4). It was also an attempt to create a buffer against the nationalistic aspirations of the Serbs and the Croats. The elevation of Muslim religious identity to the status of Muslim national identity, however, was not easily accepted by the Serbs and the Croats. For one thing, federal offices and positions were allotted in accordance with a nationality-based proportional representation. The new constitutional status of the Muslims, therefore, introduced a new factor of power in Yugoslav politics. In Bosnia Herzegovina[8] it improved the political influence of the Muslims and decreased that of the Serbs and the Croats. Serbs had yet another more specific reason to resent the

7   Malcom claims that a major reason for the improvement in the regime's treatment of Islam was due to Tito's new 'non-aligned' foreign policy. Several of his potential international partners came from Muslim-dominated countries. Muslim identity suddenly became important for working in diplomacy, even though these Muslim diplomats were also members of the Communist Party (Malcom 1994: 196-7).

8   Of the 1.9 million Muslims in Yugoslavia (8.9 % of the total population), 86 % lived in Bosnia Herzegovina according to the 1981 census (Bringa 1995: 24).

Muslims' new political influence. In the 1950s and 1960s, Bosnia Herzegovina had experienced a period of underdevelopment and poverty in relation to the other Yugoslav republics. As a consequence a lot of Bosnian Serbs had migrated to Serbia during these years. With the new census model the Serbs suddenly found themselves only the second largest population in Bosnia Herzegovina, with the Muslims as the largest (Friedman 1996: 143-77; Ramet 1992b: 176-86; Höpken 1994: 231-9; Malcom 1994: 193-212).

The recognition of the Muslims as constituting a national group was an impetus for a reawakening of Muslim religious identity. And at the beginning of the 1970s, both pan-Islamic ideas and Bosnian Muslim nationalism flourished. Advocates for the latter argued for the formation of a Muslim nation in Bosnia Herzegovina, whereas the others focused more on strengthening Islam among the Muslims of Bosnia Herzegovina (Ramet 1992b: 184-6; Bougarel 1997: 543-6). The secular wing of the Bosnian Muslims continued to be supported by the LCY, but the period also witnessed a general national awakening in Yugoslavia. As a result, the tensions in the Islamic Society between secular and more dogmatically religious trends grew. This development worried the Communist regime. Any signs of religiously motivated politics among the Muslims as well as the Serbs alarmed the Bosnian republican government. They feared that a growth in Muslim religious politics would provoke and increase Serbian nationalism. The government's anxiety about growing religious and national identification on the political scene among the Bosnian Muslims and in Yugoslavia in general led in 1983 to an attack on Muslim activists in Bosnia Herzegovina. Thirteen people, among them Alia Izetbegovic (later to become president of Bosnia Herzegovina) and three other former members of the Young Muslims, were tried for 'Islamic fundamentalism' and 'Muslim nationalism' and condemned to heavy prison sentences[9] (Bougarel 1997: 543-6; Malcom 1994: 206-8). As Ramet notes regarding the incoherent policy of the LCY towards the Muslims in this period: "The LCY, which feared the identification of religion and nationality, wanted to have it both ways: namely, to derive a new nationality from religion [the Muslims], but yet to deny that derivation and suppress demands based on it." (Ramet 1992b: 186). The attack on the Muslim doctrinaire religious wing in Bosnia Herzegovina had an intimidating effect, and it consolidated the position of the promoters of a secular Muslim national identity – a situation which was not to last for very long.

---

9   The question remains of whether these Muslims were just scapegoats in a larger political puzzle, and whether Izetbegovic's unpublished *Islamic Declaration* (completed thirteen years before) – treated by the LCY as a Muslim religious nationalist manifesto – was more than just a general discussion of politics and Islam without reference to Bosnia Herzegovina.

The SDA and the emergence of Muslim nationalism in the post-Tito period

Since the fall of the Ottoman regime, the Muslims of Bosnia Herzegovina had primarily been viewed as a religious group possessing the same privileges as other confessional groups: they could build mosques, develop and maintain religious institutions, educate according to Islam, and so on. Only in 1971 were they officially recognised in the census as constituting a nation, that is, a political group or a people. Only then did they come to represent a population with rights and privileges. However, Tito's secularisation of the Muslims of Yugoslavia had been a success. The rather substantial surveys investigating the religiosity of the citizens of Yugoslavia which were conducted from the 1950s to the beginning of the 1990s show an unmistakable trend towards a diminishment in the power of religion over people. In 1953, 86.6 % saw themselves as religious believers, whereas by 1968 only 39 % did the same. Furthermore, religious elements in national identification were giving way to more secular aspects of life. These trends were most prominent among the young, who adopted the anti-religious views of the Titoist state most easily (Cohen 1998: 47-55; Velikonja 2003).[10] From the 1950s up until the 1980s, the Muslims' interests were primarily secular, and many of Tito's most loyal followers were to be found among this group of secularised Muslims. Religious Muslims played only a secondary role in political life, and attempts at merging religion and national interest were harshly suppressed by the Communist regime, as seen in the trial in 1983. During this period, being Muslim by nationality was not the same as being Muslim by faith.

At the end of the 1980s and the beginning of the 1990s, the situation began to be reversed. Yugoslavian society was disintegrating, and the country experienced religious reawakening, party pluralism, a centralisation of power, and most of all a surge of nationalism (see Chapter 4). Just before the coming of the war and during the course of the war a rather sudden fusion of religion and nationality emerged among the Bosnian Muslims. Muslim national identity became increasingly defined on the background of faith (Islam), and religious institutions came to play a central role in the nationalist mobilisation of the Muslim community. In short, an explicit Muslim national identity emerged for the first time during this period.

In 1990, inter-ethnic relations among the people of Bosnia Herzegovina were becoming more and more tense, and the multi-party election led to the emergence of distinct political parties representing each of the Republic of Bos-

---

10 Even though the importance of religion decreased throughout these years, ethnoreligious identity was still an important factor in people's lives. This may seem contradictory. In the next section, however, I will show how such ethnoreligious identities in embedded everyday practice are rather different than when they exist in the politicised sphere of public life.

nia Herzegovina's three ethnic communities. This represented a rather crucial change in the formation of Muslim identity. As Bougarel (2001: 2) describes this development:

> The Communist period encouraged the formation of a new Muslim elite [...] and the crystallization of national identities, which until then had remained unclear and fluid as shown by the case of the Bosnian Muslims and the Albanians in Yugoslavia. But it was only after the collapse of the communist regimes in 1989/90 that these social and cultural changes got their political expression.

The Muslims' 'political expression', the Party of Democratic Action (SDA), was formed in March 1990, mainly by devout religious members of the Islamic Community who were directly involved in Islamic religious activities. Alija Izetbegovic, who had been religiously engaged all his life, was head of the party. Though the party was not given good odds, it managed to mobilise a huge part of the Muslim population of Bosnia Herzegovina in only a couple of months, and in the election the same year the SDA got 30.4 % of the votes, while the Bosnian Serb nationalist party SDS got 25.2 %, and the Bosnian Croat nationalist party HDZ 15.5 %. A collective presidency was established, consisting only of members from the three nationalist parties (Bougarel 1996: 96-7; Cohen 1998: 58-61; Malcom 1994: 218-22).[11]

---

11 How could SDA, a nationalist party, manage to obtain the majority of the Muslims' votes in such a short time? After all, only a few years before Muslims had been characterised as a very secular population with only little national consciousness. Bougarel's (1996, 1997, 2001) answers seem convincing. First, if one adds Muslim votes cast for non-nationalistic parties and the number of Muslims who did not vote, it appears that some kind of opposition existed. Second, the votes for the SDA were not uniform. SDA, which was founded on a purely ideological basis as 'a political alliance of the citizens of Yugoslavia belonging to the historical-cultural sphere of Islam', soon changed its outlook and integrated both a secular and a (pan)-Islamic wing. The SDA both strengthened Muslim nationalism by emphasising the most distinctive thing about it, its religious element, and managed to incorporate intellectuals and other prominent people from the LCY by emphasising that the SDA stood for the preservation of Bosnia Herzegovina's unique character as a multi-national and multi-religious republic (Malcom 1994: 218-219). By incorporating local intellectuals and influential people, the SDA also managed to strengthen the support of the local patron-client networks central to politics in Bosnia Herzegovina (Grandits 2007; Bougarel 1996: 96). Third, the nationalist voting pattern in Bosnia Herzegovina in 1990 had parallels to the election of representatives to the local and federal legislatures in Yugoslavia, where representation was always distributed along ethnic lines. In addition, the censuses held throughout the years were the only time people could express individual choice; the censuses were politicised as they formed the background for the distribution of national position, and the logic of these census 'votes' was national membership. Finally, with Izetbegovic in front the SDA used and enforced the fear the Muslim population of Bosnia Herzegovina traditionally had had of Serbian and Croatian nationalism, thereby contributing to the strengthening of Muslim nationalism (Cohen 1993: 145, Bougarel 1996: 98).

The division of power in Bosnia Herzegovina along ethnic lines after the 1990 election resulted in an increasingly ineffective and corrupt society. Moreover, with the break-up of Yugoslavia in June 1991, the future status of Bosnia Herzegovina became a hot topic. The SDA and HDZ insisted on sovereignty for Bosnia Herzegovina, whereas the SDS did not want Bosnia Herzegovina to secede from Yugoslavia/Serbia. The SDA's behaviour was in fact inconsistent. On the one hand, the SDA supported a united multi-ethnic Bosnia Herzegovina run by a secular Western-style government. On the other hand, it also promoted Islamic revival, in addition to contributing to and at times supporting the nationalist division of Bosnia Herzegovina.[12]

From the beginning of the war, the SDA had two potential alliance partners: Europe and Pan-Islamists (Islamic countries). And to a degree, the SDA managed to manoeuvre in this ideologically contradictory landscape of multiculturalism, pan-Islamicism, Europeanism, secularism, democracy and Muslim identity. The Bosnian Muslims' leader Alija Izetbegovic expressed the contradictory ideologies in this way:

Our folk [people] like the faith, but in faith they do not like exaggerations. They are typical folk of the great border, of the borderline between worlds. By our faith we are Easterners, by our education Europeans. With our heart we belong to one world, with our brain to the other. Well, even the ancient *Bogomil* component of forgiving and goodness is blended here. Each of us who is honest has to admit that he asks himself often to which world does he belongs. When it comes to me, I have answered myself that I am a European Muslim and I feel as comfortable in this definition as in a pair of comfortable shoes (Izetbegovic from 1994, cited in Maček 2000a: 213-4).

The SDA's identity politics, however, was not only a result of a concern for international political alliance partners, nor was it merely an attempt to reconcile the traditional tension in the SDA and Bosnian politics in general. The SDA's

---

12 Throughout the 20th century, the Muslim community of Bosnia Herzegovina had two contradictory aims: a) to preserve Bosnia as a distinct territorial unit, and b) to avoid the assimilation of the Muslim community into a larger group, be it Austro-Hungarian *bosnjastvo*, Serb and Croat nationalism, or Yugoslavism. In other words, to co-exist as an independent, sovereign, national group together in the same territorial state with other nations who do not acknowledge such claims. For instance, the tension in Bosnian political life between the SDA and the secular non-national party the SDP reflects this cleavage. The question is if this cleavage should be seen as a division between nationalists and non-nationalists, or between religious nationalists and secular nationalists. (This line of reasoning rests on personal communication with Xavier Bougarel, but see Donia and Fine (1995: 236-7) for a different claim, namely that this cleavage represents a special non-contradictory Muslim political culture).

politics also reflected the ambivalence felt by Muslims during the war, when ethnicity suddenly moved to the forefront and when people feared for their life, and when ordinary Muslims thus became both nationalists and anti-nationalists at one and the same time (Maček 2000a: 153-269).

The war – Muslim nationalism escalates

Muslim religious nationalism was further strengthened by the war. The ethnic logic of carving up the territory of Yugoslavia and Bosnia Herzegovina along ethnic lines gained more and more predominance – a development strongly supported by the diplomatic activities of the 'international community'. Assaults on Muslims by both Croats and Serbs caused leading Muslims to become increasingly separatist, religious and nationalistic, and the space left for imagining a secular multiethnic society became more and more limited. For example, Džemaludin Latić, editor of the important Muslim publication *Muslimanski glas* (Muslim Voice) warned against the secularised Muslim intellectuals who were "more dangerous to the Muslim believers than the Chetniks" (Velikonja 2003: 279),[13] and several religious leaders critical of the SDA's nationalistic politics were removed from office (Bougarel 1996: 105).

Religious Muslim nationalism spread throughout society and its institutions. The Bosnian army, which had been multi-ethnic at the beginning of the war, soon became almost completely dominated by Muslims and controlled by the SDA. Religious, spiritual and moral education was introduced into the army. Radical Islamic units appeared: they made great use of Islamic symbols and preached strict adherence to an Islamic code of conduct. Volunteer Muslim fighters from Islamic countries, the so-called *Mujahedin*, also played a role in the 'Islamicisation' of the Bosnian Army[14] (Cohen 1998: 69-70; Mojzez 1998: 95;). And though the Muslims did not commit genocide or urbicide in a systematic or programmatic fashion, there is evidence that radical Muslim fighters committed atrocities against non-Muslim populations during the war (Cigar 1995).

Religious Muslim nationalism also increased in the educational system with the introduction of Islam into most school curricula. In particular, the subjects of History and Language and Literature were changed in accordance with the ongoing ideological programme of forming Bosnian Muslim identity. This is an example from a fourth-grade history book:

---

13 See Vuković (1993) for a personal account of the impossibility of insisting on a non-national identification.

14 There are no precise figures on how many *mujahedins* participated in the war. Anywhere from 1,000 to 6,000 has been suggested (Velikonja 2003).

[In] the Middle Ages Bosnia was populated by a homogeneous Bosnian people, called *Bošnjani*…Turkish authorities populated the desolate parts of the
land (desolated because of the frequent plague epidemics and the death of
Bošnjaci on the Turkish Empire's battlefields) with Croats and Serbs from the
surrounding countries. These were mostly stockbreeders and work-elements
(serfs) … So, the *Bošnjaci* Muslims were left as the only representatives of
the Bosnian people – descendants of the Medieval *Bošnjani* (Imamović and
Bošnjak 1994, cited in Maček 2000a: 173).

Language also gained nationalist importance, which is not surprising, since
language is traditionally an important signifier in the creation and imagination
of national identities. Leading Muslims renamed their language 'Bosnian' (before Serbo-Croat), emphasising its supposed Turkish roots by introducing 'h', a
sound associated with Turkishness, into new words and using as many Turkish
synonyms as possible. Even greetings were affected: on an everyday level, the
choice of greeting became a political act and religious greetings became more
frequent. Among other symbolic gestures, the colour green (associated with
Muslim religious identity) became increasingly important, religious holidays
became increasingly popular, and TV and radio broadcasting became oriented
towards promoting a Muslim religious national identity (Maček 2000a: 172-
86).

The names of streets were changed into Muslim names. In Yugoslavia,
street names have always been a way of expressing current state ideology, so the
practice was not new, and it occurred in all parts of Bosnia Herzegovina. But
the new names reflected a rather profound change in Bosnian society.

Even streets named after partisans and Communists of Muslim nationality
were taken away, which proves the point that the shift of ideology was not
only from 'brotherhood and unity' into nationalism, but also from socialism
to capitalism (Maček 2000a: 172).

A last example of Bosnian Muslim nation-building and the politicisation of
Muslim ethnic identity is the decision taken by the Bosniak Assembly (*Bošnjački
Sabor*) in September 1993 to replace the national name 'Muslim' with the new
name 'Bosniak.' This can be seen as an attempt to resolve the issue of national
and territorial claims on behalf of the Muslims. With the new name the politicians stressed the transformation of the Bosnian Muslim community into a
political and sovereign nation, closely linked to the territory of Bosnia Herzegovina (Bougarel 2001: 8). Prior to this decision people who favoured a multiethnic state had argued that 'Bosniak' should be a national term for anyone

(Serb, Croat or Muslim) who considered him or herself to be primarily Bosnian. Others had claimed that the term 'Muslim' had been secularised enough to denominate national adherence, and that a common Bosniak identity would probably soon be co-opted by nationalist Serbs or Croats. Finally, the SDA and nationalist-minded Muslims of Bosnia Herzegovina preferred to reserve 'Bosniak' as a name for Muslims as opposed to the other ethnic groups, a name which could be used as a basis for political claims (Bringa 1995: 33-6; Bougarel 1996: 109; Hayden 2000). As Izetbegovic asserted in one of his typically ambiguous statements: "We Bosniaks, the Muslim nation of Bosnia, are predestined to be the leaders of the new integration of Bosnia" (quoted in Velikonja 2003).

Thus on a general level, despite contradictions and ambivalence, Bosnia Herzegovina witnessed the rise of a Bosnian Muslim nationalist party, the SDA, and nationalist 'Bosniak' politics within a relatively short period of time. And though secular opposition to these trends existed throughout the war both outside and inside the SDA, an antagonistic Muslim nationalism dominated many public and political settings, a situation not many people would have imagined only a few years before the beginning of the war. A war was going on, the Muslims were under attack from both the Croats and the Serbs, and the international community (apart from the Islamic world) had abandoned them. In such a situation violence contributes to creating or strengthening clear-cut identities. I therefore agree with Velikonja's (2003) analysis of the relationship between islamicisation and inter-ethnic conflict: "The invigorated religiousness of the Bosniaks was […] more a consequence than a cause of the war." Friedman sums up the difficult Muslim situation very precisely:

> Thus, the Bosnian Muslims have been caught up in a game that has been larger and tougher than their capacity to cope. Throughout their history up to the present, they were safest when they were part of a multinational coalition, with their position protected by a strong central government. Their vulnerability increased when they were recognized as a nation within Yugoslavia, because their needs had to be met and recognition meant that the Serbs and the Croats could no longer use them as subordinates. Instead, until war struck the area, the Bosnian Muslims had become equal partners in Bosnia Herzegovina and as such had to be dealt with rather than manipulated (Friedman 1995: 225).

Bosnian Muslim nationalism grew, therefore, not because it had been latent throughout the years, but because the logic of the war created it. In fact, Muslim nationalism had always been weak, in part because attempts to articulate a unifying Muslim identity had traditionally been centred on devotion, cultural traditions or pan-Islamism, all of which hindered the growth of a strong national identity (Bougarel 1996; 1997). Bringa sums up the tragic creation of Muslim nationalism in this way:

> The Bosnians have apparently been organized into tidy, culturally and ethnically homogeneous categories, and the Muslims seem finally to have become a neat ethno-national category its neighbours and the international community can deal with and understand. They have been forced by the war and the logic of the creation of nation-states to search for their origins and establish a 'legitimate' and continuous national history (Bringa 1995: 36).

Summary

I want to highlight three aspects of the last century of identity politics among the Bosnian Muslims. First, Bosnian Muslim nationalism came late. Only in the 1990s were aspects of religion, nationality, territory, language and history combined and staged in Muslim politics. Up until then Bosnian Muslim politics had been pragmatic, caught between Serbian and Croatian national aspirations. Bosnian Muslim nationalist movements had existed, but they were relatively marginal and their aims were never clearly articulated. Second, Bosnian Muslim political life has been divided into two wings, at least from the 1930s onwards: the secular and the religious. Prior to and during the war this division was played out in the conflict between (religious) nationalists and (secular) anti-nationalists, in other words between those who defended a sectional ethnic political course and those in favour of a multiethnic society. In the Tito era the secular non-nationalists were dominant. In the years up to and during the war the relationship of dominance was turned around, as seen in the politics of the SDA. The cleavage still exists, and as we shall see, it is also at play in the everyday identifications of the Muslims of Stolac. The third important point is that the promotion of a strong and politicised Muslim identity has mostly been a project of the urban elite: it is not atypical of nation-building projects in general. That granted, it still remains to address the question of the extent to which this project of creating a strong religious or national Muslim identity corresponded to the experiences of the Muslims of Bosnia Herzegovina in their everyday life. This is the question I will turn to now.

Chapter 10
Bosnian Muslim identity in everyday practice

Among (young) people in urban environments in Bosnia Herzegovina a cosmopolitan identity existed and Yugoslavism was popular, ethnic identity mattered little, and inter-ethnic marriage was common. This modern, secularised and non-sectional grouping has sometimes been taken as representative of the general Bosnian mentality. Such a view, however, neglects such tensions as the huge cleft between the rural and the urban in Bosnia Herzegovina (see Chapter 7), as exemplified by the way in which the citizens of Sarajevo (*Sarajlije*) have tried to symbolically disconnect themselves from rural culture by downplaying ethnic affiliation. However, when the focus is shifted to the countryside, it appears that ethnic identity was *a* and sometimes *the* most important identity. People knew the ethnic identity of their neighbours and inter-ethnic marriage was rare (Banac 1993). So even though Bosnian Muslim nationalism did not begin to develop in earnest until the late 1980s, this does not mean that a strong sense of ethnic belonging did not exist among the Bosnian Muslims, particularly in the countryside. But it is a sense of belonging one should not confuse with the Muslim nationalism of the late 1980s.

Several writers have argued that the political sphere of Bosnia Herzegovina has never truly been modernised. In this view, communitarianism, which gives ethnic identities priority in social relations, has continued to be the defining characteristic of society. The project of creating a strong and legitimate state never succeeded (that is, it was everywhere and nowhere), and extra-communal identifications never managed to supersede local ethnic identifications (Simić 1991; Bougarel 1996; Sunic 1998). The central element in these ethnic identifications has been religion: Serbs have been Orthodox Christian, Croats Catholic, and also for the Muslims a strong relationship between religion, faith and ethnic identity has existed. Lockwood (1975), for instance, who at the beginning of the 1970s did fieldwork in a small Muslim village, observed that religion was the most important source of identification in relation to one's ethnicity, and Bringa (1995) reported the same from a village with a mixed Muslim-Croat population twenty years later.

To clarify the characteristics of this local identification, in which religion plays a constitutive part, Bringa (1995) explores the native concept of *nacije*. At first glance one could translate the word as 'nation', but this would not capture the important distinction between *nacije* and 'nation' – especially in Yugoslavia in the late 1980s. Both Sorabji, who did fieldwork in Sarajevo in the 1980s (1993, 1996) and Bringa (1995) report that informants often asked them about their *nacije*. Bringa's initial answer was 'Norwegian', as she thought it was her nationality they wanted to know, but she learned that the answer they were after was 'Protestant' – in other words her faith. However, *nacije* is not only a religious community, even though religion is the defining element of the *nacije*, because these religious identities are also cultural and social identities. They are something to which people feel strong emotional attachment, something into which one is born and socialised, something that is normally 'inherited' from parents, something unquestionable. On the other hand, national identity in Yugoslavia was something one could choose from among the options offered by the state[1], and it often lacked the essential emotional connotations attached to *nacije* in everyday identification. Bringa (1995: 22) translates *nacije* as 'ethnoreligious identity', and concludes that the Muslims of Bosnia Herzegovina had a strong sense of ethnoreligious identity, but a weak sense of national identity. Filipovic has argued that the term 'Muslim' understood as 'nationality' did not exist among rural people even as late as 1990 in several parts of Bosnia Herzegovina (Bringa 1995: 21). This is supported by Bringa's own findings. She reports how Muslims referred to their collective identity not in an idiom "of shared blood and a myth of common origin," but "in an idiom which de-emphasized descent ('ethnicity') and focused instead on a shared environment, cultural practices, a shared sentiment, and common experience" (ibid. 30). This difference between ethnoreligious identity (*nacije*) and nationality was then exploited by the nationalist projects of the late 1980s in Yugoslavia. In Maček's words:

> [T]he new national political elites could mobilise the ethnoreligious notions of belonging into the new national projects of constitution of sovereign states for Muslims, Serbs and Croats respectively, [by] filling the new national identities with the old ethnoreligious feeling of essential belonging (2000: 157).

---

1   Note the shifting categories available over time for the Muslims of Bosnia Herzegovina: 'Serb', 'Croat', 'Yugoslav', 'Muslim undeclared', 'Muslim in the ethnic sense' and 'Muslim by nationality'.

Pre-war Muslim identity in everyday life

I will now highlight four related characteristics of the pre-war, embedded, local, everyday ethnoreligious identification.[2]

Religion as 'a domain of loose moral imperative'

First, though Islam was an important identity marker for Muslims in Bosnia Herzegovina, it should not be understood simply as a set of clearly defined rules of conduct. Religion was rather, as Sorabji (1996: 54) puts it, "a domain of loose moral imperatives." She mentions hospitality, cleanliness, generosity, honesty, kindness, courtesy, industry and the like. Though these values are central for Muslims, they are not specifically Muslim virtues; they are part of a general field of morality in which there are overlaps with the ideology of communism, the moral imperatives of which were "work hard, don't cheat your neighbours, redistribute your wealth, and so on" (ibid. 55). Sorabji seldom found that her informants evaluated each other's actions in religious terms. It was thus, as she reports, not *haram* (Arabic: forbidden by God) to slander someone, but rather *ne valja* (Serbo-Croatian: no good); it was not *sunset* (Arabic: recommended by the Prophet and pleasing to God) to wash your hands before meals, but rather *fino* (Serbo-Croatian: good) (ibid. 55). Furthermore the Islamic Community (see previous chapter) was viewed neither as a body offering guidance on matters of faith nor as the representative of Islam in Bosnia Herzegovina. Rather, the Islamic Community was perceived as no different from other (secular) authorities one might possibly benefit from or negotiate with (ibid. 56).

Likewise, Bringa (1995) found a key difference between how Muslim identity was viewed and practised by Muslims in 'her' village of Dolina and by the Islamic establishment. For the latter group, being a Muslim entailed observing the practices of Islam, whereas for her informants being a Muslim was defined primarily in contrast to the non-Muslim group closest to them, the Catholics/ Croats, and practices of identification involved both Islamic and non-Islamic elements. "The important question was therefore not whether a practice was 'according to Islam' (*po islamu*) or prescribed (*propisano*) or not, but rather that it was what Muslims in Dolina did and their next-door Bosnian Catholic neighbours did not do" (Bringa 1995: 230).

2   To my knowledge, not many qualitative studies focusing on ethnic identity in Bosnia Herzegovina have been conducted. Bcljkašič-Hadžidcdič (1998), in a survey of ethnological work in Bosnia Herzegovina from 1945 until 1988, reports that a lot of ethnography was produced in the period, but that it primarily focused on the material culture and not social organisation of the ethnic groups. The following discussion therefore rests mainly on Bringa (1995), Lockwood (1975) and Sorabji (1993, 1996), as well as on the memories of my informants.

Lockwood (1975), who did fieldwork approximately twenty years before Sorabj and Bringa, came to similar conclusions about the role of religious orthodoxy in Bosnian Muslim identity. Though Islam was much more visible and pronounced in 'his' village than in Dolina, people were still relatively indifferent to doctrine. Instead, people focused on everyday practices: "Relatively little stress is placed on religious doctrine; much more important are outward signs and symbols. In practice, a man is considered a Moslem, not because he holds to the tenets of Islam, but because he is circumcised or observes Ramazan" (Lockwood 1975: 48). Although religion was the most important element distinguishing the ethnic groups, other non-religious cultural practices which might seem trivial to an outsider, were also central to processes of identification. Lockwood mentions how clothing, eating and drinking habits and language followed a rural-urban dichotomy more than a religious one.

Religion, then, did play an important role in pre-war ethnoreligious identity. For the Muslims a non-dogmatic, locally defined version of Islam – what Bringa (1985) calls 'being Muslim the Bosnian way' – was central to their identity.

Religion, a way to maintain difference

The second characteristic of pre-war Muslim identity as it was played out in everyday practice is its contrastive aspect. Cultural differences between the ethnic groups result, as Lockwood writes:

> ... in all probability, from historical differences of origin and contact. Their persistence however, is due to their existence within relatively closed communication systems, their conscious maintenance as markers of social groups, or, most probably, the interaction of both of these principles. They function equally as focal points of ingroup sentiments and criteria of outgroup identification. They serve, in either function, to reinforce the basic belief that each religious or ethnic group constitutes a separate *nacije* (Lockwood 1975: 53).

This Barthesian (Barth 1969) understanding of Bosnian ethnic identity is also fundamental to Bringa's interpretation and findings. Within this interpretive framework, the point is not to describe how Catholics and Muslims are different *per se*, but rather to examine how they continually accentuate perceived differences as a strategy for establishing identity. Bringa describes a parallelism in the ways the two communities have constructed Otherness, where each community chose the same practices to represent its difference from the other. "We do like this, they do like that" was communicated in many different situations. However, the comparisons were actually implied contrasts which provided a justification for one's own practices (Bringa 1995: 78-84). The different ethnoreligious groups needed each other (or each other's Otherness) to construct identity, and this Otherness was embedded in a local setting and everyday practices. In other words, while elements of religious difference might have been involved in these local identity negotiations, they took place on a different level from the national identities constructed and represented in the public and national spheres. If modernisation means increased disembeddedness of social relations, then large parts of Bosnia Herzegovina cannot be considered very modern. Before the war, identity in Bosnia Herzegovina was to a great extent premised on local face-to-face interaction. Religion was not that important in itself; it mainly mattered as a way of maintaining ethnoreligious distinctions in everyday local life.

Ethnoreligious identity, one among many

A third aspect of the pre-war Muslim everyday identification is related to the fact that, even though ethnoreligious identity was fundamental in everyday life before the war, it was but one identity among many. Relatively 'ethnicity-free' zones of social interaction existed in which identification depended on the context.

In pre-war life as described by my informants, work relations and social status were highly important markers of identity. Relationships with colleagues were important social relations. Often people stressed whether someone they were discussing had been a person in a managerial position, and if so how many people he had been in charge of. Level of education and professional qualifications also stand out as important elements of identity. Usually my informants knew who had been or who still were doctors, architects or high-ranking officials, and more than once I had these people's houses pointed out to me, even though they were often only ruins. Surveying Yugoslav scholars' work on class relations in Yugoslavia, Allcock (2000: 170-211) similarly concludes that income, distribution of social power, prestige and other aspects related to class and job position were important elements in former Yugoslavian life. It was of great significance whether one was a skilled worker, unskilled worker or unemployed, if one was a peasant or self-employed, or a member of the humanistic or technical intelligentsia.

Another important aspect of identity other than the religious was gender. Bringa's (1985) thorough investigation of this matter shows how ethnoreligious identity was primarily attached to the socialisation of girls and to women's role in general; whereas boys could participate in urban, Western, non-ethnic youth cultures to a greater extent. Similarly, men could engage in networks of colleagues, get further training, work in foreign countries, and be more involved in the public sphere in general.

A third identity cutting across ethnoreligious identity relates to culture. The distinction between the uncultured and the cultured was, as argued above, very important in Yugoslavia, and though geographically related to a rural-urban dichotomy, this division should be seen more as a geographical symbolism. Culture, though sometimes attached to ethnic identity, was at other times more important in social interaction and group preferences than ethnic identity.

Ethnoreligious identification should furthermore be contrasted with higher levels of identification. In Dolina, Bringa reports, ethnoreligious identity was connected to the household, the family and sometimes one's neighbours; but at a village level a unifying localistic identification transcending ethnicity held sway. Such solidarity was created through social exchanges like regular private visits, obligations between households, evening gatherings in the village, communal voluntary work, and common house building (akcija) (1995: 65-73). The most central ethos attached to such local super-ethnic identification was that of komšiluk, hospitality and neighbourliness. The practice of komšiluk was, as Bougarel defines (1996: 98) it, a "permanent guarantee of the pacific nature of relations between the communities, and thus a security of each of them." In post-war Stolac I too found such local identification and an ethos of interethnic hospitality and mutual connexion (see also Sunic 1998). At an even higher level of identification was the Yugoslav state, which penetrated village life with its various institutions and enforced unification. We have seen how the communist regime indirectly contributed to the national tensions in Yugoslavia by dividing power along republican lines (Chapter 4). At the same time, though, the state also supported the existence of a unified Yugoslavia and of a Yugoslav identity. Bringa (1985) reports how the villagers in Dolina participated in several different spheres defined by such a Yugoslavism: the educational system, the Yugoslav People's Army, and various communist youth clubs. Additionally there were the state-controlled media as well as the various social benefits people received.

The skill of living with ethnoreligious difference

The fourth and last element relates to the skill of living with difference, an ability which many Bosnians had developed in the pre-war period. Such a competence should not be romanticised. Some experts have even questioned the very existence of such tolerance, dismissing it as a myth constructed by Western intellectuals about the presumedly tolerant Bosnian mentality. The reality is rather one of inter-ethnic distrust, it is argued (Simić 2000). After all, monoethnic communities existed all over pre-war Bosnia, and as Lockwood (1975) shows, inter-ethnic interaction in such settings as weekly markets does not necessarily lead to more profound cultural integration. Furthermore, we also have examples of villages and areas where inter-ethnic coexistence was marred by continual and cyclic outbursts of violence and inter-ethnic (blood)strifes even before the developments that led to the war (Bax 1995, 1997, 2000; Boehm 1984). Researchers have also observed how traumatic memories from the Second World War have been passed on to the younger generations (Denich 1994). I shall not enter the often intense debate in anthropology about the reality of the tolerant Bosnian mentality, a debate which has been especially fierce during and after the recent war (see Brandt 2002 for a thorough discussion). My point is rather that at the very least, it is true to say that the people of Bosnia Herzegovina regularly came into contact with members of different ethnoreligious groups in different areas, both in the public sphere and often also in the private sphere. One should not forget that the young and the middle-aged had lived in peace for almost fifty years when the war broke out in 1992. Ethnoreligious identity could have been a significant factor shaping the content and atmosphere of inter-ethnic interaction, but it was seldom a hindrance to such interaction. What is more, the interaction between the different ethnoreligious groups was often characterised by respect.[3]

Central for understanding the Bosnian skill of living with difference is that differences were not downplayed: equality as sameness was not the ideal, in contrast to some Scandinavian contexts (Gullestad 1992). Instead, differences were persistently nurtured in a way that Georgieva (1999), analysing interaction between Muslims and Christians in Bulgaria, has described as 'familiarisation of differences', that is, the network of interconnected lines that comprehends all levels of everyday life, eliminating Otherness and changing it into familiar difference. The 'others' are therefore "perceived not as a menace, but rather as an inseparable part of the complex world of everyday life" (ibid. 68). The skill of living with difference was also central in Bringa's finding:

> To most Bosnians (and particularly to the post World War II generations) difference in ethnoreligious affiliation was one of the many differences between people. [...] It was acknowledged and often joked about but it never precluded friendship. Indeed, for these Bosnians being Bosnian (*bosanac*) meant growing up in a multicultural and multireligious environment, an environment where cultural pluralism was intrinsic to the social order. Dealing with cultural differences was part of people's most immediate experience of

3   Cf. Hayden's (2002) definition of passive versus active tolerance, where the first is marked by non-interferences and the second by embrace of the Other.

social life outside the confines of their home, and it was therefore an essential part of their identity. In the village mutual acknowledgement of cultural diversity and coexistence was an intrinsic quality of life and of people's everyday experience, and therefore an important element in the process of individual identity formation (Bringa 1995: 83).

The practice of living with and managing Otherness can explain how most ordinary people were totally taken by surprise not only when war started in Yugoslavia, but also when it came to their village. Even when war had hit neighbouring villages or areas, people simply could not believe that it could come and destroy the 'familiarisation of differences' or inter-ethnic respect characteristic of their own communities (Bringa 1993; Julie 1997; Feldman 1993). This feeling of shock is also one of the central experiences of my informants.

The influence of war on Muslim everyday identity

The war and nationalist politics changed aspects of everyday identification among the Bosnian Muslims in many ways. The religious content of the ethnoreligious identities, which before the war had been a domain of loose moral imperatives, became much more closely connected to a doctrinaire reading of Islam. This happened when religion became the most central element in the construction of Muslim nationalism.

Before the war, ethnoreligious Otherness had been primarily embedded in everyday practice. That is to say, difference was mainly related to actual experiences with concrete Others. With the coming of the war and nationalist politics, Muslim ethnic identity became increasingly detached from these local contexts, and was represented in new more abstract, rigid and politicised religious categories. These categories, however, became rather real when people realised that ethnicity was – or could easily become – a matter of life or death. Before the war ethnoreligious identity had been important, but it was still one identity among others, depending on the situation. Occupation, networks of colleagues, level of education, gender and degree of cultivation were all important alternative identifications, as was the case with localistic and national (Yugoslav) identifications. But when the nationalist obsession began spreading throughout Yugoslavia, in Bosnia Herzegovina ethnic identity came to supersede all other identities, colonising every aspect of life: music, pronunciations of words, street names, love relations, choice of colours and so on.

The familiarisation of and the living with difference that had characterised respectful interethnic interaction in many parts of Bosnia Herzegovina was attacked in the war. Ethnoreligious identity, which had not been a hindrance to interaction before the war, suddenly made such interaction difficult or even impossible. In other words, though previously difference had been persistently created and reinforced, it had not posed a problem for interaction. During the war this relationship was reversed: difference was now all there was, and it posed a problem for interaction.

The following chapters will explore how much the general changes in identification described so far have penetrated my informants' everyday life, and the extent to which these identifications have rendered impossible different kinds of non-ethnic identifications. In looking at how the Muslims of Stolac identify themselves, it will become clear that although the Bosnian Muslim nationalist discourse has radically changed patterns of everyday identification, counterdiscursive practices also exist. In short, my analysis shows that although the importance of Muslim identity has increased and become much more conscious, 'Muslimness' is still not defined primarily in nationalist terms. Rather, Muslim identity is defined by reference to a rather heterogeneous group of different values, including the 'Stolac spirit' (Chapter 12), ideals of tolerance (Chapter 13), a Balkan-Europe dichotomy (Chapter 14), and a 'victim role' (Chapter 15).

Chapter 11
The national identity that failed

One might assume that nationality and religion, *Bosnia* and *Islam*, would be the most important signifiers of identity in the Bosnian Muslims' life. After all, they have experienced massive nationalist propaganda, a nationalist politics of leading Bosnian Muslims, as well as the fact that ethnic identity became a matter of life and death throughout the war. But in Stolac this is not the case. Here, Bosnia Herzegovina as a nation (language, history, symbol, territory etc.) and Islam as a dogmatic religion play only a minor role. Before I analyse the identifications that do actually matter most in my informants' everyday life, I shall clarify the Stolac Muslim lack of attachment to Bosnia Herzegovina and to Islam.

National identity
Nationalism versus survival

I was sitting with some of my informants one Saturday evening at Café Galerija. It was getting late. We were talking, joking and listening to popular Balkan-rock music. One particular new pop song from Beograd made people dance and shout. Suddenly a police car stopped outside and everybody went to the big panorama window to watch. So did the guests from the Croat cafés from across the road. The police were just stopping to report on a car that was parked illegally. Suddenly there were about fifteen Muslims standing outside the café, and outside the Croatian cafés there were about sixty Croats. The situation was getting tense. Everybody was a little nervous, especially considering an incident only a few months earlier, in which violent Croats had destroyed the Muslim café. Suddenly one of the Muslim café guests ran across the road, where he started shouting and walking in the middle of the Croatian crowd very provocatively. But nothing happened. Then after a while the waiter from the Muslem café went over to him and pulled him back, but since he was drunk and angry he ran back and started to provoke the Croats again, shouting "What is wrong with you, why do you not come over and sit at our place?" Nusret, who had served in the Bosnian Army during the war, said to me: "This is a revolt, an authentic revolt, and because of this we survived. They are over 100 people over there and we are only ten, but they are afraid, they do not dare to do anything, they know us, they know who we are. There are four million Croats in Croatia, there are seven million Serbs in Serbia, they were attacking us from both sides, but we survived, we survived. It is like the movie from Scotland, Braveheart. Have you seen it? There are many more of them than us, but we will survive." He repeated the statement, clearly proud not of the drunken man who ran alone towards the Croats, but of the symbolic messages his act carried. The incident reflected the essence of the war. Another of the guests said to me "They are the HVO [the army of the Bosnian Croats], we are *Armija Bosnia*." The tense situation continued for half an hour, during which time the police just drove off. Then slowly people began stepping inside their cafés again.

At the café there was also a young guy, rather drunk. He came from Stolac, but he was living in Germany. He was only in Stolac to visit. He was furious. His friends tried to calm him down and they started quarrelling. At one point, he shouted to everyone in the café: "So here we have the Bosnian patriots, ha! I will return to Germany tomorrow." He found the others to be cowardly for not confronting the Croats. Though he was drunk, I think his statement also indicates that unambiguous and fierce national feelings thrive best in exile. Then after a while people finished their drinks and went home. Driving back from the café, one of my informants said, "It surely has rained"; apart from that, nobody said anything.

In the days after the episode, I thought that this was the Bosnian nationalism which I had not encountered before. It only needed this provocation together with some alcohol to surface, and I started noticing other statements of the same kind. Senad, for instance, told me how he sometimes relives situations from the war and wakes up totally upset. His brother commented: "The question is if they would dare to do it again. It was the only chance they had to kill us all, they will never have such an opportunity again." And Mehmed proudly told me that:

The Bosnian people [*Bosanac*] are a very brave people. When we pursue an aim, we either get killed or reach that aim. There are no in betweens. They did not count on that. They did not expect such high morals as the Bosnian people had in this war...We succeeded, due to our reason and our strength and our braveness in creating *Armija* [Armija BiH]. It is a unique thing in the world that a people create their own army in such a short time. Often it takes six-seven-eight years to create a fully organised army. And we succeeded in two years. And with such an army we defended ourselves against Croatia, which has four million citizens, and Serbia, which has ten million citizens.

Or consider this statement by Nusreta:

> When the Muslims fought against the Croats, there was a Serbian officer in the mountains at Mostar, and he watched the battles, and he said, if only I had Alija´s [Izetbegovic's] land forces, I would conquer the whole of Bosnia Herzegovina. The Muslim soldiers were that good.

Her husband replied: "So said Karadžić."[1]

Then I started asking myself what it really was that Nusret and the others were proud of. Obviously they were proud of *Armija BiH*, and proud that as a people they could withstand both the Serbs and the Croats.[2] Seldom, however, did I hear people talk about ideals. They did not say, 'We fought for Bosnia', 'for our people', 'for our nation', and they did not refer to any national values. What people said was that they fought, and that they survived. In fact the issue of survival is very central to understanding what we for lack of a better term might call Bosnian nationalism.

In his book *Fallen Soldier*, Moose (1990) has analysed how the emergence of nationalism and compulsory military service went hand-in-hand. Formerly a soldier would risk his life for money, but with the coming of the modern nation-state the soldier was to die for his nation, and the nation would be imagined through him. Moose calls this phenomenon the cult of the dead soldier. In Stolac today people are generally proud of *Armija BiH*, or *Armija* as it is called, in which the majority of the male population served in some way or another. However, their fight, suffering and victories, and the death of relatives, are not linked to Bosnia Herzegovina as a national symbol. Their fight was for survival, not for a nation. One of my informants once said that: "Everyone who survived the war is successful." During the war, about 100,000 people were killed, and many more fled, fearing for their lives, and survival was not at all a given during the war. For many of my informants I think it is true to say that they fought for survival, for their homes, their property, their families, and, as I will later show, because they had nowhere to run to. It is my impression that national self-consciousness was not particularly strong among the Bosnian Muslims before the

---

1   The Bosnian Serb leader.

2   When the war started Bosnia Herzegovina did not have an army. It had a police force and a territorial defence (TO), which was a kind of decentralised Home Guard. Bosnia Herzegovina experienced a weapons embargo, and even though it was not totally effective, it strongly reduced the Bosnians' possibilities for arming themselves. When *Armija BiH* was established, it received some support from Islamic countries, but despite this many observers were surprised and impressed by the fact that *Armija BiH* managed to some degree to hold out against two rather mighty armies.

war, that it probably grew throughout the war, and that it has now has faded. At no time, though, has Bosnian Muslim nationalism been strong, deeply internalised and influential (see also Maček 2000a).

Emir fought in the war. Once during an interview he showed me some pictures of himself and a friend in uniform, smiling, both holding machine-guns up in the air. Emir's mother felt embarrassed and did not want me to see the pictures; Emir, on the other hand, was proud of what he and his comrades had done in the war, but his pride was not related to a Bosnian nation:

> We did not fight for any ideas at all. We did not try to create some kind of state or country; we just did it in order to survive. I fought at the front with my weapon just to prevent them from coming and taking my mother. So that they wouldn't kill her or the children who were with her. There were no ideas in my head at that time, because I was hungry and thirsty and without anything. There were people who only had ten bullets in their guns, and they fought against tanks in that way. And in that situation you do not think about creating a state…We barely survived, we did not have any adopted country, as they [Croats and Serbs] had. They closed all the outlets, from both sides. We had no food, we were barefoot and naked.

Another informat, Suljeman, felt that the war created a Muslim consciousness. He once said: "Before the war we were Bosnians, today we are Muslims," but he also thought that this was only half of the story. Survival was the other half.

TK: What about during the war, were the Bosniaks more nationalist than today?

Suljeman: Yes they were, that's normal. And it was not without reason. It was an attack. You asked yourself, what is going on? You did not believe that a war could come. A lot of people could not understand what was really happening. What the real cause was. But everybody understood it afterwards. Some understood it sooner, some later. It was an attack on the Bosnian Muslims. A lot of people went into battle just to defend themselves, and when they defended themselves, they also defended Bosnia Herzegovina. Some did not do it consciously; they just followed a stream that went forward [a nationalist stream]. But common for all is that they were just defending their own lives.

During the war the Muslims of Herzegovina were pressed from two sides: the Croatian forces from the west and the Serbian forces to the east. They could, therefore, not escape either to Sarajevo or to Croatia and then further on. Many of my informants saw this as a major tactical mistake on behalf of the Croats and Serbs. The Muslims would have escaped if only they had been given the opportunity. In this sense, they felt they became Bosnians not by choice, but by chance. They were not primarily fighting for Bosnia, but because they had nowhere to run. The Muslims, whose backs were against the wall, had a different and greater motivation to fight than did conscripts in the Serbian army. The Muslim men defended not only their own lives: they knew that their wives and children were totally dependent on them. If the men had surrendered to the Croatian and Serbian forces, they would also have given up on their families behind the lines. According to many people I talked to, this is the reason that the Muslims held out in places like the Mostar area. Nationalism might have played a role, but not being able to escape was also a factor in turning the Muslims into Bosnians.

Bosnia has no appeal

Even today the image of *Bosnia* does not function as a meta-narrative that can bestow meaning on my informants' sufferings, traumas and material losses. People are simply not proud of their country and do not identify with it. They are fed up with the corrupt and worthless politicians; the educational system functions badly and does not qualify people for jobs, only private connections do; the unemployment rate is disastrous; people do not get their paycheck or pensions on time; the division between rich and poor has increased strikingly; there is no future for the children, and so on and so forth. People also feel that Bosnia Herzegovina has lost prestige internationally. As Senida said, making a sad joke, "Today for us Albania is the West." Albania is acknowledged by all to be by far the most backward country in Europe. In this context of despair one can understand the following disillusioned statement from a Bosnian worker in the Danish Refugee Council in Mostar: "Nobody won the war. After the Dayton agreement, the weapons were silent and peace broke out." The following two statements reflect this common feeling of disillusion and identity confusion among my informants.

Fahrudin: My roots are here, and Bosnia Herzegovina is my native country. The Serbs say that their language is their fatherland, and the Croats say the same and then I ask myself: 'who am I?' I am only a fact. I am neither a Serb nor a Croat and I do not want to be one. I want to stay what I am now. It must be difficult for you to understand, it is an unclear situation and it is also difficult for me. I was born here, grew up here, and attended school here, but it is not that clear to me. And you will stay some months and of course it is difficult for you to understand.[3] The café in front of us is Croatian. But those further below are Bosniak property, but the Croats moved in during the war, and now they do not want to give them back to their owners.

Muhamed's mother: I am not an orthodox Muslim. Once in a while I go to the mosque, but I have never been a 'big Muslim' [*Veliki Muslimani*, a strong believer and nationalist-minded Muslim] and I am not today. I respect my own faith and I respect others' faith. They had a plan for annihilating the Muslims, they wanted nothing else but to exterminate us from the map of the world. Both sides, both the Serbs and the Croats wanted to annihilate the Muslims. They wanted for one of them to have one part and the other the other part of former Yugoslavia, and for Bosnia to stop existing; no more. That's how it should be. By coincidence and maybe because God helped and also some of the European countries, this plan failed. Our soldiers tried to defend us, and then came the UN soldiers and these forces separated the three military forces in Bosnia, and now we have our situation.

If one compares these statements to statements made by the ordinary Croats in post-war Croatia interviewed by Stef Jansen (2000b), the differences are striking. For Jansen's informants, nothing was 'coincidental' (cf. Muhamed's mother above). For them Croatia as a symbol of identity made total sense of the war and the present miserable social situation as well as private losses. 'We have Croatia!' as they explained to Jansen, an expression directly borrowed from official nationalist rhetoric.[4] In Stolac a statement like 'We have Bosnia' would not work. Some informants sometimes pointed out that the Muslims as a group became much more homogeneous during the war. Such unity, however, must be related to the fact that the Muslims knew who they were primarily because they had been attacked as Muslims – or as I heard it expressed sometimes, 'only because of our names.' They knew whom they fought *against*, but today many

---

3   He was right, it was difficult for me to understand. In the quotation, however, the 'it', which he refers to, is not defined and it did not link up to my question. I think this 'it' relates to the identity confusion I am alluding to.

4   One should be aware that such use of official nationalist symbolism does not automatically mean a total marriage of national ideology and the individual mind, but rather what Jansen (2006) calls 'the pragmatics of conformism'. Furthermore, not everybody interpreted the death of family members (even though they had fallen in war) in an atmosphere of national ideology. Rithman-Auguštin (1995) found, through an analysis of death notices in Croatian newspapers in 1991-92, that along with a 'heroic' discourse adopting the language of national ideology, another kind of non-nationalistic mourning existed. In these other kinds of obituaries "many families did not even mention that the deceased was a combatant. They have been just lamenting the immense loss" (ibid. 65).

are uncertain about what they are fighting *for*. I will now give some examples to show how Bosnia Herzegovina does not have any special appeal as a national symbol.

I

I did not encounter public display of nationalist symbols among the Stolac Muslims. Part of the reason for such a 'lack' is probably the fact that the Muslims have returned to their town as a minority, and have been afraid of the Croats, at least initially. But I encountered no nationalist symbols in private homes either. People are simply not proud of Bosnia Herzegovina. Although they consider its existence legitimate, it does not function as an icon of identification.

II

There is an opposition between people from Herzegovina and Sarajevo, which I think the war amplified. My informants felt that the Muslims of Sarajevo 'sold' their fellow countrymen in the war for strategic reasons. For instance, Nihad told me that a Bosnian general north of Mostar could have moved south and liberated Stolac just before the signing of the peace treaty between the Muslims and the Croats (in 1994). But the Muslim politicians in Sarajevo held him back. Nihad saw this decision as a political decision, not military strategy: "They thought that we were all going to die, so they left us to our own fate." Or as Omer once said:

> The only politician who drew attention to the fact that the Muslims were in prison camps in Herzegovina was Haris Silajdžić. SDA believed in the unity between the Muslims and the Croats, they believed it the whole time. But they did not know how we [Muslims in Herzegovina] were doing. They knew, but they kept quiet. Because they were only concerned about Sarajevo. There was a deal where our [Muslim] politicians from Sarajevo said 'If only you give us arms so we can defend Sarajevo, then you can keep Herzegovina.' They [the Croats] would definitely have occupied Mostar, if the road to Sarajevo had not been closed. We did not have any chance to leave Mostar, and that's why I stayed in Mostar and defended my family. We had nowhere to go, and that's why they could not take Mostar.[5]

---

5   According to Glenny (1996: 228), people in Sarajevo were dependent on weapons supplies coming across Croatian territory and Izetbegović did negotiate with the Croatian president Franjo Tuđman.

Sarajevo, therefore does not work for the Muslims of Stolac as an icon for im-agining a Bosnian nation.

III

According to a survey conducted in Bosnia Herzegovina in 2000 (UNDP 2000), the weak national feeling I found among my informants in Stolac was part of a broader phenomenon. 1,000 young people (ages 14 to 30) of different ethnicities were interviewed. Though the report states that as many as 85 % of the Bosniaks feel greatly or moderately attached to Bosnia Herzegovina (p. 93), family/friends, habit and local attachment account for 50 % of the respondents' incentive for continuing to live in Bosnia Herzegovina, whereas patriotism only amounts to 10 % (p. 92). Taken as a whole, the survey makes for rather disil-lusioning reading. 62 % of all the young people in Bosnia Herzegovina would leave the country if they were given the opportunity. The three most important reasons for such a wish are low standard of living (42 %), no prospects of the country (19 %), and unemployment (17 %). In sum, the report tells of a young generation which has lost confidence in the future.

IV

The Stolac Muslims' feelings about the future often swung between disillusion-ment and hope. This quotation expresses the disillusioned perspective:

Huma: He [her husband] was a soldier, I was a nurse and was working all the time at the hospital with wounded soldiers. People came into the hospital without legs, arms, totally destroyed people with psychic traumas. I gave birth to a child, and then another. We have yet another boy, but he is not here now. He is three years old. Everything is a big trauma. We stayed here the whole time as *domoljubi* [those who love their country]. We hoped things would be better. Now our country does not make sense [*bez veze*]. No law. Anarchy, anarchy, criminals. It is like the things we only saw in the movies before.

Then she talked about immigrating with their children to the USA, due to their hopeless economic situation.

Huma: We do not believe a great happiness is waiting for us. We will leave because of our children, so things can be better for them. And if we have the chance to earn some money, we will come back to Bosnia someday. We will not stay there forever. We are going in order to create a better life.

Friend (who is also planning to emigrate): I will leave because I have had enough of those idiots. I have had enough of Serbs, Croats and most of all Muslims. Something went wrong with my pretty, fine perspective on the Bosniaks. One is disappointed. And how could I not be disappointed. It is a catastrophe. My best years came to nothing.

In Stolac many talked about emigrating, and while I was there three families left the country to seek asylum before they even knew whether their applications had been turned down or not.

V

In the light of people's disappointment with their country and their politicians, it is not surprising that everyone with whom I discussed the topic wanted Bosnia Herzegovina to become a protectorate. They felt that foreign powers needed to take over Bosnia Herzegovina in order to save the country. At present the OHR is formally the highest authority in Bosnia Herzegovina, but the institution has neither the power nor the desire to control the country with an iron hand. In general, the hope of the OHR is that democracy can develop among Bosnians themselves. The Muslims of Stolac were not particularly optimistic. As Dino said "The only times there has been peace in the country have been when foreign powers controlled and ruled Bosnia Herzegovina: the Turks, the Austro Hungarians, and also Tito because he was a strict and hard leader." Seen in this light it is understandable that some of my informants feared the withdrawal of the international personnel, as such a withdrawal could lead Bosnia Herzegovina back into war.

VI

A last example of my informants' lack of identification with Bosnia Herzegovina was their attitude towards the army. Though people were proud of *Armija BiH* and believed that their army could defend them, I never traced any romantic feelings regarding compulsory conscription. In the Croat Muslim Federation there is officially a joint Croat-Muslim army, but in reality it was totally segregated. Two of my informants were to do their military service when I was in Stolac, and neither they nor the people with whom I discussed the matter had any national-romantic feelings about military service. They felt it was stupid and a waste of time that young people were forced to serve nine months in the army. A professional army would be better.

Religious identity

Religiosity today

Pre-war religious observance among the Muslims of Bosnia Herzegovina was rather low (see Chapter 9). Only 37 % claimed to be religious (Bougarel 1995: 80), and devout religiosity existed mainly among the intellectual urban elite. In everyday life, Islam was mainly used in order to construct a Muslim identity as opposed to non-Muslim groups (Croats or Serbs). During the war, religion became politicised and served as a vehicle for expressing a separate Muslim identity. Mojzes (1998: 92-96) reports that Muslim fighting units increasingly turned into purely Islamic units defending a Muslim nationalist ideology and not the multi-religious society that the Bosnian government officially defended. Vrcan (1998: 123) writes that the Muslim community vacillated between defending the idea of a Bosnian Muslim state based on Islamic culture on the one hand, and defending an independent and multi-religious, multiethnic Bosnia Herzegovina on the other hand. But as the war proceeded, there was a marked shift in the direction of a growing resistance to multi-religiosity. In her detailed ethnography of the siege of Sarajevo, Maček (2000a) also describes how religion increasingly came to signal difference between the ethnic groups rather than the groups' common background and experience. The war made people more religious, but a great portion of pragmatism continued to exist. For example, many Muslims found Catholic ancestors in their family in order to be eligible for humanitarian aid from Caritas, an organisation run by Catholics. The Muslims also wanted to keep their special Bosnian interpretation and practice of Islam. The presence, therefore, of people from foreign Islamic countries – either wanting to help or doing missionary work – in fact provoked the Sarajevans. Maček (2000a: 212) concludes: "To be a Muslim in Sarajevo one did not need to believe that there was no God but God and that Mohammed was his Prophet, but one did need to remember that faith, and reconsider what it meant for one's everyday life." In short, then, religion played an increasing role in peoples' lives because of the pressure they experienced; but at the same time people tried to keep hold of the pre-war pragmatic and tolerant attitude towards religion.

So what has happened since the end of the war? My findings suggest that today religiosity has found a level more or less equal to the pre-war situation and does not play a major role in people's everyday practices of identification.[6] For some, religious activity and ideals are important, but for most people being a good Muslim means to behave decently and does not relate to religious

6   On the background of research conducted after the war, Maček concludes the same for the Muslims of Sarajevo (Maček 2000a: 198, and personal communication), see also Bougarel (2001).

practices; for some Islam is simply unimportant. Therefore, for Stolac Muslims religious identity does not fully define what it means to be a Muslim. Several of my informants told me about how they were more religious during the war than today, they prayed more often and celebrated Ramadan more strictly. This they considered normal, due to the immense psychological pressure they endured, and consequently there was nothing strange about the decline of religious observance when the war stopped. Often people lamented the loss of the wartime sense of community and social interaction, but the issue was not religion but rather *društvo* (approximately: social intermingling). It was my impression that only a few of my informants were particularly religious. Once I said to Nihad that in Denmark people go to church three times in their lives: baptism, marriage and burial. He laughed and said that in Bosnia it was similar. I was obviously not wholly correct about Danish religiosity, and Nihad not about Bosnian, but to judge by my informants' practices and lack of talk about Islam, it seems that they had a rather pragmatic relation to their faith, as the following examples show.

I

Following the Koran one should neither drink alcohol nor eat pork. My informants did not eat pork, but the reason given was that it was repulsive.[7] The majority had a relaxed attitude to alcohol. I do not recall being in a Muslim home where I was not offered *loza* (grape brandy) and often it was homemade. Homemade wine was also highly esteemed. This is not to say that people drank a lot, but that drinking was just not an issue.

II

Only a few people regularly attended the mosque (or what was left of it), the same number of people as before the war, I was told. At the Friday service there were about five to seven young people, the remaining twenty to twenty-five persons being over sixty. And I never observed people praying during the day or in the evening.

---

7   A Bosnian refugee I interviewed in Denmark recalled a situation in which a Dane asked her why she did not eat pork, and she answered: 'I don't know, I don't like it.' But he kept asking: 'But *why* do you not eat it?' And for lack of a better answer she asked him 'Why do you not eat cats?' I think my informants could have offered a similar practical and non-religious explanation to such a question.

III

During the war language had become politicised and more Turkish words and expressions had entered the Muslims' language. Greetings had increasingly become symbols of nationality. It is my impression that this has changed again for the Muslims of Stolac. Possibly the use of religious greetings has increased from the pre-war level, but I heard them only rarely. Sometimes people would say *selam alejkum* (peace for all), and the reply would be *alejkum selam*; but mostly people said such secular and religiously neutral greetings as *dobra dan, šta ima, kako si/ste, šta radi* to each other.

IV

Before the war the children who attended *mekteb* (Koran school) would sometimes, if they had old-fashioned teachers, have to learn to recite the Koran in Arabic. Nijaz's wife Ljiljana knows some of the Koran in Arabic, but she does not get much credit for that. As Nijaz said to her once: "Well it doesn't matter, God understands all languages, why then should we pray in Arabic?"

V

The last example of my informants' pragmatic relationship to their faith refers to Ramadan [*Ramazan*], which took place in November and December 2000, when I was doing fieldwork. Ramadan is the main event in the Muslim ritual calendar. It occurs in the ninth month of the Muslim year, and is observed as a month of fasting during which Muslims abstain from eating, drinking and sexual intercourse between sunrise and sunset. As a codified ritual in Islam, it is an individual statement of one's personal commitment and it could easily be used as a way to identify and collectively emphasise Muslim identity. But not many people in Stolac observed the fast. Some did so on some days, while others ate and drank less in the period. Often only one or two in a family would be fasting or partly fasting. Actually, it was not a big issue. On a number of occasions I heard people making jokes about those who fasted. Once when Mensur's mother talked about waking up before sunrise to have something to drink, her husband laughingly replied "this is definitely not for me", and later when she told me that smoking is not allowed during Ramadan, her husband said, "Well, then Ramadan is good for something." Their daughter-in-law was a smoker. Muhamed was also fasting, and his friends once said to me while we were having coffee together (with the exception of Muhamed): "He is not allowed to eat, or even drink coffee, he cannot smoke, or even drink water, and he is not allowed to make love to his wife for a whole month", and then they all started laughing. Those who fasted or partly fasted focused mainly on practical aspects: how it is easier to fast in the wintertime as the days are shorter, how to wake up at four o'clock in the morning to have a morning coffee, how drinking a little water is allowed if one needs to take pills, and so on. Or they said that they did it because it was a nice tradition. Two of my informants who observed the fast gave more ideological explanations for observing the ritual. They focused on how it made one feel good, how one could handle things more easily, how one got energy after a couple of days, and how it helped one to be a better human being. Irrespective of their attitude towards the fast, everybody looked forward to the Bajram (*ramazanski bajram*), when the fast was over and people visited each other and had cakes (especially *baklava*), juice and coffee.

Dissociation from religious dogmatism

These examples are not meant to illustrate that Islam does not have a place in people's lives. Many people saw themselves as believers and respected their God. Being a believer, however, was about being a decent human being, behaving properly, taking care of one's family and fellow man and so on. It was not about knowing the Koran, praying, fasting, attending the mosque, greeting people in the right way and so on. In fact, I often heard people dissociate themselves from more dogmatic religious manifestations. Instead, they wanted to stick to what they regarded as the typical Bosnian way of practising religion. Ljubica was what one could regard as a normal believer, to the extent that such a concept makes sense. She believed a little, fasted a little during Ramadan, and she knew the Koran a little:

> The Muslims here in Herzegovina were not particularly devout. Maybe it is different north of Sarajevo. The Serbs aren't devout either, but the Croats go to church every Sunday. During the war, then we were more religious, we were scared. Before the war I never saw anyone with a veil, but during the war there were quite a few donations from Saudi Arabia and Iraq, and they brought the custom with them. But it is not autochthonous [authentic]. The Muslims here are different. It seems as though everybody today is afraid of Islam, but our Islam is different from the Arabic countries, we are not particularly devout.

In Sarajevo, Maček (2000a) observed a similar attitude. People distinguished between 'real Muslims' and 'April Muslims'; the latter being the ones who discovered their religiosity at the beginning of the war (April 1992). People respected the 'real Muslims', but often the newly awakened Muslims were looked on with contempt. Throughout the war and afterwards, religious symbols had been manipulated, religious differences reinforced, and many people had been killed or had to flee in the name of religion. Today many of the Muslims in Stolac are tired of politicians' nationalistic-religious rhetoric. As I have already shown, the Croats use nationalistic and religious symbols in abundance. This is what Muhamed's mother said:

> When one enters the hospital [run by Croats] there is a huge picture of Tuđman, and below it says 'Tuđman is my president.' And there is a big cross with Jesus on it, and you should not do such a thing in a public place. When you enter a hospital in eastern Mostar [the Muslim part of Mostar] the only thing you can find on the walls are children's drawings, you do not see a cross or crescent and stars. It is all right if you wear a cross on yourself, that is your right, because it is something that is your own. And you have the right to wear it. But it is not all right if you place it somewhere where it doesn't belong. Jesus Christ, I salute him, but he should not be in the places where he doesn't belong. His right place is in the Church and they shouldn't play with him.

People not only disapprove of the misuse of religious symbols by others. Their 'own' religious symbols and practices are also rejected if viewed as too dogmatic. I shall give some examples.

I

One day while shopping in a local shop in Stolac where people sometimes hang around, a man wanted to teach me a Muslim greeting. Another of the men present said, "No, you can't teach him that, that's a religious expression you know, that's not a good thing." I found it a little strange, since the man who protested was one of the more devout people I knew. But he automatically dissociated himself from what he sensed could be interpreted as a religious/nationalistic statement. This is not to say that he did not appreciate such religious statements, but rather that he wanted to show that he did not find them appropriate. I experienced a similar situation one evening during a private visit. One of those present used an old Turkish word (I cannot recall the word), and another man jokingly said that he should not be teaching me such words, as I would then think they were Muslim fundamentalists. Behind the joke I think he was also concerned with the picture I got of them as Muslims. He did not want me to see them as particularly devout.

II

One evening Nihad and I were talking about what it meant to be a Muslim, and he light-heartedly said: "We are Muslims, we don't eat pork, but we drink a lot of *loza* [grape brandy]. During the war we received some dates in the aid packages from Saudi Arabia and we used them for making *rakija* [spirits]. We did not have food, but we had cigarettes and *rakija*, we needed something to soothe the nerves." Besides being funny, the story also communicated how Bosnian Muslims are not very religious, at least not as religious as 'those from Saudi Arabia'.

III

Another example of my informants' rejection of a dogmatic interpretation of Islam relates to how those who showed off their religion too much were not well respected, such as women who wore veils or *mujahedins* who stayed on in the country after the war. One evening I did an interview in a home where one of the women present was a firm believer and not allowed to touch men other than her husband. I was therefore instructed by the informant I conducted the interview with not to offer her my hand on entering. I was only to say *dobro veče* (good evening). After the interview, I told some people about the woman who would not shake hands and one of the men commented "well, she would probably do it if you had a DM100 note in your hand", and another man replied, "You would probably only need DM10."

IV

The last example relates to the rebuilding of mosques throughout Bosnia Herzegovina. One might assume that such rebuilding was popular, as the destruction of the many mosques during the war was a symbol of the destruction of the Bosnian Muslim people. Reconstruction of mosques could be seen as rebuilding dignity and Muslim identity signalling 'we have not given up.' The Muslims of Stolac, however, simply found such rebuilding to be a total waste of money. The Muslims in Stolac I talked to all agreed that they did not want the rebuilding of the mosques, they wanted investments. While I was in Stolac there were plans to rebuild the mosque in the centre of town. Talking to Emir about the matter, I said that I thought it was a good idea. Rebuilding the mosque would be a statement saying that the Muslims also have the right to live in Stolac. Emir, however, did not agree. He definitely preferred jobs and factories to a symbolic manifestation saying 'we have returned.'[8]

One could have assumed that national and religious identity would have been used by my informants to define Muslim identity, considering the all-pervasiveness of powerful ethnoreligious nationalist politics prior to and throughout the war. In addition, Muslim identity has been extremely important, as the killings and expulsion of the Muslims solely referred to ethnic identity. The

8   The mosque has now been reconstructed.

Muslims of Stolac strongly felt themselves to be Muslims, and to be a Muslim in Bosnia Herzegovina refers both to the practice of Islam and to national identity (*narod*). In spite of all these factors, however, religion and national identification only played a minor role in my informants' identifications; these two aspects could not alone fill up the 'container' called Muslimness. People did not identify much with their country, neither during the war when they mainly fought for survival and not for a state, nor when I did fieldwork when the positive symbolic value of Bosnia Herzegovina was slight. Religion was more important: I only met a few people who declared themselves to be atheists. Their religious identity, however, had not colonised more of their identity as Muslims than it had done before the war; on the contrary, it seemed that people distanced themselves from a radical and dogmatically religious Islam. In the remainder of Part III, I shall analyse how the Muslims of Stolac defined themselves as Muslims, considering the fact that national and religious identities are but a part of the overall Muslim identification.

Chapter 12
Localistic identifications

During and after the war, *Jugo-nostalgija* was a label used by nationalists to tag people they considered critical of the nationalist vision. The label, however, was soon taken over by those targeted by it. According to Jansen (2000a), *jugo-nostalgic* displays of the past and the imagination of Yugoslavia as a common cultural space where everyone lived well were used as critical commentary on the present. First, because the story of the good times in Yugoslavia was a story of remembering, in opposition to the nationalistic regimes' amnesia and break with the past. Second, by conceptualising a shared space (the Yugoslavian past) it became possible to "access a common ground where a host of different desires might meet and be articulated into a potential dynamic of change" (ibid. 217). Reconstruction of the past, in other words, had the potential to enable a political vision of a better future. Similarly, Velikonja (2002) has shown how *jugo-nostalgija* in Slovenia has become a vehicle for a critique of the present regime's uncritical embrace of a Western-style future. In Stolac people talked a lot about the past. Sometimes, like Jansen's informants, they explicitly talked about Yugoslavia and the cultural space connected with it. More often, they talked about Stolac, or the 'Stolac spirit' as they sometimes called it, but even so some of the same dynamics analysed by Jansen existed. My informants' strong local patriotism focusing on Stolac as a centre of open-mindedness, a meeting point for different cultures and ethnic groups, and a unique and beautifull town provides a source of identification and resistance to the nationalist vision, and is thus part of the counterdiscourse. At times, though, it also serves as a critique of the Croats, who are considered blameworthy.

The Stolac spirit

Three aspects characterised people's talk about the Stolac spirit, and all hoped this spirit would return.

Coexistence

The ideal of coexistence was of central importance to the Muslims of Stolac, and was often associated with a typical Stolac mentality: people from Stolac are simply seen as predisposed to co-exist, and multiculturalism runs in the 'cultural genes' of the people. My informants saw Stolac as a crossroads for different cultures, and stressed that all newcomers have been welcomed. People mentioned the Jewish grave just outside town, which commemorates the Rabbi Mosha Danon from Sarajevo, who died on his way to Jerusalem and was buried here in 1830. Or they refer to an ornament on one of the world-famous *Stećaks* (medieval Bosnian tombstones) at the *Necropolis Radimlja* two kilometres outside town. This headstone is decorated with the figure of a standing man whose hand is lifted upwards at the elbow and whose palm is open, greeting the spectators. This gesture is read by the Stolac Muslims as meaning that all strangers are welcome. Salko expressed his idea of local inter-ethnic coexistence in Stolac in the following way:

> Our wish is that people would return. We want the Stolac spirit to return. And that spirit is the citizens who lived here before the war *bošnjaki, i serbi, i hrvati.*[1] And those coming from outside [*strani*], the best thing would be if they left.[2]

An interview I did with a Croat woman shows that this idea of a Stolac spirit was not reserved for Muslims. It is for everybody to identify with.

> When I returned to Stolac three years ago, I met a Muslim, and I inquired about all my neighbours, and then we talked for a while, and when we split up I said: 'Greet everyone who drank from our river.' It doesn't matter if they are Serbs, Croats or Muslims. Because everyone is the same and has the same problems. Compared to other cities where people built big houses, in Stolac they built small houses, but the heart was big. The neighbours are tolerant towards us, and we towards them. If you do not want to live in this way, you shouldn't come back to Stolac. If I only wanted to live with Serbs or Croats I would never have returned. We have to live together and not beside each other. Because if we live beside each other, we can live here for 1,000 years without talking to each other. When I stayed in Zagreb, nobody greeted or talked to each other. It is better to live together. It is beautiful. That's the way I was raised.

---

1   The reason why I write this in the source language is that I often heard precisely this expression: 'Bosnjaks, and Serbs and Croats'. It seemed to be a deeply felt and engraved turn of phrase.

2   He refers to Croats from central Bosnia.

The beauty and economic strength of Stolac

The second element of the Stolac spirit relates to the feeling of unity with the beauty of the town. Pictures of pre-war Stolac show that it was a very beautiful and architectonically harmonious town. On a number of occasions I was reminded that before the war Stolac was a candidate for UNESCO's list of cities worthy of preservation. People proudly told me about the four picturesque mosques, *Stara Tepa* (the big town market built in old Ottoman style), *Begovina*, the old watermills, the Hotel Bregava (a newly constructed but architectonically well-integrated building), all the cafés, the shops and so forth. Today everything is mined or burned. They told me about the lovely Mediterranean climate. They talked about the River Bregava, which runs through the town, where one can swim and fish and which provides water for the gardens situated on its banks. They described all the fruits they could grow: "In the summer fruit is so plentiful you don't have to go hungry, we have kiwi, peaches, apricots, figs, apples, grapes, pomegranate, plum," as Mensur's mother said. And they told me about all the industries and factories in town, which employed a lot of people and exported goods to the whole of Yugoslavia and abroad. In short, they were/had been very proud of their town.

The reason why I write 'were/had been' is that people often had ambivalent feelings about their town. Visual memories from before the war, pictures from pre-war Stolac, present images, dreams – they all merged together. Some said they could not remember what the town looked like before the war; others said they could not drive through the town without seeing the 'real' Stolac in their mind's eye. Everybody felt the town had become ugly, but nonetheless I was asked – often in the expectant way one normally asks visitors to one's town – how I liked the town, and it was obvious that the appropriate and polite answer would be 'It is very nice.' I just could not say it, because Stolac was ruined, dirty and ugly. And when I said that, people sometimes became quiet for a while and then said, "Yes, that's right." Despite such contradictory feelings, Stolac was generally constructed in people's minds as a beautifull and unique town. When people were in a realistic mood, their Stolac did not exist any more; instead they saw an ugly town dominated by Croats. But when they talked about Stolac in a more insubstantial but still physical manner, it was as though the old 'real' Stolac rose from the dust, and people were again full of pride for their town. They considered it the best place on earth. In this way the beauty of the town coalesced with the spirit of coexistence, and together these visions functioned as a symbolic cultural space or an idea with which one could identify.

Mehmed was a member of the SDA, and as such supported a more explicit Bosnian Muslim national identity. His statement below, however, regards local and not national identity.

We *Stočani* [citizens of Stolac] wish, even though I will not live long enough to see, but my daughter will live long enough to see Stolac become Stolac again: the old town that you have seen in pictures. We *Stočani* want such a town again. Life here is unique compared to the whole rest of Bosnia. Stolac as Stolac with its own way of life, and all *Stočani* want it to be so again.

Mehmed's wife: And those people from Kakanj [Croats from central Bosnia], they just have to go back to where they came from.

Mehmed: Everyone should have the opportunity to go back to their own homes, and one's property should be one's own again. And those people from Kakanj, if they don't want to go back, nobody says they can't stay, but they have to live in their own houses, not in mine. My house was given to me by my father, and I will not let someone else live in my house. It is mine and it is my life. For me Stolac is the most beautiful town in the whole world, although it's destroyed. And the same goes for Bregava [the city river].

Raha was a woman who loved her town. In this excerpt from an interview, she is talking about *Stara Tepa*, the pre-war market in Stolac. There was widespread agreement about such a market's potential for facilitating interethnic interaction. A special aspect of this quote is the way the speaker mixes past and present tense, which reflects people's ambiguous feelings for their town.

It's expensive in the shops and the market is much cheaper, and therefore we want one. And we called it *Tepa*. The things one can buy there are handmade by the people producing them, and there is no tax, that's why it's cheaper. The only thing they must pay for is the stand. Every week people came from all over, and one could buy meat and the quality is the best in the whole of Herzegovina. We have a flower in Herzegovina, and when the goats eat it the quality [of the meat] is the best. And the honey is the best and most expensive due to this flower [*zanovijet*].

Besides being a source of identification, picturing pre-war Stolac was also a critique of the Croats who demolished the old Ottoman-inspired town and dominate it today, and who were trying to create a new Catholic and modern Stolac. Stolac was destroyed after the fighting with the Serbs in 1992-93. When the Muslim men had been expelled and only women and children were left, the mosques were razed, and the old houses, private libraries and priceless cultural artefacts were burned. And when the Muslims started to return in 1997, ordinary Muslim houses were mined and burned. The meaning of the violence was clear: to extinguish everything reminiscent of the Muslims/Ottomans/Turks – and later to prevent the return of the Muslims. Physical traces of the past were removed or destroyed, and the town was to be constructed in a new image. Flags were raised, the street names changed, and a bust was erected in front of the school where the old Partisan memorial had been. An even more grotesque denial of the town's past appeared, so I was told, on TV. Following the expulsion, only very few Muslims remained in Stolac, all women in mixed marriages. One Muslim family did stay, though, as members of the family had saved a Catholic bishop from the Partisans during the Second World War.[3] The man in the family was forced to confirm on television that there had never been any mosques in Stolac, which naturally was very odd for the Stolac Muslims to watch or hear about. The Muslims' active remembering of pre-war Stolac is therefore not only a matter of nostalgia and identification, but also a resistance to the Croats' destruction of the old Stolac and their vision of a new town. For this reason, even talking about the past and pre-war Stolac is a strongly political act.

Sometimes the criticism of the Croats is more explicit. People say that the Croats do not love the town, or that they do not have any real attachment to it. If they did, they would not have treated it the way they did. Broken bricks, pieces of glass, ruined houses used as dumps, car wrecks in the river or in gardens, old faded graffiti: this is what characterises Stolac. And the Croats responsible for most of this mess, and who have lived in it since the war, have done nothing to clean it up. As Suljeman said: "They want a dump rather than cultural monuments", implying that the Croats do not deserve the town. Ibro and his wife expressed this criticism very directly during an interview.

Ibro: When I returned last year, I went out to see to the river, but the river was wild. You couldn't see the water because the shores were polluted. We used to clean the river every year, every spring, so the river would be clean, because it is the mirror of the town.

Wife: None of the young people will do it now, and we elderly, we can't. I am not a pessimist; I hope it will be good again. Come back to Stolac in five years and see how it is. A lot of young people are returning, but you can't live here if you don't love this town. When you live in your own town, you take care of it and love it, and I can see that it hasn't been taken care of during the war. And this is because the ones who lived here during the war, they did not love it, they did not take care of it. They threw old cars in Bregava. In the river lived fish, snakes and frogs, and now there is nothing. There were many water mills on the river. Everything is destroyed, but it will be again [the town will be beautiful again].

3   See: http://www.haverford.edu/relg/sells/stolac/stolacrab.htm

The homemade and local

The last element in Stolac Muslims' local patriotism has to do with the value attached to everything *domaci* (homemade/local), in particular local food. People would proudly let me know that the bread, the cheese, the yogurt, the juice, the *loza* (grape brandy) they served me were all *domaci*. Homemade food from the Stolac area was by definition better quality and preferable. People told me how the local food products were produced without chemicals or fertilizers, which in turn made the *domaci* clean (*čisto*). Some emphasised that their cows did not have mad cow disease, as they moved freely around in the mountains; others told me that eggs from the chicken farms smelled so strange. Of special importance was the pomegranate [*šipak*], which grows in abundance. It is tasty and full of vitamin C. I was kindly given several bottles of *šipak* juice, and when I went home to Denmark I was asked to take *šipak* juice to people's relatives there. The positive connotations of everything homemade affected other kinds of classifications. In Chapter 8, we saw how people said that they did not have problems with Croats from Stolac, labelling them '*naši domaći Hrvati*': our hometown Croats.

The struggle for local identity

There are only a few visible markers of Muslim identity in Stolac: the Croats dominate the public space, and the Muslims do little to change this. Many are probably afraid of the reactions that visible demonstrations could provoke (see e.g. Mahmutcehalic 2001), but more importantly this attitude is in line with the Muslims' self-perception. The Muslims identify themselves by the fact that they *do not use* the same methods and rhetoric as the nationalists. Waving a flag or drawing nationalistic graffiti simply would not be respected. The few physical markers of identity I did encounter are rather part of the Muslims' localistic identifications.

I

Before the war, a modest local historical pamphlet was published in Stolac with illustrated articles on the history, archaeology and architecture of the area. After the war and the total destruction of the Stolac heritage, these booklets suddenly gained new importance. In 1997, some prominent people from Stolac initiated the reprinting of these booklets, along with a section with comparative photographs of Stolac then and now, in the format of a book (Slovo Gorčina 1997). The book was evidence of a time and a town which no longer existed. The articles, which hardly anyone read before the war, now became an important source of identity for people living in Stolac, since the book helped them to mentally (re)construct the picture of beautiful pre-war Stolac that the Croats had destroyed and now deny ever existed. Without these publications, the ethnic and cultural cleansing of Stolac would have been total. The free distribution of the book to the citizens of Stolac was intended to help them remember their town. However, the book was probably also meant as a kind of propaganda, to play a part in the imagination of the 'real' Stolac, as it was not particularly attractive for people to return in 1997-98 due to such problems as violence, threats and unemployment. In this sense, the political motive behind the book's publication was to help motivate people to return, so that Stolac could again become Muslim.

II

Another source of local identity was the River Bregava, which runs through town. People often talked about the river and would sometimes say, 'at least we have Bregava.' I think that the Bregava functioned as a central component in the Muslims' identification with Stolac and the Stolac spirit. Here is a small excerpt from my notebook written after a conversation with Anvere:

> [S]he was laughing a little at the name Sanpero, the name of the restaurant where the cultural centre had been before. She also said that before [the war] there had been a gallery next to Café Galerija, where artists from Stolac exhibited. She then told me that it was so strange to realise that all this is destroyed and gone. The town really had soul before, a spirit: 'now they have destroyed everything, the mosques, Begovina…Bregava is the only thing which they haven't destroyed.' When she said this, I realised why people talked about Bregava so much; maybe they had done so before, but now it was of extra importance, because it was the only thing people have left. It was like a symbol saying 'We have not given up.' The Bregava is what was left of the real Stolac. Or as Enver replied when I asked him if the River Bregava is the spirit of Stolac, 'Yes, it is the only thing left that is ours.'

One of the Muslim cafés in Stolac is called Café Benat. The name refers to the place in town where the river is most scenic. And the name was not chosen arbitrarily; rather it is part of the appropriation of the symbolic/physical space of Stolac.

III

Another Muslim café in Stolac, Café Galerija, marked a more contested struggle to regain a territorial marker. The café, located in the centre of town opposite three Croatian cafés, was popular. The owners of the place spent a lot of energy on making it a cosy and pleasant place to be. It had big panorama windows so that one could overlook the centre, outdoor tables, flowers on the tables, and beautiful black and white drawings of pre-war Stolac on the walls, drawings which were part of the mental (re)construction of pre-war Stolac. The café had been destroyed twice by Croats. I think that the Muslim café in the centre of town was seen as a provocation by the Croats, and as a symbolic invasion of territory. Accepting the café would be tantamount to accepting the presence of the Muslims in Stolac. It should also be taken into account that Muslim houses were also repeatedly mined or burned (especially in 1996-98) in order to frighten the Muslims and prevent them from returning. On both occasions the café was reopened. For the Muslims the re-openings were a symbol of the integration of the town and the possible coexistence of the ethnic groups in Stolac rather than a sign of antagonism. Some said that Croats also patronised the café. Although, I never met any. I suppose that people wanted them to come to Café Galerija, thereby legitimising it and doing their part in (re)constructing the Stolac spirit. Recall also (Chapter 11) the night at Café Galerija where one of the Muslims provoked the Croats on the other side of the road. He repeatedly shouted, "Why don't you come and sit with us", meaning something like why do you not want to help reconstruct the Stolac spirit. This is an excerpt from an interview with Alija, one of the owners of Café Galerija. He hoped the café could play a part in reintegrating people in Stolac, seeing it as a fight for the town and the Stolac spirit of coexistence.

TK: Has the café also been a fight for your country?

Alija: What happened during the war was a fight for the country[4]. But the thing about the café was a fight for this town, and everybody who comes to the café understands it in that way.

TK: Do you think the Croats will come to the café in the future?

Alija: Yes. Listen, the good Croats already come, so do the Serbs. When they are in town, they naturally go down to Galerija…I hope the café can play a part in integrating people living here in Stolac…You have been at the cafe, what is your experience, do you think people enjoy themselves, is there a good atmosphere?

---

4   He says *drzava, opstina, naroda* right after each other, so it is difficult to translate.

IV

Alija also played a central role on two other occasions when a fight for the physical/symbolic space of Stolac was going on. First, he initiated a tidying-up of one of the *haremi* (Muslim graveyards) in town. Before the war the scouts normally did this, as well as cleaning the river. Since the expulsion of the Muslims, however, the *harem* had been left unattended. Grass, trees and bushes had grown wild. One day a group of people, among them Alija, made a poster asking everybody to come and spend a day cleaning the place. Around 80 people, mostly men of all ages, turned up. The atmosphere was great and everybody seemed to enjoy the work, especially because they were finally able to do something, accomplish something, take up some space in Stolac, saying indirectly: this is also our town. Everybody was working hard, cutting, sawing, weeding and raking, and there were a lot of bonfires. Suddenly a big beautiful tree caught fire. Edin, however, just laughed and said "save nature." Then he and another person started making fires next to trees in other places. I said: "Isn't it a pity to do so?" "No!" Edin replied, "So many shells have fallen here, the place needs to be cleaned up." People laughed and kept working, and I do not think Edin was alone in thinking that the best thing would be if one could burn it all down, like a symbolic purification. The *harem* was already defiled and had lost some of its sacredness. Nijaz's father showed me his father's grave, a big marble slab with an engraving of a picture of his father. He pointed at the holes in the slab (approximately ten holes, each the size of a small coin) made by the shells, and said nothing. I think the anarchistic cleaning and burning gave the *harem* some of its value back.

V

The last example of the physical/symbolic recapturing of Stolac and the con-current construction of the Stolac spirit is rather tragic. Alija again played a central role, but this time in a sad and involuntary way. One morning the tel-ephone rang and my landlady answered it. She did not really say anything. She just sighed and then said "Oh no!" Alija's younger brother had died. A couple of days before he and some friends had driven off the road. Perhaps the road had been icy. He died in a hospital in Sarajevo. After hanging up my landlady said: "Imagine, surviving the war and then he dies now, it is a tragedy, it is life!" Her husband did not say anything. Tears just ran down his cheeks. The follow-ing day the funeral (*dženaza*) was held. A lot of people attended the ceremony at the only functioning mosque in town, actually a reconstructed room in a demolished mosque, and afterwards everybody walked through town down to the *harem*. I think 500-800 people were present. It was quite a sight when everybody walked in procession through the town, all these people through the narrow streets. More importantly, though, it was the first time since the war that people had *walked* through town at a *denaza,* which was customary. I do not think it was meant as a provocation. Rather it was a way of saying 'we also live here', 'we have the right to be here.' Furthermore, this manifestation was in accord with the deceased's spirit. He was known as a lively person who always held his head high. I was told that at the beginning of the Muslims' return to Stolac everybody had been afraid of going to the centre, but Alija's brother walked gaily: he was always whistling. Talking about the *denaza* with people in the days that followed, I was reminded on several occasions that: 'The Croat shops were closed when we passed', and 'The Croats didn't play music [in the cafés] when the procession passed through town', and 'Croats attended the funeral and put flowers on the grave' and 'In the car on the day of the accident were also two Croats and two from mixed marriages.' I think for many Muslims the *denaza* was special. First of all it was tragic, but it was also a day when the Muslims took up space in town and the Croats accepted it, which they showed by closing the shops, turning off the music, and attending the funeral. All of these actions were interpreted as signs of respect. As Emir said: "We cannot forget all the time we have lived together, and neither can they." In short, the *denaza* played a part in the Muslims' construction of the Stolac spirit.

These five examples are some of the few visible attempts at redefining the physical/symbolic space of Stolac that I encountered.[5] In addition there are all the minor daily acts, which are primarily about creating an everyday world, but which nonetheless also relate to the creation of the Stolac spirit. It is difficult to establish a dividing line between the everyday construction of small life-worlds and the more visible conquests of local physical/symbolic space. For instance, there were families who kept the road outside their house and garden extremely clean by sweeping it every day, even though the house next to them lay in ruins with a huge pile of litter in front. Are they just fastidious people trying to keep some dignity in an ugly and ruined town? Or is it possible to see such acts as efforts to clean up (parts of) Stolac in order to create a contrast to the state of total decay in which the Croats have left the town? I think that both alternatives are

---

5   On the Internet, one also finds Stolac homepages. These are important statements of identity, but were not really relevant for the Muslims of Stolac. Firstly, only a few people in Bosnia Herzegovina had access to the Internet, and secondly, the pages consisted of hardly anything but expressions of opinion from people living outside Stolac, and many also outside Bosnia Herzegovina. Furthermore, the tone and the statements on the homepages were much more antagonistic and fierce and the criticism of the Croats more explicit than is the case in Stolac. Again one finds that nationalism is often stronger in exile, perhaps because people in exile do not have to live with the consequences of their own actions. This observation is supported by the research project I did in Denmark among Bosnian refugees (see Introduction).

true. And what about such gestures as returning to a demolished house, reconstructing buildings, insisting on being positive about the future for the sake of the children, opening shops, baking cakes for a birthday party,[6] tidying op the street, planting flowers, tilling the soil, paying visits – all these actions attempt to recreate and normalise life, which also relates to creating the Stolac spirit.

The chapter has analysed my informants' identification with the town, mainly the 'Stolac spirit', important for the Muslims' work of working out their new position in town. The Stolac spirit is about the creation of a physical/symbolic space – that is, spaces existing in reality like Bregava, Galerija, the mosques – and a cultural space, which is more a (re)construction of ideals and the aesthetics of the town with which one can identify. The creation of a cultural space is simultaneously a struggle for physical space, and the struggle for physical space is also an attempt to reconstruct Stolac as a cultural place and thereby as a source of identification. The Stolac spirit probably existed before the war, but has gained new significance. The Muslims returned to a town from which they were expelled, their houses were ruined and/or looted, everything Muslim was destroyed and the Croats now controlled all public administration and buildings. So it was no longer certain what being a *Stočani* meant. Hence, just to talk about the beauty of the town, the excellent climate, or the native and tolerant soul of Stolac, to open a café, stroll through the streets, use the River Bregava, produce and praise homemade food, identify *naši domaći Hrvati* and so on, now have some degree of political significance. The Stolac spirit is a source of identification, but it is also a sort of political manifestation saying we (also) have the right to live here. However, it is important to distinguish such a local identification from a nationalistic or religious one. Localistic identification and the evocation of the Stolac spirit is not about being Muslim, but about being a Muslim citizen of Stolac. The Stolac spirit redirects focus from a nationalistic identification towards a local one, and is thus part of my informants' counterdiscourse.

6   During and after the war many housewives did not bake cakes, as cakes symbolise joy and celebration.

Chapter 13
Ideal of tolerance and coexistence

The Muslims of Stolac subcribed to an ideal of tolerance and wish for coexistence with the other ethnic groups. Often this ideal was expressed through people's talk about the past, focusing on how everybody lived peacefully together and how ethnicity did not matter. People always talk about the past from a particular perspective, and talking about the past also exposes the present. I therefore have no hesitations about grouping people's illuminations of the past together with statements about the present, and viewing both as part of an ideal of tolerance and coexistence.

I analyse my informants' use of the past and the connected ideal of tolerance and coexistence in three different ways. First, people's nostalgic relationship to the past was used as a way of comprehending the war, or more precisely of creating a space uncontaminated by the war. Second, talking about the past was also a political commentary on the present. Third, and most important, my informants were rather conscious of the ideal of tolerance and coexistence when it was used in a self-reflexive manner to identify Muslimness and criticise ethnic Others, the Croats in particular. The fusion of the past, tolerance and coexistence thus became a source of identification defining Muslim identity. In all three instances, my informants' use of the past and their ideal of tolerance and coexistence became a way of criticising the intolerant nationalist vision of ethnic segregation, thus forming part of the Muslims' counterdiscourse.

The trouble-free past: a space uncontaminated by the war

Sometimes people, mostly the elderly, regarded the past as a trouble-free, harmonious and pleasant time, from which all problems and sorrows had been weeded out. Such a sentimental relationship to the past can be seen as a kind of escapism (Chase and Shaw 1989), brought about by an escessively dominant present. However, creating/remembering a harmonious past is also a way of coping with actual problems and overwhelming memories. For the majority of the Muslims of Stolac, their experiences from the war were so terrible that they were not able to talk about them (see Chapter 2). Instead they tried to forget or develop mechanisms for handling the violent memories. The creation of an undamaged and uncontaminated past was such a mechanism. It became an ocean to dive into, a place where the nightmarish present was sealed, set apart from the war and its tragic consequences. Sometimes people also projected the past into the present, and lived for a moment in the belief that soon everything would be as before. In this way memories of the past offered an alternative to the depressing future and the sad memories from the war.

Once I was watching sports on television together with Enver and Alen. Then their mother Ljubica came home and after a while she said: "Come on, change the channel, you are always watching sports." Enver shifted to a some-what nostalgic TV programme; such programmes were broadcast once in a while. A singer known from before the war was singing with a picture of old Sarajevo in the background. After that there was poetic scenery from the park where the River Bosna has its source (*Vrelo Bosne*): children playing, flowers, slowly running water, a swan swaying idyllically in the light breeze. Everything was from before the war. "Oh, this is lovely, it's so beautiful" Ljubica comment-ed to herself. The programme certainly did have a nice atmosphere. It was as if I could feel Ljubica's longing for this peace and quiet, this beauty and balance, where children play untroubled, the time before the world was out of joint, the non-chaotic state. Am I interpreting too much? I do not know, but my inter-pretation has to be related to Ljubica's other expressions. She was often very despondent, resigned and tired: "The war Nicolas, you cannot imagine what it has changed, before we lived so well, now …"

Though nostalgic use of the past was mostly reserved for the elderly, who had memories from before the war, and for whom it was not a sign of weakness to dwell on the past and the sad fate of the Muslims, young people could also enter this mode. Here is an example from an interview with a woman in her late 20s. She had been talking about the war crimes of the Croats and how it would be possible to live with the Croats again when her objective account slid into a kind of world beyond:

Lamira: But before the war it was so beautiful in Stolac. We had poetry evenings at the Stecći [a place with a huge collection of medieval tombstones outside town] where poets from all over came and read poetry out loud. Then there was Bregava, it was so beautiful in the summer. We bathed, and the boys who had – you know boys' bicycles they have such a crossbar – the boys who had such a crossbar, they could give their girlfriend a ride. My boyfriend had such a bicycle, and I could sit on it when he drove us down to Bregava. There was about three kilometres to walk, so it was nice. We also did theatre in the school, and we made a small newspaper that we sold, and the profit went to the 'children's embassy' in Sarajevo. I was also a Girl Scout, and we went on a lot of lovely ex-cursions. We went to cafés and acted like real ladies, sitting and having coffee.

Photographs were also used as an entrance to this nostalgic world. People often showed me pictures of their family, their schoolmates, their friends etc. from birthday parties, excursions, holidays etc. On several occasions only the first pair of pictures was shown to me before memories took over and people faded into another world. Such a creation of a nostalgic past did not work out for all. Thinking about how everything had been became too intense. In such cases the past was not an ocean to dive in to, but a direct road to the traumatised memories from the war. Once when I was visiting Džanana I noticed the book *Slovo Gorčina* (see above), which is filled with beautiful colour photos of Stolac from before the war. I fetched it, looked in it and asked Džanana if she could remember the old Stolac. She said she would rather not. Her daughter then looked at the pictures, and after a while Džanana looked as well, but she had to stop. She excused herself with tears in her eyes, explaining that it was too sad to look at the pictures.

The past as a political comment on the present

The nostalgic use of the past served other functions than sealing off violent memories. When people told me about how the three ethnic groups lived together harmoniously before the war, they were also expressing that it is possible to live that way again. Evoking the past in this way was a political comment on the present, resisting the nationalist ideology. Though people were disillusioned and did not believe that things would be as they were before, the construction of a harmonious past keeps reminding people that things could be different. As Mila, an elderly woman, expressed it:

> I want things to be as they were before the war. I had a good time. And I have lived what I needed to live. I was well off and I think that everybody [all ethnic groups] was well off, if they were to tell the truth. We had work, we built our houses, we lived well together. My husband and I had a job where both Croats and Muslims worked. Believe it or not, we had both Serbs and Croats coming to our house, they visited us at festivals and we visited them. I want these times to come back…Deep down in my soul I love all three nations [*nacije*]. I pray to my God that the time that was will come back. I could sleep on the asphalt, in the middle of the road, because I was not afraid of anybody. That's how we lived. The place you fell asleep was where you slept. Nobody hit you or frightened you.

I will not offer further examples. Analysing people's use of the past as a political comment on the present could fill a whole book. This section is intended only as a reminder of the complexity attached to my informants' use of the past and their ideal of tolerance and coexistence.

Tolerance and coexistence as sources of identity

In the rest of the chapter, I will show how the Muslims of Stolac resist the nationalist ideology of ethnic separation by identifying themselves as a tolerant people wishing to coexist. Again, the past is drawn upon, but contrary to the more nostalgic use of the past, memories generate a conscious identification, in which the past is not just the 'good old days', but rather represents ideals synonymous with Muslimness. These ideals of tolerance and coexistence make up the second part of my informants' counterdiscursive identifications.

I see some ethical challenges here. The war killed hundreds of thousands of people. The nationalist and prejudiced policies which continue even today have destroyed the lives of even more. Bosnia Herzegovina is a country filled with distrust, despair, and corrupt politicians living off the hate they can create between the ethnic groups. What is needed is a great portion of tolerance and a will to coexist and rebuild society together. To a certain extent this attitude exists among the ordinary Muslims of Stolac. But in this chapter I will be implicitly devaluing this attitude due to a necessary analytical distance, necessary because the ideal of tolerance plays such a great part in the Muslims' conscious self-identification. Talking to employees in various international organisations present in Bosnia Herzegovina I sometimes encountered a cynical approach in which the tolerant attitude of the Bosnian Muslims was seen as more or less hypocritical. The following example about the use of the school in Stolac reveals such an attitude, as well as introducing a discussion, running through the rest of the chapter, of the actual content and reality of the ideal of tolerance and coexistence among my informants.

The school in Stolac

When the Muslims started to return to Stolac in 1997, they were not allowed by the Croats to use the school, and therefore had to use an improvised, reduced 'house school.' The mothers accompanied their children to school, waited for them and accompanied them back, because they were afraid the children would be attacked by local Croats trying to frighten them. As more Muslims returned, the problem of the lack of school facilities grew. Before the war the school had had 1,340 pupils, but after the war only 4-500 Croatian children attended it. Not allowing the Muslims to use the school facilities was an act of sheer discrimination. Carina, an English employee in the OHR who had Stolac as her field of responsibility, once told me about the negotiations which ultimately led to an opening of the school for the Muslim children.

Carina had been very personally engaged in the attempt to facilitate the Muslims' return to the school facilities. Initially there had been many political tugs-of-war with the HDZ, and the changing mayors of Stolac (all members of the HDZ) had argued that 'house schools' were common in Bosnia Herzegovina, so why all the fuss, and why not in Stolac? But after some intricate negotiations, in which Carina invested a lot of time and all her political skill as well as putting her prestige at stake, the reintegration of the school was accepted at last. So she was happy the day when all kinds of prominent people, including some high up in the OHR, went to Stolac to officially celebrate the reunion. The following day the more concrete aspects of the deal were to have been agreed on, but then the Bosniaks[1] suddenly wanted much more than was realistic. The problem was that though the deal was in place, there were no exact references to what the Bosniaks should get. At this point in the story, Carina added that though the Croats are hard to negotiate with, the Bosniaks are definitely no better than they should be. They wanted half of the school and they wanted a separate entrance. Carina said to them: "Now you are pressing too hard. You only have eighty-five pupils, so you cannot get everything you demand and you can forget the thing about the separate entrance. We are about to make a good deal so do not destroy it." And the mayor (Croat) was becomming furious. Alone with him Carina said: "You have to stick to it. They will not get their demands, but you have to hold out." And to the Bosniaks she said: "You have twenty minutes to sign, otherwise there will be no deal, and we can skip it all and everything else in the future. And the thing with the two entrances you can forget about, one of the reasons why the OHR intervened was that this could be a project of reconciliation." Carina knew that the Bosniaks who were present did not have the final say, so she told them to call X (someone higher up in the hierarchy) and tell him that it was now or never. Then they signed and they all went together to the school. Here the Bosniaks started again: "We want these particular rooms. They have to be painted ..." The mayor was ready to jump out of his skin. The Bosniaks were so disrespectful, Carina said. They pointed to things in the school and said: "We want this and this." When finally the deal was settled and they came out of the school, one of the Bosniaks pointed at Carina and commented: "We are not satisfied!" Despite the importance of this agreement – it was the first of its kind in Bosnia Herzegovina – there were no thanks, Carina told me.

---

1   She used the term Bosniak and not Muslim.

The autumn of 2000, then, was the first time after the war that Muslims and Croats sent their children to the same school. While I was in Stolac, the Muslims had four classrooms and the Croats had sixteen. Because there were too many Muslim children to fit in so few classrooms, they had to use the school in shifts, from 8 am to 12 noon and from 1 pm to 5 pm. Furthermore, only the Croats were allowed to use the huge gym. The secondary school was only for Croats as well; starting in 7th grade Muslim children had to go to Mostar by bus every day.

Carina's experiences call the Muslims' tolerance and will to co-exist into question. Why were they not satisfied? Why were they not grateful? If they were as tolerant as they claimed, they would have signed the deal without comments. I have two answers. First, when analysing the ideal of tolerance and coexistence, I am not, as Carina did, referring solely to the political scene. On the everyday level things are different simply because they are less conscious and deliberate, as I will elaborate below. Second, Carina's story does actually touch on the content of the Muslims' tolerance to some extent, but to understand this better we also have to listen to the other side of the story. That is, how the Muslims of Stolac saw the school. For them, the school was very problematic. Their main experience in relation to the school was one of discrimination. They were often indignant about the situation of the Muslim children: 'Why is it that we only have four rooms when we have as many kids as they do?' 'Why can't our kids use the gym?' 'Why can only Croatian kids go to secondary school in Stolac?' 'What happened to all the equipment?' And so on. Furthermore, many of my informants attended school in Stolac, and have recollections from that time. People also told me that their parents helped build the school after the Second World War. Some have traumatic memories from the time it was used as a barrack during the recent war, as well as being the place where Muslim women were searched and robbed before the expulsion. And people also told me that the school was renovated in 1997 with help from the state. As one said: "Izetbegovic [the former president of Bosnia Herzegovina] helped pay for the renovation of the school and still we only have four rooms." In short, for them there was no reason to be grateful. When looked at from the perspective of the political sphere where Carina works, the reintegration of the school was an important success for the OHR. Looked at from the point of view of the Muslims who live in Stolac, the deal was merely a continuation of the Croatian discrimination in Stolac.

All my informants with whom I spoke about the school wanted it to be integrated so that Croat, Muslim and Serbian children could attend school together. They saw the school as an important place for the creation of a future without ethnic discrimination, and a lack of integration in the school as the major hindrance to the reunion of Stolac.

Muhamed: Imagine that in one part of the school we have the Bosniak children and in the other the Croat children, and that's idiocy. For instance in the second class, if anyone asked my daughter if she is Muslim she would say 'Yes I am', but she would not know what it means. She doesn't know. And it would be the same if you asked the question to a little Croat. In fact they do not know what it means. The stupid parents tell their children 'You are Croat or Muslim and you are not allowed to play with the others.' And time passes and the children who are raised in that way become encapsulated [*zatvoren*]. The Indians[2] are much better than them [the parents]. That's how it is. The teachers who work at the school, if they go to their class and say 'Hello, you are Muslims and you shouldn't play with the Croats or be together with them', then the children will be like that.

The Muslim teachers in Stolac I talked to all wanted the instruction of the ethnic groups to be integrated. They were aware that history, music and Croatian/ Bosnian/Serbian language had to be taught separately, but English, biology, geography, physical education and other such neutral subjects should be taught jointly. As Mehmed, a teacher who had also taught at the school before the war, answered when I asked him if the Croat and Muslim teachers talk together:

> There are no official contacts, because they don't want them. I wish there would be, so that the kids could be together and attend the same classes. So that the English teachers can teach both Croats and Muslims, that they can have maths and physics together, and the subjects common to all they should be taught together, with respect for the subjects that are national. I also teach gym, and the Croatian children who are free for the day come to the schoolyard where I teach and they ask if they can join, and I say it is OK. Maybe some fall in love during such meetings. Children think in a different manner. They are not bad. But the parents do not allow them to play with the Muslims. And that's the problem.

On the one hand, then, the Muslims talked about ethnic coexistence in the school, while on the other hand they appeared to be backward-looking, ungrateful and discontented in Carina's story. Both attitudes are relevant when describing my informants' identification with an ideal of tolerance and coexistence. As Džanana, once said, in a way synthesising the two different attitudes: "I

2   People frequently used evolutionary schemes when evaluating behaviour. Indians are normally placed at the bottom of the scheme, but here Muhamed places the nationalist-minded parents even lower. See also Chapter 13.

can live together with anybody, as long as the situation is just." For the Muslims, tolerance is not the same as compliance (Carina's interpretation). Neither is it confrontation. There is a rather large and murky middle ground between the two poles of compliance and confrontation. In the rest of the chapter, I will try to clarify this middle ground and thus the Muslim understanding of tolerance. I will focus on how tolerance and a wish for coexistence featured in everyday life among the Muslims of Stolac. I have arranged the sections around some of the themes which people persistently evoked when talking about the past and about the Muslims' tolerant character.

Differences were an advantage

When talking about the past, my informants often stressed that cultural diversity enriched everyday life: people learned from each other, had more festivals in which to participate, and a large social network. Ethnicity mattered, not in relation to a larger political nationalistic framework, but in relation to everyday habitual practices of identification (see Chapter 10). Today people mourn the loss of these differences, or rather the loss of their respectful and habitual handling. The war both highlighted and created ethnic differences, but it also changed the positive connotations related to these differences and instead promoted an ideology in which ethnic dissimilarity was seen as a hindrance to interaction and a threat to cultural survival. Therefore, talking about ethnic differences in a positive manner was a means to resist the rhetoric of ethnic separation that nationalistic politics communicated in Stolac. And for the Muslims it was a way to identify themselves by saying, 'We have no problems interacting with the different ethnic groups; we are a tolerant people.'[3] Take Emir, who reports how the Muslims' tolerant attitude during the war was turned against them:

---

3   Džanana's story below is an example of a story about respectful and tolerant interaction among the three ethnic groups:
       "Our whole family was mixed. It didn't matter if one was Serb, Croat or Muslim; everybody was good enough. When my oldest brother was going to be married, he came with his bride, and her name was Olga, and I knew her from before. We used to go down to *Videvo Polje*, and there she saw me with my son. 'Well you know who I am'. 'Yes, you are going to marry my brother'. When my brother came, he said to me: 'Go to our father and tell him that I will be coming with my bride. How is he going to react when he hears that?' I went home and told him, and my father said: 'Why are you asking me? If he loves her, so do I. If he can sleep with her, I can dine with her'. My sister-in-law says that she can never think of my parents without starting to cry. She also says that they received her well and weren't too religious, and that it did not bother them at all that she was Serb. And my uncle, he married a Croat woman. We took good care of each other. And one of my uncle's daughters married a Serb and they lived in Serbia. And another one married one from Montenegro...Now I can't remember them all. Everything was mixed in our family."

In school I had Serbian and Croat friends, and for instance on Bayram, I invited my Serbian and Croat friends home, and at Christmas time, on 25th [of December] and 7th January, the Muslims were invited to their homes to roll eggs, but you could not do that today; it is unthinkable. Before the war the other cultures were an advantage for us: if there were only Muslims everybody would know one another, but with other religious communities we learned from each other – it was enrichment. Differences did exist, but it was a difference that enriched us. But with the war the differences became our disadvantages. We were conscious about being different before the war, but it was a difference that enriched us. With the war this difference was turned against us [exploited by nationalist politics].

Suljeman answered in a similar manner when I asked him how people had perceived these differences before the war – were they seen as positive?

Yes of course. It is an advantage; differences are an advantage. Life is richer, people are also richer with these differences, but now the Serbs and Croats try to throw these differences out, it just has to be the same [ethnic homogeneity]. They have destroyed the good things about Bosnia Herzegovina. Before the war Bosnia Herzegovina was much more beautiful and the relations [between the ethnic groups] were much better. Now the relations have suffered.

As Suljeman, Emir and the most of my informants saw it, difference, respect and tolerance were three inseparable issues. However, even if the Croats opened up for interaction tomorrow, I think many Muslims would find interaction difficult. More to the point, then, the Muslims (want to) perceive themselves as tolerant and ready to resume interethnic relations, whereas they maintain that other ethnic groups do not hold the same ideal. Recollecting and stating that differences were/are no hindrance to interaction, therefore, is also an act of identification.

Nationality did not matter

People also said that before the war everybody lived together and had a good time, and no one cared about ethnicity. At first glance this would seem to contradict the views expressed above, but in fact they are rather similar. When my informants said they were not aware of ethnic affiliation before, it is probably not true: they knew which religious community people came from, but this is not the point. What they were expressing is that they did not care. This is in keeping with the official ideology of the Yugoslav regime (Brotherhood and Unity), which tried to make ethnicity a thing of the past, and to many of the

Bosnian generations from after the Second World War a pan-ethnic Yugoslav identity was important. Mustafa, a man of about thirty-five, depicted the days before the war as joyful, a time when ethnicity was unimportant. I think this memory was important to him, enabling him to imagine a better future and reminding him of what he is, of his values, as he now lives in a totally different context.

TK: Do you remember what life was like before the war?

Mustafa: Let me tell you one thing: everybody had their life. We had work – I began building my house before the war. I also started with my business and I was about to open a coffee bar. Things were going well for me. I had a good group of friends. You are born here in Stolac, grow up together and have the friends until you get married, and I married before the war. We had a circle of friends. And that's enough…You have a job, family, some everyday obligations; it was a normal life. You knew where to go in the evenings, and that you would meet your friends at that place. Then the war came and turned everything upside down. Now I can find some of my friends all the way from Canada to Australia. And not only Bosniaks, also Serbs and Croats. I had a big circle of friends. There were between ten and twenty of us in that circle. Before the war it did not matter if you were Serb, Muslim or Croat. You did not know what people were, you were not weighed by it…When I got married, my best man was Croat, and at my son's first birthday his godfather was Serb. Now they live in Canada. That's how it was.

Mustafa's statement entails a contradiction. One the one hand he said, "You did not know what people were." On the other hand, he told me – in line with the tradition of respectful interaction between the different ethnic groups – about the deliberate choice of a Croat and a Serb to be best man and godfather, respectively. This contradiction, however, does make sense. Firstly, claiming to be unaware of the ethnic identity of one's friends simply expresses indifference. Secondly, after the war the habitual pre-war pattern of tolerant and respectful inter-ethnic interactions has been objectified and constructed by many Muslims as conscious knowledge, relevant in identifying present Muslim identity. This should become more evident in the following examples.

I was once shown a photo from a school excursion of five pupils sitting on a war monument, and the person who showed it to me commented: "This guy he is Serb, he now lives in Beograd", and "She is Croat, she was one of my best friends." Another photo I was shown was from a party, everybody seemed to be in high spirits, cheering at the photographer, and the comment: "Look he is a

Serb, we were best friends," and "We were all together, Serbs, Croats and Muslims; nobody cared." Mostly when people showed me photos they explicitly told me about the nationality of the ones depicted. Besides mourning times past, such commentaries also expressed the spirit of interethnic tolerance which today forms part of the Muslims' self-identification.

People sometimes told me they had Croat friends, mingled with Croats, and went to Croatian cafés and shops and vice versa. Sometimes this was not quite correct. It was as if people wanted to assure me and themselves that they still upheld the ideal of tolerance and inter-ethnic interaction. When I first met him, Safet told me that he had several Croat friends and acquaintances. But some months later, when I asked him if he knew some Croats I could interview, he said that he did not really know any. And once when I invited Mensur, who had told me that he frequented the Croatian cafés, for a cup of coffee as we were standing outside a Croatian coffee bar, he said "Yes, but then we will go to Galerija," which was the nearest Muslim café, even though he was in something of a hurry. I do not think people were lying as such, but more central for my argument, the point is that it was important for people to state that they were tolerant and to identify with the ideal of coexistence, even though in practice this was rather difficult.

Alija, the owner of the Muslim Café Galerija, who wanted the café to be a symbol of (Muslim) tolerance, once proudly told me how six Catholic nuns from Dubrovnik (Croatia) had entered the café and had some cakes. Obviously, they did not know it was a Muslim café. Besides being a funny story (I also heard it from other people), it also demonstrated for people that ethnic tolerance still exists or is at least possible. In the telling of the story the local Muslims and the nuns were somehow made conspirators, excluding the obdurate Croats who were left behind in their antiquated politics of separation.

A last example of how the ideal of tolerance and coexistence is first objectified and then related to Muslim identity relates to inter-ethnic marriages (*mješovit brak*). Such marriages were often highlighted as a symbol of unproblematic interethnic coexistence. I do not have the figures for the frequency of interethnic marriage in Stolac before the war. When I compare the ones I know of with the high number people sometimes referred to, I think that there is a discrepancy. Again, one could say that people were only telling about the 'many' interethnic marriages in order to construct a past that never existed. What is more interesting, however, is what people want to communicate in constructing such an idyllic past. Interethnic marriage was a symbol of coexistence, so by saying that Stolac was one of the cities in Bosnia Herzegovina with the highest rates of interethnic marriage, one also states that: 'We were able to live together and even marry each other', or 'Tolerance is what characterises the true inhabitants of Stolac', or 'If we were able to live together before, why not now.' On several occasions I heard the story of the three sons (Muslims) from Begovina: one married a Catholic from the Czech Republic, the second a Serb, and the third a Muslim. Besides resembling a fairytale, this and other evocations of the powerful symbol of interethnic marriage form part of the ideal of tolerance and coexistence which the Muslims construct and identify with. At the same time they say that the Croats and the Serbs were the ones who broke the 'promise of marriage' which the ethnic groups had made.

I will end this section with a quote from an interview with Zahida, who wanted to pass on to her children the same ideals of tolerance she herself was brought up with, knowing that they are neither unambiguous nor easy to adopt in the present situation. On several occasions her children communicated a more antagonistic attitude towards the other ethnic groups than she found suitable. She struggled to believe in and identify herself with the ideal of tolerance:

> I was born after the Second World War and I have felt the consequences of the Second World War. My parents told me what had happened and I lived together with the Serbs up there [the village where she originated from]. And then Tito came to power and we lived well together and we helped each other when we worked in the fields. And therefore I think that we elderly people are able to live together again. But Amira [her daughter] was only nine years old, and the only thing she knew was how to play, and somebody came and interrupted that game. Until that moment she did not know she was Muslim, but she does know now. We did not teach our children that they were Muslims and that the others were Croats or Serbs. It was as if you erased these differences. And now the children have difficulties understanding why these things were done to them. They could not see any reason for it, they do not understand. The young have a much harder time understanding why it happened than the old.

Her statement puts the ideal of tolerance I have touched on into perspective, when she indicates that the older people have somehow been through it all before. The young were raised to consider ethnicity unimportant, whereas the older people had to push the memories from the Second World War into the background. The older people, while upholding an ideal of tolerance and coexistence, also knew how ethnicity suddenly could be made important.

Criticism of the Croats – identification of the Muslims

In talking about past inter-ethnic interaction or present tolerance, sometimes the Muslims blame the other ethnic groups – especially the Croats – for abandoning these ideals. This blame and the implicit identification of oneself as tolerant is part of the same logic. Below is an excerpt from an interview with a schoolteacher and one of her colleagues. She lived outside Stolac in an area with many Croats. She hoped for a better future but was rather despondent. Interaction with the Croats was rare in that area, and at the small school where she taught, the Croat children left when the Muslims arrived. Croat nationalist symbols in and at the school communicated ethnic separation and indicated for her the Croats' lack of willingness to intermingle.

Colleague: In the previous state in Yugoslavia, we went in for brotherhood and unity

Teacher: The worst thing is that those times were the best in my life. In former Yugoslavia ordinary people, the workers, had their rights, I think that everybody was better off in comparison to now.

Colleague: Except the criminals.

Teacher: Yes, of course, those mafia people. Before one could travel, for instance to Belgrade. We made trips together, everywhere. Nobody stopped you on the street. You could sleep in the car, or in the middle of the road, and nobody would touch you. Those were untroubled times. You can't describe the difference compared to today. Terrible, terrible!

TK: Did you know who was Muslim or Serb or Croat before the war?

Teacher: Yes, I did, but there were no differences; it did not matter. In the street in Stolac where I lived, there lived Serbs, Croats and Muslims. You received the flats from the factory where you worked and nobody asked about who the neighbours were – if you were Serb, Croat or Muslim. There were also mixed marriages. And nobody felt it mattered. We were all as one. My first neighbour was Croat, and my sisters and I looked after their children. We were close. Not a day went by without visiting each other. We talked about everything. We knew each other's problems. Today she [the Croat neighbour] doesn't even bother to visit my parents, or even to talk to them. Our window is next to their terrace; you can jump from our apartment to their flat. It is senseless when you realise all these things. You have to hope but it is difficult.

The teacher was criticising the Croats for not living up to the ideal of respectful interethnic interaction, which she implicitly claimed was still current among the Muslims. Other examples touch more explicitly on the issue of identification. People said, for instance, that "Muslims read Serbian or Croatian literature but they do not read ours", or "We read Cyrillic letters but they do not learn our alphabet", or "We listen to their music, but they do not listen to ours."[4] Comparisons of this sort meant that 'our' tolerance in fact exists as a function of 'their' intolerance. Whether the intention was to criticise them (Croats and Serbs and the whole nationalistic project) or define what it is to be Muslim is hard to tell. It is probably both.

One evening while I was visiting Muhamed, we were watching a music programme on TV.

Muhamed: This is a Serbian programme, and my children like these songs. They know them all by heart. They are all Serbs and I don't mind.

Wife: And I do not forbid them to watch these programmes.

Samir: But with them it is not like that. Šerif Konjević and Safet Isović, who are Muslim folk singers, they do not listen to them. They [the Croats] are their own enemies [dušman, that they do not want to be together].

A last example of how tolerance, by criticising what is seen as the nationalist attitude of the Croats, is used as a way of identification comes from an interview in which two of my informants were discussing traditions of cooking and school politics. Before the war everybody in Yugoslavia learned Serbo-Croatian and everybody learned to read and write in both the Cyrillic and Roman alphabets. Since the war, language has become an important element of cultural identification. Serbs only use Cyrillic, and Croats only use Roman letters. Muslims use Latin letters, but also learn Cyrillic.

Nijaz: The Muslims and the Croats have common traditions, but there are also some differences. For instance, regarding what is permissible and forbidden to eat and drink. Our faith tells that we may not eat pork or drink alcohol. Islam forbids it, but it is not forbidden for the Croats. Wine is the blood of Jesus Christ. And the traditional cakes [Baklava] we talked about, we got them from the Turks and now they are part of traditional Bosnian cooking, and the Croats have their traditional cooking. And these traditional differences

---

4   In Café Galerija they often played Western as well as 'Yugoslav' music. Often I heard tapes with Serbian pop and rock singers, as I was told: 'As long as the music is good, we play it'.

were used in the political life. These differences between the traditions were respected before the war, but not during the war. A people which can write two alphabets and a people which has three religious communities, I consider to be a rich people. We learned both alphabets and our Bosnian pupils learn them also today, even if it is said that the Cyrillic is Serbian.

Amira: It is a good thing. If you go to Belgrade for example, you can read everything and find your way, and if you want to read some of the books in Cyrillic you can do that.

Nijaz: The Croatian children do not read Cyrillic, but we read both.

Coexistence is our fate

People sometimes said that it was the fate of the inhabitants of Bosnia Herzegovina to live together. For the Muslims of Stolac it was absurd to discuss ethnic separation, and for them coexistence was an obvious reality: the people of Bosnia Herzegovina have to live together. Such talk of inescapable coexistence makes sense when related to the Muslims' general political situation in Bosnia Herzegovina, especially during the war. For the Bosnian Serbs and the Bosnian Croats, visions of a greater Serbia/Croatia were in the air, whereas for the Muslims visions of a greater (Muslim) Bosnia never really crystallised (as discussed in Chapter 9). One might say that the Muslims defended what they had (a multiethnic Bosnia Herzegovina), whereas the other two groups fought for something more (including the elimination of multiethnic Bosnia Herzegovina). Coexistence was hence an important political card for the Bosnian Muslims. The policy pursued by the Muslims rested on the other ethnic groups, whereas the Croats' and the Serbs' political visions excluded the Muslims.

The political rhetoric of the Muslim politicians with their insistence on a multiethnic Bosnia was reflected in many of my informants' statements. They never talked about a pure Muslim Bosnia Herzegovina, or a Stolac only for Muslims. Instead, they stressed that the three ethnic groups belonged together, and that they simply had to learn to coexist again. "Stories of people's own lives melt into the general themes of a collective narrative" as Malkki writes (1995: 56). Furthermore, as the Muslims also held the position of minority returnees in Stolac, arguments of coexistence can also be seen as legitimising their return and their re-assimilation into the Stolac community. In short, my informants' ideal of tolerance and coexistence is connected to political life and it is impossible to fully separate the one from the other. A first example of how coexistence is perceived as a matter of fate comes from a talk I had one day with Nijaz.

TK: Did you have Croat friends before the war?

Nijaz: Yes, lots. One of them pointed the gun at me when we were forced into the truck. He was a good friend and he stood there pointing the gun at me.

TK: Don't people feel hatred afterwards? Today don't you feel hatred towards the Croats?

Nijaz: You can't have that. We Muslims only have Bosnia. The Croats have Croatia, and the Serbs Serbia. We have to live together, and the children have to get on together, so hatred is of no use.

In his utterance Nijaz implicitly defines Muslim character as tolerant, but it is a tolerance which is entwined in the Muslims' political situation in Bosnia Herzegovina. Salko, a prominent member of the local SDA, expressed the relationship between a Muslim ideal of coexistence and coexistence as fate very clearly:

> Something very terrible happened to us. 200,000 were killed. Most of them were Bosniaks. We have to tell our children what happened, we have to say that they have to be very careful, so that the same will not happen to them. We must never forget. Those who did this, it was totally individual, and the war criminals have to face justice and go to jail. You can't say that a whole nation is bad, because it is totally individual. Our fate is to live together. When you listen to the tape again, you will hear that I never said that we should be segregated. We have been living together for many years, why should we not be able to do so again? People have to live together, but at the same time we have to be aware that we do not again come to experience the ugly things that happened. I believe that Bosnia has a future even though many are ready to divide Bosnia. And this vision of dividing Bosnia [between Serbia and Croatia] will exist for ever [...] but I hope it will never be fulfilled. Bosnia will survive and will always be three different peoples. The war created the ethnic division, but it was the war that created it [implying that it was not something ordinary people wanted]. The majority of the Serbian population will never come back to Croatia, and many of the Bosnian Croats will buy these Serbian properties and move to Croatia. Let us be realistic – if I were a Croat, and Croatia were so close, I would move to Croatia. But even if I were to move to another place in the world, Denmark for example, I would always be Bosniak, even if I were to go to Croatia I would be Bosniak. We Bosniaks have no alternative than to stay here. It is my fate to die here. Also before the war, when my schoolmates were going to study, the majority of the Stolac Croats went to Zagreb and the Serbs to Belgrade. And the ones who had the opportunity to work in Belgrade or Zagreb, they would never come back. Well, that's how it is. But the most

important is that we give some hope to the people who do return. If a Serb has the will to return [to Stolac] he should be given the chance to do so [only few Serbs return]. I think that the majority of the Serbs will never return, but I wish that all would come back. It is only the old people who return – they will die in a couple of years, and then I think the children will sell [their houses]. Some [Serbs] are already selling their houses now, it is, it is…If we had another native country as the Croats have, then we might also move. But we only have Bosnia and that's why we are here.

This is the articulate statement of a politician. A plainer one comes from Osman, who though he described himself as an ordinary person with only little schooling, nevertheless communicates more or less the same ideal of tolerance and coexistence. As a Muslim, Osman both believes in it and has no other imaginable options (coexistence as fate).

My family and I really want the past to come back [*prošlo vrijeme*], and that people should be unified again, united. And if it is not going to be so, I cannot imagine that we can have a good future. If our school, factories and hospitals stay as they are [divided] you can't expect things to be better. Especially in a shared town, where three different nations live, like in Stolac […] Nobody can say on behalf of others how many want a real peace and union in this town. I can only say what I think. I think we should live together again and be together again and create a better future for our kids, *a boga mi* [he reveals his own scepticism towards his own hopes]. The problem is that our children are divided, and while they are divided you can't expect things to become better. When the children play together and the Croats say *balija* and the Muslims say *ustaše* [both are ethnic insults] I can't see how it can be better. Maybe the solution is that the children should be together in school and get to know each other, and when they grow up they will behave as they learned in school.

The merging of tolerance and Muslim identity

In this chapter I have analysed a further aspect of my informants' self-identification. The first was the localistic identification, the second relates to an ideal of tolerance and coexistence. The war has forced people to reflect on pre-war practices in order to make some sense of it all. Ethnic difference, including the way this difference was nurtured, articulated and created before, has become objectified and part of the Muslims' conscious identification. The Muslims call this tolerance; I call it the *ideal* of tolerance. In short, practices of interaction (such as the 'familiarisation of difference' described in Chapter 10) have become ideals of identification. The tolerant and respectful way characterising the different ethnic groups' interaction before the war is now increasingly seen by the Muslims as a specific Muslim quality, partly because the other ethnic groups are seen as having abandoned the respectful pre-war attitude. But persistently highlighting the trouble-free and joyful interaction among ethnic groups in the past, and stressing the possibility of resuming this interaction in the future, is also a way to handle the traumatic experiences from the war, and more importantly a way of rejecting the nationalistic rhetoric and practice of ethnic exclusiveness. The ideal of tolerance and coexistence is thus an important part of the Muslims' counterdiscourse. Though the Muslims' ideals of tolerance and coexistence are intertwined in this mix of political life, identification, nostalgia, visions of a future and resistance, this does not mean that these ideals are not deeply felt. Feelings are not something you can isolate from the rest of the social world: instead they are connected.

Chapter 14
The Balkans – Europe

We are European Muslims. That is our destiny. We want to be Muslims and Europeans. I personally feel most comfortable when I say that I am a European Muslim, because that's what I am. When I go to the East, I am disturbed by some things there, some things disturb me also when I go to the West. I feel best here, in Bosnia. Probably because it is East and West, and the good that exists on both sides. (Izetbegovic, former President of Bosnia Herzegovina, 1996 from an SDA meeting, quoted in Maček 2000a: 213).

If we have to fight, well then we will fight. But I hope they are not going to be crazy enough to fight with us. For if we don't know how to work and produce that well, at least we will know how to fight well. (Slobodan Milošović, former President of Serbia, 1991, quoted in Cohen 1993: 223).

The next identification relevant for the Stolac Muslims' attempt to identify themselves and comprehend the war relates to a pair of geographical symbols: the Balkans vs. Europe/the West.[1] This is a conflicting discursive field in which my informants were entangled. Rather than taking solid and consistent positions, they had to make their identifications in the middle of an existing quandary. Sometimes Europe was decadent and cold, at other times it was the future and the civilised. Sometimes the Balkans was authentic and honest, at other times it was violent and crude, and sometimes it was associated with an unavoidable destructive force. Whereas the ideals of tolerance and coexistence and, as I show in the next chapter, the victim identity relate directly to what my informants see as characteristics of Muslims in Bosnia Herzegovina, and localistic identifications relate to being a Muslim in Stolac, identifications with the Balkans or Europe are more general. The Others are not so much the ethnic Others (Croats and Serbs), as European Others. Entering this space of identity, people are more focused on defining what it is to be a Balkan Muslim than a Muslim. My informants' uses of the Balkans-Europe dichotomy thereby evades nationalist thinking and forms part of the Muslims' counterdiscourse.

---

1   Both the West and Europe are in play. Europe, however, is the label most commonly used by my informants.

I start by looking at the cultural construction of the Balkans-Europe dichotomy, and then move on to focus on how it is used among the Muslims of
Stolac and forms part of their counterdiscourse.[2]

The discursive construction of the Balkans – Europe

From without

In his polemic of the geographical metaphor 'the Oriental', Edward Said (1985)
showed how this concept is much more than a designation of an area; it is rather a Western cultural construction of the 'Other.' Whereas the Orient as a place
has changed, its status as Other has remained more or less intact. The same
seems to hold true of the Balkans. Most people probably have an idea of what
the Balkan mentality is, but few know exactly where the Balkans start or stop.

Inspired by the debate about Orientalism, the Bulgarian-American historian Todorova (1994) has analysed how the Western construction and image
of the Balkans came into being. She argues that the Balkans as a distinct geographical area with specific cultural traits was not discovered/invented before
the end of the 18th century, mainly through European travel literature, which
became very popular at that time. The Balkans was increasingly associated with
the traditional, the non-civilised, tribalism (political underdevelopment), and
the rural and uneducated. During the Balkan wars and World War I, a further
ingredient was added to this mixture: violence. In fact violence has been a leitmotiv of the idea of the Balkans ever since. After World War II a new demon,
communism, was grafted onto the image of the Balkans (see also Bakic-Hayden
1992: 3-4). And during the recent war in former Yugoslavia the image of the
Balkans came full circle, since Western observers have explained the war as if
not unavoidable then at the very least typical evidence of the Balkan mentality.
For example, in an article in *The New York Review of Books* from 1993 George
Keennan explains the war by referring to the Balkan wars of 1913. On both occasions the conflict was inevitable because of the Balkan mentality:

---

2   I am restricting myself to outlining the discursive construct of the Balkan-Europe dichotomy,
but I am aware that the creation and maintenance of this opposition also relates to tangible
economic interests. As Allcock (2000) argues, the Balkans stand in a 'semi-peripheral' relationship to a capitalist world system, and if the Balkans have come to signify conflict and
fragmentation: "This is because the region has been the arena in which the larger conflicts of
European powers have been concentrated and, to some extent, conducted by proxy" (ibid. 24;
see also Schierup 1991).

Eighty years have now passed since the Carnegie commissioners[3] paid their visit to that region. And this writer knows of no evidence that the ability of the Balkan peoples to interact peaceably with one another is any greater now than it was those eighty years ago. (1993: 7).

In a recent book with the telling title *Balkan Ghosts,* Robert Kaplan continues the Western essentialisation of a presumed Balkan mentality, which he identifies with everything violent. A quotation from the book gives an impression of his views.

> Twentieth-century history came from the Balkans. Here men have been isolated by poverty and ethnic rivalry, dooming them to hate. Here politics has been reduced to a level of near anarchy that from time to time in history has flowed up the Danube into central Europe.
>
> Nazism, for instance, can claim Balkan origins. Among the flophouses of Vienna, a breeding ground of ethnic resentments close to the southern Slavic world, Hitler learned how to hate so infectiously. (Kaplan 1993: xxiii).

Considering such stigmatising denunciation of the Balkan people, one can understand Todorova's opinion:

> The Balkans have been ill served by discovery and invention. Balkanism and its subject are imprisoned in a field of discourse in which 'the Balkans' is paired in opposition to the 'West' and 'Europe', while 'Balkanism' is the dark other of 'Western civilization.'

In fact the people of the Balkans have been even worse off than those caught in the discourse of 'Orientalism', she continues:

> When the Balkans were part of the scatter pattern of invective aimed at the east and 'Orientalism' was the other necessary for the self-essentializing 'West' and 'Europe', there existed the prospect of their rediscovery in a positive fashion. With the rediscovery of the east and orientalism as independent semantic values, the Balkans are left in Europe's thrall, anti-civilization, *alter ego*, the dark side within. (1994: 482).

---

3   The Carnegie Commission was charged with the task of giving the West a clear and reliable picture of what was going on in the affected area.

A minor and rather innocent example of how the people of the Balkans have had a hard time escaping the discourse that partly created them is seen in the shifting European perception of coffee. At first traveller reports from the mid-17th century from the Balkans depicted the Turkish drink called coffee as a dark, disgusting drink which was 'hell-like.' Later, when the drink became popular in Europe, possible chains of positive associations between the Balkans and Europe were cut by referring to the *motive* behind the intake of coffee. In Europe the drink was valued for its energy-creating effect, whereas the Balkan people were seen as drinking it only for pleasure. That is, they did not in a rational way use the drink's stimulating potential, rather coffee drinking was just seen a part of a general Balkan mindset: relaxation, laziness and unproductiveness (Božidar 2001).

From within

Besides being a part of the self-construction of the West, since its invention 'the Balkans' has also been used politically by people inhabiting the area. Even back in early twentieth century some of the first famous scholars from respectively Serbia (Jovan Cvijić 1865-1927) and Croatia (Dinko Tomašić 1902-1975) contributed to and used the Balkan discourse. Cvijić for his part embraced and positively valorised the characteristics stigmatised in the West. The 'Dinaric type' (one of four basic types he operated with) was seen as a lively, intelligent and sensitive type growing very enthusiastic or angry without much effort, and he praised its military qualities, opposing the virtues of this type to the decadent and degenerating urban population. Tomašić, on the other hand, distanced himself from the qualities of the Dinaric type, opposing them with a democratic mentality which he claimed existed mainly in northern Croatia, while the more violent and uncivilised types lived in the Dinaric mountains, which were populated mainly by Serbs and Montenegrins (Kaser 1998; Bougarel 1999; Ritman-Auguštin 1995). Despite differences in sympathies, both scholars used the mentalities they studied politically and tended to 'ethnicise' features of the Balkan discourse (Bougarel 1999: 161).[4]

Basic-Hayden (1992, 1995) has analysed what she calls a symbolic geography in Yugoslav politics, a geography which forms a hierarchy in which Europe and the Balkans, West and East are valorised in terms of religion. This symbolic geography is an opposition which can be used on all levels of society, with primitive and conservative values increasing the further 'East' you go ('nesting orientalism' she also calls it (1995)). Islam is generally less favourably viewed

---

4   Both writers have recently had a renaissance because they so easily entered into (post-)Yugoslav nationalistic polemic and politics.

than Orthodox Christianity, whereas in the West the Protestant tradition is generally jugded more positively than Catholicism. This symbolic geographical opposition was and is part of the Yugoslav and Ex-Yugoslav everyday life, with Slovenia being seen as the more civilised, educated, developed and Western country, and going south and south-east the pictures changed proportionally.[5]

In the recent conflict images of civilisation and Europe versus barbaric, violent and Balkan-like were used abundantly. Croatian and Slovenian politicians engaged the Balkan discourse in their attempts to legitimise their secession from Yugoslavia. As a result, the Orthodox Christian tradition and the Serbs were depicted as authoritarian, patriarchal, power-hungry and aggressive, whereas the Croats and the Slovenes were depicted as embracing democracy and Western values (Bougarel 1999; Bakic-Hayden and Hayden 1992; Bakic-Hayden 1995; Ritman-Auguštin 1995; Zarkov 1995). As an article by the HDZ stated, seeing its victory in the elections of 1990 as the ultimate step in:

> the inclusion [of Croatia] in the states of central Europe, the region to which it has always belonged, except for the recent past when balkanisms and the forcibly self-proclaimed national representatives have constantly subordinated the Croatian state territory to an *Asiatic form of government*, while the justified anger and protests of certain Croatians have been qualified as terrorism and even fascism. (Quoted in Bakic-Hayden and Hayden 1992: 9).

And during the Muslim-Croat confrontation in 1993 a Croatian general warned that it was necessary to:

> Distinguish the essentially different mental makeup and value system of the writer of the Islamic declaration [an allusion to Bosnian President Alija Izetbegovic] and his followers from those of European-oriented Christians, even if the latter are on the margins of civilization [an allusion to Orthodox Christian Serbs]. (Bakic-Hayden 1995: 929).

The symbolic geography has also been reversed. Internalising and positively valorising a Balkan identity, which at the outset is negatively assessed, can be traced from Cvijeć´s analysis (see above) up until the recent war. Based on eth-

---

5   Consider this joke told to me by a Bosnian: A Slovene, a Croat and a Bosnian had an audience with God. The Slovene asked God: "When will we reach European standard?" "In ten years' time" God answered, then the Slovene cried. Next, it was the Croat's turn. Standing in front of God, he asked: "When will we reach European standard?" "In fifty years' time" God answered, and the Croat cried. Finally, it was the Bosnian's turn, and he asked: "God, when will we reach the European standard?" Then God cried.

nographic fieldwork in Novi Sad in Vojvodina, van de Port (1998) has shown how the local Serb population is caught between two discourses. By day they try to be civilised city people (*fine ljudi*), or as van de Port calls them, a 'Balkan Bourgeoisie', embracing what they see as European values and distancing themselves from the brutal and uncivilised Balkan mentality. But at night they frequent gypsy bars, singing and drinking and living out another identity: the emotional, violent and primitive, but at the same time authentic and genuine Serbian Balkan identity. The internalisation of this 'Balkan identity' is, as van de Port sees it, partly due to a European refusal to accept the Serbs as civilised Westerners, but also due to continued experiences with the devastating forces of war.

Consequently, the discursive construct the Balkans-Europe – like *kultura-nekultura* (see Chapter 7) – offers a dichotomy which can be used to evaluate behaviour in almost all situations, in which the context determines the use and not so much one's geographical position.

Balkan identifications in Stolac

Everyday Balkanism

When the category 'Balkan' was used by my informants in everyday life to evaluate and categorise behaviour and attitudes, it often bore negative connotations, being associated with such qualities as laziness, callousness, disrespect and violence, and with things being unstructured, complicated, corrupt and unpleasant.

I

One morning after Nijaz and I had taken a stroll through town, we went to the café, where we sat down to talk. All of a sudden the music started to play. It was loud rock music, much too loud for the small speakers, which distorted the sound and made conversation almost impossible. "Typically Balkan", Nijaz said. On our way home we passed the school and the gym. "Do you play basketball?" I asked, pointing at the gym. "No!" Nijaz answered: "The sports hall is only for Croats, but it is about to change, I think it will change in a couple of months, but it takes time, if it had been in Denmark [read Europe] it would have been fixed at once, but here it takes time; Balkan mentality!"

II

A couple of times I taught in the school in Stolac. Once one of the boys was sitting with his feet on the table when the teacher and I entered the room. The teacher told him to take them down, and after the lesson he excused the 'Balkan attitude' the boy had displayed.

III
Nusret, Suljeman and I were talking one day about taking a short trip to Croatia. But Suljeman said that he could not go because he did not have a passport. "Typically Balkan" Nusret commented: "He doesn't care, he will have to stay here, he never manages to organise such things."

IV
One evening I was sitting with Mensur and his family watching a Croat film on a Croat TV channel. The film was about a Croat living in Germany who pretended to be dead so his wife could obtain his pension. He therefore had to be transported to Croatia in a coffin by an undertaker. The film then showed all the crazy and stupid entanglements this led to, all the not very clever solutions sought, and several instances of random violence. Several times during the film Mensur commented: "Balkan, Balkan. And they [the Croats] say they are a part of Europe, they are as Balkan as we are."

Balkan, something in the air

In everyday conversation 'Balkan', then, is used as a negative adjective. But 'Balkan' is also used in a more profound way to explain and comprehend the war and the post-war violent and complicated situation. 'Balkan' becomes associated with violence, rudeness and brutality, with madness, insanity and death. On several occasions I heard people saying in a despairing manner that down here (in the Balkans) people did not care about things or humans.

I
One evening I was eating frog drumsticks and drinking homemade white wine with my landlords. One of their sons had been down to Bregava to catch the frogs. I told him that in Denmark frogs are protected, at least some species. My landlady then replied: "They are not protected here, here [in the Balkans] nothing is protected, neither animals nor humans." She then laughed a sad laughter.

II
People also said that this war was a typical Balkan war because of the many dead, the viciousness, and the insanity.

Dino: This war could never have occurred in Europe. It is a typical Balkan war. It's insanity and savagery – we have to try to get rid of it, this Balkan-ness, but it is a part of us.

III

Once Asim expressed something similar down by the River Bregava. He started to tell me about the destruction of the town by the Croats in a desperate manner, but ended up ascribing the devastation to a Balkan mentality, which he himself found that he could not escape. In this way, ethnic denunciation was replaced by Balkan identification. This is how I remembered his words subsequently:

They have destroyed everything, grenades, bombs, mines…Boom! Look at the house over there [in ruins], why? Ugh! Fascists! Ruined everything. Before the war we had everything, we had a good life together. I was director of a big company, I had three TVs in my apartment and a piano, everything. Look at me now. Now I am walking with an old iron that is broken [which he wants his brother to repair]. Look at my clothes, Ugh! When they came to get us [when they were expelled], we couldn't even take a plastic bag with us.

Why, why should they destroy everything? The Balkan mentality, it is not good, Balkan people are not good. This couldn't happen in Europe, France, England. This is Balkan mentality; it is Mediterranean. We are not normal. During the war here in Bosnia 300,000 people died and 300,000 people were wounded, and everybody has been damaged psychologically. Why? Europe didn't do anything; it is only because of America that it didn't get even worse. Europe was sleeping. They didn't do anything. They did not care. If they had intervened, it wouldn't have looked like this, destroyed houses. They should go to The Hague, all the criminals. 10,000 of them. They could build a whole town there [he is laughing].

Today there is nothing here in Bosnia; the industry is destroyed. The machines are destroyed by grenades, rusted away, or they are obsolete, and the market – before we could sell to all of Yugoslavia, now…And today everything is with computers, and we have no computers. Computers, internet. We have nothing. Before everything was good, can you imagine?

IV

Connected to this idea of a specific Balkan mentality, people seemed to think that foreigners could not understand what is going on in Bosnia Herzegovina. Perhaps people from the Balkans do not understand it intellectually either, but nevertheless, as they see it, the war has become part of an implicit shared experience, as this part of a conversation shows:

Miho: How can one kill a little child? Imagine, in Mostar many children were killed, how can you explain it? People must be sick in their heads. How can they come and set houses on fire, steal windows, doors, everything? It is hard for a Westerner to understand.

TK: But isn't it hard to understand for you as well?

Miho: Yes it is. But in our country we often have war.

It is this kind of knowledge van de Port calls implicit social knowledge, that is, knowledge gained through experiences of successive generations, often impossible to articulate (van de Port 1998: 100). Personally I doubt the significance of such a cultural logic. Many of my informants did not have prior experiences of war. Rather I believe that the Balkan metaphor is employed to make some kind of sense of the madness, with one element in this Balkan discourse being that people in the Balkans are used to recurrent insane violence – in short they know it by heart. In a similar vein, I occasionally heard people say that every 25 years or 30 years there is war, or that: "We build up everything – houses, family, economy – and then we destroy it all."

One might have expected that the Muslims of Stolac would have associated the other ethnic groups with this Balkan mentality, and used the label as an ethnic condemnation in disguise. But they seldom did. The war was typically Balkan, rather than being typical of specific ethnic groups. It is my impression that people perceived 'the Balkan mentality' as an independent force operating in the Balkan areas that makes people act insanely. People do not positively embrace this violent and destructive Balkan mentality, but they do not feel they can evade it either. The Balkan mentality is an unavoidable aspect of living in the Balkans. People sometimes describe themselves as crazy Balkan people, but they are not the subjects that act: it is the Balkan mentality and its irreversibility that are acting through them. As one of my informants said when talking about this mentality: "Maybe it is something in the air, or maybe in the cigarettes, maybe they put marijuana in the cigarettes here in Bosnia." The wild and chaotic Balkan mentality is thus enclosed in the middle of culture, but at the same time it is not part of the ordinary. It has its own secret life and its own dynamic, so the normal and ordered world can be upheld. The war's incomprehensibility is not set apart or isolated outside culture, it is encapsulated inside culture. Such an identification with a Balkan mentality on behalf of all groups in Bosnia Herzegovina (the Balkans) forms part of the Muslims' counterdiscourse, as it makes ethnically based condemnations irrelevant.

Balkan, the authentic

Besides its everyday use and its status as an unavoidable mad mentality, 'Balkan' also occasionally has positive connotations. When compared to European mentality it sometimes represents the authentic, warm, real, impulsive and unpretentious, whereas Europe represents the decadent, commercial, false and cold. I have heard people say that it was only after the war, with the presence of the international community, that drugs and prostitution entered Bosnia in earnest; that Westerners are often very patronising and condescending; that the kind of democracy that, for example, America defends only pretends to be democracy, and so on.

The owner of a local shop where I often did some shopping or just came to talk clearly saw me as representing Europe, and he often wanted to compare life in Bosnia Herzegovina with life in Denmark/Europe. He wanted me to taste his *pršut*, a kind of air-dried meat. I told him it tasted delicious and he replied: "Our cows have plenty of space, they live naturally, they don't grow fast and never become bigger than 250 kilos, but the meat is the best, they do not have any diseases [he referred to mad cow disease, which was a big theme in Europe], as your cows have. You only have industry, right? We don't, but our quality is better." Or he wanted to talk about how we treat the elderly in Europe. "In Bosnia the family sticks together and people take care of their parents, in Denmark you send the old to a nursing home. I have heard that people in Denmark spend more time on their pets than they do on their parents." And he was not alone in making such comparisons. Many people loved to engage the well-known stereotypes that oppose cold (Northern) Europe and the warm and hospitable Balkans.

The following is an excerpt from an interview with a couple in their mid-thirties and two of their friends. Stereotypes here are free range ignited by my presence as a European, showing how Europe is a central 'Other' in my informants' self-understanding.

Huma: Yes, our mentality is different compared to your Scandinavian mentality. We are warm people. We are hearty. We are hospitable. We will give everything.

Friend: For instance today you say you like *sarma* (a dish) and tomorrow we'll invite you for *sarma*. And they [people from Europe] say we are crazy.

Huma: We don't arrange our visits.

Nedžad: When you have arrived at someone's house you are welcome.

Friend: We would never show that we did not want you to come. We are happy that you came, because Nedžad is our friend and you came with him. It doesn't matter who he brings, we would treat him as a friend.

Nedžad: A friend's friend is also a friend.

Huma: This is not how it is like for you. I do not like that, but such things await me in America [she is planning to emigrate]. We like having company, going out, spending some money if we have any; if we don't, we are happy anyway. We are not together because of the money. If our neighbour is sick it would be unimaginable not to go over with cakes and some juice. Where you come from you can live 30 years next to your neighbour without knowing him. We also like *sijaset* [to have and make fun]. Then we say all kind of things, true and false.

Friend: We like to interfere in each other's lives.

Huma: We are also different when it comes to marriage, it is impossible [to imagine] for us to get divorced so much as you do in Europe.

On other occasions people told me that they were more impulsive than Europeans, or that they had more time, not being so stressed, or that they were more emotional. In short, people embraced the positive stereotypes which are also connected to a Balkan mentality.

Embracing Balkan insanity

Balkan identity is complex and contradictory. It is both a violent and destructive force, and an authentic and creative attitude. And sometimes people embrace the contradictions and adopt the wild and chaotic madness because it also represents something real, that is non-European. This aspect of Balkan identification I mainly (but not solely) found among the younger male population. I will start with two excerpts from my diary:

He [Nusret] tells me that: 'People in the West look at us and think we are crazy, they all think we are crazy', and he says something like: 'Our mentality is different', He does not directly refer to a Balkan mentality, but it is something like it. This thing where you at one at the same time hate your culture, the Balkan-like, which is the chaotic, crazy, violence, war, the incomprehensible, and if not love it then identify with it. It is like saying: 'I am crazy, insane and I am proud of it.' Like when we hear this powerful and crazy yell from down the road and you think some kind of catastrophe has happened, and I ask what it was, and he replies: 'Nothing, it is normal here.' And then they laugh a strange laughter, but also one that is meant to tell me [as a European]: 'This is how we are, we are wild and we are proud of it.' It is this embrace of the otherness they are perfectly aware that a Westerner sees in them. As when Edin says: 'People from the West look at us and say we are crazy, abnormal, but here everything is abnormal, that's why I feel normal.'

[At the Café Galerija] Edin rose and danced a little; those at the table next to us did the same, and they sang. I said something like I had never felt unsafe in Bosnia, and Suljeman replied: 'That's how the Balkans are, here you can do what you want, you can sing, shout, dance, but nothing ever happens. Never. We never have fights in a place like this. Never.' We talked a great deal about the Balkans, or rather Safet did. He identifies with 'Balkan.' For him 'Balkan' is something crazy, beautiful, insane, real, authentic; he often uses the words 'authentic Balkan.' He is Balkan, or as he said when Edin was dancing with his hands raised above his head – this was after he had stubbed out the cigarette on his tongue – 'He is a Balkan boy.' 'Balkan' is the thing that explains the insanity in his life; it explains the war, that nothing works, his fear, his dis-like, everything. 'Balkan' explains without having to be explained itself. As he clearly said himself: 'Balkan is Balkan, you cannot explain it.' […]

When we were talking about music he [Safet] said: 'This music you do not find other places, it is real Balkan music'. He said the same thing about the Bosnian cafes. 'Like we are acting right now, you only find this in Bosnia. People are happy, they are crazy. You can shout in here (he shouts), you can enter without clothes, you can do what you want, nobody would ever harm you, we never have fights. We are a peaceful people and then suddenly war comes, it comes every 20-30 years and then we run totally amok (he beat his fists against each other in a very telling manner) aaaahhh! 30 years of peace, without the slightest violence, everybody lives well together and then comes total war, everybody runs amok. It is Balkan, it is crazy.' He laughs, but the laughter passes into a cheerless and despairing attitude. We listen to more music, and some *novakomponovana narodna muzika* [new-composed folk music] is played; he does not like it. The authentic is important. Balkan is war and chaos, and it is beautiful and sentimental. I say that it is crazy and beauti-ful at the same time. He totally agrees.

A final example comes from an interview with a young man called Edin, and it depicts, among other thing the tension which is so characteristic in people's identification with everything 'Balkan.' Edin seeks both the Balkan wildness and the European orderliness. But he cannot have both.

TK: How is the Balkan mentality different?

Edin: I don't know…Germany, Denmark, there is law and order. But here in the Balkans there is nothing. Here everybody can do as they please. People, like you coming from Denmark, think: wow what kind of animals live here. It has always been like that, before the war, in the war and after the war. It will always be like that. It will never change. There is a difference. You can see it. For instance yesterday you and I drank beer, and in Denmark when you drink beer, you talk, smoke, you are calm, normal, nothing special. But here when you drink beer wow! *Hajde!* [meaning something like: come on! Yeah!] do you understand? It is Balkan. Aaaaaarg! [shouting]. You know what I mean.

TK: Feelings?

Edin: Feelings are different. Here you feel strong, very strong. If I came to Denmark and had done like that: *hajde!* People would have said what kind of idiot, a fool, then the police come and drive you to the hospital.

TK: And that is positive [the feelings in the Balkans], you think?

Edin: Yes.

TK: But does 'Balkan' also have negative dimensions?

Nijaz: Negative? Yes, many. I tell you again, there is no law and order, you can do what you like. Here there is no law. There are a lot of drugs, a lot of mafia […] But it was not good before the war either. With Tito the Balkan mentality was the same, *aj gotovo!* [meaning something like: to hell with everything!] If only we had good law and order, everything would be fine. Everything is for sale: here you make counterfeit money, if you do that you will have inflation, like in Russia. In Germany there is no counterfeiting, everything works, computers control everything. If we had another kind of law and order it would be perfect here; people would be different.

Balkan, then, is negative and positive, and also unavoidable. It is the opposite of the European mentality – sometimes better, sometimes worse. It is destructive and creative, and it is used to understand the war, violence and destruction. The question of wheter to be or not to be (or rather how to be) Balkan is not something one normally relates to Muslim ethnoreligious identity. For the Muslims of Stolac, however, it was a central question, which they answered in contradictory ways. Furthermore, the central elements in the Western discourse on the Balkans, such as violence, passion, emotion and so on, were also the ones that entered into the examples just given. One thing, though, uniting my informants' different use of Balkan mentality is the absence of a linkage with ethnicity. This kind of linkage was made extensively throughout the war on the political level, as previously discussed, so one might also have expected that my informants would have associated negative aspects of the Balkan mentality with the Croats or Serbs, and positives characteristics solely with Muslim mentality. This, however, was only seldom the case. When entering the Balkans-Europe dichotomy, my informants entered a higher level of identification at wich the sparring partners were European Others, not ethnic Others, and the madness of the area related not to one ethnic group, but to the whole populace. The contradictory Balkan identifications, therefore, form yet another part of the Muslims' counterdiscourse.

European identifications in Stolac

Opposite the Balkans is Europe. And Europe is contradictory just as the Balkan picture is. The Muslims of Stolac had three ways of comparing and identifying themselves with Europe: as lagging behind, as being like, and/or as being better – not by being Balkan but by being more European than Europeans.

Lagging behind Europe

Many of my informants associated Europe with peace, prosperity and orderliness, and believed it could offer a better life. 'Towards Europe', as an election poster stated it in the general election in November 2000. Europe was a dream, and for many an unattainable one. Bosnia Herzegovina was seen as lagging behind materially and technologically, as well as in regard to the legal system and societal development.

I

I remember once Rasim showed me some pictures, one of which was of his family during the war. Its quality was bad. The background was a wall with graffiti on it. His children, who looked sad, were wearing ragged clothes, and everything seemed to be run down. Another picture was taken inside an apartment, in front of an empty peeling wall; one of the boys was sitting on an old mattress full of holes. That is all. Right next to these pictures in the album was one taken by his sister, who lived in Germany. The home was pretty and the quality of the picture was good. The children were well dressed and well groomed, pictures were hanging on the wall, and there was nice furniture and china on the table. Everybody looked healthy and lively. Rasim's comment was: "It's the same, right? Totally the same; can't you see it?" He laughed a little, I know he dreamt of being able to give his children and himself such a future. In fact, he emigrated with his family to Sweden two months later.

II

On many mornings my landlady's child watched the British children's programme *Teletubbies*. Besides the small puppets, there were scenes with children from the UK and Germany playing in nice kindergartens, beautiful private houses, tidy streets etc. Often I heard the boy's mother sighing in the background. I guess she was wishing and dreaming for, and perhaps also recalling such material surroundings and orderly conditions. Watching such a programme in Stolac, where so much was destroyed and people's living standard so low, seemed more or less surreal. Compare this to the time Mensur and I stopped to buy petrol at a garage. It was a new one: everything worked and the place was clean. After filling the car Mensur said that this was a good garage, orderly and fine, like in the West.

III

The Muslims of Stolac very clearly operate with an evolutionist paradigm, evaluating countries and cultures on a time scale, as the following utterance by Munir shows.

> The situation we have now is one Western Europe experienced a couple of hundred years ago. Western Europe has experienced nationalist fights from the time of the French Revolution. And now we have it, after 150 years we have it. In Western Europe they are throwing out the borders, but here we create more borders than existed in the whole of Europe.

The idea that Bosnia Herzegovina is placed on a lower evolutionary stage than Europe also runs as a theme in many of the jokes people tell about themselves. Bosnians are here characterised as being simple, unsophisticated and primitive. I referred to one above about the Slovene, Croat and Bosnian talking to God. Another one goes like this.

A Bosnian man had taken his grandmother [Balkan] to Scandinavia [Europe]. The man stopped at a cash dispenser and got out of the car to withdraw some money. The old lady saw how he just went to the cash dispenser and got a lot of money. When he returned she asked him to see the money. She counted it and said: "Why did you only take so little, why did you not take some more?"

The next joke was told to me by a young woman. When I asked her if such a thing as a Balkan mentality existed, she answered by telling three jokes and ended by saying that she was so fed up with this lousy, criminal Bosnian mentality: "Mujo has moved to USA, to an apartment where everything is electric [symbol of Europe/the West]. Suljo[6] comes to visit him. At one point he has to go to the toilet, but he cannot get it to work with all those buttons and electrical installations. At night when the others are asleep he therefore gets up and tries to find a bucket, but does not find any. So he takes a plant and all the soil out of its pot and shits in the pot and puts the soil and the plant back in place. The day after he tells Suljo that he is going home; the place is not for him. After he returns about three weeks pass, and he receives a telegram from Mujo that says: "Tell us where you have shit, we have moved three times, but the place still smells of shit."

At the same time as the jokes depict Bosnians as 'below' Europe, they also to some extent embrace the primitiveness associated with the Balkans (as described above).[7] It is as though the primary characters are saying: "We are lagging behind the whole world, but we don't care." This is the case in this joke, which many people probably know with other characters: A Dane, a Swede and a Bosnian were in a sauna. The Dane talks proudly about his tiny cellphone, which one can hardly see. The Swede then says that he has had a cellphone operated into one of his teeth; he just has to chew to make a call. The Bosnian waits a little, then he presses and shits, and says: "Aha! I just received a fax." It is as if people in the jokes degrade themselves with ill-concealed satisfaction: "When the world once is destroyed with a big crash, Bosnia will survive for another 100 years (as they lag 100 years behind)."

We are Europeans, normal people

On other occasions when Muslims compared the Balkans with the charged symbol of Europe, they did not depict themselves as lagging behind, but rather as being no different. They stressed that it was the other peoples in Europe who deemed them to be underdeveloped and abnormal. As Mensur once said, "The Bosnian Muslims are the most intelligent and most educated Muslims in the world, probably because we are from Europe." Sometimes I was confronted

---

6   Mujo (Muhamed) and Suljo (Suljeman) are recurrent characters in many jokes, they are archetypical Bosnians associated with primitiveness and a Balkan mentality.

7   For instance, this one: It was during the war, there were a lot of snipers in Sarajevo, Suljo runs into the street and suddenly a sniper fires and shoots off one of his ears. He takes cover. Mujo says: "Oh! Your ear is shot off, what are you going to do." "Fuck the ear," Suljo replies "I had a cigarette behind the ear." Se also Maček's (2000a: 60-63) interpretation of some of the Mujo and Suljo jokes in relation to everyday life under siege in Sarajevo.

with the view – contrary to the Balkan explanation – that the war could have occurred anywhere, that Europe also has a bloody history, or that it was all due to international as well as national politics, a view with which people resisted attempts at linking up the war with a typical Balkan mentality.

Mensur often, when talking about aspects of Bosnian culture, used the expression: "it is the same as in the West", as if to convince me that the societies and mentalities were the same, and that he (they) were not Balkan. Once, for instance, he told me how male chauvinistic people were before: "If the wife was sick they would go to the doctor, but it was the man who would be riding. To-day it is not like that, now both the man and the woman help, like in Europe."

In the following quote from an interview with Muhamed several different identifications are at play. He calls himself a European, a Balkan man, and also just normal/ordinary. And though he sees the standard in Bosnia Herzegovina today as lagging behind that of many other countries, he does not perceive the culture or mentality to be second rate.

Muhamed: In Denmark everybody thinks that we fight, as if we were some kind of tribe in Africa, as if there were a civil war. We are not. What did people say when you were about to travel down here? That you would be robbed, killed, that it was dangerous?

TK: Yes.

Muhamed: Yes I know, I know the propaganda in the West, but we are ordinary people. Maybe you should arrange for a tourist bus to come down here, then people could have a look, and we could tell about the war…

The majority of the Bosniaks who live abroad, who I talk to say that the Danes think that this war was like a tribal war [*plemenski rat*], like Indians. People in the West see us as a tribal people [*domorodac*]. But we are not. We are a normal people, a European people. I speak a little English, but we have people who speak good English and German. For instance the Bosnian children in the Danish schools, they are very clever, our children. They have a broad perspective, so it is, but you have to show it [people in the West do not know]. People in the West are afraid to invest their money here, because we are a risk area. […]

We are not Iranians. I do not wish for Bosnia Herzegovina to be an Islamic country, I do not need it. I am not a man of the East. I am a man of the Balkans. Neither am I a man of the West, but I want my children to have the same life as Westerners have and it shall be here. […]

Well, I've never been in Denmark. Our houses may not look like Danish houses; maybe you have bigger living rooms in Denmark. Maybe you have a fireplace in the house. There is a difference between you and us, but if you travel to Albania, the Albanians they have it much harder than us, and it is the same in Bulgaria and Rumania. […] Before the war when we were in Yugoslavia, those people from the Czech Republic, Slovakia, Albania, and the other countries from the Eastern block, in comparison to them we were the West. When Poles came to Yugoslavia, four of them would sit and share one beer, they would have four glasses. And when we travelled to Poland with KM200 [€100], we were like a host [*gazda*]. But now, it is totally opposite. For instance the Czechs and Hungarians have it much better than us. The only republic from the former Yugoslavia that is progressing is Slovenia. Serbia, Macedonia – it is a catastrophe.

For Muhamed Europe or the West are persistently used as sparring partners, and it is clear that he has no respect for the condescending attitude of Europeans. Bosnians are Europeans too.

We are more European than you

The last aspect of the comparison between the Balkans and Europe is when people stated that Bosnians are in fact better than Europeans, not because they are more authentic, emotional and hospitable, as was the case when the Balkan discourse was embraced and the Otherness internalised, but because they are more European. The main arguments employed to support this identification relate to education and general knowledge.

Nusret's father, for instance, clearly placed Bosnia Herzegovina at the top of Europe. He was a well-read man[8] and was part of an intellectual group in Stolac which does not exist any more because, as he said, the majority of the intellectuals have left the country. He often talked about the high intellectual level of former Yugoslavia: "We had one of the best school systems in Europe, philosophy, architecture, mathematics. Plato, Aristotle, everything", and he told me that the West does not reckon the people in the Balkans as capable of anything. One day he told me about a Spanish SFOR soldier who used to come and visit him: "I asked if he knew [he mentioned a Spanish writer whose name I did not catch]; he didn't, so *I* had to teach *him* Spanish literature." He also talked about civilisation, that a culture has to settle. He said that civilisation has existed in Bosnia and in Yugoslavia for many years, which may be regarded as a tree

---

8   The first time we met he excused himself for not having read Kierkegaard, and on his table I have for instance seen: *The Will to Power* and *Madness and Civilisation* in Cyrillic, a biography about Freud as well as his *Interpretation of Dreams*, a book about German grammar and a book about Horcheimer and Adorno.

with close rings, while American culture is of the same quality as a tree growing very fast. He speaks Russian and taught himself German from a tape. One day he told me about the superiority of the letter *c* in the Bosnian language: "In German you need three letters to create the same sound: *sch*."

The following quote is from an interview with Amela, a young schoolteacher. It shows how Europe can be used as the basis for an evaluation of the perceived superiority of Bosnian culture, educational system and civilisation.

TK: Why did you return from Germany?

Amela: I returned because I couldn't [stand] be[ing] there any more. I had a good education. When I came [to Germany] they treated us as the lowest class. You could only get the jobs the Germans did not want themselves. […] There, nobody respects you. They don't respect our educational system, even though our school system had a greater capacity than the German, or that of other European countries. That's our problem. We learn a lot in the school and many people go to the university, but in Europe it doesn't count. They think we're on a lower level. For instance when I was in primary school I read at least 200 books. We had to, it was a must. Whereas in the European schools the children read two books in ten years. […]

I couldn't get another job in Germany and then I cleaned for a German. I spoke to her in English, because I couldn't speak German. She asked me where I had learned English, because she didn't know anything about us. She couldn't understand that we were capable of doing anything. She gave me a vacuum cleaner and showed me how to turn it on. She also had a vase, which was antique and she explained that the vase was valuable, as if I did not know. She didn't think that I knew anything because I came from some country at war. […]

If we had the same conditions as one has in the European countries, if I had good conditions, if I had a good salary, I would battle to learn even more. They [Europeans] stagnate. They stop with only minimal education. They are content with what they have got, but for us it is not like that. We fight to take yet another step forward, while they remain with what they have got. For instance, our men in Germany who worked building houses – Germans were foremen, and if some tool was lacking they would go to a shop to buy it, while our people would always improvise something to replace the missing tool. Why buy it? The Germans said it was the Balkan system, that is, improvising. We like improvising. If we don't have a table we would not go to a store to buy a new one, we would try to make something. We can fix things with fewer resources. We improvise everything in life. I don't know where we learned it from, maybe from the old system [in Yugoslavia]. Germans work with *one* thing in *one* way. For us it is not like that. [...]

Nobody respects us because they don't know how much we are capable of. When we started at the university a professor from USA came to teach us. We were scared because we thought we were going to read thick books in English, and then he brought some thin books. Like books for children. His way of teaching was so simple. Our school is difficult and we laughed when we saw the books he brought with him. Their students learn from those books. That is to say, it's much easier to study there. After a while it was decided that he should not teach any more, and then another one came and he brought some thick books. [...]

My son is in first grade. In the West when you are in the first grade you play with your friends; my son is taught simple equations in mathematics. He has to write whole sentences without errors. He has to. I believe it is different for you.

Reading the quotation, a 'Westerner' cannot help being a little provoked or amused. Naturally, Amela's thinking relates to Yugoslav and post-Yugoslav pedagogical traditions of knowledge and teaching. But other things are also at stake. Amela felt like a European, but did not feel that she (and the Bosnian people in general) were accepted as such. This is why she employed these occasionally dubious arguments. In as much as these arguments were justifications for herself and her culture and a criticism of Europe and European civilisation/education, they were expressions of the dilemma inherent in the discourse of the Balkans-Europe.

In their attempt to define their identity as Muslims, my informants drew on the discursive construction 'the Balkans versus Europe', which during the war became even more relevant due to extensive use of the metaphors the Balkans and Europe by almost everyone involved: ex-Yugoslav politicians trying to legitimise succession; Western politicians, journalists and academics trying to 'Balkanise' the war and thereby legitimise non-interference; and civilians trying to grasp the madness by encapsulating the violence, seeing it as the result of some kind of unavoidable Balkan mentality. The Muslims' dilemma of being (n)either Balkan (n)or European was a central aspect in everyday processes of identification, and the Muslims of Stolac employed the opposition in different and rather incongruous ways. Often the same persons made different statements depending on the situation or the topic discussed. However, the different Balkans-Europe identifications avoided ethnic connotations, as they were placed beyond ethnicity by my informants, on a higher level of comparison.

To be a Muslim of Stolac means to continually place oneself somewhere in the discursive tension of the Balkans-Europe dichotomy, and by so doing ethnic affiliation becomes less relevant. As this, moreover, opposes the way the Balkans-Europe discourse was employed in other spheres of society, I see it as part of the Muslims' counterdisourse.

Chapter 15
The role of the victim

In contrast to the previous identifications I have discussed, the Muslims' identification of themselves as victims – victims of both Serbian and Croatian aggression and the cynical politics of the West – functioned as an explicit criticism of the Croat/Serbian Other. The role of the victim explicitly set the Muslims apart and reinforced the nationalistic rhetoric of exclusiveness and ethnic separation. The Stolac Muslims' recurrent talk about themselves as victims of the war was a mutual confirmation of their own fate and their communality as Muslims. The establishment of the victim's role was a way of representing identity and an attempt to come to terms with the unmaking of the world. In short, the statement 'we are victims' became an answer to the questions the Muslim population of Stolac was continually faced with: who are we (as a group), why did these things happen to us, what does it mean to be Muslim, how can one make sense of the ruined world?

The role of the victim is linked to national political rhetoric. Though not well documented, it seems that Muslims as a group were promoted as victims in Bosnian politics by Muslim politicians throughout the war in order to gain international sympathy and to legitimise the preservation of an ethnically heterogeneous Bosnia Herzegovina (Velikonja 2003; Bougarel 1996: 108-109). For instance, when we look at the terrible rapes committed during the war, it appears that the raped Muslim women only became important politically when they disappeared as individuals and were transformed into a symbol of the raped nation (Meznaric 1994; Morokvasic 1998; Olujic 1998). As Olujic (1998: 45) writes, "The rapes of individual women were microcosms of the larger invasions of territory."

The role of the victim in Stolac is, however also ambivalent and contradictory. By identifying with a role as victims, one also *remembers* the atrocities, thereby poisoning the present with hate: the recalcitrance of the tragedy, as Das and Kleinman call it (2001: 14-16). Facilitating inter-ethnic interaction and a comparatively normal life demands forgetting, especially in Bosnia Herzegovina, where no public processes of reconciliation by remembering have been set in motion. Again I am faced with an ethical problem. My analytical focus centres solely on how my informants *use* their actual fate as victims as a source of identification and a way of comprehending their unmade world. Implicitly, such an analytical position questions the Muslims' actual status in the war. On the other hand, stating that the Muslims *are* victims would not explain why and how they themselves stress this matter, or what identity is sought by such a strategy. Even though they are victims, they did not have to focus on it, and when they do there are many ways of constructing oneself as the injured party.[1] My informants' accounts were variations of the same story again and again: "We didn't start the war, we did not commit any atrocities, we did not burn down any churches, we showed our true nature in the war, no Muslims stand charged in The Hague, we are still victims". Hereby the role of the victim communicates central values relevant for the Muslims of Stolac, especially their righteousness as Muslims. What is more, identifying with the role of the victim is also a way – more or less the only one – of making a more direct criticism of the ethnic Others.

The conspiracy

One aspect of the role of the victim concerns the Muslims as victims of conspiracy. Almost everybody I talked to recalled how the war came as a surprise (see Chapter 2), and they explained this by saying that it was all a conspiracy and that they were betrayed. People believed in Yugoslavia, in Brotherhood and Unity (*bratstvo i jedinststvo*), in their army JNA (Yugoslav People's Army), and later when the war had started they believed that they and the Croats were facing the same enemy – the Serbs. But when the war started, the Muslims realised that the Serbs had been planning it for a long time, and the Croats had intended to go against the Muslims even when the two groups were still allied in 1992-93.

I

Nihad often talked about the deceit he, his family and the Muslims had experienced; a feeling which was probably amplified by the fact that he, like all other adult men in Stolac, had not been able to defend himself and his family when he was arrested (see Prologue). Some observers of Balkan culture say that the ability to defend and revenge one's kin is very central in these areas (Boem 1984; Bax 2000b). I do not know if such attitudes are more pronounced here than

---

1   A victim role is probably a universal role (Buruma 1995), but its actual manifestation and function is culture specific and linked to the social situations in which it is articulated. The Palestinians, for instance, construct a victim role which is used as a way of gaining individual merit, part of an initiation rite, and there are degrees of victimhood, as seen in the practice of acknowledging martyrdom (Ladekjær 2002).

elsewhere. Rather, I believe that frustration is a universal feeling when you are under pressure and without options for acting (Jackson 2002). This at least was Nihad's situation, and probably the reason why the deceit was felt so deeply. Let me add that when the male Muslim population was released from the prison camps many went to the Mostar area, where they were met with a contemptuous attitude from the local Muslims and accusations of not having defended themselves against the Croats (or the Serbs for that matter when they occupied Stolac in 1992). So for the second time many Stolac Muslims were placed in the front line in military operations (the first time was when they fought together with the Croats). At least this was what people told me.

Nihad: The Croats had planned it all far in advance. Before the war, in 1991-92 they had already begun printing their own birth certificates. It was all planned. The Serbs and Croats had a deal. The Serbs were to get the territory to Neretva [the great river running through Herzegovina and also Mostar], and the Croats the territory from Neretva. What about us then? We were supposed to end up in the river.

Wife: Nihad, he didn't think there would be a war; he just worked all the time. He thought that as long as he worked nothing would happen. At that time, in 1991, he helped a friend build a house in Dubrave. Then a Croatian friend of ours came by and asked, 'Why are you working, Nihad; the war will still come and destroy everything.'

Nihad: I was standing there by the road working, and he passed and asked, 'Nihad why are you working; the war will soon come and everything will be destroyed.' I didn't take any notice of him; he has always been a little nervous. It was all planned. The Croats, they stabbed us in the back.

II

Omer expressed the feeling of betrayal by the Croats and the theory of the conspiracy between the Serbs and the Croats in this way:

Omer: When the war started between Muslims and Croats in Konjic [central Bosnia], the Croats from Konjic were driven on trucks through Serbian territory to Stolac. And in return the Croats drove food to the Serbs in the same vehicles. The Serbs also received gasoline and diesel in return for allowing the Croats to drive through their territory. It was in 1993.[2] All the time during the

2   See Glenny (1996: 197) for an explanation of the deal between the HVO and the Serbs.

war a part of Konjic was under Croatian control. They were surrounded by
Muslims on the one side and Serbs on the other. And if they were not on good
terms with the Serbs they could not receive supplies from their base, and they
would have been in the same situation as we were in Mostar.

TK: When did you know that the Croats would expel you?

Omer: When they expelled us. Maybe you suspected it a little earlier, but you didn't
really believe it. When we were arrested, all the Muslims were in a row, and we
all had to put our guns on the ground [...]...It was like cheating.

People also felt that the West let them down by not intervening soon enough,
by not allowing the Muslims to arm themselves (due to the weapons embargo),
and by pretending not to know what was going on in Bosnia Herzegovina (especially the existence of the Croat prison camps). They felt as though they were
part of a political game that they were unable to see through: old alliances, territory, military access to the sea, international politics, arms deals and so on.
On the other hand, people stressed that it was the West that finally ended the
war and ensured peace. People are grateful, yet they still ask themselves why the
West did not intervene long before, thereby saving thousands of lives.

Salko: It took a long time to explain to the Europeans that it wasn't a civil war but
an aggression, that they [Serbs and Croats] would exterminate [*unište*] the
Muslims.[3] But the West gave the go-ahead to the Croats and the Serbs to exterminate us. You can still read some of these thinkers in the newspapers, for
example Robert Owen, he still thinks in that way. I have read a letter that John
Major wrote to Douglas Hurd, which says that that Bosnian Muslims should
be exterminated. And of course the Muslim countries entered the conflict,
Saudi-Arabia and Iran, and they are economically very strong countries, and
it became a fight against America.

Stolac Muslims, then, have a feeling of being betrayed by everyone and only
having oneself to turn to. At the same time people kept on expecting the international community to sort out their present problems. It was as though they
felt that the West 'owed them' for having let them down in the war.

Another aspect of the role of the victim is that when talking about the
betrayal, people represent themselves as credulous and naive. They ask themselves why they did not see things coming, why they believed the Croats, and

3   See for instance Cigar (1995) regarding how Lord Owen considered it to be a civil war.

why they did not make military preparations. But at the same time this naiveté is also read as evidence of the Muslims' trustworthiness and decency. Consider here what Muhamed's mother once said:

> In the beginning it was the Serbs [who started the conflict] and then they per-suaded the Croats to do the same. Tuđman and Milošović were in Karadjor-djevo, where they were planning how to divide the country. Then Milošović said to Tuđman: 'You can have your country to Neretva, you can have half of Bosnia Herzegovina and then I want half of Bosnia Herzegovina, then we'll make a deal and then we will kill all the Muslims.' We Muslims did not know anything about the deal at that moment. We are decent people and want a good relationship with everybody. There is one word very characteristic of us Muslims and that is *merhametli* [roughly: to be helpful]; we are not bad people. We cannot all be brothers and sisters, but we have to be good friends, we have to understand each other, take care of each other and be together, communicate. And if I do not have anything today and you do, you should help me, and tomorrow if you do not have anything I'll help you.

One of my informants once said that "Some think we were too *merhametli* during the war and that's why all this happened; we were too tolerant." In the quote Muhamed's mother clearly communicated the feeling of deceit, and the sense that the Muslims were victims, and with a starting point in this fate she moves towards a definition of Muslimness: a deceived, naive, but decent people.[4]

A final element of people's talk about the betrayal is their lack of trust in the Croats: they can live together, but will not trust each other again. And many felt an obligation to tell their children the truth, so the war will not repeat itself. When we discussed the curriculum in the school, Amira, a schoolteacher, made the following remarks:

> You have to realise our problem. It was the Muslims who suffered most in the war. In the school where I work we are forced to have a joint school pro-gramme. They [the OHR's educational section] threw everything Muslim out of the books. But it is only Muslims who live up to the plan that Petrich [Wolf-

---

4   During Muhamed's mother's talk about proper behaviour and Muslim identity, Muhamed and his friend (both around 35 years of age) were talking about prices in the shops. They probably agreed with her, but had heard it all before, and more importantly the elaboration of the victim role is mostly done by the older generation. For the young there is not much prestige or future in pursuing the role of victim.

gang Petrich; OHR] wants. In the Croatian schools they teach their children the way they want.

I cannot teach my child to forget it all. My mother never taught me about the things that happened before [Second World War], and that's why these things happened to us. If we were a little stronger and if we did not believe in everything they say…The worst thing is that we believed them. We paid the highest price because we believed them. We shall never forget. If we forget, it will happen again. They raise their children to become the greatest Croats or the greatest Serbs, and things will remain the same until they change their education.

Criticism and decency – mosques and churches

The different elements in the role of the victim (we were deceived by everybody; we were naive but decent; we are not like them/we will never trust them fully again) all fit together, and by referring to one you refer to them all. One can enter the role of the victim through any one of them, and often one does not have to say a lot in order to implicitly refer to a much broader framework. By saying, for instance, "We did not destroy any churches" or "We did not commit any war crimes", people were also implicitly talking about such issues as physical violence, the looting of houses, the present political violence of the Croats, the insufficient support from the West, and so on, as these assertions belong to the same cluster. Below are examples of such assertions, which taken together constitute additional parts of the Muslims' role of the victim.

We were not guilty

The Muslims definitely saw themselves as victims who had been robbed of everything: material goods, their past, their present, political influence, and so on. They saw the war as an aggression, an attempted nationalistic genocide, for which they had no responsibility themselves. They did not feel they had anything to be ashamed of. And they felt neither ashamed nor embarrassed about the pre-war years, when they trusted the other ethnic groups and lived peacefully and well together. What they wanted was for the Croats (and the Serbs) to face their misdeeds, because, as the Muslims saw it, they were the ones who rightfully should feel embarrassed.

Fahrudin was one of the first Muslims to return to Stolac after the war. He believed in the future, or at least he wanted to. But he also had his souvenirs from the war, as he called them. All his front teeth are artificial: a Croat from Stolac smashed his real teeth out with a rifle butt during the expulsion.

TK: Is it difficult to live together again?

Fahrudin: It is not that difficult to live with them, but it is difficult [for them] to face the truth. On a political level Croatia hasn't apologised for what they did against the Muslims in Herzegovina, and the same goes for Serbia. And the people in Croatia have to say to themselves that they have done wrong. I didn't kill anybody; I didn't do anything bad to other people. I can look them in the eyes [*pogledaj ga u oči*]. But there are people here in Stolac who can't. I didn't burn down any houses, and I didn't mine any churches. And on a general level *Amija BiH* didn't do things like that. Those who say that we can't live together are chauvinists and nationalists. If we could live together for 50 years, why can't we then continue?

We did not destroy any churches

I often heard the statement: "We did not destroy any churches." The destruction of cultural artefacts, especially religious buildings, was a very widespread practice during the war. Stolac's four mosques were destroyed. Altogether an estimated 1,000-1,500 mosques were destroyed during the war in Bosnia Herzegovina (about two-fifths of them all) (Velikonja 2003). The destruction of the mosques became a symbol of the destruction of the Muslim people. At the same time, according to my informants the Muslims did not destroy churches, and if they did it was a matter of individual cases and not part of a war strategy of ethnic and cultural cleansing. By dissociating themselves from the practices of the others, the Muslims at one and the same time were able to demonise and criticise the ethnic Other and stress their own decency and tolerance, as this excerpt from an interview with Salko shows:

> We have shown in this war that we are not like them. We haven't killed as they have killed. We haven't razed churches. Once when I was in Sarajevo during the war, I heard the bell from the cathedral and the Catholic church. And I have to say that it made me shiver. In the centre of Sarajevo there is a Catholic church, and in my hometown there isn't one mosque. And that's the way we Bosniaks are – we do not want to be like them.

The next example comes from an interview with Muhamed, talking about the moral support *Armija BiH* had.

Muhamed: Let me tell you about Armija BiH. For instance if we two got into in a car and drove to Mostar, to Jablanica, drove to Konjic, Sarajevo, or to any town which was under *Armija's* control – in all these towns, you will find churches, everywhere. We did not touch the churches. There was no destructions of churches. None. But here in Stolac you can't find a single mosque. I lived in Konjic during the war, and when there were clashes between HVO and Armija, policemen from Konjic guarded the church. And do you know why they did that? They were afraid that some Croats would set the church on fire.

Friend: That is the truth.

Muhamed: There were Franciscans, and there were nuns there all the time, and that is the army you asked about [*Armija BiH*].

Friend: For instance in Bugojno the Croats themselves threw bombs at the Catholic church to show that the Bosniaks did it [give them the blame].

Muhamed: All mosques were destroyed during the war, and that's why they wanted to show that the Muslims did the same to their churches. […]

Friend: In comparison to what they did to us, we were the best.

Muhamed: For instance I lived in Stolac. And I knew what the Croats did in Stolac and then I went to Konjic, where there lived Croats, but I never considered at all doing anything bad against them. What kind of person would I be if I did?

During the war the Muslims did not commit the same number of atrocities as the Serbs and Croats did. These differences are used by the Muslims of Stolac as a way of identifying themselves as well as labelling the others.

During the war, Blagaj was the outermost isthmus of the Muslim-controlled area, and the place to which many of the Muslim women and children from Stolac were expelled in 1993. The mosques in the area were all destroyed (some have been rebuilt since), and at least one Serbian church was hit by Croatian fire. When I visited Blagaj the Catholic church in town was still standing. It had not been touched, not even by graffiti, and this in an area totally under Muslim dominance. I think that part of the answer is that for the Muslims, the church was and still is a visible symbol of the Muslim mindset: they can point to the church and say "We are not like them."

We did not commit any war crimes

The Muslims considered that they showed their true nature during the war by not 'talking' the same language as the other two ethnic groups, that is destruction, looting, and killing of civilians. People felt innocent and were astonished by the violence in the war: "How can anyone kill innocent children and women?" "We didn't commit any war crimes," "We showed our nature by not being inhuman."

Once I asked Emir why the Croats behaved so cruelly towards the Muslims in the prison camps. He answered: "I don't know, if I knew I would be like them." A central strategy was to turn the wrongdoers' actions back on themselves. The misdeeds affected the Muslims, but they spoke about their perpetrators. At the same time, the contours of Muslim mentality were delineated.

My informants did not believe that the International Criminal Tribunal for the Former Yugoslavia in The Hague could bring any justice or redress, as it was regarded as working too slowly and not charging the big shots (Milošović was not on trial when I was doing fieldwork). But in establishing themselves as victims and identifying Muslimness, the tribunal had a place. On several occasions I heard people saying something like: "All war criminals should be sent to the Hague, but notice that only two Muslims stand accused: the rest are Serbs and Croats." For the Muslims The Hague became a symbol of their role as victims, and the injustice they had experienced. The following excerpt from an interview with Omer is an example of how the others' misdeeds, one's own decent behaviour and one's status as a victim are all used as ways of identifying Muslim mentality.

Omer: I was up at Treskavica [a mountain near Sarajevo] and it was during the war between the Serbs and the Muslims. And if some of our soldiers found some of the enemy soldiers wounded, they didn't kill them, but brought them to our hospital [*sanitet*]. Once they brought me a wounded Serbian soldier, but he was dead when he came to the *sanitet*. And even though they found him five hours' walk away from the *sanitet*, they brought him to me, because they hoped that I could help him. But all our soldiers who fell into their hands were killed. On both sides [both Croatian and Serbian]. Every single soldier they caught was killed.

Friend: Our soldiers respected the Geneva Convention; if you find a wounded soldier you should exchange him.

Omer: Once three Serbian soldiers were caught during battle; they were brought to Mostar and later exchanged. But in Srebenica they have killed 10,000 people.

We want to move on

One last part of my informants' construction of their role as victims centres around how they want to rebuild a peaceful and democratic future in contrast to the other ethnic groups. Implicitly, one senses that the Muslims feel that it is not possible to suppress their decency and righteousness. Mustafa had a small business producing articles for all three ethnic groups. The business was built on savings made during the time he was in exile. He wanted to move ahead, forget about the war and ethnicity and create a future, and this was naturally important if his business was to succeed.

Mustafa: It is true that the Croats have stolen from me. You can't say when a customer comes, 'You are Croat, I don't want to make anything for you', and the same goes if he is Serb. If you did that it would be stupidity. If you looked at things that way nobody would be able to do anything. There would be no commerce, nothing. We would each be in our trench. Life goes on.

Generational lopsidedness

By identifying themselves as victims, the Muslims at one and the same time criticised the ethnic Other (mostly Croat) and set themselves apart as decent, honest and naive people. By entering the role of the victim, my informants stereotyped the other ethnic groups, as well as setting themselves apart as a single ethnic group. This identification works counter to the other Muslim identifications I have outlined. Whereas the 'Others' in the previous identifications have been for instance European, the nationalists, or those coming from central Bosnia, the Otherness related to the role of the victim is the general mentality of the different ethnoreligious groups. The role of the victim, however had a generational lopsidedness.

The young wanted to forget as much as possible, both about the war and the past. They did not want to live on the nostalgic memories of the older generation. The young had had enough of this talk about the past and this self-victimisation; they wanted to get on with their lives. They wanted a future, and they wanted to listen to music, buy a car, and watch sport on television. They did not oppose the role of victim, but on the other hand they did not find it of special use in their lives. It gave no status.[5] The ideal of tolerance and coexistence was more relevant, not as a kind of nostalgic clinging to the past, but more as a way to get out of 'all this' and start afresh. The localistic identification was

5   One day when I was talking with my landlady about my trip back home to Denmark, I said that taxis were very expensive in Sarajevo, but were the only way to get from the hotel to the airport. My landlady replied: "Why don't you just take the bus to the bus terminal and from there it's only a 250-300-metre walk. Everything is destroyed there, but just follow the road, because there are mines, so don't go off the road." Her son, who had overheard our conversation, interrupted and said: "There *are* no mines, mother." And she replied: "Yes there are. A lot of things were destroyed during the war; the frontline was there, there are mines." And her son said, a little resignedly: "Mother there is no war any more, the war is over!"

often central for the young, but again more as a territorial marker than a recollecting of the 'beautiful old Stolac.'

The old were often poor and many had poor health. Old people with children and/or grandchildren abroad suffered from a huge sense of absence, but could at least be pleased that their children or grandchildren often had better opportunities in foreign countries. In general, however, the old had had their lives. Remembering the old times may be painful, but the old were able to construct a parallel world which could supplement the real one. The victim identity, the ideal of tolerance and coexistence, and especially the Stolac spirit were of central importance in their practices of identification.

The middle-aged were caught in between: they were despairing, despondent and bitter. In particular, the sad future of their children tortured them, and their own inability to offer them the conditions for a good life. The middle-aged often entered a discourse of problems. From the young people's point of view the old were too nostalgic and the middle-aged too depressed by problems. The middle-aged definitely saw themselves as victims not only during the war but also after. I think many wanted to break out of this persistent focus on and talk about problems, but they were rarely able to do so.

Common to all is the dilemma of forgetting versus remembering. The creation of a possible future demanded that the war be put behind you, but fear of repetition and the sense of justice demanded that the offences be retold and remembered. The young, though, were more concerned about forgetting (it all), whereas the middle-aged wanted to remember; their whole life had been destroyed. They could not live with oblivion.

Summary of Part III

In comparison to the two other national groups (Serbs and Croats), the religious nationalism of the Bosnian Muslims came rather late. Nevertheless, throughout the war it soon came to dominate Bosnian Muslim politics. And though the Muslim religious nationalism was definitely more ambiguous than were Serbian and Croatian nationalism, because it adhered to an idea of both ethnic coexistence and ethnic exclusion, it definitely had its say in putting ethnic identity to the forefront. Before the war Muslim ethnic identity was mainly embedded in everyday life: respectful modes of interethnic interaction existed which familiarised differences, and ethnic identity made up only one identity among others. The war-related violence, especially the practice of ethnic cleansing, and the nationalist discourse in the public realm, changed this. By fully objectifying ethnicity, making it the absolutely most important identity, the Muslims' awareness of themselves as constituting a separate ethnic group became enormously heightened. One might then expect that national and religious adherence would have constituted the major part of the Muslims present identification of themselves as a group. As I have shown in Part III, this was not the case.

National identifications were more or less non-existent, and the Muslims' religiosity had presumably found a level relatively equal to the pre-war period. My findings show that instead of national and religious attachments, my informants were attached to what they call a Stolac spirit, characterised by a strong local patriotism. This identification excluded the Croats who had destroyed this spirit, and it was used to carve out a physical space for the Muslims, but it did not exclude the ethnic Other as such. Rather a spirit of ethnic interdependence was highlighted. On a more general level, the Muslims of Stolac upheld an ideal of tolerance and coexistence. The wilful remembering of past respectful interethnic coexistence made up a central part of this ideal, and I concluded, on the background of Chapter 10, that former practices of interaction had become ideals of identification. That is, the tolerant and respectful way the different ethnic groups interacted before the war is increasingly seen by the Muslims today as a specific Muslim quality. Nevertheless, this ideal completely contradicts the nationalist ideology of ethnic exclusion and must be seen as part of the Muslims' counterdiscourse. The Muslims' use of the pair of geographical concepts the Balkans-Europe was inconsistent and many-sided. Sometimes my informants saw themselves as no different from other Europeans; at other times they embraced an endemic, authentic Balkan mentality. These identifications, however, all surpassed ethnicity; it was Europe and not the other ethnic groups which made up the Other. This in itself makes this identification part of the counterdiscourse, and it is increased by the fact that the discursive construct the Balkans-Europe was highly ethnicified by all sides throughout the war.

The Muslims' use of 'the role of the victim' was the only identification I encountered in Stolac which seriously stands in opposition to the Muslims' counterdiscourse and where something resembling a Bosnian Muslim national character was constructed. By persistently identifying themselves as victims, the Muslims perpetuated ethnic tensions and problematised coexistence. Perhaps a role as victims has a universal character. What, however, characterised my informants' identification with the role of the victim was the way the Others' atrocities became proof of the Muslims' righteousness. Seeing oneself as a victim, however, also has its limitations. For many, especially the young, such an identification carries little prestige and is rejected, whereas for the middle-aged and the old it was an identification they could not escape from. This generational dilemma reflected a broader predicament seen in other post-war societies: a dilemma of forgetting versus remembering, or one could say between facilitating future coexistence versus a feeling of justice.

To sum up, the Muslims of Stolac answered the question which the unmade world has produced – who are we, since this was done to us? – mainly by engaging non-ethnic identifications, some of which have links back to pre-war inter-ethnic life. And these identifications can therefore be understood as part of their counterdiscourse.

Conclusion

In my analysis I have presented three concepts central to understanding post-war life among the Stolac Muslims: remaking, identification, and counterdiscourse. In short, I have looked at patterns of *identification*, which make up a central element in the process of *remaking*. I have analysed these identifications resisting the nationalist paradigm in central ways, a resistance I call *counterdiscourse*. Let me summarise the main argument of the book.

Inspired by contemporary anthropological studies of the experience of war and violence, I have stated that a major proportion of my informants' everyday lives have been unmade by the war and post-war violence. I have focused on people's experiences of how the very foundation of existence has been questioned; how the stories and values governing normal social life have been damaged; how the loss of epistemological frameworks has made communicating about the traumatic experiences difficult; and how Stolac is pervaded by a feeling of loss, which continues (though in a diminished way) the world's unmaking. This unmaking had forced my informants to question central categories of human experience in fundamental ways in order to remake their shattered world. One of these categories relates to identity: the identity of oneself and of the Other. For my informants this has meant answering two fundamental questions: *Who are they, the ones who did this to us?* And: *Who are we, since this was done to us?* In the study I have analysed the way in which my informants have answered these questions.

In particular, I have discussed the role of nationalist discourse in my informants' remaking of their world, as one might expect that the nationalism which had infected the whole area would have been the central constituent in the remaking of my informants' lives – or in the work of Elaine Scarry, the Truth which has alleviated the pain. However, this has not been the case. This avoidance of the massive nationalist pressure I have termed counterdiscourse. Theoretically, this counterdiscourse has several characteristics. First, it only exists when viewed against (counter-) the nationalist discourse. As such it is not an independent feature; it only manifests itself in resisting the nationalist discourse's search for hegemony, for instance by offering alternative non-nationalist contexts for explaining and identifying. Second, such anti-nationalist identifications rest upon already existing cultural categories and social identities, as well as drawing upon experiences from pre-war habitual inter-ethnic interaction. The cultural part of this counterdiscourse is therefore not necessarily new, but the context in which it is employed is new. Former categories and ways of interacting obtain new values in this process. For example, I have shown how a local-patriotic framework ('the Stolac spirit') could be used to express values of ethnic coexistence. Similarly, the cultural category of the 'non-cultured' has been used to explain the war and the destruction of Stolac without resorting to ethnicity, just as former respectful inter-ethnic patterns of interaction have become objectified as part of the Muslims' identification with an ideal of tolerance and coexistence. Third, I maintain that the value of the counterdiscourse should not be evaluated in terms of authenticity. Instead of seeing my informants' conflicting values and contrasting practices in terms of real and false, I analyse them as evidence of the coexistence of contested discourses – in Stolac, a nationalist discourse and its counterdiscourse. Throughout the study, I have pointed out such tensions, repeatedly stressing that they are a characteristic of post-war life in Stolac. People both resist the nationalist framework and use it when remaking their world.

In Chapter 4 and Chapter 9, I have given a historical account of the emergence of nationalism in Yugoslavia generally, and in Bosnia Herzegovina more specifically. A discourse of nationalism spread throughout former Yugoslavia, leaving hardly any area of life unaffected; a nationalism which, when linked up with the violent practices of the war, had ethnic cleansing as its aim and method. According to this antagonist nationalism, the different ethnic groups could no longer live together. Bosnian Muslim nationalism, came late, but managed for the first time in the history of Bosnia Herzegovina to link territory and national identity with religion (Islam). Only from around 1991 did it make sense for the Muslims of Bosnia Herzegovina to envision an independent Muslim territory of Bosnia built upon Islam. In the ambivalent political strategies of leading Bosnian Muslim politicians, such national-religious exclusiveness became one of the war strategies. The other aim was continued inter-ethnic coexistence. I have also shown how this Bosnian nationalism, this new version of Muslimness, collided with pre-war habitual practices of inter-ethnic identification and interaction. From being a domain of loose moral imperatives, religion became much more closely connected to a more fundamentalist reading of Islam. Ethnic Otherness, which before the war had been embedded in everyday practices, became dissociated from its context and represented in new, rigid and politicised religious categories. Ethnic identity changed from being one facet of identity among others to being the most defining one. Finally, respectful modes of inter-ethnic interactions were destroyed.

Therefore, if one considers the following four aspects: the rise of nationalistic thinking on the political level in former Yugoslavia as well as in Bosnia

Herzegovina; the violent practices of ethnic cleansing throughout the war; the ethnic division of the public space in Stolac (institutionally as well as symbolically, see Prologue); and the unmaking of my informants everyday world, then one can understand that many of my informants' identifications of both themselves and the Other must be seen as resistance to the nationalist picture of the world. I have outlined various ways in which my informants practised this resistance or counterdiscourse.

First, they did it by *recontextualising* the narratives of destruction, which I also called non-ethnic condemnation. That is, when accounting for the war and the present sad situation, my informants often refrained from using the ethnic Other as an explanatory framework. Instead, possible non-ethnic Others were presented such as *politika* and the immoral world of politics, a category which was constructed as an autonomous force accounting for ungraspable aspects of the unmade world. The category of decent people (*pošteni ljudi*) was used to deliberately categorise acquaintances of other ethnic affiliation as decent people, thereby legitimising and facilitating interethnic interaction. The category of the non-cultured (*nekultura*) – clearly connected to pre-war social and cultural changes, mainly urbanisation and education – was also used to explain the war by reference to non-ethnic Others; instead allusions were made to the uncivilised and the rural. And finally, the notion of the Balkan Other has been used to account for a destructive and violent force existing inside Bosnian culture, a force which is only occasionally linked up with a particular ethnicity.

Second, even though ethnic labels were sometimes employed to account for the world's unmaking and the present sad situation, such labels were complex and situational, and a different moral value was attached to each ethnic category. This *complexity* marks a second way of practising the counterdiscourse. I have shown how my informants operated with dissimilar kinds of Croats: Croats from central Bosnia, from the countryside, from Stolac, from Croatia, good Croats, and so on. When my informants did criticise the Croats in general, this was mostly done in a context with reference to violence and discrimination.

A third counterdiscursive practice relates to more deliberate and obvious *anti-nationalist demonstrations*. The outright criticism of nationalist politicians, including 'one's own', was an example. Another was my informants' dissociation from the newly constructed Bosnian Muslim national identity. I have termed this the national identity that failed. People told me how they fought for survival, not for Bosnia. In general the state of Bosnia Herzegovina had no appeal. In the same way, my informants distanced themselves from religious fundamentalism. They considered themselves to be believers; but in line with pre-war religiosity, being a good Muslim meant adhering to an everyday moral code of conduct, not visible religious displays.

A fourth way in which my informants contributed to the counterdiscourse was by identifying with *values of ethnic tolerance and coexistence*, in total contrast to the exclusive, antagonist nationalist discourse. The Stolac spirit (part of the localistic identifications) centred on the positive aspects of the co-existence between the three ethnic groups – Croats, Serbs and Muslims. And pre-war embedded practices of respectful and tolerant inter-ethnic interaction have become objectified ideals of identification for the Muslims. Ethnic tolerance is seen as a primarily Muslim quality, as the other groups have abandoned that ideal. Nevertheless, stressing and identifying an ideal of tolerance and highlighting the trouble-free and joyful interaction among ethnic groups in the past, as well as pointing to the possibility of future interethnic coexistence, works counter to the nationalist discourse.

Finally, I have argued that for the most part my informants identify themselves in *non-antagonist* and *non-exclusive* ways. In fact some of their identifications are able to encompass members of the other ethnic groups, as is the case with aspects of the localistic identifications, in which one's status as 'real Stolac citizen' is more important than one's ethnic affiliation. As with the Balkans-Europe identification, the different positions in this geographical symbolism referred not to ethnicity but to being Bosnian. The role of the victim, however, was a more exclusive Muslim identification, setting the different ethnic groups apart. On the other hand, it primarily existed among the older generation, as did a general preoccupation with the past, especially the idea of the good old days.

Before the war ethnic identity in Bosnia Herzegovina was only one identity among others, and ethnic differences were embedded in everyday practices. Today ethnic difference is all there is. The Muslims of Stolac are fully aware that as Muslims they constitute a totally separate group, and that ethnic identity is by far the most important form of identity in present-day Bosnia Herzegovina. In that regard the nationalist project has succeeded. Such a crystallisation and explication of identity fits in well with the structurally inspired anthropology of war and violence, which theorises that the function of violence is to create unambiguous identities. However, my study has shown that for the Muslims of Stolac, the creation of unambiguous ethnic identities is only half the story. Looking at my informants' everyday identifications, one sees a move in the opposite direction as well. It is a move which blurs as well as breaking down ethnic differences, makes ethnic labelling complex, and in fact creates resemblances: in sum, it resists the importance of ethnic identification. But as I have also argued, such a move (or counterdiscourse) is not a fully conscious or deliberate strategy. The resistance to the antagonist nationalist discourse and the prevalence of exclusive ethnic thinking should be seen not as deliberate or ideological tolerance, but as a necessity, as my informants have to live with the ethnic Other as well as with the consequences of their own actions. Ethnic hatred is a luxury they cannot afford.

Bibliography

Abbink, J. 2001. 'Violence and Culture: Anthropological and Evolutionary-Psy-
chological Reflections on Inter-Group
Conflict in Southern Ethiopia', in B.
Schmidt and I. Schröder (eds.), *Anthropology of Violence and Conflict*. New
York: Routledge.

Abu-Lughod, L. 1986. *Veiled Sentiments.
Honour and Poetry in a Bedouin Soci-
ety*. Berkeley: University of California
Press.

—. 1990. 'The Romance of Resistance: Trac-
ing Transformations of Power through
Bedouin Women', *American Ethnologist*, 17(1): 41-55.

Allcock, J.B. 2000. *Explaining Yugoslavia*.
London: Hurst & Company.

Allen, T. and Seaton, J. (eds.) 1999. *The Media
of Conflict. War Reporting and Representations of Ethnic Violence*. London:
Zed Books.

Anderson, B. 1991. *Imagined Communities.
Reflections on the Origin and Spread of
Nationalism*. London: Verso.

—. 1992. *Long-Distance Nationalism: World
Capitalism and the Rise of Identity
Politics. The Wertheim Lecture 1992*.
Amsterdam: Centre for Asian Studies
Amsterdam.

Andrić, I. 1993. *Broen over Drina*. Copenhagen: Gyldendal.

Appadurai, A. 1999. 'Dead Certainty: Ethnic
Violence in the Era of Globalization',
in B. Meyer and P. Geschiere (eds.),
*Globalization and Identity. Dialectics
of Flow and Closure*, 305-24. London:
Blackwell.

Babuna, A. 1999. 'Nationalism and the Bosnian Muslims', *East European Quarterly*, 33(2): 195-218.

Bakic-Hayden, M. 1995. 'Nesting Orientalism.
The Case of Former Yugoslavia', *Slavic
Review*, 54(4): 917-31.

Bakic-Hayden, M. and Hayden, R.M. 1992.
'Orientalist Variations on the Theme
'Balkans': Symbolic Geography in Re-
cent Yugoslav Cultural Politics', *Slavic
Review*, 51(1): 1-15.

Baldwin, J.D. 1986. *George Herbert Mead: A
Unifying Theory for Sociology*. London:
Sage.

Banac, I. 1993. 'Bosnian Muslims: From Reli-
gious Community to Socialist Nation-
hood and Postcommunist Statehood,
1918-1992', in M. Pinson (ed.), *The
Muslims of Bosnia-Herzegovina. Their
Historic Development from the Middle
Ages to the Dissolution of Yugoslavia*.
Massachusetts: Harvard University
Press.

Barth, F. 1969. 'Introduction', in F. Barth (ed.),
*Ethnic Groups and Boundaries. The So-
cial Organization of Culture Difference*,
9-38. Oslo: Universitetsforlaget.

Bauman, Z. 1994. *Modernitet Og Holocaust*.
Copenhagen: Hans Reitzels Forlag A/S.

Bax, M. 1995. *Medjugore: Religion, Politics, and
Violence in Rural Bosnia*. Amsterdam:
VU Uitgeverij.

—. 1997a. 'Civilization and Decivilization in
Bosnia. A Case-Study from a Mountain
Community in Hercegovina', *Ethnolo-
gia Europaea*, 27: 163-76.

—. 1997b. 'Mass Graves, Stagnating Identification and Violence: A Case Study in the
Local Sources of "The War" In Bosnia
Hercegovina', *Anthropological Quarterly*, 70(1): 11-20.

—. 2000a. 'Planned Policy or Primitive Bal-
kanism? A Local Contribution to the
Ethnography of the War in Bosnia-
Herzegovina', *Ethnos*, 65(3): 317-40.

—. 2000b. 'Warlords, Priests and the Politics
of Ethnic Cleansing: A Case-Study
from Rural Bosnia Hercegovina', *Ethnic
and Racial Studies*, 23(1): 16-36.

Beljkašič-Hadžidedič, L. 1988. 'Ethnological Work in Bosnia and Herzegovina from 1945 to the Present', *Etnološki Pregled*, 23-24: 65-73.

Bennett, C. 1995. *Yugoslavia's Bloody Collapse. Causes, Course and Consequences*. New York: New York University Press.

Blok, A. 2000. 'Relatives and Rivals: The Narcissism of Minor Differences', in H. Driessen and T. Otto (eds.), *Perplexities of Identification. Anthropological Studies in Cultural Differentiation and the Use of Resources*, 27-55. Aarhus: Aarhus University Press.

Boehm, C. 1984. *Blood Revenge. The Anthropology of Feuding in Montenegro and Other Tribal Societies*. Kansas: University Press of Kansas.

Bogdanović, B. 1993. *Die Stadt Und Der Todt*. Klagenfurt: Wieser Verlag.

Botev, N.W., Richard 1993. 'Seeing Past the Barricades: Ethnic Intermarriage in Yugoslavia During the Last Three Decades', *Anthropology of East Europe Review*, 11(1-2, Special Issue: War among the Yugoslavs).

Bougarel, X. 1995. 'Ramadan During a Civil War (as Reflected in a Series of Sermons)', *Islam and Christian-Muslim Relations*, 6(1): 79-103.

—. 1996. 'Bosnia and Hercegovina – State and Communitarianism', in D.A. Dyker and I. Vejvoda (eds.), *Yugoslavia and After. A Study in Fragmentation, Despair and Rebirth*, 87-115. London: Longman.

—. 1997. 'From Young Muslims to Party of Democratic Action: The Emergence of a Pan Islamist Trend in Bosnia-Hercegovina', *Islamic Studies*, 36(2): 532-49.

—. 1999. 'Yugoslav Wars: The 'Revenge of the Countryside' between Sociological Reality and Nationalist Myth', *East European Quarterly*, 33(2): 157-75.

—. 2001. 'Islam and Politics in the Post-Communist Balkans (1990-2000)', *Draft*.

Bourdieu, P. 1995. *Outline of a Theory of Practice*. Cambridge: Cambridge University Press.

Bowman, G. 1994. 'Xenophobia, Fantasy and the Nation: The Logic of Ethnic Violence in Former Yugoslavia', in V. Goddard, J. Llobera and C. Shore (eds.), *The Anthropology of Europe. Identity and Boundaries in Conflict*, 143-71. Oxford: Berg.

—. 2001. 'The Violence in Identity', in B. Schmidt and I. Schröder (eds.), *Anthropology of Violence and Conflict*, 25-47. London: Routledge.

Božidar, J. 2001. 'Where Paradise Was but a Sip of Hellish Brew Away. A Story of Coffee in the Balkans', *Ethnologia Balkanica*, 5: 193-207.

Brandt, E. 2002. *On War and Anthropology. A History of Debates Concerning the New Guinea Highlands and the Balkans*. Amsterdam: Rozenberg.

Bringa, T. 1993a. 'We Are All Neighbours', in D. Christie and T. Bringa (eds.), *Disappearing World*: Granada Television.

—. 1993b. 'Å drive ut den bosniske sjelen', *Nordisk Østforum*, 23(29-35).

—. 1995. *Being Muslim the Bosnian Way. Identity and Community in a Central Bosnian Village*. Princeton: Princeton University Press.

—. 2002. 'Averted Gaze: Genocide in Bosnia-Herzegovina, 1992-1995', in A.L. Hinton (ed.), *Annihilating Difference. The Anthropology of Genocide*, 194-225. Berkeley: University of California Press.

—. 2004. 'The Peaceful Death of Tito and the Violent End of Yugoslavia', in J. Borneman (ed.), *Death of the Father*, 148-200. Oxford: Berghahn Books.

Brubaker, R.D.L. 1998. 'Ethnic and Nationalist Violence', *Annual Review of Sociology*, 24: 423-52.

Burkitt, I. 1991. *Social Selves: Theories of the Social Formation of Personality*. London: Sage.

Buruma, I. 1995. *The Wages of Guilt: Memories of War in Germany and Japan*. London: Vintage.

Buur, L. 2000. 'Institutionalising Truth. Victims, Perpetrators and Professionals in the Everyday Work of the South African Truth and Reconciliation Commission', *Department of Ethnography and Social Anthropology*. Aarhus: University of Aarhus

Carneiro, R. 1996. 'War and Peace: Alternating Realities in Human History', in S.P. Reyna and R.E. Downs (eds.), *Studying War. Anthropological Perspectives*,

3-29. Langhorne: Gordon and Beach Publishers.

Chase, M. and Shaw, C. 1989. 'The Dimensions of Nostalgia', in M. Chase and C. Shaw (eds.), *The Imagined Past: History and Nostalgia*, Manchester: Manchester University Press.

Cigar, N. 1995. *Genocide in Bosnia. The Policy of 'Ethnic Cleansing'*. Texas: A&M University Press.

Cohen, L. 1993. *Broken Bonds. The Disintegration of Yugoslavia*. Boulder: Westview Press.

—. 1998. 'Bosnia's 'Tribal Gods': The Role of Religion in Nationalist Politics', in P. Mojzes (ed.), *Religion and the War in Bosnia*. Atlanta: Scholars Press.

Cohen, S. and Taylor, L. 1972. *Psychological Survival: The Experience of Long-Term Imprisonment*. Harmondsworth: Penguin Books.

Čolović, I. 2002a. *The Politics of Symbol in Serbia. Essays in Political Anthropology*. London: Hurst & Company.

—. 2002b. 'Who Owns the Gusle?' in S. Resic and B. Törnquist-Plewa (eds.), *The Balkans in Focus. Cultural Boundaries in Europe*, 59-83. Lund: Nordic Academic Press.

Corbey, R. 2000. 'On Becoming Human: Mauss, the Gift, and Social Origins', in A. Vandevelde (ed.), *Gifts and Interests*, 157-74. Leuven: Peeters.

—. 2006. 'Laying Aside the Spear: Hobbesian Warre and the Maussian Gift', in T. Otto, H. Trane and H. Vandekilde (eds.), *Warfare and Society. Archaeological and Social Anthropological Perspectives*, 29-37. Aarhus: Aarhus University Press.

Coward, M. 2002. 'Community as Heterogeneous Ensembles: Mostar and Multiculturalism.' *Alternatives*, 27: 29-66.

Cusman, T. and Mestrovic, S. G. (eds.) 1996. *This Time We Knew. Western Responses to Genocide in Bosnia*. New York: New York University Press.

Das, V. 1990. 'Our Work to Cry: Your Work to Listen', in V. Das (ed.), *Mirrors of Violence: Communities, Riots, and Survivors in South Asia*, 345-98. Oxford: Oxford University Press.

Das, V. and Kleinman, A. 2001. ‚Introduction', in V. Das, A. Kleinman, M. Lock, M. Ramphela and P. Reynolds (eds.), *Remaking a World. Violence, Social Suffering, and Recovery*, 1-31. London: University of California Press.

Das, V., Kleinman, A., Lock, M., Ramphela, M. and Reynolds, P. (eds.) 2001. *Remaking a World. Violence, Social Suffering, and Recovery*. London: University of California Press.

Dedijer, V. 1992. *The Yugoslav Auschwitz and the Vatican: The Croatian Massacre of the Serbs During World War II*. Buffalo: Prometheus Books.

Denich, B. 1993. 'Unmaking Multi-Ethnicity in Yugoslavia: Metamorphosis Observed', *Anthropology of East Europe Review*, 11(1-2, Special Issue: War among the Yugoslavs).

—. 1994. 'Dismembering Yugoslavia: Nationalist Ideologies and the Symbolic Revival of Genocide.' *American Ethnologist*, 21(2): 367-90.

Denitch, B. 1994. *Ethnic Nationalism. The Tragic Death of Yugoslavia*. London: University of Minnesota Press.

Desjarlais, R. and Kleinman, A. 1994. ‚Violence and Demoralization in the New World Disorder', *Anthropology Today*, 10(5): 9-12.

Devic, A. 1997. 'Anti-War Initiatives and the Un-Making of Civic Identities in the Former Yugoslav Republics', *Journal of Historical Sociology*, 10(2): 127-56.

Dimitrijević, V. 1995. 'The 1974 Constitution and Constitutional Process as a Factor in the Collapse of Yugoslavia', in P. Akhavan (ed.), *Yugoslavia the Former and the Future. Reflections by Scholars from the Region*: The Brookings Institution/Washington and the United Nations Research Institute for Social Development/Geneva.

Dizdar, M., Mulać, S., Pirie, A., Rizvanbegović, F. and Sator, M. (eds.) 1997. *Slovo Gorčina*. Mostar: Stamparija Islamskog Centra Mostar.

Donia, R.J. and Fine, J.V.A. 1994. *Bosnia and Hercegovina: A Tradition Betrayed*. New York: Colombia University Press.

Drakulić, S. 1995. *Balkan express. Fragment från andra sidan kriget*. Stockholm: Ordfronts Förlag.

Dreyfus, L. and Rabinow, P. 1982. *Michael Foucault: Beyond Structuralism and Hermeneutics*. Brighton: Harvester Press.

Feldman, A. 1991. *Formations of Violence. The Narrative of the Body and Political Terror in Northern Ireland*. Chicago: The University of Chicago Press.

Feldman, L.Č., Prica, I. and Senković, R. (eds.) 1993. *Fear, Death and Resistance: An Ethnography of War: Croatia 1991-1992*. Zagreb: Institute of Ethnology and Folklore Research.

Ferguson, R.B. 1984. *Warfare, Culture, and Environment*. Orlando: Academic Press.

Foucault, M. 1982. 'The Subject and Power', in L. Dreyfus and P. Rabinow (eds.), *Michael Foucault: Beyond Structuralism and Hermeneutics.*, Brighton: Harvester Press.

—. 1991. *Discipline and Punish: The Birth of the Prison*. London: Penguin.

—. 1994. *Viljen til viden [Trans.: La Volonté De Savoir]*. Copenhagen: Det Lille Forlag.

Friedman, F. 1996. *The Bosnian Muslims. Denial of a Nation*. Boulder: Westview Press.

—. 1998. 'The Bosnian Muslim National Question', in P. Mojzes (ed.), *Religion and the War in Bosnia*, 1-10. Atlanta: Scholars Press.

Frykman, M. 2001a. 'Construction of Identities in Diaspora and Exile. Croats in Sweden in the 1990s', in M. P. Frykman (ed.), *Beyond Integration. Challenges of Belonging in Diaspora and Exile*, Lund: Nordic Academic Press.

Frykman, M. P. 2001b. 'När våldet tar plats. Platser och identiteter', in K. Hansen and K. Salomonsson (eds.), *Fönster mot Europa*, 125-67. Lund: Studentlitteratur.

—. 2002. 'The War and After. On Anthropological Research in Croatia and Bosnia-Herzegovina', *Wenner-Gren Workshop 'Suffering and Recovery'*.

Gal, S. 1993. 'Diversity and Contestation in Linguistic Ideologies: German Speakers in Hungary', *Language in Society*, 22: 337-59.

—. 1995. 'Language and the 'Arts of Resistance'', *Cultural Anthropology*, 10(3): 407-24.

Gallagher, T. 1997. 'My Neighbour, My Enemy: The Manipulation of Ethnic Identity and the Origins and Conduct of War in Yugoslavia', in D. Turton (ed.), *War and Ethnicity. Global Connections and Local Violence*, 47-75. New York: University of Rochester Press.

Garfinkel, H. 1963. 'A Conception of and Experiments with 'Trust' as a Condition of Concerted Stable Actions', in O. Harvey (ed.), *Motivation and Social Interaction*, 187-238. Ronald Press.

—. 1967. *Studies in Ethnomethodology*. Englewood Cliffs: Prentice-Hall.

Geertz, C. 1973. *The Interpretation of Cultures*. London: Hutchinson.

—. 1986. 'From the Native's Point of View. On the Nature of Anthropological Understanding', in C. Geertz (ed.), *Local Knowledge. Further Essays in Interpretive Anthropology*, 52-72. New York: Basic Books.

Georgieva, C. 1999. 'Coexistence as a System in the Everyday Life of Christians and Muslims in Bulgaria', *Ethnologia Balkanica*, 3: 59-84.

Giddens, A. 1985. *The Nation-State and Violence. Volume Two of A Contemporary Critique of Historical Materialism*. Cambridge: Polity Press.

—. 1987. *Social Theory and Modern Sociology*. Cambridge: Polity Press.

—. 1991. *Modernity and Self-Identity: Self and Society in Late Modern Age*. Cambridge: Polity Press.

Gilliland, M.K. 1995. 'Reclaiming Lives: Variable Effects of War on Gender and Ethnic Identities in the Narratives of Bosnian and Croatian Refugees', *Anthropology of East Europe Review*, 13(1).

Glenny, M. 1996. *The Fall of Yugoslavia*. London: Penguin Books.

Gluckman, M. 1995. *Custom and Conflict in Africa*. Glencoe: Free Press.

Goffman, E. 1971. *The Presentation of Self in Everyday Life*. Harmondsworth: Penguin.

—. 1974. *Stigma. Notes of the Management of Spoiled Identity*. Harmondsworth: Penguin.

—. 1983. 'The Interaction Order', *American Sociological Review*, 48: 1-17.

Good, B. 1994. 'The Body, Illness Experience and the Lifeworld: A Phenomeno-logical Account of Chronic Pain', in B. Good (ed.), *Medicine, Rationality and Experience. An Anthropological Perspective*, Cambridge: Cambridge University Press.

Gow, J. 1997. 'After the Flood. Literature on the Context, Clauses and Courses of the Yugoslav War - Reflections and Refractions.' *The Slavonic and East European Review*, 75: 446-84.

Grandits, H. 2007. 'The Power of 'Armchair-Politicians': Ethnic Loyalty and Political Factionalism among Herzegovinian Croats', in X. Bougarel, E. Helms and G. Duijzings (eds.), *The New Bosnian Mosaic. Identities, Memories and Moral Claims in a Post-War Society*, 101-23. Hampshire: Ashgate.

Grandits, H. and Carolin, L. 1999. 'Discourses, Actors, Violence - the Organization of War-Escalation in the Krajina-Re-gion in Croatia 1990/1991', *Potentials of (Dis-)Order. Former Yugoslavia and Caucasus in Comparison*, 23. Institute for East European Affairs/Institute of Ethnology of Free University, Berlin.

Green, L. 1995. 'Living in a State of Fear', in C. Nordstrom and A. Robben (eds.), *Fieldwork under Fire. Contemporary Studies of Violence and Survival*, 105-29. London: University of California Press.

Guha, R. 1997. *Dominance without Hegemony. History and Power in Colonial India*. London: Harvard University Press.

Gullestad, M. 1992. *The Art of Social Relations: Essays on Culture, Social Action and Everyday Life in Modern Norway*. Oslo: Scandinavian University Press.

Gutman, R. 1993. *A Witness to Genocide. The First inside Account of the Horrors of 'Ethnic Cleansing' in Bosnia*. Shaftes-bury: Element.

Hacking, I. 1986. 'The Making of People', in T. Heller, M. Sosna and D. Wellbery (eds.), *Reconstructing Individualism*, Stanford: Stanford University Press.

—. 1994. 'Memoro-Politics, Trauma and the Soul', *History of the Human Sciences*, 7(2): 29-52.

—. 1995. 'The Looping Effects of Human Kinds', in D. Sperber, D. Premack and A. Premack (eds.), *Causal Cognition: A Multidisciplinary Debate*, Oxford: Clarendon Press.

Hajer, M.A. 1995. *The Politics of Environmental Discourse. Ecological Modernization and the Policy Process*. Oxford: Claren-don Press.

Halpern, J. and Kideckel, D. A. (eds.) 2000. *Neighbours at War. Anthropological Per-spectives on Yugoslav Ethnicity, Culture, and History*. Pennsylvania: Pennsylva-nia State University Press.

Hammel, E.A. 2000. 'Lessons from the Yugo-slav Labyrinth', in J. M. Halpern and D.A. Kideckel (eds.), *Neighbours at War. Anthropological Perspectives on Yugoslav Ethnicity, Culture, and His-tory*, 19-39. Pennsylvania: Pennsylvania State University Press.

Hardin, R. 1995. *One for All. The Logic of Group Conflict*. Princeton: Princeton University Press.

Harrison, S. 1993. *The Mask of War. Violence, Ritual and the Self in Melanesia*. Man-chester: Manchester University Press.

—. 1999. 'Identity as a Scarce Resource', *Social Anthropology*, 7(3): 239-51.

Hastrup, K. 1988. 'Etnografiens udfordring. Fortællingen om det anderledes', in K. Hastrup and K. Ramløv (eds.), *Feltar-bejde. Oplevelse og metode i etnografien*, Copenhagen: Akademisk Forlag.

Hayden, R. 1996. 'Imagined Communities and Real Victims: Self-Determination and Ethnic Cleansing in Yugoslavia.' *Ameri-can Ethnologist*, 23(4): 783-801.

—. 2000. 'Muslims as 'Others' in Serbian and Croatian Politics', in J. Halpern and D. Kideckel (eds.), *Neighbours at War. Anthropological Perspectives on Yugo-slav Ethnicity, Culture, and History*, Pennsylvania: Pennsylvania University Press.

Hayden, R.M. 2002. 'Antagonistic Tolerance. Competitive Sharing of Religious Sites in South Asia and the Balkans', *Current Anthropology*, 43(2): 205-19.

Hedtoft, U. 1990. *War and Death as Touch-stones of National Identity*. Aalborg: Department of Language and Intercultural Studies, University of Aalborg.

Heelas, P. 1989. 'Identifying Peaceful Societies', in S. Howel and R. Willis (eds.), *Societies at Peace. Anthropological Perspectives*. London: Routledge.

Helms, E. 2007. 'Politics Is a Whore': Women, Morality and Victimhood in Post-War Bosnia-Herzegovina', in X. Bougarel, E. Helms and G. Duijzings (eds.), *The New Bosnian Mosaic. Identities, Memories and Moral Claims in a Post-War Society*, 235-55. Hampshire: Ashgate.

Helsinki Watch 1992. *War Crimes in Bosnia-Hercegovina*. Human Rights Watch.

Hoare, Q. and Malcom, N. (eds.) 1999. *Books on Bosnia*. London: Bosnian Institute.

Hodson, R., Sekulič, D. and Massey, G. 1994. 'National Tolerance in Former Yugoslavia', *American Journal of Sociology*, 99(6): 1534-58.

Howel, S. and Willis, R. (eds.) 1989. *Societies at Peace. Anthropological Perspectives*. London: Routledge.

Höpken, W. 1994. 'Yugoslavia's Communists and the Bosnian Muslims', in A. Kappler, G. Simon and G. Brunner (eds.), *Muslim Communities Re-emerge. Historical Perspectives on Nationality, Politics and Oppositions in the Former Soviet Union and Yugoslavia*, 214-47. Durham: Duke University Press.

Haas, J. (ed.) 1990. *The Anthropology of War*. Cambridge: Cambridge University Press.

Jabri, V. 1996. *Discourses on Violence. Conflict Analysis Reconsidered*. Manchester: Manchester University Press.

Jackson, M. (ed.) 1996. *Things as They Are: New Directions in Phenomenological Anthropology*. Bloomington: Indiana University Press.

—. 2002. *The Politics of Storytelling. Violence, Transgression, and Intersubjectivity*. Copenhagen: Museum Tusculanum Press.

Janić, D. 1995. 'Resurgence of Ethnic Conflict in Yugoslavia: The Demise of Communism and the Rise of the 'New Elites' of Nationalism', in P. Akhavan (ed.), *Yugoslavia the Former and the Future.*

Reflections by Scholars from the Region: The Brookings Institution/Washington and the United Nations Research Institute for Social Development/Geneva.

Jansen, S. 2000a. 'Anti-Nationalism. Post-Yugoslav Resistance and Narratives of Self and Society', Doctoral Dissertation. Hull: University of Hull.

—. 2000b. 'The Violence of Memories: Local Narratives of the Past after Ethnic Cleansing in Croatia', *Intersecting Times: The Work of Memory in Southeastern Europe*, Swansea.

—. 2006. 'The (Dis)Comfort of Conformism. Post-War Nationalism and Coping with Powerlessness in Croatian Villages', in T. Otto, H. Trane and H. Vandekilde (eds.), *Warfare and Society. Archaeological and Social Anthropological Perspectives*, 433-46. Aarhus: Aarhus University Press.

—. 2007. 'Remembering with a Difference: Clashing Memories of Bosnian Conflict in Everyday Life', in X. Bougarel, E. Helms and G. Duijzings (eds.), *The New Bosnian Mosaic. Identities, Memories and Moral Claims in a Post-War Society*, 193-208. Hampshire: Ashgate.

Jenkins, R. 1992 'Doing Violence to the Subject', *Current Anthropology*, 33 (2): 233-5.

Kaplan, R. 1993. *Balkan Ghost. A Journey through History*. New York: St. Martins Press.

Karćič, F. 1999. *The Bosniaks and the Challenges of Modernity*. Sarajevo: El Kalem.

Kaser, K. 1998. 'Anthropology and the Balkanization of the Balkans', *Ethnologia Balkanica*, 2: 89-101.

Keegan, J. 1994. *A History of Warfare*. New York: Vintage Books.

Keennan, G.F. 1993. 'The Balkan Crisis: 1913 and 1993', *The New York Review of Books*, 3-7.

Keesing, R.M. 1992. *Custom and Confrontation. The Kwaio Struggle for Cultural Autonomy*. Chicago: University of Chicago Press.

Kleinman, A. 1992. 'Pain and Resistance: The Deligitimation and Relegitimation of Local Worlds', in M.-J. DelVecchio Good, P. E. Brodwin, B. J. Good and A. Kleinman (eds.), *Pain as Human Expe-*

rience: An Anthropological Perspective, 169-97. University of California Press.

Kleinman, A. and Kleinman, J. 1995. ,'Suffering and Its Professional Transformation. Toward an Ethnography of Interpersonal Experience', in A. Kleinman (ed.), *Writing at the Margin*. London: University of California Press.

Knudsen, A. 1989. *Identiteter i Europa*. Copenhagen: Christian Ejlers Forlag.

Kolind, T. 2002a. 'Non-Ethnic Condemnation in Post-War Stolac. An Ethnographic Case-Study from Bosnia-Herzegovina', in S. Resic and B. Törnquist-Plewa (eds.), *The Balkans in Focus. Cultural Boundaries in Europe*, 121-37. Lund: Nordic Academic Press.

—. 2002b. 'Vold, identitet og modstand i Bosnien-Hercegovina', *Jordens Folk*, 27(2): 51-57.

—. 2006. 'Violence and Identification in a Bosnian Town. An Empirical Critique of Structural Theories of Violence', in T. Otto, H. Thrane and H. Vandkilde (eds.), *Warfare from the Perspectives of Archaeology and Social Anthropology*, 447-69. Aarhus: Aarhus University Press.

—. 2007. 'In Search of 'Decent People': Resistance to the Ethnicization of Everyday Life among the Muslims of Stolac', in X. Bougarel, E. Helms and G. Duijzings (eds.), *The New Bosnian Mosaic. Identities, Memories and Moral Claims in a Post-War Society*, 123-38. Hampshire: Ashgate.

Krohn-Hansen, C. 1997a. 'The Anthropology and Ethnography of Political Violence', *Journal of Peace Research*, 34(2): 233-40.

—. 1997b. 'The Construction of Dominican State Power and Symbolisms of Violence', *Ethnos*, 62(3-4): 49-78.

Lacan, J. 1956. *The Four Fundamental Concepts of Psycho-Analysis*. London: Penguin.

Laclau, E. and Mouffe, C. 1985. *Hegemony and Socialist Strategy: Towards a Radical Democratic Politics*. London: Verso.

Lagos, M.L. 1993. 'We Have to Learn to Ask': Hegemony, Diverse Experiences and Antagonistic Meanings in Bolivia', *American Ethnologist*, 20(1): 52-71.

Lampe, J.R. 2000. *Yugoslavia as History. Twice There Was a Country*. Cambridge: Cambridge University Press.

Larsen, E.L. 2002. 'Because of the Situation: An Ethnographic Analysis of Violence in Everyday-Life in the Palestinian Westbank', *Department of Ethnography and Social Anthropology*, 59. Aarhus: University of Aarhus

Last, M. 2000. 'Reconciliation and Memory in Postwar Nigeria', in V. Das and A. Kleinman (eds.), *Violence and Subjectivity*, 315-32. London: University of California Press.

Laušević, M. 2000. 'Some Aspects of Music and Politics on Bosnia', in J. M. Halpern and D. A. Kideckel (eds.), *Neighbours at War. Anthropological Perspectives on Yugoslav Ethnicity, Culture, and History*, 289-301. Pennsylvania: Pennsylvania State University Press.

Lockwood, W. 1975. *European Moslems. Economy and Ethnicity in Western Bosnia*. New York: Academic Press.

Löfving, S.I.M. 2000. 'On War - Revisited', *Antropologiska Studier*, 66-67: 2-13.

Lutz, C. and Abu-Lughod, L. (eds.) 1990. *Language and the Politics of Emotion*. Cambridge: Cambridge University Press.

Maček, I. 2000a. 'Breaking the Silence', *Antropologiska Studier*, 66-67: 34-49.

—. 2000b. *War Within. Everyday Life in Sarajevo under Siege*. Uppsala: Acta Universitatis Upsaliensis.

—. 2001. 'Predicaments of War: Sarajevo Experiences and Ethics of War.' in B. Schmidt and I. Schröder (eds.), *Anthropology of Violence and Conflict*, 197-225. London: Routledge.

Mahmutcehalic, R. 1999. 'The War against Bosnia-Herzegovina', *East European Quarterly*, 33(2): 219-32.

—. 2001. 'The Agony of Stolac', in *Oslobodjenje*. Sarajevo.

Malcom, N. 1994. *Bosnia. A Short History*. New York: New York University Press.

Malešič, M. (ed.) 1993. *The Role of Mass Media in the Serbian-Croatian Conflict*. Stockholm: Styrelsen för psykologisk försvar.

Malkki, L.H. 1998. *Purity and Exile. Violence, Memory, and National Cosmology among Hutu Refugees in Tanzania*. Chicago: University of Chicago Press.

Margold, J.A. 1999. 'From 'Cultures of Fear and Terror' to the Normalization of Violence. An Ethnographic Case', *Critique of Anthropology*, 19(1): 63-88.

Martin, J. 1992. 'When the People Were Strong and United: Stories of the Past and the Transformation of Politics in a Mexican Community', in C. Nordstrom and J. Martin (eds.), *The Path to Domination, Resistance and Terror*, 177-90. Oxford: University of California Press.

Mattingly, C. 2001. *Healing Dramas and Clinical Plots. The Narrative Structure of Experience*. Cambridge: Cambridge University Press.

McCarthy, J. 1993. 'Ottoman Bosnia, 1800 to 1878', in M. Pinson (ed.), *The Muslims of Bosnia-Herzegovina*, 54-84. Massachusetts: Harvard University Press.

Mead, G.H. 1967. *Mind, Self, and Society. From the Standpoint of a Social Behaviourist*. Chicago: Chicago University Press.

—. 1982. 'A Behaviourist Account of the Significant Symbol', in J. Curtis and J. Petras (eds.), *The Sociology of Knowledge: A Reader*, London: Duckworth.

Mehta, D. and Chatterji, R. 2001. 'Boundaries, Names, Alterities: A Case Study of a 'Communal Riot' in Dharavi, Bombay', in V. Das, A. Kleinman, M. Lock, M. Ramphela and P. Reynolds (eds.), *Remaking a World. Violence, Social Suffering, and Recovery*, 201-50. London: University of California Press.

Mertus, J. (ed.) 1997. *The Suitcase. Refugee Voices from Bosnia and Croatia*. Berkeley: University of California Press.

—. 2000. 'National Minorities under the Dayton Accord', in E. A. Hammel and D. A. Kideckel (eds.), *Neighbours at War. Anthropological Perspectives on Yugoslav Ethnicity, Culture, and History*, Pennsylvania: Pennsylvania University Press.

Meznaric, S. 1994. 'Gender as an Ethno-Marker: Rape, War, and Identity Politics in the Former Yugoslavia', in V. Moghadam (ed.), *Identity Politics and Women. Cultural Reassertions and Feminisms in International Perspective*, 76-97. Boulder: Westview Press.

Mojzes, P. 1994. *Yugoslavian Inferno. Ethnoreligious Warfare in the Balkans*. New York: Continuum.

—. 1998a. 'The Camouflaged Role of Religion', in P. Mojzes (ed.), *Religion and the War in Bosnia*, 74-99. Atlanta: Scholars Press.

—. (ed.) 1998b. *Religion and the War in Bosnia*. Atlanta: Scholars Press.

Morokvasic, M. 1998. 'The Logic of Exclusion: Nationalism, Sexism and the Yugoslav War', in N. Charles and H. Hintjens (eds.), *Gender, Ethnicity and Political Ideologies*, 65-90. London: Routledge.

Mosse, G.L. 1990. *Fallen Soldiers. Reshaping the Memory of the World Wars*. Oxford: Oxford University Press.

Nagengast, C. 1994. 'Violence, Terror, and the Crisis of the State.' *Annual Review of Anthropology*, 23: 109-36.

Natsoulas, T. 1985. 'George Herbert Mead's Conception of Consciousness', *Journal for the Theory of Social Behaviour*, 15(1).

Nordstrom, C. 1997. *A Different Kind of War Story*. Philadelphia: University of Pennsylvania Press.

—. 2000. 'Finding the Frontlines', *Antropologiska Studier*, 66-67: 15-33.

Nordstrom, C., and JoAnn Martin 1992. 'The Culture of Conflict: Field Reality and Theory', in C. Nordstrom, and JoAnn Martin (ed.), *The Path to Domination, Resistance, and Terror*, 3-18. Berkeley: University of California Press.

Nordstrom, C. and Robben, A. (eds.) 1995. *Fieldwork under Fire*. University of California Press.

Oberschall, A. 2000. 'The Manipulation of Ethnicity: From Ethnic Cooperation to Violence and War in Yugoslavia', *Ethnic and Racial Studies*, 23(6): 982-1001.

Olujic, M. 1995. 'Coming Home. The Croatian War Experience', in A. Robben and C. Nordstrom (eds.), *Fieldwork under Fire. Contemporary Studies of Violence and Survival.*, 186-206. Berkeley: University of California Press.

—. 1998. 'Embodiment of Terror: Gendered Violence in Peacetime and Wartime in Croatia and Bosnia-Herzegovina',

Medical Anthropology Quarterly, 12(1): 31-50.

Ortner, S. 1989. *High Religion. A Cultural and Political History of Sherpa Buddhism*. Princeton: Princeton University Press.

—. 1995. 'Resistance and the Problem of Ethnographic Refusal', *Comparative Studies in Society and History*, 37(1).

Otto, T. 1997. 'Informed Participation and Participating Informants', *Canberra Anthropology*, 20(1 and 2): 96-108.

Otto, T., Trane, H. and Vandekilde, H. (eds.) 2006. *Warfare from the Perspectives of Archaeology and Social Anthropology*. Aarhus: Aarhus University Press.

Pavlowitch, S. 1996. 'The History of Bosnia and Herzegovina', *Ethnic and Racial Studies*, 19(1): 186-92.

Pedersen, P. 1989. 'The Nature of Anthropology: From Description to Action', *Folk*, 31.

Perera, S. 2001. 'Spirit Possessions and Avenging Ghost. Stories of Supernatural Activity and Mechanisms of Coping and Remembering', in V. Das, A. Kleinman, M. Lock, M. Ramphela and P. Reynolds (eds.), *Remaking a World. Violence, Social Suffering, and Recovery*, 157-201. London: University of California Press.

Pick, D. 1993. *War Machine. The Rationalisation of Slaughter in the Modern Age*. Yale University Press.

Pinson, M. (ed.) 1993a. *The Muslims of Bosnia-Herzegovina*. Massachusetts: Harvard University Press.

—. 1993b. 'The Muslims of Bosnia-Herzegovina under Austro-Hungarian Rule, 1878-1918', in M. Pinson (ed.), *The Muslims of Bosnia-Herzegovina. Their Historical Development from the Middle Ages to the Dissolution of Yugoslavia*, Massachusetts: Harvard University Press.

Povrzanović, M. 1993. 'Ethnography of a War: Croatia 1991-92', *Anthropology of East Europe Review*, 11(1-2 Autumn).

—. 1997. 'Identities in War. Embodiment of Violence and Places of Belonging.' *Ethnologia Europaea*, 27: 153-62.

—. 2000. 'The Imposed and the Imagined as Encountered by Croatian War Ethnographers.' *Current Anthropology*, 41(2): 151-62.

Ramet, S. P. 1992a. *Balkan Babel. Politics, Culture, and Religion in Yugoslavia*. Boulder: Westview Press.

—. 1992b. *Nationalism and Federalism in Yugoslavia, 1962-1991*. Bloomington: Indiana University Press.

—. 1996. 'Nationalism and the 'Idiocy' of the Countryside: The Case of Serbia', *Ethnic and Racial Studies*, 19(1): 70-87.

Rapport, N. 1999. 'The Narrative as Methodology and Ethnomethodology: Individual Belonging in a Post-Cultural World', in N. N. Sørensen (ed.), *Narrating Mobility, Boundaries and Belonging*, 7-27. Centre for Development Research, Denmark.

Reyna, S.P. 1994. 'A Mode of Domination Approach to Organized Violence', in S.P. Reyna and R.E. Downs (eds.), *Studying War. Anthropological Perspectives*, 29-69. Langhorne: Gordon and Breach.

Riches, D. 1986. 'The Phenomenon of Violence', in D. Riches (ed.), *The Anthropology of Violence*, Oxford: Basil Blackwell.

Ritman-Auguštin, D. 1995. 'Victims and Heroes. Between Ethnic Values and Construction of Identity.' *Ethnologia Europaea*, 25(1): 61-67.

Rosaldo, M. 1984. 'Toward an Anthropology of Self and Feeling', in R. Shweder and R. Levine (eds.), *Culture Theory. Essays on Mind, Self, and Emotion*, 137-57. Cambridge: Cambridge University Press.

Rose, N. 1996. *Inventing Our Selves: Psychology, Power, and Personhood*. Cambridge: Cambridge University Press.

Ross, F.C. 2001. 'Speech and Silence. Women's Testimonies in the First Five Weeks of Public Hearings of the South African Truth and Reconciliation Commission', in V. Das, A. Kleinman, M. Lock, M. Ramphela and P. Reynolds (eds.), *Remaking a World. Violence, Social Suffering, and Recovery*, 201-50. London: University of California Press.

Said, E. 1985. *Orientalism*. Harmondsworth: Penguin.

Scarry, E. 1985. *The Body in Pain: The Making and Unmaking of the World*. New York: Oxford University Press.

Scheper-Huges, N. 1992. *Death without Weeping: The Violence of Everyday Life in Northeast Brazil*. Berkeley: University of California Press.

Schierup, C.U. 1991. 'The Post-Communist Enigma: Ethnic Mobilization in Yugoslavia.' *New Community*, 18(1): 115-31.

Schröder, I. and Schmidt, B. 2001. 'Introduction: Violent Imaginaries and Violent Practices', in B. Schmidt and I. Schröder (eds.), *Anthropology of Violence and Conflict*. London: Routledge.

Scott, J.C. 1990. *Domination and the Arts of Resistance. Hidden Transcripts*. New Haven: Yale University Press.

Selby, H. 1974. *Zapotec Deviance. The Convergence of Folk and Modern Sociology*. Texas: University of Texas Press.

Shotter, J. 1989. 'Social Accountability and the Social Construction Of "You"', in J. Shotter and Gergen (eds.), *Texts of Identity*, 133-52. London: Sage.

Shoup, P. 1992. 'Titoism and the National Question in Yugoslavia: A Reassessment', *Yearbook of European Studies*, 5: 47-72.

—. 1995. 'The Bosnian Crisis in 1992', in S. Ramet and L. Adamovich (eds.), *Beyond Yugoslavia. Politics, Economics, and Culture in a Shattered Community*, Boulder: Westview Press.

Shweder, R. and Bourne, E. 1984. 'Does the Concept of the Person Vary Cross-Culturally?' in R. Shweder and R. Levine (eds.), *Culture Theory. Essays on Mind, Self, and Emotion*, 158-99. Cambridge: Cambridge University Press.

Símić, A. 1973. *The Peasant Urbanities. A Study of Urban-Rural Mobility in Serbia*. New York: Seminar Press.

—. 1991. 'Obstacles to the Development of a Yugoslav National Consciousness: Ethnic Identity and the Folk Cultures in the Balkans', *Journal of Mediterranean Studies*, 1(1): 18-36.

—. 2000. 'Nationalism as a Folk Ideology. The Case of Former Yugoslavia', in E. A. Hammel and D.A. Kideckel (eds.), *Neighbours at War. Anthropological Perspectives on Yugoslav Ethnicity, Culture, and History*, 103-15. Philadelphia: Pennsylvania University Press.

Simons, A. 1999. 'War: Back to the Future.' *Annual Review of Anthropology*, 28: 73-108.

Sluka, J. 1992a. 'The Anthropology of Conflict', in C. Nordstrom and J. Martin (eds.), *The Path to Domination, Resistance, and Terror*, 18-36. Berkeley: University of California Press.

—. 1992b. 'The Politics of Painting: Political Murals in Northern Ireland', in C.J.M. Nordstrom (ed.), *The Path to Domination, Resistance and Terror*, 190-219. Berkeley: University of California Press.

—. 2000. 'Introduction: State Terror and Anthropology', in J. Sluka (ed.), *Death Squad. The Anthropology of State Terror*, 1-46. Philadelphia: University of Pennsylvania Press.

Sofus, S.A. 1996. 'Culture, Politics and Identity in Former Yugoslavia', in B. Jenkins and S. A. Sofus (eds.), *Nation and Identity in Contemporary Europe*. London: Routledge.

—. 1999. 'Culture, Media and the Politics of Disintegration and Ethnic Division in Former Yugoslavia', in T. Allen and J. Seaton (eds.), *The Media of Conflict. War Reporting and Representations of Ethnic Violence*, 162-75. London: Zed Books.

Sommelius, S. 1993. *Mediernes krig i forna Jugoslavia*. Stockholm: Styrelsen för psykologisk försvar.

Sorabji, C. 1993. 'Muslim Identity and Islamic Faith in Sarajevo': Cambridge University.

—. 1995. 'A Very Modern War: Terror and Territory in Bosnia-Hercegovina', in R.W. Hinde, Helene (ed.), *War: A Cruel Necessity. The Bases of Institutionalized Violence*, 80-99. London: Tauris Academic Studies.

—. 1996. 'Islam and Bosnia's Muslim Nation', in F.W. Carter and H.T. Norris (eds.), *The Changing Shape of the Balkans*, 51-62. London: University College Press.

Stefansson, A.H. 2000. 'Det fremmede hjem. Bosniske flygtninges illusioner om hjemlandet', *Tidskriftet Antropologi*, 41: 47-60.

—. 2007. 'Urban Exile: Locals, Newcomers and the Cultural Transformation of

Sarajevo', in X. Bougarel, E. Helms and G. Duijzings (eds.), *The New Bosnian Mosaic. Identities, Memories and Moral Claims in a Post-War Society*, 59-79. Hampshire: Ashgate.

Sunic, T. 1998. 'From Communal and Communist Bonds to Fragile Statehood: The Drama of Ex-Post-Yugoslavia', *The Journal of Social, Political, and Economical Studies*, 23(4): 465-75.

Taussig, M. 1987. *Shamanism, Colonialism and the Wild Man: A Study in Terror and Healing*. Chicago: University of Chicago Press.

Taylor, C. 1992. *The Ethics of Authenticity*. Cambridge: Harvard University Press.

Todorova, M. 1994. 'The Balkans: From Discovery to Invention', *Slavic Review*, 53: 453-82.

—. 1997. *Imagining the Balkans*. New York: Oxford University Press.

Turner, V. 1956. *Schism and Continuity in an African Society: A Study of Ndembu Village Life*. Manchester: Manchester University Press.

Turton, D. 1997. 'Introduction: War and Ethnicity', *War and Ethnicity. Global Connections and Local Violence*, 1-47. Rochester: University of Rochester Press.

UNDP 2000. 'Human Development Report Bosnia and Herzegovina 2000 - Youth', 114. Sarajevo: Independent Bureau for Humanitarian Issues (IBHI).

van de Port, M. 1998. *Gypsies, War & Other Instances of the Wild. Civilisation and Its Discontents in a Serbian Town*. Amsterdam: Amsterdam University Press.

Vayda, A. and Rappaport, R. 1968. 'Ecological, Cultural and Noncultural', in J. Clifton (ed.), *Introduction to Cultural Anthropology*, Boston: Houghton Mifflin.

Velikonja, M. 2002. 'Ex-Home: 'Balkan Culture' in Slovenia after 1991', in S. Resic and B. Törnquist-Plewa (eds.), *The Balkans in Focus. Cultural Boundaries in Europe*, 189-209. Lund: Nordic Academic Press.

—. 2003. *Religious Separation and Political Intolerance in Bosnia-Herzegovina*. Texas: Eastern European Studies.

Vrcan, S. 1998. 'Religious Factors in the War in B&H', in P. Mojzes (ed.), *Religion and the War in Bosnia*, 108-32. Atlanta: Scholars Press.

Vukovic, Z. 1993. *Mordet på Sarajevo*. Copenhagen: Brøndum Aschehoug.

Vulliamy, E. 1994. *Seasons in Hell: Understanding Bosnia's War*. New York: Simon & Schuster.

Warren, K. B. 1993. 'Interpreting 'La Violencia' in Guatemala: Shapes of Mayan Silence & Resistance', in K. B. Warren (ed.), *The Violence Within. Cultural and Political Opposition in Divided Nations*, 25-56. Boulder: Westview.

—. 2000. 'Mayan Multiculturalism and the Violence of Memories', in V. Das, A. Kleinman, M. Ramphela and P. Reynolds (eds.), *Violence and Subjectivity*. London: University of California Press.

Woodward, S. L. 1995. *Balkan Tragedy. Chaos and Dissolution after the Cold War*. Washington DC: Brookings.

—. 2000. 'Violence-Prone Area or International Transition', in V. Das, A. Kleinman, M. Ramphela and P. Reynolds (eds.), *Violence and Subjectivity*, London: University of California Press.

Zarkov, D. 1995. 'Gender, Orientalism and the History of Ethnic Hatred in the Former Yugoslavia', in L. Helman, A. Phoenix and N. Yuval-Davis (eds.), *Crossfires. Nationalism, Racism and Gender in Europe*, 105-20. London: Pluto Press.

Zur, J. 1998. *Violent Memories. Mayan War Widows in Guatemala*. Boulder: Westview Press.